The Early History of Greater Mexico

The Early History of Greater Mexico

Ida Altman
University of New Orleans

Sarah Cline
University of California, Santa Barbara

Juan Javier Pescador
Michigan State University

Prentice
Hall

Upper Saddle River, NJ 07458

Library of Congress Cataloging-in-Publication Data

Altman, Ida.
    The early history of greater Mexico / Ida Altman, Sarah Cline,
Juan Javier Pescador.
      p. cm.
    Includes index.
    ISBN 0-13-091543-2
    1. Mexico—History—To 1810. I. Cline, S. L. II. Pescador, Juan Javier.
III. Title.

F1219.1 .A442 2003
972—dc21
                                                        2002020705

Acquisitions editor: Charles Cavaliere
Production editor: Laura A. Lawrie
Manufacturing and prepress buyer: Sherry Lewis
Copy editor: Laura A. Lawrie
Editorial assistant: Adrienne Paul
Permissions research: Cheryl J. Gilbert
Cover image specialist: Karen Sanatar
Image permission coordinator: Nancy Seise
Cartographer: Alice Thiede/CARTO-GRAPHICS
Line art manager: Guy Ruggiero
Cover design: Bruce Kenselaar
Cover art: Pyramid at Teotihuacan, Mexico.
    Spanish Conquest of Mexico (*Codex Florentino*: SAHAGUN Lam CXLI, Libro
    XII, No. 25, LC Shelf No. F 1219 S1313 Copy 2.
    Cathedral, Mexico City.
    All images courtesy of Library of Congress.

This book was set in 10/12 Palatino by DM Cradle Associates,
and was printed and bound by Courier Stoughton.
The cover was printed by The Lehigh Press, Inc.

© 2003 by Pearson Education, Inc.
Upper Saddle River, New Jersey 07458

Printed in the United States of America

10 9 8 7 6 5 4 3 2 1

ISBN 0-13-091543-2

Pearson Education LTD., *London*
Pearson Education Australia PTY, Limited, *Sydney*
Pearson Education Singapore, Pte. Ltd
Pearson Education North Asia Ltd, *Hong Kong*
Pearson Education Canada, Ltd., *Toronto*
Pearson Education de Mexico, S.A. de C.V.
Pearson Education--Japan, *Tokyo*
Pearson Education Malaysia, Pte. Ltd.
Pearson Education, *Upper Saddle River, New Jersey*

We dedicate this book to our parents:
Teresa Cantón Abes;
and, in loving memory,
Ralph Altman and Jeanne Weinberger Altman;
Howard F. Cline and Mary W. Cline;
and Emilio Pescador Magallanes

Contents

Preface   *ix*

Part I: 1325–1598

1   Mexican Peoples and Cultures   3
2   Spain in the Era of Expansion   27
3   Conquest and Colonization   53
4   Narratives of Conquest   73
5   Mexico and the Columbian Exchange   97
6   Christianity in Colonial Mexico   115

Part II: 1598–1700

7   Mesoamerican Indians under Colonial Rule   143
8   Economy and Society in the Middle Period   162
9   The Northern Frontier   185
10   The African Presence in New Spain   204
11   Elite and Popular Culture   225
12   Rebellion and Crime   242

Part III: 1700–1824

13   Race, Class, and Family   261
14   Economy and Society in the Late Colonial Period   282
15   The Bourbon Era   300
16   The Northern Borderlands   320
17   The Struggle for Independence   341
18   Colonial Legacies   362

Suggested Reading in Spanish   *379*
Index   *387*

Preface

This volume is intended to serve as a basic text for courses in Mexican history, as well as others in which the history of Mexico plays an important part. The general reader wishing to learn more of Mexico's early history and development also may find this book to be a useful introduction and guide to the fascinating story of a country that shares a border and much history in common with the United States but in many senses remains little known or understood in this country.

Mexico's history is immensely rich and diverse, and writing it offers great challenges. Here we will consider the peoples and cultures who inhabited Mesoamerica before the arrival of Europeans; the Spanish conquest and subsequent clashes and interactions among groups as they all adjusted to a changed and changing context; the rapid economic and institutional development of the colony that the Spaniards called the Kingdom or Viceroyalty of New Spain; the expansion of Hispanic society and culture from central Mexico into remote areas of the north and south; and the growing complexity of society and economy over the centuries of Spanish rule. In this volume, we examine Mexico's early history by focusing on a series of topics treated within a chronological framework, dividing the colonial period into three periods that correspond roughly to the three centuries of colonial rule. This approach makes it possible to give due consideration not only to better-known events and aspects of that history—such as the Aztec empire and the Spanish conquest, or the establishment of the Roman Catholic church—but also to introduce the reader to important topics such as the role of Africans in colonial Mexico, the nature of marriage and family, the form and implications of interactions among different ethnic groups, and the causes and significance of disorder and rebellion, both before and during the wars for independence. We also have made an effort to take a balanced approach to regional diversity and development.

No single, relatively brief volume can claim to offer a comprehensive history of colonial Mexico. This text attempts to combine existing knowledge with the most recent scholarship in the field. Thus, we can only provide an introduction to ongoing research that is constantly modifying our understanding of colonial society. Some of the more recent trends in scholarship include the following: the use of indigenous texts to study sociopolitical structures, language patterns, gender roles, economic activities, and cultural change and continuity among Indian groups during the colonial period; the use of microhistorical analysis to understand complex socioeconomic and political processes; and a new effort to examine and integrate previously less studied groups—women, people of mixed racial and ethnic background—and relatively neglected regions (the far north and south) into the mainstream of Mexican history. At the same time, incorporation of recent scholarship should not mean the neglect of essential older works that by no means have been superseded. With respect to the rich historiography of colonial Mexico, we have endeavored to take a balanced approach as well.

The authors acknowledge a number of individuals who have contributed their time, effort, and expertise to this book. Todd Armstrong, formerly of Prentice Hall, first suggested to us the idea of writing a textbook on colonial Mexican history; his successor at Prentice Hall, Charles Cavaliere, has been most helpful in seeing the project through to completion, as has Laura Lawrie. We wish to thank Pedro Santoni of California State University at San Bernardino, William C. Olson of Marist College, and John Sherman of Wright State University, who reviewed the original proposal. Patrick Grant of the University of Victoria and Michael Polushin of the University of Southern Mississippi read the entire manuscript and provided invaluable comments. William B. Taylor of the University of California at Berkeley and James Lockhart of the University of California at Los Angeles also were kind enough to read all or part of the manuscript on very short notice and to share with us their responses and suggestions.

We also wish to acknowledge the understanding and encouragement of our families, friends, and colleagues. As is often true for worthwhile projects, this one took longer and proved to be far more demanding of everyone's time and patience than anticipated.

Ida Altman
University of New Orleans

Sarah Cline
University of California, Santa Barbara

Juan Javier Pescador
Michigan State University

Modern Political Boundaries of Greater Mexico

The Early History of Greater Mexico

Part I

1325–1598

One

Mexican Peoples
and Cultures

A Spanish Conqueror Sees the Great
Aztec Market, 1519

On reaching the great marketplace, we [Spanish conquerors] were astounded at the great number of people and the quantities of merchandise, and at the orderliness and good arrangements that prevailed, for we had never seen such a thing before. . . . Every kind of merchandise was kept separate and had its fixed place marked for it.

Let us begin with the dealers in gold, silver, and precious stones, feathers, cloaks, and embroidered goods, and male and female slaves who are also sold there. They bring as many slaves to be sold in that market, as the Portuguese bring Negroes from Guinea. Some are brought there attached to long poles by means of collars around their necks to prevent them from escaping, but others are left loose. Next there are those who sold coarser cloth, and cotton goods and fabrics made of twisted thread, and there were chocolate merchants with their chocolate. In this way you could see every kind of merchandise to be found anywhere in this land, laid out in the same way as goods are laid out in my own district in Medina del Campo [Spain], a centre for fairs, where each line of stalls has its own particular sort. So it was in this great market.

They have a building there also in which three judges sit, and there are officials like constables who examine the merchandise . . .

We turned back to the great market and the swarm of people buying and selling. The mere murmur of their voices talking was loud enough to be heard more than three miles away. Some of our soldiers who had been in many parts of the world, in Constantinople, in Rome, and all over Italy, said that they had never seen a market so well laid out, so large, so orderly, and so full of people.

Bernal Díaz del Castillo, *The Conquest of New Spain* [abridged edition of *The True History of the Conquest of Mexico*], trans. J. M. Cohen (London, 1963), pp. 232–5.

Conqueror Bernal Díaz del Castillo's 1519 description of the market in the Aztec capital of Tenochtitlan conveys Spaniards's amazement at the opulence of the capital of the Aztec Empire. The city's huge, regulated, permanent marketplace dramatically exemplified the complexity, richness, and

Figure 1-1 **The founding of Tenochtitlan.** The wandering Mexica of Aztlan believed that they would establish a settlement where they saw an eagle perched on a cactus. Stylized burning temples indicate two Aztec conquests; symbols of the Mesoamerican calendar form the border. Permission granted by the Bodleian Library, University of Oxford, for reproduction of MS.Arch. Selden. A. 1, fol. 2r.

high degree of development of society in central Mexico, comparable to that of Spain itself and other great centers of the Christian world such as Rome and Constantinople (which by then had fallen to the Turks).

When Spaniards arrived in central Mexico in 1519, they found virtually all the hallmarks of a complex society. These included well-built cities with temples, palaces, and central markets; stratified social systems similar to their own, with nobles, commoners, and slaves; a structured political state with fully developed systems of taxation and law; a privileged military group; far-reaching trade networks; a religious cult with high priests; and a system of writing. True, the natives had no metallurgy or beasts of burden, and their religion called for human sacrifice, but clearly the Aztecs had achieved a high level of civilization as Spaniards understood it.

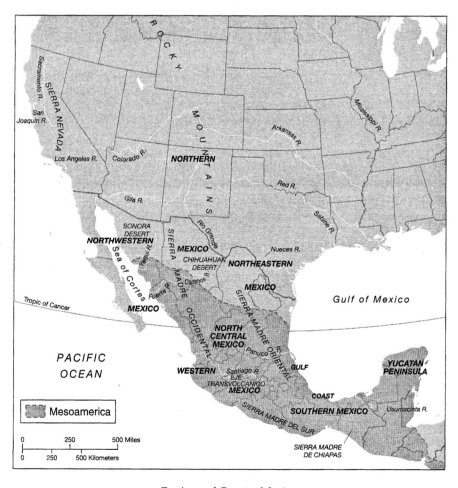

Regions of Greater Mexico

The "discovery" and conquest of central Mexico fulfilled Spaniards' dreams of empire. Mexico offered treasure to be seized and divided, dense populations accustomed to obligatory work and payment of tribute, and rich mineral resources to exploit. Spaniards established themselves on the ruins of the Aztec Empire and from there launched further expeditions of exploration and conquest. Elsewhere in Greater Mexico they found other, organized societies as well as mobile, fierce groups that resisted conquest for a long time. Because the indigenous populations of Mexico shaped Spanish colonial rule profoundly, it is essential to understand how their cultures developed before European contact.

Terms of Reference

In this book, we will examine Greater Mexico from the period before the arrival of the Spaniards in 1519 until Mexico achieved its independence from Spain in 1821. **Greater Mexico** is used here to refer to the huge territory over which the Spanish Crown claimed sovereignty which today encompasses both the modern nation-state of Mexico and the southwestern United States, which scholars in the United States often call the **Spanish borderlands**, a region that includes modern Texas, New Mexico, Arizona, Nevada, Colorado, and California. Mexico City, built on the site of the Aztec capital of Tenochtitlan, became the administrative capital of what the Spaniards called the kingdom of **New Spain**.

One of the important geographical and cultural zones within Greater Mexico is **Mesoamerica**. This term refers to the area south of the great northern desert that includes the central plateau and extends southward to Central America. There the densest populations were found and complex societies evolved during the **prehispanic era** (the period preceding the arrival of the Spaniards in the early 1500s). During the centuries of Spanish rule, the **colonial era** (1521–1821), Greater Mexico was under the jurisdiction of the **viceroyalty** of New Spain with its capital in Mexico City. The southern portion of the territory constituted the virtually autonomous Captaincy General of Guatemala that had jurisdiction over Chiapas and Central America, regions largely outside the scope of this textbook.

Two further terms of reference are **Old World** and **New World,** which came into use among Europeans during the colonial era. The Old World comprises Europe, Asia, and Africa, regions that were in contact with one another in the period prior to 1492 and which to some degree formed a unified arena for the diffusion of disease and technology as well as genetic mixing. The **New World** is the Western Hemisphere, including the continents of North and South America and the Caribbean islands. Although some scholars have begun to abandon this terminology, these designations have the virtue of being easily recognized and understood. Nonetheless it should be noted that recent archeological work has produced solid evidence that advanced societies developed in the Western Hemisphere much earlier than once thought, so traditional ideas about the relative "newness" of American societies and culture must be discarded.

"*Indians.*" A number of possible terms may be used to refer to Greater Mexico's indigenous populations before and after the conquest. From the time of Christopher Columbus to the present, Europeans and others have called the peoples of the Americas "Indians" (because of Columbus's belief he had reached the East Indies), but the "Indians" never thought of themselves as constituting a single group. Even settled agriculturalists living in narrow geographic areas and speaking the same language considered themselves different from one another; their allegiance was to their local community. Profound differences existed between hunting and gathering groups (with no fixed villages), slash-and-burn agriculturalists (whose village sites shifted over time), and sedentary cultivators (with fixed villages and fields cultivated over generations). Although the term "Indian" has obvious problems, it has remained in use as a relatively neutral means of designating people of the Western Hemisphere, along with terms such as "natives," "indigenous peoples," "Native Americans," and "Amerindians." In this textbook, all of these terms for the peoples of Greater Mexico may appear, but in discussing a particular group, the group's standard designation—often the name of their language—will be used.

The major group that Spaniards encountered in central Mexico spoke Nahuatl. The divisions among Nahuatl speakers, the Nahuas or "Aztecs" (a modern term not used by them), directly affected the Spanish military campaign that toppled the Aztec Empire. During the colonial era, Spaniards called many indigenous groups by terms the Aztecs used. Three examples show the enduring influence of the Aztecs. One of the important groups in the Oaxaca[1] region called themselves the Ñudzahui, but the Aztecs called them the "Mixtecs" ("cloud people"); the major group in Michoacan called themselves the Purepecha, but the Aztecs designated them "Tarascans." The Aztecs called the mobile northern peoples "Chichimecas," a collective term for linguistically diverse groups. In all these cases, the Spaniards adopted the Aztec designations and for the most part they remain in use in both scholarly and popular literature.

The Aztec Empire. In central Mexico, Spaniards encountered the Aztec Empire, a confederation of three city-states (the Triple Alliance) that controlled the fertile central plateau and collected tribute from conquered regions in southern and eastern Mesoamerica. The Triple Alliance city-states of Tenochtitlan,[2] Texcoco, and Tlacopan grew rich on tribute from nearby conquered city-states and others far outside the central plateau that were

---

[1] Pronounced waHAka. The spelling is based on sixteenth-century Spanish spelling conventions that have been retained in the postindependence era.
[2] Pronounced differently in Nahuatl (Te-noch-TI-tlan) than in Spanish (Te-noch-ti-TLÁN), with a written accent. In Nahuatl, the accent is standardly on the penultimate syllable. Throughout the textbook, names of indigenous people, places, and languages are written without accents.

Indigenous Groups in Greater Mexico

dominated by Nahuatl speakers. Because of the Aztecs' imperial expansion, their language, Nahuatl, had become the common tongue for rulers, merchants, and traders far beyond central Mexico. The city-states of Texcoco, the cultural capital of the alliance, and Tlacopan were on the mainland in the central lake region, while the dominant power at the time of the Spaniards' arrival, Tenochtitlan, was an island city and capital of a far-flung empire.

The story of Greater Mexico's indigenous peoples before European contact is important for understanding its colonial history. Mexico's prehispanic history is complex, the product of Greater Mexico's distinctive geography and cycles of cultural and political development, expansion, displacement and assimilation.

The Geography of Greater Mexico

Physical Geography. By the time Spaniards arrived in the early 1500s, Greater Mexico's peoples had adapted to a range of environments and forged varied lifestyles, from the hunting and gathering societies of the north to the complex societies of Mesoamerica. Greater Mexico stretches from what is now the Southwestern United States to the jungles of Central America, a large area with diverse geographical and environmental zones. Mountains and desert separate regions and prevent easy contact between human settlements. Mexico's vast northern desert lies between the temperate highlands of central Mexico and the broad temperate plains of North America. Dense jungles in the south resist easy human habitation. In the southern highlands, people settled in temperate valleys separated from one another by the mountainous terrain.

Greater Mexico lacks major rivers. There are no easily accessible transportation routes that connected one region with another or major river valleys that gave rise to integrated systems of irrigated agriculture, which in many places promoted the formation of centralized bureaucracies. The equivalent on Mexico's central plateau was the inland lake system formed by Lake Texcoco. It became a major center of human settlement, with city-states along the lakeshore linked by canoe and foot traffic. The freshwater southern portion supported labor-intensive agriculture. This area was not, however, the oldest center of urban culture in Mexico, a distinction belonging to the Olmec society that arose in the coastal area of the Gulf of Mexico around 1200 B.C.

Greater Mexico has lengthy coastlines on the Gulf of Mexico and Pacific Ocean, but ancient (and modern) Mexicans for the most part were not seafarers. There is evidence of ancient maritime contacts between Peru and western Mexico, but they were not crucial to the evolution of Mexican culture.

Regional distinctions in climate, soil, vegetation, and animal life developed over the millennia before humans arrived in Greater Mexico around 20,000 B.C. Most of Greater Mexico lies in latitudes 15 to 30 degrees north of the equator, the same broad band where complex societies evolved in Egypt and the Middle East, China, and India. *Homo sapiens* originated in the Old World, probably Africa. Humans arrived in the Americas relatively late, crossing the Bering land bridge from northeast Asia as early as 35,000 B.C. That land bridge submerged around 9000 B.C. as sea levels rose at the end of the last Ice Age, preventing continued relatively easy migration from Asia.

When humans arrived in North America, they found many large mammals, including mammoths and giant bison. The complete extinction of many animal species, including the horse, coincided with the arrival of humans in the Americas. The remaining array of animals did not include such easily domesticable and useful ones as cattle, sheep, goats, pigs, and chickens. These animals aided Old World peoples not only by supplementing or replacing human muscle power for work but also by providing food, hides, and wool.

Scholars see complex societies in the Old World as having arisen from settled agriculture and the practice of herding animals (pastoralism), as cultivated plants and grazing animals were reliable food sources that could support large settled human populations. The kind of organization that such settlements required, together with their ability to produce agricultural surpluses, fostered the development of managerial groups and division of society into classes. Mexican cultures, however, developed in the complete absence of pastoralism, a notable achievement. Settled agriculture produced surpluses that could support nonagriculturalists, such as rulers, priests, and artisans. In Greater Mexico, the area most conducive to the development of thriving agricultural societies was Mesoamerica.

Geographical Zones. Mesoamerica had considerable but not uniformly favorable conditions for the development of settled societies. It has both highland and lowland geographical zones with differing agricultural potential. In the highlands, the most important region for settlement is the temperate zone (*tierra templada*), with elevations between one thousand and two thousand meters above sea level. Tierra templada exists in the central plateau and a broad band through the southern highlands from Chiapas down to Nicaragua in Central America. The temperate regions of the highlands have fertile soils created by volcanic ash and sediments from ancient lakebeds, which could support large agricultural populations.

Some highland areas of Mesoamerica had climates too extreme for settled agriculture and dense human populations. At the higher elevations of mountain ranges that run north to south, the Sierra Madre Occidental and the Sierra Madre Oriental, and of the east–west range, the Sierra Madre del Sur, lies the "cold land"(*tierra fria*) at 2,000 to 2,800 meters above sea level.

Steamy lowlands called the "hot country" (*tierra caliente*), occupying zones from sea level to one thousand meters, are found along both coasts down to the Isthmus of Panama. They have more variable soils than the temperate highlands. Fertile lowland areas benefited from alluvial deposits from rivers flowing to the Caribbean and the Pacific, bringing soil from the richer highlands, and supported substantial agricultural populations.

The Yucatan peninsula is geographically isolated from central Mexico, a limestone escarpment protruding into the Caribbean. Despite its thin soils, Yucatan had significant agricultural populations that gave rise to Maya culture. Although Yucatan has no rivers, the large number of *cenotes* or water-filled sink holes and underground streams allowed substantial numbers of agriculturalists to thrive.

The earliest complex societies in Mexico, the Olmec and the Maya, evolved in lowland areas. This fact long confounded scholars, until archeological fieldwork found evidence of multiple food sources available to support large populations and linkages to other regions. People who settled in the coastal lowlands adapted to the environmental constraints by developing slash-and-burn agriculture, which allows for cultivation of crops on nutrient-poor soils for a period of time before it is exhausted. Then farmers would move elsewhere, sometimes returning to the same site when soils recovered fertility a decade or more later. Farmers also expanded productive land through terracing, raised fields in wetlands, kitchen gardens, and fruit orchards.

Lowland areas supported the cultivation of many crops, but most importantly corn or maize, which was the staff of life for most settled populations in Greater Mexico. Tropical lowland areas supported cacao orchards that produced exotic and valuable chocolate beans. The lowlands of southern Mexico also were home to untamable animals, such as the jaguar, ocelot, and the quetzal bird whose pelts and feathers were highly valued and used as ornamentation on the regalia of nobles and priests.

Greater Mexico's mountainous topography limited contact between regions and hampered the diffusion of new crops, domesticated animals, and technology. Despite geographical barriers, however, Mesoamericans developed advanced cultures over time in several regions, that came into contact through trade and conquest and exerted considerable influence over one another. By the time the Spaniards arrived, regional centers of power had formed in several places and a number of societies had risen, flourished, and in turn been supplanted by other powers.

Population size. In the period before Europeans arrived in the early 1500s, Greater Mexico had a population numbering in the millions, although exactly how many is a matter of lively scholarly debate. Some estimates for the whole area are as high as twenty-five million. At European contact there were major metropolises in central Mexico. Tenochtitlan had as many as 150,000 people in 1519 and Tzintzuntzan in the Purepecha (Tarascan) area of Michoacan fifteen to twenty thousand. In the Maya region of southern Mexico, cities also reached considerable size, although by the time Spaniards arrived, the Mayas had abandoned their large ceremonial complexes and the population lived in scattered small villages.

Although large urban centers existed from early times, the population of Greater Mexico was unequally distributed. The greatest concentrations were in Mesoamerica in the highlands of the central plateau, Oaxaca, and western Mexico (in what is now Michoacan), Yucatan, Chiapas, and the highlands of Central America, all of which supported the growing of corn. The deserts and mountains of northern Mexico, which were unsuitable for agriculture, had the lowest numbers. Mobile hunting and gathering groups dominated most of the region except the river valleys of the northwest and in New Mexico, where farmers grew and processed corn as did Mesoamericans.

Agriculture and Trade

Agriculture. Archeologists estimate that humans in Mesoamerica domesticated plants somewhere between 8000 and 2000 B.C. During this period, there was a worldwide climatic shift that resulted in expansion of the environment suitable for the grassy ancestors of modern grain crops, including wheat, rice, and maize. By 5000 B.C., the standard Mesoamerican diet of cultivated corn, beans, and squash had emerged. By around 1500 B.C., full-time farming had supplanted a lifestyle that depended on a mix of agriculture, hunting and gathering.

The long delay before fully sedentary agriculture replaced hunting and gathering likely was due to a combination of factors. Corn varieties with high enough yields to sustain settled populations probably developed very slowly. The corn grown at the time of Spanish contact in the 1500s was far different from its ancestor *teosinte* (*Zea mexicanus*), a small-headed grass that in its original form did not reliably produce surpluses. By around 5000 B.C., people had developed maize or Indian corn (*Zea mays*), with its large seeds and higher protein content, through selective breeding.

Given the geographical barriers to the diffusion of innovations, the spread of maize cultivation throughout Greater Mexico was slow compared to the relatively rapid adoption of sedentary agriculture in much of Eurasia. Although corn cultivation had developed fully in central and southern Mexico by 1500 B.C., it did not spread to the plains of North America until around A.D. 900, when the Mississippi Valley peoples adopted it.

Corn shaped human life in Mexico. Corn requires human intervention at every point of its seasonal cycle. Corn kernels are firmly attached to the fibrous cob, so humans must remove them in order to plant the next crop. Corn must be planted rather than left on the soil surface to germinate. The soil must be prepared for planting in full sun, requiring the complete clearing of fields. Harvesting maize requires that the ears be picked by hand, a labor-intensive task. Despite the high labor demands at certain times, corn otherwise requires little care between planting and harvest and will produce an abundant crop with sufficient rainfall. In some areas mild temperatures make it possible to plant and harvest two or even three crops annually.

While corn is relatively easy to grow, preparing it for consumption is as complicated as it is necessary. In Mexico the endless task of preparing corn was (and is) literally the daily grind for women. Dried corn kernels are removed from the cob, soaked in lime or ashes, then ground into corn flour on a broad flat stone called the *metate* (from the Nahuatl word *metlatl*) with a stone grinder, the *mano* (Spanish for "hand"), a process not mechanized until the twentieth century. If the kernels are not soaked, thus breaking down the chemicals to release niacin and amino acids otherwise inaccessible during human digestion, corn is poor in nutrients. Omitting this stage of preparation can cause pellagra, a nutritional disease caused by lack of niacin. Just how Mesoamericans learned to soak corn kernels in lime is a mystery. The exponential growth of highland Mexico's human population may owe as much to the mastery of corn processing as to its initial domestication.

The development of settled agriculture based on corn had implications for gender relations in Mexico. In hunting and gathering societies, women gatherers often contribute more to the sustenance of their families than do male hunters. With the transition to agriculture families came to depend on crops produced by men and food prepared by women. In settled agricultural societies, men generally control land and cultivate the crops, while women depend on men's labor to support them and their children. Mesoamerican women's work shifted from gathering to preparing food. The change from foraging to farming allowed for larger families, but relations within the family became less egalitarian and more hierarchical. The development of a hierarchy based on gender may have foreshadowed or contributed to the formation of other social and political hierarchies.

Abundant corn harvests not only fed the households that produced them but also supported nonagriculturalists. As early as the Olmecs, Mexico's earliest civilization (1300–500 B.C.), society was divided into classes, with rulers and priests supported by food produced by others. From that period onward, even settled farming families could pursue other kinds of tasks, such as hunting or fishing, part-time crafts (weaving, basket-making, pottery-making, mat-making), community labor (building and maintaining roads, temples, and palaces), and military service. These nonagricultural activities also followed gender lines, with women being part-time weavers of fine cotton cloth for household needs. Cloth also became an important trade and tribute item. The main nonagricultural duty of men was to perform labor on public works projects.

Trade Networks. Greater Mexico's diverse climatic and ecological zones and unevenly distributed natural resources fostered the early development of local and regional trade networks. Expansion of settled agriculture and the resulting surpluses allowed for growth in population and socioeconomic complexity that gave the highland regions a competitive advantage, allowing nonagriculturalists to develop crafts and long-distance traders to deal in the goods they fashioned. The discovery of artifacts, especially durable ones such as carved stone or pottery, far from their point of origin makes it possible for archeologists to identify trade networks. Obsidian arrow points are found throughout Mesoamerica but are produced in only a few sites.

Goods were also redistributed through tribute, a major factor in the political economy of Mesoamerica. Individual households and communities as a whole were required to deliver specific types and quantities of goods to tax collectors. A subordinate community would send tribute goods, sometimes over considerable distances, to their overlords to be used by the rulers, given as gifts, sold or traded. In this way products from individual households ended up far from where they were produced, carried by porters (called in Nahuatl *tlameme*).

Markets were important in Mesoamerica. Some were permanent centers, such as the great market in the Aztec capital that Bernal Díaz described, but periodic markets were more typical. Because many towns or regions specialized in particular crafts, people seeking specific products would travel to the appropriate town on its market day, which was set according to the solar-based calendar in use throughout Mesoamerica. Women as well as men bought and sold in the marketplace. Long-distance merchants were probably exclusively male, but there is evidence from Aztec times that women of the merchant group invested in trade.

While barter was probably a feature of Mesoamerican markets, by Aztec times and perhaps before two items had come into use as money—cacao beans (chocolate) and standardized lengths of cotton cloth. Cacao was a trade and tribute item from the southern tropics, which also came into use as a medium of exchange. Chocolate beans are convenient and fairly uniform in size, do not easily rot even without refrigeration, and are intrinsically valuable as food. The Aztecs promulgated written laws that regulated market exchanges in order to promote fair commerce, imposing severe penalties for sharp practice and theft.

The Rise of Mesoamerican Cultures

Almost all our information about ancient Greater Mexico comes from archeological data, as written texts exist for only a few regions and times. Archeologists use artifacts to reconstruct complex pictures of cultures and societies. Settlement patterns can reveal the density and size of populations at particular sites, the existence of social distinctions as reflected in hierarchical residential patterns, and human reshaping of the naural landscape as evidenced in terracing and road-building. The remains of tools and material

Mexican Cultures

Olmec	Gulf Coast	1300–500 B.C.
Monte Alban	Oaxaca	500 B.C.–500 A.D.
Classic Maya	Chiapas, Guatemala	200–900 A.D.
Teotihuacan	Central Plateau	1–700 A.D.
Toltec	Central Plateau	1000–1100 A.D.
Anasazi	New Mexico	1100–1300 A.D.
Chichen Itza Maya	Yucatan Peninsula	1000–1250 A.D.
Aztec	Central Plateau	1300–1521 A.D.

culture provide evidence of settled agriculture and crafts such as weaving, pottery, and feather work. From the remains of buildings archeologists learn about architecture, engineering, transportation of construction materials, methods of construction, and the purposes that different buildings served. As a result, we know a tremendous amount about Mexico's evolution over centuries.

The Olmecs. Olmec society began developing on the Gulf Coast of Mexico as early as 1500 B.C. At San Lorenzo, the Olmecs created huge public works, largely without stone, reshaping whole hillsides. Huge stone heads carved from massive blocks of basalt, probably depicting rulers, are the best-known remains of the Olmecs. They also constructed the first known ball courts for a game that spread throughout Mesoamerica and as far north as New Mexico and endured until the Spanish conquest. All evidence points to a society with a population large enough to support an elite group of rulers and priests and provide mass labor power for public building projects.

The Maya. Maya peoples dominated the southern highlands and lowlands during the period from A.D. 200 to 900, constructing impressive stone pyramids, palaces, and astronomical observatories. The cultural flowering of this period saw the development of a system of writing, a sophisticated calendar, detailed study of the movement of the planets, the creation of a mathematical system with a zero, and the architectural innovation of the corbeled arch, forming a vault. The Maya were sedentary agriculturalists who engaged in expansionist warfare and sacrificed prisoners, although not on the scale later seen among the Aztecs. The region was one of city-states that lacked a unifying and integrating state structure. The Maya city-states were abandoned for complex reasons. Population growth, climate change, and ecological decay in a fragile zone probably all contributed to this decline, together with foreign intrusion and warfare that was increasing in scale and destructiveness. Tikal in Guatemala, Palenque in Chiapas, and Copán in Honduras were important Maya centers in this period.

Teotihuacan. Teotihuacan, the remains of which still astound visitors, dominated the central plateau. Having reached its height with a population of 150,000 around 500 A.D., it had collapsed completely by about 700. Teotihuacan was a huge urban complex with wide boulevards and two enormous pyramids, called in modern times the Pyramids of the Sun and the Moon. Temples, elite residences, a central market, and dense apartment compounds were laid out in well-ordered quarters. Craftsmen living in the apartment compounds produced obsidian tools, ceramic pots, decorative figurines, and jewelry. Teotihuacan clearly played an important political and economic role in the central plateau, and its traders were active in many parts of Mesoamerica. In the seventh century, Teotihuacan's residents suddenly burned the religious and administrative structures. Scholars are still trying to piece together plausible explanations for this turn of events.

Toltecs. In the tenth century, Tula emerged as an important center on the central plateau. Tula was a major ceremonial site, with pyramids, columns, sculptures, ritual ball courts, and other evidence of substantial settlement. In the Aztecs' oral histories, recorded in pictures and alphabetic writing in the early Spanish period, they traced their cultural ancestry and kin connections to the Toltecs, although to date nothing in the archeological record supports that tradition. Tula was abandoned around 1150 A.D.

Anasazi. In the area of present-day New Mexico and Colorado, agri-culturalists now called the Anasazi or "Ancient Ones" created dense settlements. They reshaped the landscape to provide enough water for their staple crop of corn and made beautiful as well as serviceable baskets and superb pottery. Around 1100 A.D. they began building huge settlements in the cliffs near their fields with multistory structures of stone, wood, and mud plaster. Some dwellings could house up to 150 people; when the wooden ladders used to reach their houses were removed, they were secure from attack. Around 1300, the major Anasazi sites were entirely abandoned, perhaps because of climatic changes. Another theory is that invaders dese-crated the sites by practicing human sacrifice. Modern Pueblo and Hopi peoples claim cultural connections to the Anasazi.

Mesoamerican Society and Culture

Social Structure. How elite groups gained the power to command common-ers to pay tribute and provide labor service is a question hotly debated by scholars, but agricultural surpluses led to the division of Mesoamerican societies into classes as early as the time of the Olmecs. Rulers were sup-ported by lands cultivated by free commoners or dependent laborers who were attached to the households of the nobility. With the exception of the Mixtecs (Ñudzahui) in Oaxaca, where a man and woman jointly held the throne, Mesoamerican dynastic rulers were male. A ruler usually fulfilled several important functions, serving as political head of state, patron or priest of the religious cult, and military leader. Among the Aztecs demon-strations of valor in battle could elevate commoners to the ranks of the nobility, but just prior to the arrival of the Spaniards, this avenue to high social status was shut.

The largest group in Mesoamerica were the free commoners (called *macehualtin* by the Nahuas) who tilled the soil. With the transition to set-tled agriculture, control over resources shifted exclusively into men's hands. Land was held by clans or kin networks, called *calpulli* in Nahuatl. Households worked individual plots held by the calpulli. Failure to culti-vate the plot meant that it could be reassigned to landless or land-poor members. Free commoners were required to pay tribute in crops, especially corn and lengths of woven cotton. Households paid tribute to officials who delivered it to the local ruling elites. Community labor service also was important. Men participated in the construction and maintenance of public works, and women also performed tasks outside the household for the public good, such as food preparation, sweeping, and other domestic activities. Religious ideology created the rationale for such labor demands, so that commoners performed this work with a sense of higher purpose.

In addition to the basic division of society between nobles and commoners, there were two other groups in Mesoamerican society: merchants who constituted a wealthy elite but were not considered to be nobles, and dependent laborers and slaves attached to noble households. Long-distance merchants (the *pochteca*) were particularly important in the Aztec Empire, going on trading expeditions to distant lands, which also served as reconnaissance missions for the Triple Alliance. Merchants were important economically and politically, but they enjoyed their wealth privately rather than flaunting it. In the military culture of the Aztec Empire, the nobility and warriors were privileged over the wealthy commercial class, a pattern also found in Western Europe.

At the other end of the social scale were the dependent laborers and household slaves. Landless people in central Mexico often became dependents of a nobleman, cultivating his fields in exchange for reduced tribute requirements. Slaves also served in noble households. Although they were not free vassals, they retained some rights and could not be killed with impunity. Orphans and people suffering economic duress could sell themselves into slavery. Excessive gambling losses also could lead to enslavement.

In the hierarchical social structure of the Aztecs, rules stipulated who could wear particular clothing. Noblemen wore finely woven cotton capes, often elaborately embroidered, a breach clout and sandals, while noblewomen wore fine, often embroidered, cotton skirts and a loose cotton top called *huipil*, still worn by many Mexican Indian women. Commoner men and women usually wore clothing of rough cloth made from cactus fiber. Married women of all stations wore their hair up, while unmarried women wore it loose. For both men and women, having one's head shaved was a severe form of punishment.

Writing Systems. Mesoamericans created pictorial systems of writing, allowing the creation of written histories, record keeping, and transmission of news. The earliest surviving written records are carved stone glyphs, which have survived the ravages of tropical climates. The Olmecs developed ideograms during the period 1500–900 B.C., which spread throughout Mesoamerica, but the Mayas were responsible for true writing. In the Maya region, stone-carved stele, temples, and palaces record important rulers and dates. At some point the Mayas gave the pictograms phonetic content.

When the Spaniards arrived in Mesoamerica, they encountered glyphic texts written on fig bark paper (*amatl*), deerskin screen-folds, and cloth as well as stone. Unfortunately, they destroyed much of this written material.

In Mesoamerica, the existence of writing systems and survival of scribes trained in the written tradition allowed Mesoamericans to adopt European forms of writing and record keeping easily.

The Aztec Empire

Rise of the Aztecs. In 1400, the site of the future Aztec capital of Tenochtitlan was a desolate, snake-infested island in the middle of the central lake system of the central plateau. How did Tenochtitlan become the powerful head of a huge empire ruled by the descendants of wandering hunters and gatherers? The pictorial history known as the *Tira de Peregrinación* depicts the Aztecs' journey, beginning around 1100 A.D., from their homeland in a remote desert area called Aztlan, perhaps in northwestern Mexico, to the central plateau. The early Aztecs or Mexicas were hunters and gatherers. By the time the Mexicas arrived in the Valley of Mexico, they had assimilated the lifestyle of settled agriculturalists and spoke Nahuatl, the major language of the central region. Mexicas served as mercenaries to existing powers in the region, including Culhuacan, a refuge for the Toltecs after they abandoned Tula.

In 1325, the Mexicas retreated to an island in the middle of Lake Texcoco, forced to flee because they had sacrificed a daughter of the ruler of Culhuacan who had married the Mexica leader. Legend has it that the Aztecs saw an eagle perched on a prickly pear cactus (*nopal*) devouring a snake, a vision their god Huitzilopochtli foretold, showing them where they should settle permanently (see Figure 1-1). The island city-state of Tenochtitlan became the Mexicas' home, and they continued to act as mercenaries to other powers in the region. When the ruling line of Azcapotzalco, one of the regional powers they served, ended in 1428, the Mexicas of Tenochtitlan seized the opportunity to become a power in their own right, allying with Texcoco and Tlacopan to form the Triple Alliance in 1430. The Mexicas reconciled with the rulers of Culhuacan and intermarried with their ruling dynasty, allowing them to claim a direct connection to the Toltecs.

Mexica rulers enhanced their reputation and the empire's fortunes through military conquest. Since each Mexica ruler was expected to build on the accomplishments of his predecessors, new rulers sought further conquests. In 1502, the council of noblemen chose a new ruler. Looking for the ablest leader among possible candidates, they picked thirty-four-year-old Moctezuma, nephew of the recently deceased ruler and son of another ruler. Electors saw him as mature, pious, wise, proud, and brave. By the time of Moctezuma II's rule, the status of the Mexica monarchs verged on divine. They were thought to have special powers of prophecy and the ability to interpret omens, a role that played some part in the Spaniards' conquest of Mexico.

Aztec Kings

Acampichtli	1375–96	Axayacatl	1469–81
Huitzilihuitl	1396–1417	Tizoc	1481–6
Chimalpopoca	1417–27	Ahuitzotl	1486–1502
Itzcoatl	1427–40	Moctezuma II	1502–20
Moctezuma I	1440–69	Cuitlahuac	June–October 1520
		Cuauhtemoc	October 1520–August 1521

Although Tenochtitlan became the senior partner in the Triple Alliance, the city-state of Texcoco remained important and its ruling line exerted considerable influence over Tenochtitlan. Texcoco was the cultural capital of the Triple Alliance, and it was there that the Aztec legal code was written. Texcoco's greatest ruler was Nezahualcoyotl ("hungry coyote"), reputed to be a poet-king. His son, Nezahualpilli ("hungry lord"), also was highly revered, although during his early years as ruler Tenochtitlan gained ascendance over Texcoco. Under Nezahualpilli, Texcoco ceased to participate in Tenochtitlan's military campaigns, because they no longer brought Texcoco material gain. His death in 1515 precipitated a succession crisis that was ongoing when the Spaniards arrived.

The Aztec Empire. When Spaniards landed on the Gulf Coast of Mexico in the early sixteenth century, the Aztec Empire controlled a large expanse of central and southern Mexico. Several important areas lay outside its power, most notably the Purepecha (Tarascan) state in west-central Mexico and the Nahua city-state of Tlaxcala. Tribute officials collected a rich array of goods for the Triple Alliance, with the lion's share going to Tenochtitlan.

The Aztec Empire was made up of a number of political units, city-states that themselves usually controlled smaller political units. The internal structure of even subordinate city-states remained largely intact after conquest, so local elites maintained their positions while continuing to mobilize tribute and labor for both themselves and their overlords. The Triple Alliance did not garrison soldiers in conquered city-states but instead relied on other strategies to maintain control, including speedy deployment of warriors to quell rebellions. The threat that rebellious warriors faced of ending up as human sacrifices to the Aztec gods might well have acted as a deterrent to revolt. Another strategy was the marriage of key noblewomen to the rulers of the Triple Alliance, which solidified alliances at the top.

Since city-states maintained a high degree of internal integrity and usually longed for a return to political autonomy, the Aztec empire was fragile. The empire worked well as a tribute-collecting confederation, but the lack of political integration of conquered city-states, as well as the Triple Alliance's failure to maintain a permanent military presence, meant that subordinate city-states often revolted if given the opportunity. People remained loyal to their local community, not to the larger state. Although religion was important, a city-state's defeat did not mean its deities were overturned; rather, the conquerors' principal gods were added to the pantheon.

Tenochtitlan. As with other city-states in the Valley of Mexico, the island capital of Tenochtitlan was divided into quarters. The Great Temple was built at the intersection of the city's four quarters, reflecting the Aztec concept that the world was divided into four parts. Each quarter itself had a temple and palace complex, as well as a market. Although Tenochtitlan was not self-sufficient in food, some commoners cultivated *chinampas*, fertile and well-watered gardens artificially created in the lakes that produced fresh vegetables. Lakeside city-states such as Xochimilco and Culhuacan also practiced this labor-intensive but highly productive form of agriculture. Tenochtitlan's control over these towns brought it additional tribute and created a secure zone for the capital.

Lake Texcoco was easily traversed by canoe, and the movement of people and goods to Tenochtitlan kept the island city-state well supplied. Tribute from nearby conquered city-states as well as goods destined for markets made the island capital a great emporium. Causeways also linked Tenochtitlan to the mainland. Built with removable sections, the causeways allowed the Mexica to control access to their island. It was not until Spaniards built brigantines with cannons mounted on them for the siege of Tenochtitlan (1520–1) that the Mexicas were threatened by water. Native canoes were adequate for transporting goods, but they were not stable, maneuverable, or large enough to allow enemies to attack Tenochtitlan successfully by water.

Aztec Law and Religion

Legal Code. Reinforcing social order in the Aztec sphere were written laws that survive in pictorial form and show how the state regulated a variety of activities, including marriage, public drunkenness, and robbery. The Aztec law on adultery prescribed that both men and women were to be punished by death if they were married.

High status did not protect those who violated the law. Shortly before the arrival of the Spaniards, there was a spectacular adultery trial that involved the legitimate wife of Texcoco's ruler, Nezahualpilli, recorded by one of his descendants in the sixteenth century, Don Fernando de Alva Ixtlilxochitl. The adulteress was a woman of the highest status, the daughter of Tenochtitlan's ruler Axayacatl named Chalchiuhnenetzin ("precious jade-stone"), who took a series of lovers. She had them killed and placed their images in her chambers, telling her husband that they were her gods. Her downfall was to leave three lovers alive after their identifiable images joined her "pantheon." She was convicted at a public trial and executed, despite the breach it created between Texcoco and Tenochtitlan.

Religion. Mesoamericans worshipped a pantheon of gods and goddesses. They had a priesthood and large and beautiful temples as well as local and domestic cults. A ritual calendar linked to a solar calendar governed religious life. Deities were believed to hold power over the universe, nature, and affairs of humankind, and humans were concerned with propitiating them. Many deities were linked to the elements necessary to sustain agriculture, such as rain. Religion served the ruling elites well, with conquests marked by religious celebrations, rulers' positions sanctioned by the deities, and rituals that underscored the power and sacredness of the political order.

The Aztecs' religious system was built on traditions and beliefs that had evolved over a long period in Mesoamerica. Certain deities that had similar attributes and cults, such as the rain god (Tlaloc in the Nahua region, Chaac in the Maya), were especially widespread. The cult dedicated to the Aztecs' principal god, Huitzilopochtli, who represented a fusion of traits associated with militaristic deities, justified conquest, tribute, and the power of the nobility.

Another important deity was Quetzalcoatl ("feathered serpent"). His image decorated temple complexes as early as the Olmec era (c. 800 B.C.), and spread to the central plateau, where it is found in Teotihuacan. Around A.D. 900, a priest-king born in Tula took the name of the diety; he was called Quetzalcoatl Topiltzin ("our revered lord"). Later the cult of the deity and the priest-king apparently merged, so that in postconquest indigenous and Spanish accounts the creator god and priest-king became one. The priest-king Quetzalcoatl Topiltzin was chaste and opposed to human sacrifice. Tricked into defiling his sister while drunk, he exiled himself from Tula, departing to the east. According to one legend, he vowed to return. Because the Mexica of Tenochtitlan claimed Toltec lineage, some scholars argue that when the Spaniards appeared on the Gulf Coast in 1519, soon after a new fifty-two-year cycle began, they believed Cortés to be Quetzalcoatl Topiltzin returning to claim his throne.

Human Sacrifice. Human sacrifice has been practiced in various places worldwide. The Aztecs offered human hearts to their god Huitzilopochtli to propitiate him and ensure that the sun would continue on its daily course. On the platform of the great temple of Tenochtitlan the gods Tlaloc and Huitzilopochtli had adjoining altars.

Human sacrifice was an important part of Aztec religion. Other Mesoamericans also practiced it, including the Mayas, but not on a comparable scale. The Aztecs' main sacrificial victims were warriors captured on the battlefield, and apparently the main objective of some wars was to capture warriors. In these so-called "flowery wars" (*xochiyaotl*), warriors captured but did not kill their enemies. Some scholars have speculated that the Nahua city-state of Tlaxcala was allowed to maintain its independence despite its proximity to the Triple Alliance city-states so that Aztec warriors could not only gain experience on the battlefield close to home but also have a source of human offerings to the gods.

Human sacrifice ceased with the Spanish conquest, not only because it horrified the Christian conquerors who vigorously prohibited it but also because Aztecs generally sacrificed outsiders and conquered peoples. Mesoamericans did not volunteer themselves for sacrifice no matter how strong their allegiance to the old gods, although many continued to follow rituals of bloodletting for years after the Spanish conquest.

Warfare: The Aztecs and Regional Powers

The Aztecs were a militaristic society, with an elite warrior group organized into units called the Eagle and Jaguar Warriors. These warriors dressed to resemble these beautiful but lethal animals. Since Mesoamerica lacked metallurgy, all weapons were made of wood and stone. Bow and arrow was the standard weapon of commoner warriors, while leaders wielded heavy wooden clubs called *macanas* with sharp obsidian imbedded in the edges, capable of taking a man's head off at a stroke. A spear thrower, called an *atlatl*, sent projectiles into enemy forces from a distance. Combat took place on foot, generally on open plains.

Aztec warriors fought to acquire more tribute-paying states for the Triple Alliance and victims for human sacrifice, as well as to demonstrate personal valor, highly valued in militaristic societies. Often an initial test of strength would decide the outcome of the battle, with an early capitulation ensuring better terms for the defeated power.

Tenochtitlan did not conquer all of Mesoamerica. The Purepecha of western Mexico remained independent. Located in the modern state of Michoacan, the Tarascan empire was an important center whose capital Tzintzuntzan had a population of around thirty-five thousand in 1519. Unlike central Mexico, where a large number of city-states vied for power, there were no other competing states in western Mexico to challenge the Tarascans within that region. Since they were neither imperialistic nor interested in creating a commercial network, they did not seek external contacts or conflicts and experienced relative internal peace. The Aztec's campaigns against them forced them to build up their military defenses, but the Purepecha more than held their own against the Triple Alliance. Although the Purepecha shared many traits of Mesoamerican culture, they conspicuously lacked a system of writing, probably an outgrowth of their xenophobia.

When the Spaniards arrived the Maya zone consisted of three core areas, whose inhabitants all spoke variants of Mayan. In the southern high-

Figure 1-2 **Aztec cannibalism**. Ritual sacrifice and cannibalism were an integral part of Mexica religion, shown here with the god, Mictlantecuhtli, lord of the dead. From *The Book of the Life of the Ancient Mexicans*. Part I, Facsimile. Berkeley: University of California Press, 1903. Republished 1983, p. 61/73 (two different systems of pagination). Boxed set with *The Codex Magliabechiano*, edited by Elizabeth Hill Boone, University of California Press, 1983.

lands of present-day Chiapas and Guatemala and the tropical lowlands of Petén, Belize, and the Yucatan peninsula regional states held sway over their surrounding regions. The Quiché Maya of the southern highlands created an empire centered at Utatlán. The Aztecs sought trade and conquests in the region, and the Quiché and Mexica royal families intermarried, perhaps to ease military tensions and facilitate trade. Trade between the Maya region, Oaxaca, and central Mexico was extensive. These trade networks, however, never consolidated into political confederations.

The Aztec Empire was not prepared to resist a major challenge from the outside, particularly one launched by invaders who arrived literally armed with superior technology, as Europeans did in 1519. For a century militaristic Nahuas had conquered and controlled large sections of central and southern Mesoamerica. The Aztec Empire did not integrate its territories politically, failed to disarm conquered city-states, and did not garrison soldiers. As a result the empire was quickly built but vulnerable to swift disintegration. Its efficiency in using existing hierarchies to extract tribute from conquered city-states made the Aztec Empire rich. It became the prize that Spaniards had long sought in the Americas.

Glossary

Aztec Empire   dominant empire of central Mexico in 1519
calpulli   kinship and landholding group or local district of the Nahuas
cenote   sinkhole characteristic of Yucatan, usually filled with water
chinampas   artificially created farmland, erroneously called "floating gardens"
Mesoamerica   area of sedentary Indian settlement from just north of the Valley of Mexico to southern Central America
Mexica   Aztecs, also called Tenochca
Nahuas   Nahuatl-speakers, often called the Aztecs
Nahuatl   language of central Mexico, spoken by the Aztecs
New Spain   Spanish Crown's designation of its territory in North America
pochteca   Nahuatl word for long-distance merchants
Purepecha   indigenous group of western Mexico, often called the Tarascans
prehispanic era   before the arrival of the Spaniards
Tenochtitlan   most powerful polity when the Spaniards arrived
tlameme   Nahuatl term for porters

Questions for Discussion

1.   How did climate and environment affect the development of cultures in Greater Mexico?

2.   Why was the domestication of maize so important?

3.   What role did the Aztecs play in the history of Greater Mexico?

4.   What were some of the social and cultural patterns that European and Mesoamerican peoples shared? In what ways did they differ?

5.   What kinds of comparisons to the Old World did Bernal Díaz del Castillo make in describing the market in Tenochtitlan?

Suggested Reading

Primary Sources

Coruña, Fray Martín de Jesús de la. *The Chronicles of Michoacán* [1541]. Trans. and ed. by Eugene R. Craine and Reginald C. Reindorp. Norman: University of Oklahoma Press, 1970. Account of the history and culture of the Tarascan (Purepecha) state in western Mexico.

Durán, Fr. Diego. *The History of the Indies of New Spain* [1581]. Trans., annotated and with an introduction by Doris Heyden. Norman: University of Oklahoma Press, 1994. An account of the Aztecs compiled by a sixteenth-century Dominican friar from native sources.

Sahagún, Fr. Bernardino de. *General History of the Things of New Spain* [1576] (12 volumes). Trans. and ed. by Arthur J. O. Anderson and Charles Dibble. Salt Lake City: University of Utah Press, 1952–80. The richest source of information on Aztec culture, compiled in Spanish and Nahuatl by a Franciscan in the 1570s, and based on native sources.

Secondary Sources

Adams, Richard E. W., and Murdo J. MacLeod, editors. *The Cambridge History of Native Peoples of the Americas,* (vol. II) *Mesoamerica.* Cambridge: Cambridge University Press, 2000. Articles by leading scholars summarizing archeological and historical information on Mesoamerica, and includes extensive bibliographic essays.

Anawalt, Patricia. *Indian Clothing before Cortés.* Norman: University of Oklahoma Press, 1981. Important examination of Mesoamerican clothing and its significance.

Aveni, Anthony F. *Skywatchers of Ancient Mexico.* Austin: University of Texas Press, 1980. Major work on astronomy in ancient Mesoamerica.

Berdan, Frances F. *The Aztecs of Central Mexico: An Imperial Society.* New York: Holt, Rinehart, and Winston, 1982. Excellent summary by an ethnohistorian dealing with all aspects of the Aztecs before the conquest.

Carrasco, David, ed. *The Oxford Encyclopedia of Mesoamerican Cultures.* New York and Oxford: Oxford University Press, 2001. Major reference work.

Carrasco, Pedro. *The Tenochca Empire of Ancient Mexico: The Triple Alliance of Tenochtitlan, Tetzcoco, and Tlacopan.* Norman: University of Oklahoma Press, 1999. Thorough discussion of the political and territorial structure of the empire.

Cline, Howard F., ed. *Guide to Ethnohistorical Sources, Handbook of Middle American Indians,* vols. 12–14. Austin: University of Texas Press, 1972–75. A major bibliographic source for central Mexican Indian history which has been updated periodically by new volumes in the series.

Edmonson, Munro. *The Book of the Year: Middle American Calendrical Systems.* Salt Lake City: University of Utah Press, 1988. Thorough analysis of Mesoamerican calendars and their importance.

Hassig, Ross. *War and Society in Ancient Mesoamerica.* Berkeley and Los Angeles: University of California Press, 1992. Analysis of the role of warfare by an anthropologist specializing in Aztec ethnohistory.

León-Portilla, Miguel. *Aztec Thought and Culture.* Norman: University of Oklahoma Press, 1963. Important synthesis by a major scholar.

Marcus, Joyce. *Mesoamerican Writing Systems: Propaganda, Myth and History of Four Ancient Civilizations.* Princeton, N.J.: Princeton University Press, 1992. Examination of Mesoamerican traditions with an emphasis on genealogies among the Maya, Zapotec, Mixtec, and Nahuas.

McVicker, Donald. "Quetzalcoatl," *The Encyclopedia of Mexico,* vol. 2, pp. 1211–14. Chicago: Fitzroy Dearborn Publishers, 1997. Concise discussion of key areas of confusion in interpreting history and myth.

Offner, Jerome A. *Law and Politics in Aztec Texcoco.* Cambridge: Cambridge University Press, 1983. Prize-winning analysis of Aztec legal structures and political dynamics based on close reading of written and pictorial sources.

TWO

Spain in the Era
of Expansion

Just as it is essential to understand the indigenous societies and cultures of the Americas, it is important to know something about the history, culture, and experiences of the people of Spain who directly and indirectly contributed to and participated in the forging of a new society in Mexico. The circumstances of the conquest of Mexico and the resulting contacts among Europeans, Indians, and Africans in one way or another affected everyone who was involved. As they adapted to the new situation, all of colonial Mexico's peoples would strive to maintain and elaborate their particular norms and lifestyles, although often they only succeeded in part. This chapter provides a brief introduction to the history and society of Spain, with particular attention to those aspects of the Spanish experience that would have greatest relevance to the conquest and settlement of Mexico.

1492: A Watershed

Three critical events occurred in 1492 that had a decisive impact on Spanish history. They symbolized and signaled a break with Spain's ethnically and religiously diverse medieval past and heralded a new direction for the future. In January 1492, the forces of King Ferdinand and Queen Isabel conquered Granada, the last Muslim kingdom in the Iberian peninsula. This victory brought to a close a difficult and expensive decade-long military campaign and the centuries-long reconquest, in which Christians reestablished control over territory that had been ruled by Muslims since the early eighth century. Less than three months later, at the end of March 1492, the sovereigns, whose triumph over Granada earned them the papal title of the "Reyes Católicos" (Catholic Monarchs), signed the decree expelling all remaining Jewish subjects from their kingdoms. Within a month of that act, the Catholic Monarchs made their fateful agreement to sponsor the westward voyage of Columbus.

Rather than reaching their intended destination, Asia, with its wealthy trading peoples and exotic wares, after crossing the Atlantic Columbus and his men made landfall in the Bahamas in mid-October of 1492. This voyage initiated a continuing and increasingly close connection between Europe and the Americas that would utterly transform both.

Although certainly not as decisive as these three events, one other achievement associated with the rise of Spain, and specifically of Castile, to power also would be realized in 1492: the completion of Antonio de Nebrija's grammar of the Castilian language, which he dedicated to Queen Isabel. On the publication of this grammar, the first of any modern language, Nebrija not only expressed his expectation that Castilian would expand at the expense of other languages within Spain itself, but also pointed out that "language has always been the companion of empire." Perhaps he had in mind the classical examples of the spread of Greek in the east after Alexander's conquests and later of Latin in the lands ruled by Rome. Thus, even scholarship helped to usher in the new age of expansion.

The Legacy of the Past

From ancient times the Iberian Peninsula, lying at the westernmost end of the Mediterranean and nearly touching North Africa at its southern tip, attracted outsiders and became home to representatives of many cultures. Celts settled mainly in the north and west, and over time they probably mingled with peoples already living there. The Basques, whose origin is a mystery, already were living in the western Pyrenees when the Celts arrived. The people called Iberians, who lived along the Mediterranean and south Atlantic coasts, spoke non-Indo-European languages. They came into contact with people from the eastern Mediterranean when Greeks and Phoenicians, attracted by Iberia's mineral wealth and agricultural potential, established colonies on the eastern and southern coasts in the tenth through sixth centuries B.C.

As the power of Phoenicia in the western Mediterranean waned, its North African colony of Carthage grew and began to exert more influence over the Iberian peninsula. The defeat of Carthage by Rome in the first Punic War (241 B.C.) had significant consequences for Spain, as the Carthaginians started extending their control over the Iberian peninsula as a counterweight to Roman power. The expanded Carthaginian presence embroiled Spain in the second Punic War, which brought two Roman legions to the east coast in 218 B.C. The Romans would remain for another six centuries, leaving a strong imprint on everything from the languages, laws, and religion of Iberia to the sites of cities and network of roads that connect them. Roman occupation did not go unopposed, however. Although over time much of the Iberian peninsula would be thoroughly Romanized, it took nearly two centuries before the Romans could claim uncontested authority over Spain.

Visigothic Rule. With the disintegration of the Roman empire in the west the Visigoths established themselves on Iberian soil in the second half of the fifth century A.D. The Visigoths were not the first Germanic invaders to cross the Pyrenees, having been preceded by the Alans, Sueves, and Vandals, all of whom occupied parts of the Iberian peninsula for some time. After forming a kingdom in southwestern Gaul in the fifth century, the Visigoths extended their control over the Iberian peninsula, initially as the allies of Rome. Perhaps the most Romanized of the Germanic groups, the Visigoths in many ways assimilated and preserved the Roman tradition in Spain. By the beginning of the sixth century the Visigoths had been pushed out of Gaul, after which they maintained their kingdom in Spain, making the centrally located city of Toledo their capital in the mid-sixth century.

The Visigoths were Christians, although in the fourth century they had converted to Arianism, a variant form of Christianity that was later declared heretical by the Roman Catholic church. Their Hispano-Roman subjects were Roman Catholics. Late in the sixth century, the Visigoths formally converted to Catholicism, a process that in any case had been under way as they increasingly mingled and intermarried with the local population. Under the leadership of the bishops, first of Seville (the most notable being the influential and prolific Isidore) and then of Toledo, the Spanish church played a prominent role during the Visigothic period.

The Visigothic kings compiled several law codes, the most important of which became known as the Visigothic code or *Fuero Juzgo*, promulgated in 654. It remained in effect in many parts of Christian Spain until at least the thirteenth century. The law code known as *Siete Partidas* that King Alfonso X "el Sabio" (the Learned) sought to impose as the uniform law of the land in the thirteenth century, although mainly based on Roman law, also drew in part on the Visigothic code, which itself had incorporated a great deal of the old Roman law.

During the seventh century Spain's Jewish population, which was sizeable in the east and south, became the target of legislation that restricted their rights or even attempted to force them to convert. It has been suggested that Visigothic persecution of the Jews in this period predisposed them to support and aid the next wave of invaders who entered the Iberian peninsula, this time from the south. These were the Muslims.

Islamic Spain. In 698, as part of the astonishingly rapid and successful expansion of the Muslim empire in the east and west, Arabs completed their conquest of North Africa, which then became the staging ground for yet another swift movement of conquest and expansion. Armies of North African Berbers (often called Moors), led by Arabs, crossed the Strait of Gibraltar into southern Spain, conquering Toledo in 711 (or possibly 712), reaching Zaragoza in the northeast by 714, and overcoming the last Visigothic stronghold in 720. In later years, Christians would look back to their victory over Muslims at Covadonga in northern Spain (more a skirmish than a real battle) as having marked the beginning of successful Christian resistance to Muslim occupation of the peninsula, although at the time it probably was not very significant.

The Muslims eventually reached and crossed the Pyrenees but never really established a presence in the north. The Roman network of roads facilitated movement and conquest, and many of Islamic Spain's cities had once been Roman towns. The Muslims called their Spanish realm "al-Andalus," a name that apparently derived from one of the Germanic tribes—the Vandals—that once occupied southern Spain. The area of greatest Muslim strength and influence lay in the center and south of the Iberian Peninsula, reflecting Islamic Spain's ties with, and orientation toward, North Africa. Although Toledo remained important, the Muslims shifted their center of administration to the south, first Seville and then Córdoba, both on the Guadalquivir River. In the tenth century, an independent caliphate (Muslim state) with Córdoba as its capital was established by the Umayyad dynasty (929–1031). Although the united caliphate lasted barely a century, the subsequent political fragmentation of Muslim Spain by no means slowed its development. The economy, based on irrigated agriculture, silk production, and brisk international commerce that tied al-Andalus to the Muslim world, flourished. A sophisticated Islamic culture, centered in the major cities and sustained in large part by the patronage of the wealthy rulers of the states that replaced the caliphate, also developed.

Under the Muslims, Spanish cities became great centers of learning and education in fields such as botany, medicine, mathematics, astronomy, and philosophy. Córdoba had a library with four hundred thousand books at a time that the largest libraries in western Europe could boast no more than a couple of thousand. Toledo became a center for translation. Gerard of Cremona (1114–87), one of the leading Christian scholars who worked there, initiated the translation of the works of Aristotle, Galen, Ptolemy, and other Greeks from Arabic into Latin.

Two of the influential intellectuals of the era, Moses Maimonides and Averroës (Ibn Rushd), both born in Córdoba in the twelfth century, exemplified the scholarly and philosophical achievements of Islamic Spain. Maimonides (1135–1204), a leading authority on Jewish law, medicine, and philosophy, left Spain to live in Egypt, where he became the court physician to Saladin, the great Muslim general who retook Jerusalem from the Christian Crusaders. Maimonides wrote *Guide of the Perplexed*, his best-known work, in Arabic; it was translated into Hebrew during his lifetime and into Latin in the thirteenth century. The scholarly work of his Muslim contemporary Averroës (1126–78), also a physician, included a medical encyclopedia and treatises on astronomy, grammar, and law; but his greatest contribution to scholarship consisted of voluminous commentaries on Aristotle and Plato. Translated from Arabic, these works would have enormous influence on Latin scholars in the medieval period.

Probably the majority of the residents of al-Andalus—especially city dwellers—eventually converted to Islam. Arabic became the language of everyday life in Muslim Spain. Muslim influence was reflected in place names; loanwords that entered the Romance languages of the Iberian

Peninsula; the form, function, and even the officials of cities; architecture; and agricultural technology. Christians continued to live in Muslim-ruled areas, many of them absorbing a substantial degree of Muslim cultural influence as reflected in their language, diet, and dress. These Christians, known as Mozarabs, later would play an important role in the development of the emerging Christian kingdoms of the north, as many left Muslim-ruled states to live in Christian-controlled territory or remained in formerly Muslim areas when Christians gained control.

Jews, present in the peninsula since Roman times, continued to live in Islamic Spain, and probably more arrived from North Africa after the Muslim conquest. In the Middle Ages there were Jewish communities living in territories ruled by both Christians and Muslims. Mainly urban in their residence and occupations, most Jews made their living as shopkeepers, artisans, and merchants, although in some areas there were Jewish farmers. A small number achieved influence and wealth as the financial and political advisors of kings. Prominent Jews also served as tax collectors and physicians.

Muslims allowed both Christians and Jews to practice their own religions, although they required them to pay special taxes. Although the three religions remained sharply differentiated, Muslim, Christian, and Jewish scholars and artisans at times collaborated with and influenced one another, and members of the different groups did business together and associated in various ways. Inevitably there were social contacts and even intermarriage, even though all three religions strongly opposed it.

Through most of the Middle Ages, religious toleration usually, although not invariably, prevailed; the term *convivencia* ("living together") is often used for the accommodation these religious and ethnic groups made with one another. In the later Middle Ages, however, tolerance began to break down. Serious outbreaks of Christian violence against Jews, beginning in 1390, not only nearly eliminated the thriving Jewish communities of the largest cities but also resulted in significant numbers of conversions to Christianity in the following decades. Many of these converts, called *conversos* or "New Christians," continued to associate closely with their Jewish kin and friends, and members of the Christian community often viewed them with suspicion.

The Reconquista. The sporadic conflict known as the *Reconquista,* or Christian reconquest, of the Iberian Peninsula initially did not necessarily stem from religious fanaticism or hatred. For a long time it probably was as much motivated by the quest for land, cattle, and booty and the political and personal ambitions of kings and fighting men as it was by religious objectives. By the twelfth century, non-Iberian Christians had joined the struggle, while on the other side Muslims had regained their military strength and initiative with the arrival from North Africa of militant new groups. With the arrival of these outsiders, the Reconquista began to take on more of the character of a crusade or holy war. It always retained, however, some of the distinctive qualities that arose from centuries of convivencia, and foreigners who came to aid Spaniards in their "crusade" at times were scandalized by the tolerance and apparent leniency that Iberian Christians exhibited in their dealings with the Muslim enemy.

The northern part of the peninsula, sparsely populated and rural at the time of the eighth-century invasion from North Africa, never came under Muslim rule. Christian principalities began to take shape there in the eighth century. Asturias in the northwest claimed a connection to the old Visigothic monarchy. East of Asturias, in the western Pyrenees, a Basque principality later formed the basis for the kingdom of Navarre. In the eastern Pyrenees, in Catalonia, the Frankish king Charlemagne organized several counties into the Spanish March, which by around 900 essentially had become independent of the Carolingian monarchy. Of these, the Asturian kingdom expanded most rapidly, both southward and westward, giving rise to Castile to the east and Portugal to the west. Although the Christian-occupied north was rural and its economy agrarian, by the ninth and tenth centuries the populations of these kingdoms had increased to the point that they were pressing southward.

Despite the backwardness of Christian Spain in the early medieval period, it was never entirely cut off from the rest of Christian Europe. Its relative isolation soon would end with the development of what would become Christendom's third most important religious shrine, which transformed northern Spain into a major destination for pilgrims. In the early ninth century the discovery of what was believed to be the tomb of one of the apostles, St. James or Santiago, was made in Galicia in the northwest. The site of his tomb, Santiago de Compostela, began to attract pilgrims from across the Pyrenees; by the eleventh and twelfth centuries they were arriving in great numbers. Towns such as Pamplona, Logroño, León, and Burgos that were located along the pilgrimage route—the Camino de Santiago—grew, as not only pilgrims but also French and Jewish merchants arrived from across the Pyrenees. Many of them settled in the towns as shopkeepers and artisans.

The French exerted notable influence over the medieval church in Spain, especially in establishing new monasteries. French architects designed the new cathedral of Santiago de Compostela, built between 1078 and 1124. Nevertheless the cult of St. James retained a distinctly Spanish character. As the "Moorslayer" (Santiago Matamoros) St. James became the symbol of the Christian struggle with the Muslims and later would be invoked during the Spanish conquest of Mexico. Spaniards made other significant contributions to Roman Catholicism in this period as well. The Castilian Domingo de Guzmán (1170–1221, canonized St. Dominic in 1234), became the founder of a new order that emphasized preaching. Committed to the campaign against heresy, Dominicans became influential intellectuals within the church.

Figure 2-1 **Saint James the Moorslayer** (*Santiago matamoros*), patron saint of Spain, is a potent symbol of militant Christianity, shown here with fallen Muslims during the Christian reconquest of Spain.
From Copilaciõ de los establecimientos de la Orden de la Cavalleria de Santiago de la Espada. Seville, 1503. Library of Congress, Rare Book and Special Collections.

As the Christian kingdoms expanded southward, new towns were established. They played an important role in reoccupying and holding territory claimed by Christian kings. In order to attract settlers to these frontier towns kings granted charters (*fueros*) that usually conceded the right to self-government through an elected town council. They also offered potential *vecinos* (citizens, householders) incentives to settle, such as tax breaks, grants of urban and rural property, and access to municipal commons (which generally included pastures and woodlands). The fueros also often gave towns and cities jurisdiction over their surrounding territories, which could include smaller towns, villages, and other settlements. A thriving town could be a considerable asset to a king. Many maintained militias that participated actively in skirmishes with the Muslims and thus provided crucial support in military campaigns that yielded booty and profits that played an important role in the medieval economy.

Independent towns and cities were not, of course, the only entities exercising dominion in the countryside. Kings granted towns, land, and jurisdiction over territory to high-ranking nobles in return for military services and financial support. Some areas came under the jurisdiction of high church officials, such as the Archbishop of Toledo. Military orders—the Knights of Calatrava, the Order of Alcántara, and the Order of Santiago— were founded in the twelfth century, modeled on crusading religio-military orders such as the Templars. Membership conferred great prestige and often considerable wealth and power as well. As the Christian kingdoms expanded south of the Tajo River, the Spanish military orders received jurisdiction over extensive territories, especially in the southwest (Extremadura), in return for their services.

By the latter part of the Middle Ages, the Spanish kingdoms had become jurisdictionally very complex, with territory variously controlled by towns and cities and lay and ecclesiastical lords. Whether one resided in royal, noble, or ecclesiastical dominions, however, did not necessarily make a great deal of difference in terms of either lifestyle or financial and tax obligations. Usually people were free to leave one locality to go to live in another. This lack of constraint would have important implications for physical mobility, population shifts and the founding of new settlements, and eventually for emigration abroad.

By the middle of the thirteenth century, only one Muslim kingdom remained in the Iberian peninsula, Granada. Most of the rest of the peninsula had been absorbed into three major Christian kingdoms: Portugal along the Atlantic seaboard; Castile, which had both Atlantic and Mediterranean coasts and ports; and the eastern kingdom of Aragón, which with its great port cities of Barcelona and Valencia long had been active in the trade and politics of the Mediterranean. Of the three kingdoms, the largest and most populous was Castile. This kingdom participated most actively and directly in the Spanish conquest and settlement of the

Americas, ultimately having the greatest influence on Spain's overseas empire.

Government and Politics in the Era of Expansion

The Catholic Monarchs. Prince Ferdinand, heir apparent to the crown of Aragón, married Princess Isabel of Castile in 1469. Although Isabel's bid to claim the Castilian crown was contested, ten years after marrying both Ferdinand and Isabel succeeded to their respective thrones. The marriage created a Spanish monarchy, uniting the crowns of the two largest Iberian kingdoms, which thereafter would be held by all successive monarchs. Between 1580 and 1640, the Spanish crown also ruled Portugal. The kingdoms remained separate in most senses, retaining not only their distinct political institutions but even different monetary systems. The various kingdoms and provinces continued to be linguistically, culturally, and economically diverse, although in general they shared a common Iberian culture rooted in religion (Roman Catholicism), social structure, and political and historical experience.

Although they remained monarchs of their respective kingdoms, Ferdinand and Isabel pursued a policy of joint rule. Because of their remarkable success in bringing order to their kingdoms, which had suffered from political weakness and conflict in the fourteenth and fifteenth centuries (and, in the case of Aragón, economic decline), the Catholic Monarchs often are considered to have been great innovators. In fact, in institutional terms they introduced relatively little that was new. Nonetheless, by strengthening and extending existing institutions and pursuing a policy of centralization, they made considerable strides toward consolidating and restoring prestige to the monarchy and bringing stability to their kingdom. They traveled constantly to enforce their rule, often spending a week or more in the key towns and cities of their realms, especially Castile. In the latter years of their reign, and particularly after Isabel's death in 1504, some of the progress they made toward achieving a balance of power between an ambitious nobility and independence-minded towns began to erode. In the long run, however, their successors upheld their policies, which to a great extent continued to shape government and administration in the sixteenth century in both Spain and America.

The Catholic Monarchs relied heavily on the Royal Council, which was advisory in function and also served as the highest judicial court of appeal. There also were *chancillerías*, high courts, located in Valladolid and Granada, and secondary high courts known as *audiencias*. Other councils subsequently came into existence, some of them dealing with specific sectors of government (such as the Council of Finance, created in 1524 by Charles V) and others with particular territories (such as the Council of the Indies, also established in 1524). This conciliar form of government could be cumbersome and slow. Yet, despite the inefficiencies that resulted from duplication of, or conflicts over, function, the overlapping responsibilities of the councils created a system of checks and balances in which the Crown in effect could act as the ultimate adjudicator. From the time of Ferdinand and Isabel the Spanish monarchs increasingly appointed university-trained lawyers, *letrados*, to their councils. These lawyers formed the basis for an educated and competent professional bureaucracy that could expand to staff agencies of royal government in the Americas as well. By appointing a viceroy for Aragón the monarchs also set a precedent for governing kingdoms in which the monarch was not present, which later would be followed in Spanish America.

Royal government also incorporated a representative element, the importance of which varied considerably. Assemblies, or *Cortes*, represented the nobility, clergy, and towns. These were powerful institutions in the Crown of Aragón, where Aragón, Valencia, and Barcelona each had a Cortes that met on a regular basis and had legislative power. The Castilian Cortes never achieved comparable independence from the monarchy, which did not have to summon the assembly on a regular basis, although by the middle of the thirteenth century it was customary for the Crown to obtain its consent for new financial exactions. In the fifteenth and sixteenth centuries the Crown increasingly derived its income from taxes that were not controlled by the Castilian Cortes, above all the *alcabala*, or sales tax. Lacking any equivalent means to bypass the political institutions of the Crown of Aragón, the monarchy came to rely heavily on Castile for its revenues.

During the reign of the Catholic Monarchs, the church began to recover much of the prestige and influence that it had lost during the preceding period of royal weakness. Enjoying a close relationship with the papacy, the monarchs in 1501 received the power of patronage, the *patronato real*, over ecclesiastical appointments in the newly acquired territories of the Americas. The patronato real in effect gave the Spanish Crown control over the church in all matters except doctrine. The monarchs, especially Isabel, promoted church reform through the work of Cardinal Francisco Jiménez de Cisneros (1436–1517), who became Isabel's confessor in 1492, Archbishop of Toledo in 1495, Inquisitor General in 1507, and regent of Castile in 1516. He founded the new University of Alcalá de Henares, which opened in 1508 and became a center for humanistic thought in Spain. Although Cisneros espoused an intolerant and zealous form of Catholicism (actually leading an army of fifteen thousand into Africa to capture Oran from the Muslims when he was seventy-three years old), he was interested in religious reform and welcomed the ideas of humanists such as Erasmus. By the late 1520s, however, Erasmian ideas about church reform had become increasingly (if erroneously) associated with Lutheranism and therefore suspect.

The generally low educational and other standards for priests improved little during the reign of the Catholic Monarchs. Far more significant were reforms undertaken by the mendicant orders, particularly under the growing influence of the Observants, who called for stricter observance of rules. This movement affected the Franciscans, Dominicans, and Augustinians. Another important development of the fifteenth century was the rapid expansion of the Jeronimite Order, founded in 1373. With its emphasis on prayer and return to older forms of worship this order influenced the Observants and hence reform in the mendicant orders. The "hermit friars," as the Jeronimites were known, also became closely associated with the Spanish monarchy.

The Catholic Monarchs were responsible for establishing the Spanish Inquisition in the 1480s. Its main purpose was to eliminate clandestine Jewish practices and beliefs among people who had converted to Christianity. Given the circumstances under which many Jews had converted—they often faced real or threatened violence or the choice between leaving their homes or staying—not surprisingly many conversions had been more expedient than sincere. In its early years, the officials of the Holy Office of the Inquisition performed their assigned task with a grim thoroughness that on the whole succeeded in eliminating the problem. The establishment of the Supreme Council of the Inquisition also provided the Catholic Kings the opportunity to create the only royal institution that encompassed all the Spanish kingdoms.

Despite the work of the Holy Office of the Inquisition in the 1480s, the problem of Spain's Jewish population remained. As Jews increasingly became targets of popular resentment and violence and of onerous restrictions or even expulsions at the local level, the monarchy finally interceded by declaring the edict of expulsion in 1492. The evolving sense of Christian superiority, exclusivity, and intolerance also affected the recently defeated Muslim population of Granada, which after 1501 also was required to convert. Paradoxically, however, Spaniards could not accept converts as fully Christian because they equated religion with race, and race was hereditary. The concept of *limpieza de sangre*, purity of blood, was the product of that equation; it could only be achieved through "pure" and untainted ancestry. By the sixteenth century, Spaniards increasingly were using the standard of purity of blood to prevent converts from participating in a range of activities.

Charles V. After the reign of Ferdinand and Isabel a significant change occurred that affected the future of the Spanish monarchy. Their daughter Juana married Philip the Fair, son of the Holy Roman Emperor, the Habsburg Maximilian, and Mary of Burgundy. Her parents never had expected Juana to reign, but when her other siblings died Juana became with her husband heir apparent to the Spanish throne. Philip, however, died suddenly in 1506. King Ferdinand had continued to rule Castile as well as Aragón after Isabel died, until his own death early in 1516. Considered incompetent to reign because of her apparent psychological instability, Juana "la Loca" ("the Mad") lived out her life in a convent in Tordesillas, retaining the title of Queen but never actually ruling.

The Spanish Crown instead passed to Juana's eldest son Charles, who also was elected Holy Roman Emperor in 1519 after his grandfather's death. Charles grew up at his Habsburg grandfather's court and spoke no Castilian when he arrived in Spain. Initially disliked as a foreign interloper, his accession to the Spanish throne was marred by the outbreak of the *Comunero* revolt in which many towns of the north and center participated. The causes of this revolt, led by members of the urban governing and commercial groups, had as much to do with abuses towns suffered at the hands of the expansionist nobility as it did with resentment of the new king. Charles was able to suppress the revolt and reach an accommodation with his Castilian subjects, on the whole taking few reprisals against the majority of the participants in the revolt. By 1522, his reign was secure.

The establishment of the Habsburg dynasty, with its many possessions and interests in central Europe, greatly altered Spain's position in European affairs. Although when Philip II succeeded to the throne in 1556 he did not become Holy Roman Emperor, the Spanish monarchy nevertheless retained significant holdings and interests in the Low Countries (the Netherlands and Belgium) and Italy. Thus, well before the end of Charles V's reign the Spanish Crown stood at the head of a world empire that stretched from Italy to Mexico and Peru (this empire reached even farther when Spain occupied the Philippines in the 1560s) and encompassed much of Europe, which by then was torn by religious and ethnic conflict. Castilian had become the language of diplomacy and empire, and the ambitions of other western European powers impinged on, and were shaped by, the power and possessions of Spain.

Municipal Government. The political life of Spain was by no means confined to the workings of the royal government and the Cortes. Cities and towns had their own councils that affected many aspects of daily life. The councils were responsible for maintaining and regulating access to common lands and deciding how to use the income from municipal properties. They adopted ordinances relating to the practice of various trades and often set prices for wheat and bread, provided subsidies for religious institutions and hospitals, and employed lawyers, physicians, and schoolteachers who provided services to the townspeople. Despite the authority that most municipalities exercised, they were not independent of outside control. By the late fifteenth and sixteenth centuries a royally appointed *corregidor* (district administrator) presided over the councils of many towns and cities. They presided over council meetings and could veto their decisions. They also acted as the conduit through which royal ordinances or financial or other exactions (such as military levies) were conveyed to the municipalities to be implemented at the local level. Although not all towns had these officials, they nonetheless represented an important extension of royal power to the level of local government.

By the sixteenth century, the composition and structure of municipal councils varied considerably. In the older towns and cities of the north and center councils continued to include a representative element and officials rotated in office. Women never were eligible to serve in political office. If they were *vecinas* (citizens), they could participate in elections, but only through male proxies.

In contrast, in many of the towns and cities of the south municipal government was relatively closed and proprietarial and often entirely monopolized by the men of local noble families. In these municipalities the councils typically consisted of eight, twelve or more *regidores* who held their offices for life and could pass them along to sons or other relatives or in effect sell them. Although in principle the Crown appointed the members of the councils in the municipalities under its jurisdiction, royal approval normally hinged upon payment of a fairly substantial fee. Significantly, it was the closed, proprietarial municipal council, rather than the more open and representative one, that was transferred to the Americas.

The Spanish Economy

As in most of Europe in this period, the mainstays of the Spanish economy in the late medieval and early modern period were farming and pastoralism. There was industry as well, especially cloth production, and significant commercial exchange through ports on both the Atlantic and Mediterranean coasts. If agrarian pursuits predominated, nonetheless Spaniards participated in a range of trades and occupations, most of which they would carry to America as well.

Wool production and the trade in wool probably constituted the single most important sector of the economy. Uniquely suited to both the ecology and historical development of Spain, sheep raising was well established in the Iberian Peninsula by the eleventh century. Spain is very mountainous, and much of it is semi-arid. Herding in many ways proved to be an ideal and profitable way to use relatively scarce manpower and marginal land.

As more territory came under the control of Christian kingdoms, long-distance transhumance, the seasonal movement of flocks, developed. Herders annually moved their flocks of sheep from the cool, mountainous pastures of the north, where they grazed in the summer, to spend the winter in the milder climate of the grassy southern plains. The introduction of merino sheep, which produced a particularly fine and soft wool and for centuries were raised only in Spain, helped to establish Castile as one of the major suppliers of wool to the industrial centers of Europe, especially Flanders and Italy. As transhumant herding became increasingly important, disputes inevitably arose between migratory herders and municipalities seeking to protect their lands (both agricultural and grazing) and resources; organization and regulation were needed. In the mid-thirteenth century (the exact date is not known) King Alfonso X established the transhumant stockraisers' association called the *Mesta Real*, intended to protect migratory flocks and to mediate disputes.

The majority of agriculturalists were farmers, *labradores*, who principally cultivated wheat and other grain crops such as oats and rye, using plows drawn by mules or oxen, on land that they generally owned or rented (in some cases it was possible to farm land that belonged to municipal commons, or unassigned royal lands called *tierras baldías*). Most labradores diversified to some degree, so that they also might produce small amounts of grapes, olives, nuts, fruits, or vegetables (generally in irrigated gardens or orchards, known as *huertas*) or keep bees, chickens, pigs, and a cow or goat or two. Some people specialized in garden crops, and in the south especially the commercial production of grapes and olives was important. Not everyone who worked in agriculture was a labrador. In some regions there were substantial numbers of landless rural laborers, both men and women, who worked for better-off farmers and might migrate seasonally to perform agricultural labor.

Although sheep raising and wheat farming predominated in much of Castile, given the geographic and climatic diversity of the peninsula other economic activities also were important locally or regionally. The Basques of the Pyrenean region mined and exported iron and engaged in commercial fishing, Valencia produced rice and oranges, tuna fishing was important in Seville and Cádiz, silk production continued to flourish in the south, especially in Granada and Murcia, and cities like Toledo and Segovia manufactured woolen textiles on a considerable scale. Cattle ranching and pig farming were important in the south and southwest. Basque, Castilian, Catalán, and Andalusian merchants were active in regional and international commerce in both the Mediterranean and the North Atlantic, although foreign merchants also played a significant role in Spanish trade.

Despite Spain's varied resources, its economic development was subject to some significant limitations. Spain was large by European standards, with relatively few navigable rivers and a mountainous terrain; overland transportation was expensive and slow, largely conducted on the backs of mules. Agricultural production frequently suffered from drought and other problems; shortages of wheat, the basic staple of most of the peninsula, were common. The combined effects of governmental policy and an unequal social structure also could undermine the economy. Although the extent to which royal protection of wool production proved detrimental to agriculture probably has been exaggerated, increasingly heavy taxation during the sixteenth century clearly had a negative impact on small farmers in many parts of Castile. Official decisions, such as the expulsion of the Jews in 1492 and the deportation of the *Moriscos* (descendants of the Muslims still living in Spain) from the Alpujarras region near Granada after an unsuccessful rebellion in 1568–70 and ultimately from all of Spain in the early seventeenth century, also had negative, if mainly localized, economic consequences.

The Organization of Society

After the early sixteenth century Spain officially was entirely Christian, but the pluralism of the Middle Ages left a legacy of ethnic and social diversity. Moriscos, the descendants of the Muslims, and conversos, converted Jews or their descendants, formed significant minorities that were not always easily assimilated or accepted in Christian society. In the late middle ages, gypsies crossed the Pyrenees into the Iberian Peninsula, where they continued to lead their customary itinerant existence, attracting the suspicion and hatred of both authorities and the general populace. From the middle of the fifteenth century increasing numbers of African slaves began to arrive in the peninsula via the Portuguese trade with Africa. As a result of conflicts with the Muslims and, later, Morisco rebellions, Spaniards still held Morisco slaves well into the sixteenth century; but African slaves soon outnumbered them. The latter became a substantial presence in Seville, where they could be found working in artisans' shops and domestic situations. Elsewhere in Spain Africans were seldom numerous, but upper-class households might include several slaves who functioned much as did other servants.

In addition to these groups large numbers of foreigners came to live in the peninsula. Thousands of people emigrated from France, settling above all in the kingdom of Aragón, and Portuguese commonly crossed the border into Castile. The establishment of the Habsburg monarchy with the succession of Charles V and foreign participation in Spanish commerce brought Italians, Greeks, Britons, Germans, and eastern Europeans to Spain, where they principally resided in the cities. Some of these people remained only temporarily, or lived in their own distinct communities (this was especially true for foreign merchants), but many simply settled in, intermarried, and became indistinguishable from their Spanish neighbors.

Spanish society was strongly urban in orientation. Governmental, religious, and educational institutions concentrated in towns and cities, which were the focal points for local and regional economies. Weekly markets drew people and products from the countryside; annual trade fairs attracted buyers and sellers from much farther away. Even in rural areas, people in most of Castile did not live in scattered farmsteads but, rather, in small towns or villages, going out to work their fields in the morning and returning at night.

Nobles often had "country houses" on or near their rural estates, but they usually maintained impressive residences in town where they spent much of their time. People tended to identify strongly with their particular place of origin and residence——their *pueblo* (which means both a place and the people who live there) and its surrounding area, or *tierra*. The sixteenth century was a period of urban growth, with many cities and towns doubling in size, probably in large measure due to migration from smaller communities in the countryside. By the end of the century, Seville had over one hundred thousand people and probably was twice the size of any other Castilian city. Even much smaller cities, however, played an important role within their regions.

As was true of most of Europe in this period, Spanish society was divided between nobles and commoners. By law and tradition members of the *hidalgo* or noble group enjoyed inherited privileges (and responsibilities) that set them apart from, and above, the rest of society. Among their privileges was exemption from most forms of taxation; among their duties were military service owed to king and country and the obligation to attain a certain level of education. While the highest-ranking nobles were wealthy and powerful, the hidalgo group encompassed a wide range of statuses and resources. At the upper end of the spectrum were the great titled nobles; at the lower end, modest hidalgos much resembled their labrador or artisan neighbors in both their occupations and their lifestyle. Very likely the majority of hidalgos owed their privileged status to ancestors who had been ennobled by virtue of their military services and financial contributions to the crown. The nobility, in other words, for the most part had arisen from the common estate, meaning that in many ways the two social classes were closely connected. Both hidalgos and commoners participated in, and contributed to, a shared Spanish culture. Ties of patronage, employment, common interest, friendship, and sometimes kinship bound members of different socioeconomic and even ethnic groups to one another.

Commoners paid the taxes. They also performed most of the productive work for society. They could be professionals in law and medicine, clergymen, merchants, farmers, artisans, urban or rural day laborers, servants, or slaves. Wealthy merchants, high ecclesiastics, and successful professionals, regardless of their social origins, could attain a lifestyle much like that of the nobility, with whom they might intermarry. In the sixteenth century, the same would be true for people who returned from the Americas with wealth. Commoners in fact spanned the range from great wealth to extreme poverty. The largest numbers of people, however, worked in agriculture, and even individuals with skilled or specialized occupations might be part-time agriculturalists.

The class division of society was far from being absolute. People of all ranks moved up and down the social and economic scale. Literacy, which could foster upward mobility, increased considerably in the sixteenth century. Primary education generally could be obtained from tutors, members

of the clergy, or schoolteachers for fairly modest fees, and many municipalities established secondary schools that young men also could attend for a
fee (probably few women outside the hidalgo group or convents received
any formal schooling). Both hidalgo and middle-class families sent their
sons to study at universities like Salamanca, Valladolid, or Alcalá de
Henares, or in seminaries to prepare for the priesthood. A certain economic
fluidity characteristic of much of the middle class of farmers and artisans
also could result in upward mobility. Although families tended to concentrate in certain occupations, people often took advantage of opportunities to
invest in activities other than their principal enterprise, and in this way they
sometimes improved their economic situation. In order to enter into or
invest in some line of business other than their primary one, individuals
needed capital, credit, or advantageous personal or business connections.
Many people lacked all of these, and some lacked any reliable source of
income or financial support. Censuses taken in Castilian cities, towns, and
villages in the sixteenth century typically categorized substantial numbers
of people as paupers.

Society in late medieval and early modern Spain often is described as
"corporate." At all levels of political, economic, social, and religious life people pursued and expressed their collective interests through groups and
associations, or corporations. Family members worked together, defended
one another's interests, and maintained strong emotional bonds even when
separated. Beyond the family stretched a network of related kin. The extent
to which people dealt closely with their kin probably depended in some part
on such factors as geographical proximity, common interest, and the amount
of wealth, property, and influence a family commanded.

Practices were developing among noble families in the late fifteenth
and sixteenth centuries that in some respects set them apart from the families of commoners. In most of Castile, a parent's legacy was divided equally
among all legitimate children—both sons and daughters—in a practice
known as partible inheritance. Illegitimate children who had been acknowledged also received a share, although smaller than that of legitimate heirs. It
was possible, however, to set aside a larger portion of the estate for a designated heir. In that case, although all children still received something, obviously one would stand to inherit much more than the others. People at any
level of society could and did avail themselves of this option in determining
the distribution of their estates, but noble families in particular adopted this
practice of favoring one heir, usually a son.

It also was possible to obtain royal authorization to entail the bulk of
the estate, which then could not be subdivided. Most entails favored the oldest son and male line, but this was not always the case. This modified form
of inheritance had a substantial impact on upper-class families. While a family's estate essentially survived intact, many children could not expect to
replicate the lifestyle of their parents solely through inheritance. The result

was that younger (or illegitimate) sons had to seek alternative careers, often entering the church, joining the army, serving in another noble household, or pursuing university studies in hopes of launching a bureaucratic career. In the sixteenth century, emigration to America offered another attractive option for young men who did not anticipate a substantial inheritance.

Women in Spain were entitled to a range of legal rights and protections. Both men and women were considered to reach the age of majority at twenty-five years. By then, most women were married. If she were single or widowed, a woman of twenty-five or older could conduct all legal and financial transactions in her own right. A married woman had to obtain her husband's permission to do so, but once she had this authorization she could function independently. As a result adult women at all levels of society owned property, invested money, and ran businesses. When a woman married her family normally provided a dowry. The dowry, sometimes supplemented by a donation from her husband (the *arras*), remained a woman's property, which she later could bequeath as she wished, although her husband could use his wife's dowry and unfortunately squander it as well. Nonetheless, a widow had to be repaid the equivalent of the dowry after her husband's death; she also was legally entitled to one-half of the financial gains made during her marriage.

In principle, then, women enjoyed guarantees of their right to property, which normally should have protected them from impoverishment in the event that their husbands died before them. In reality, widows at the lower end of society often were left quite poor, because married couples might never accumulate much in the way of property or investments. The situation of upper-class women normally was different. Wealthy widows could function quite successfully on their own and avoid compromising their independence through remarriage. Nonmarrying daughters in noble families often entered convents, usually located in their home towns or nearby. In these institutions they might not only live in comfort in the company of a number of their female relatives but also acquire an education and avail themselves of opportunities to exercise administrative and management skills.

In sum, Castilian women at all levels of society were economically active. In the working groups, they formed an essential part of the domestic economic unit, often working alongside their husbands in the family business or in cultivating the land as well as performing the multitude of tasks associated with maintaining a household and raising children. Women (especially widows) not infrequently became the principal breadwinners and effective heads of household. Nonetheless, women of the working classes could end up destitute, and women of all ranks could find themselves manipulated to their disadvantage by husbands, fathers or other male relatives or become victims of sexual and other kinds of violence. Women also faced constraints on their freedom of choice and action imposed by custom and sexual double standards. Divorce was rarely obtainable, but women sometimes escaped unhappy or abusive marriages if they could find a safe refuge (sometimes by emigrating to America).

Religious Life

Religion and the church played a vital role in the lives of Spaniards. Cities and towns had large religious establishments that included parish churches, monasteries, and convents; larger cities that were the seats of bishoprics had cathedrals and seminaries for training priests. During the sixteenth century the church and its clergy were expanding both in size and influence. The Holy Office of the Inquisition, having dealt with the *converso* problem in the early years of the century, turned its attentions toward enforcing orthodoxy and discipline among both lay people and the clergy. In general, the Inquisition had little if any impact on most Castilians, and holding a position as an agent of the Holy Office (lay people could serve as *familiares*, clergy as *comisarios*) conferred prestige.

The reforms adopted by the Council of Trent had a substantial impact on the Spanish church. This council, organized in part in response to the threat posed by the expansion of Protestant Christianity in Europe, met in three sessions between 1545 and 1563. Standards for clerical education (and to some extent behavior) rose, liturgy was standardized, parish priests began maintaining systematic records, and the clergy devoted greater effort to the basic indoctrination of lay people. Another new development was the establishment of the Society of Jesus by the Basque Ignacio de Loyola (1491–1556), who produced a manual entitled *The Spiritual Exercises*. Approved by the pope in 1540, the order sent missions to Asia; but above all the Jesuits played a crucial role in the Counter, or Catholic, Reformation in sixteenth-century Europe and helped restore several areas to the Catholic Church. In the 1580s, the extraordinary St. Teresa of Avila founded another influential order, the Discalced Carmelites.

For most people in Spain religious life centered on religious holidays and festivals and the fulfillment of vows and devotions to particular saints and shrines. In any given community, the sacred calendar probably included officially designated church holidays as well as locally recognized ones. Festivals could be celebrated in a variety of ways, from organizing processions in which the images of saints or the Virgin Mary were carried, to bull fighting, providing charitable feasts, or staging religious dramas performed by professional players or amateurs. Lay people joined religious associations known as *cofradías* or confraternities that normally were dedicated to a particular saint, the Virgin Mary, or, increasingly in the sixteenth century, to Jesus Christ. Many confraternities accepted members from all social and occupational groups, women as well as men, and membership dues usually were low. Priests could belong but they did not control these lay associations. In addition to their religious activities, confraternities performed charitable work and aided their members in times of illness. When a member died, the confraternity would see to the funeral and burial.

The church and religion permeated Spanish society; politics, religion, and social life were closely intertwined. Town councils provided funding for churches, monasteries, and hospitals and often undertook the organization of major festivals like Corpus Christi; a religious vow made to a saint frequently took the form of an official legal act. Members of the clergy exercised considerable political, social, and economic influence in local society. At the level of royal government high-ranking ecclesiastics served on royal councils or as the special representatives of the Crown. The monarchy exerted a great deal of influence over the church in Spain, as it later would in Spanish America, and derived a substantial income from it.

Overseas Expansion

Creation of an Overseas Empire. Spaniards had not yet completed the Reconquest of the peninsula when they began to expand beyond it. King James I of Aragón conquered Mallorca, Menorca, and Ibiza (the Balearic Islands, off the coast of Valencia) in the thirteenth century. Castilians—along with the Portuguese and French—became interested in the Canary Islands in the Atlantic (southwest of Spain and close to the African coast) in the fourteenth century. The conquest and occupation of the Canaries was a protracted, piecemeal affair in which Castile established its preeminence only gradually and with considerable effort over the course of the fifteenth century.

Castilian control of the Canaries proved to be highly advantageous in the long run, not so much for the islands' intrinsic value as for their strategic location on the route across the Atlantic. The settlement of the Canaries and treatment of their inhabitants (people called Guanches, who probably had originated in North Africa) had a striking connection to the Americas in another sense. They provided a number of precedents for Spanish activities in the next set of islands they would occupy, in the Caribbean. The Genoese played a vital role as merchants and financiers in the Canaries, as they subsequently would in the early years of Spanish settlement of the Caribbean. The prospect of gaining access to African gold, which Spaniards (as others) hoped that control of the Canaries would facilitate, was a strong motivating factor in the campaign, resumed in 1478 by Ferdinand and Isabel, to conquer the largest and richest islands. Similarly, the search for gold would take Columbus from island to island in the Caribbean. The final campaigns of conquest in the Canaries met with stiff resistance. They took years to complete and at times entailed considerable brutality. The conqueror-settlers exported large numbers of native Canarians as slaves, introduced sugar cane cultivation to the islands, and on Tenerife witnessed the devastation that epidemic disease could wreak on a previously unexposed population. The parallels to the early Caribbean are chilling.

Effective Spanish occupation of the Caribbean began in 1493. On his second voyage across the Atlantic, Columbus carried with him the basic necessities for real settlement: livestock, seed, equipment. Discovering that the crude fort of Navidad, which he had left manned when he returned to Europe from his first voyage, had been destroyed, Columbus established Isabela on the north coast of Hispaniola, the island that today is divided between the countries of Haiti and the Dominican Republic. The Spaniards would concentrate their efforts on Hispaniola for more than twenty years. During that time they reconnoitered the other islands of the Greater Antilles (Cuba, Puerto Rico, Jamaica) and the coast of the circum-Caribbean region and engaged in slave raiding. They needed slaves for labor because the indigenous population of Hispaniola, which has been estimated at anywhere from one hundred thousand to eight million at the time of contact, disappeared with horrifying speed, due to famine, disease, warfare, and mistreatment at the hands of Spaniards.

The settlers' immediate need was to find something of value that they could export, not only in order to import necessary staples but also to pay off their debts and realize profits substantial enough that they could continue to explore and occupy the newfound lands. Columbus, who anticipated establishing trade with wealthy Asian states, found disappointingly little in the way of viable commercial products on the islands. One possibility was to send the people from the islands to Spain as slaves, but Queen Isabel quickly put a stop to this practice. The inhabitants of the islands, the Tainos, were agricultural villagers organized into chiefdoms under rulers called *caciques*. They used some gold for ornamentation but were not accustomed to producing it in any quantity. In order to obtain gold in larger amounts, Spaniards had to go into mining for themselves, which meant forcing the men to work for them. Spaniards who rebelled against Columbus in the mid-1490s settled in Taino villages, dividing them among themselves in allotments called *repartimientos* that entitled them to use the labor of the men, who at least in principle remained free and continued to live in their villages. In fact, the Spaniards exploited and abused the Tainos with little restraint, disrupting both family life and the agricultural cycle (precipitating famine) by moving men away from their homes to work in the mines.

By the time the Spanish Crown sent its first real governor, Fray Nicolás de Ovando, to Hispaniola in 1502, this system for granting labor was entrenched. Ovando formalized it by calling the grants *encomiendas*, a term that in Spain referred to the jurisdiction granted to members of the military orders. The holder of an encomienda was called an *encomendero*. Although clearly in the Indies (as Spaniards would refer to the new overseas territories, since Columbus had expected to find Asia, and to the people as "Indians" for the same reason) encomiendas differed considerably from the Spanish precedent, these grants served a similar purpose—to reward people for services to the Crown.

In order to gain control over and pacify island societies, Spaniards under Columbus's direction began organizing military campaigns and using terror and coercion in the mid-1490s. Although Columbus forged alliances with some of the caciques, other caciques formed a coalition to oppose the intruders. By the time of Ovando's governorship much of the cacique group had been eliminated, making any kind of organized resistance on the part of the Tainos very difficult. The indigenous populations of the other islands might have fared slightly better than those of Hispaniola, but on the whole the experience of the island peoples is a story of devastation and virtually untrammeled exploitation and abuse.

Fray Antonio Montesinos's Denunciation of Spanish Cruelty, 1511

Sunday having arrived, and the time for preaching, [Dominican] Friar Antonio Montesinos rose in the pulpit, and took for the text of his sermon what was written down and signed by the other friars, "I am the voice of one crying in the wilderness." He began to speak of the sterile desert of the consciences of the Spaniards on this isle [of Hispaniola], and of the blindness in which they lived, going about in great danger of damnation and utterly heedless. "This voice," said he, "declares that you are in mortal sin, and live and die therein by reason of the cruelty and tyranny that you practice on these innocent people. Tell me, by what right or justice do you hold these Indians in such cruel and horrible slavery? By what right do you wage such detestable wars on these people who lived mildly and peacefully in their own lands, where you have consumed infinite numbers of them with unheard-of murders and evils? Why do you so greatly oppress and fatigue them, not giving them enough to eat or caring for them when they fall ill from excessive labors, so that they die or rather are slain by you, so that you may extract and acquire gold every day? And what care do you take that they receive religious instruction and come to know their God and creator, or that they be baptized, hear mass, or observe holidays and Sundays? Are they not men? Do they not have rational souls? Are you not bound to love them as you love yourselves? How can you lie in such profound and lethargic slumber? Be sure that in your present state you can no more be saved than the Moors or Turks who do not have and do not want the faith of Jesus Christ." Thus he delivered the message he had promised, leaving his [Spanish] hearers astounded. Many were stunned, others appeared more callous than before, and a few were somewhat moved; but not one, from what I [Bartolomé de las Casas] could later learn, and was converted [to the idea of better treatment of the Indians.] When he had concluded his sermon, he descended from the pulpit, his head held high, for he was not a man to show fear, of which indeed he was totally free, nor did he care about the displeasure of his listeners, and instead did and said what seemed best according to God. . . . After he had left, the church was so full of murmurs that . . . they could hardly complete the celebration of the masses of the grave sins in which they lived and died.

Benjamin Keen, ed., *Latin American Civilization: History and Society 1492 to the Present* (Boulder, 1986), pp. 63–4.

As the gold gave out and Hispaniola's population all but disappeared within a generation, Spaniards began to conquer and settle the other large islands and make tentative moves to the adjacent mainland. Despite economic decline a stable Spanish society nonetheless developed in Hispaniola, centered on the city of Santo Domingo, which became the seat of the first *audiencia* or high court in the Indies. Spaniards began to import African slaves, mainly to work on sugar estates, and all the large islands soon came to have mixed populations of European, African, and indigenous origins. Cuba and Puerto Rico developed along much the same lines as Hispaniola, with their fast-diminishing indigenous populations allotted in encomiendas and modest economies based on ranching and agriculture. Cuba's capital of Havana, with its splendid harbor, became the most important Caribbean port, rather than Santo Domingo. In the future, Havana would be closely linked to the principal eastern port of Mexico, Veracruz. Hernando Cortés, the conqueror of Mexico, was an encomendero in Cuba, and the conquest of Mexico was, in essence, a Cuban undertaking.

The Movement of People to America. Almost from the outset, a broad spectrum of people emigrated to Spain's new territories in the Americas. The very wealthiest nobles and most destitute paupers did not go, but nearly everyone else did—artisans, farmers, priests, notaries, merchants, bureaucrats, and professionals, along with their wives, sisters, and daughters. Because of the costs of the journey (which included obtaining a license from the authorities of the House of Trade in Seville, established in 1504), many people traveled as the servants or employees of better-off emigrants. After arriving, however, they seldom remained in service, given the kinds of opportunities that awaited them. There were, of course, large numbers of young men among the emigrants, since people not yet established with families were in a good position to relocate. Yet, even among the young single men, few actually went by themselves. Instead, they traveled with relatives, friends, or employers, or went to join someone already in the Indies. Over time, increasing numbers of women, married couples, and families emigrated. Emigrants came from all over Spain, although preponderantly from the south, southwest, and center. Overall, the largest numbers would go to Mexico, perhaps because of its greater accessibility and stability compared to the second major destination for emigrants, Peru.

The people who went to America brought with them their experiences and background—their language, religious beliefs and practices, notions of family and kinship, political institutions, loyalty to home, and understanding of themselves in relation to the larger world—as well as their expectations of what they could accomplish in their chosen destination. Few evinced much curiosity about the new lands and peoples they would encounter; they were drawn to the Indies by the prospect of a better life for themselves and their children. Generally, this meant trying to replicate as much of their old lives as possible but in much improved economic circumstances.

Nonetheless in Mexico, as elsewhere in the Indies, they were forced to adjust to life in a quite different context.

Glossary

alcabala   sales tax
alcalde   magistrate
audiencia   secondary high court
cacique   chief or ruler among the Tainos
chancillería   high court
cofradía   confraternity, lay brotherhood
converso   converted Jew, Spaniard of Jewish descent
convivencia   living together
corregidor   royal municipal administrator
Cortes   legislative assembly
encomendero   holder of an *encomienda*
encomienda   grant of right to Indian labor and tribute
fuero   written charter of privileges
hidalgo   member of the nobility
huerta   irrigated garden or orchard
labrador   farmer
letrado   university-educated lawyer
limpieza de sangre   purity of blood
Mesta   stockraisers' association
Moor   term often used to refer to Spanish Muslims
morisco   converted Muslim, Spaniard of Muslim descent
New Christian   converted Jew or descendant of converts
Patronato Real   royal power of ecclesiastical patronage
pueblo   village or town; people who live there
Reconquista   Christian reconquest
regidor   town councilman
repartimiento   assignment of a group of Indians to perform labor; later
   called encomienda
tierras baldías   unassigned royal lands
vecino   citzen, householder

Questions for Discussion

1.   What was the impact of the integration of much of Spain into the Islamic world in the middle ages?

2.   In what ways did Christian Spain become increasingly tied to the rest of Christian Europe during the middle ages?

3. What policies did Ferdinand and Isabel, and later Charles V, pursue that extended and strengthened monarchical authority?

4. What was the basis for the Spanish economy and how did it vary regionally?

5. What were the connections between the reconquest and the beginnings of overseas expansion to the Canary Islands and the Caribbean?

6. How did Fray Antonio Montesinos criticize Spanish treatment of the Indians in the Caribbean?

Suggested Reading

Altman, Ida. *Emigrants and Society: Extremadura and Spanish America in the Sixteenth Century*. Berkeley and Los Angeles: University of California Press, 1989. Study of the impact of emigration to Spanish America on two cities in southwestern Spain.

Boyd-Bowman, Peter. *Patterns of Spanish Emigration to the New World (1493–1580)*. SUNY at Buffalo, Special Studies No. 34, Buffalo, N.Y., 1983. Study based on analysis of passenger lists and other sources demonstrating basic patterns of the sixteenth-century movement to Spanish America (chronology, timing, demographic composition, regional origins, and choice of destination).

Carr, Raymond, ed. *Spain: A History*. Oxford: Oxford University Press, 2000. Includes articles by leading scholars on different periods of Spanish history.

Christian, William A. *Local Religion in Sixteenth-Century Spain*. Princeton, N.J.: Princeton University Press, 1981. Study of local religious practices and beliefs, mainly based on the "Relaciones geográficas."

Dillard, Heath. *Daughters of the Reconquest: Women in Castilian Town Society, 1100–1300*. Cambridge: Cambridge University Press, 1984. Study of the role and legal status of women in early medieval Castilian society.

Fernández-Armesto, Felipe. *Before Columbus: Exploration and Colonisation from the Mediterranean to the Atlantic, 1229–1492*. London: Macmillan Education, 1987. Traces the connections between expansion within the Iberian peninsula and expansion overseas.

Kamen, Henry. *Spain, 1469–1714: A Society of Conflict*. London and New York: Longman, 1983. Basic survey of early modern Spanish history emphasizing socioeconomic development.

Liss, Peggy K. *Isabel the Queen*. Oxford: Oxford University Press, 1992. Biography of the influential monarch.

Nader, Helen. *Liberty in Absolutist Spain: The Habsburg Sale of Towns, 1516–1700*. Baltimore, Md.: Johns Hopkins University Press, 1990. Study of the establishment of municipalities and their changing status.

Pike, Ruth. *Aristocrats and Traders: Sevillian Society in the Sixteenth Century.* Ithaca, N.Y.: Cornell University Press, 1972. Study of the great port city that served as the hub for trade and movement of people to and from the Indies.

Sauer, Carl O. *The Early Spanish Main.* Berkeley and Los Angeles: University of California Press, 1966. Study of the Caribbean at the time of contact and early development of Spanish society in the islands based principally on early accounts and histories.

Vassberg, David E. *Land and Society in Golden Age Castile.* Cambridge: Cambridge University Press, 1984. Looks at patterns of land ownership and use in early modern Castile.

Three

Conquest
and Colonization

The defeat of the Aztecs of Tenochtitlan at the end of a two-year struggle (1519–21) is the most famous episode of the Spanish conquest of Mexico. Extension of Spanish control over Greater Mexico, however, took significantly longer, with conquered areas serving as jumping off points for subsequent expeditions. Some regions were not pacified until the end of the 1500s.

Spanish Background to the Conquest of Mexico

The Spanish conquest of Mexico came after twenty-five years of Spanish exploration and settlement in the Caribbean. Previous experience in exploring new territory, conquering or subduing indigenous peoples and exploiting their labor via the encomienda, and establishing permanent Spanish settlements provided ample precedent for the conquest of Mexico. For that reason, while the events of the conquest of central Mexico and the personalities of the conquerors and leaders of the indigenous groups are particular to Mexican history, the patterns they reflect in themselves were not unique to Mexico. The Christian reconquest of Iberia from the Muslims, Spanish conquest and settlement of the Canary islands, and Portuguese maritime explorations down the coast of Africa that culminated in the establishment of lucrative routes to the spice-rich Indies shaped Spaniards' expectations and sense of possibility. In short, Spaniards went to the Americas to enrich themselves, to rise to the challenge of conquest, and to spread Christianity: gold, glory, and God. Compared to the Caribbean, the size, complexity, and wealth of the Indian civilizations they found in Mexico were unprecedented.

For indigenous populations in the Americas, Spaniards represented an intrusive force, but Indians' resistance or alliance and accommodation also followed certain patterns. Dominant groups in a region tried to maintain control and resisted conquest, while secondary groups often allied with Spaniards in pursuit of their own goals. The complex but fragile structure of the Aztec Triple Alliance dominated by Tenochtitlan meant that indigenous factors played an important role in the events that unfolded in the early sixteenth century.

Spanish Voyages of Exploration. Through the expedition (*entrada*) of exploration, conquest, and settlement Spaniards gained control of territory and indigenous populations, expanding Spanish sovereignty without expending the crown's money. Although participation in an entrada was risky, with injury or death a real possibility, many men were willing to play those odds. A man of substance petitioned the Crown to lead an expedition. If successful he was named the *adelantado*. As such, he usually assumed the greatest financial risk by investing in equipment, such as cannons, and contracted for ships, since early expeditions usually took the form of coastal probes of new territory. The Crown granted privileges to the adelantado, stipulating a region to be conquered and the rewards to be granted if the expedition succeeded. Many leaders of entradas were hidalgos, members of the lower ranks of the nobility. Both the Crown and the aspiring conquerors hoped for financial gain from an expedition, with the *quinto*, one-fifth, of the profits earmarked for the Crown. Participants were rewarded according to the size of their investment in the enterprise, with horsemen (*caballeros*) receiving two shares (one for the horse, the other for the rider) and those who fought on foot one share each.

Typically, an established settlement served as the staging ground for expeditions into unknown territory. In the conquest of Mexico the group that sailed west from Cuba in 1519 to the Gulf Coast of Mexico included men experienced in the Indies, such as Hernando Cortés, Pedro de Alvarado and his brothers, and the well-known "common man" conqueror, Bernal Díaz del Castillo. Conquerors generally became a new region's first settlers, reserving for themselves encomiendas and positions on the cabildo. The adelantado ruled in the name of the Crown, usually being appointed governor once the military phase of conquest was over.

Cortés and the Conquest of Mexico

Background and Initial Stages. The conquest of Mexico is a well-documented historical event for which we have written accounts by both Spanish conquerors and their Indian allies and opponents (see Chapter 4). The two-year campaign was complex, but reflected basic patterns that had developed during the twenty-five years that Spaniards spent in the Caribbean. Capturing the cacique to facilitate conquest, making alliances with disgruntled secondary powers to wage war on more powerful rivals, and superior Spanish military technology and battlefield tactics all fostered Spanish military success. Divide and conquer is classic military strategy, but Europeans' policy of waging all-out war rather than following the rules of ritual combat contributed to their initial success.

Two expeditions set out to explore coastal Mexico. The first, under Francisco Hernández de Córdoba (February to April 1517), ended badly for

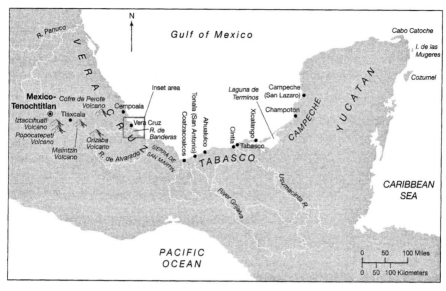

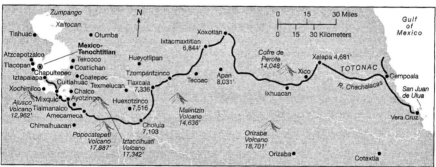

Route of Hernando Cortés

the Spaniards, with nearly half of the 110 men killed by Mayas at Champoton. The second voyage, under Juan de Grijalva, left Cuba in May 1518, returning nearly a year later. Both expeditions brought news to Spaniards in the Caribbean of promising lands to the east. Grijalva's probe actively avoided engaging hostile forces, landing only to secure supplies. Aztec officials who spotted the Grijalva ships reported the information to Moctezuma, ruler of Tenochtitlan, the senior city-state in the Aztec Triple Alliance. The lengthy absence of the Grijalva expedition prompted Cuba's Governor Velázquez to authorize a third expedition in 1519. Hernando Cortés leapt at the opportunity to lead this entrada. Hernández de Córdoba's and Grijalva's expeditions were intended to be solely exploratory and were not authorized to establish settlements. The third expedition under the leadership of Hernando Cortés differed significantly in its outcome—the conquest and settlement of central Mexico—because Cortés decided to go well beyond his official authorization.

Hernando Cortés (1485–1547) is famous for the conquest of the Aztecs, but he was a typical leader of an expedition: mature in years, experienced in the Indies, well connected politically, solvent, and ambitious. Born in Extremadura in southwestern Spain, Cortés was the legitimate son of an hidalgo family. He was literate and conversant with legal culture, having lived with a maternal uncle who was a notary. Arriving in Santo Domingo in 1504 at the age of nineteen, he associated himself with Diego Velázquez, who later became governor of Cuba. Receiving an encomienda and becoming the notary of a cabildo, Cortés followed Velázquez to Cuba and became his secretary. In the same period, he married Catalina Suárez, daughter of a prominent local family.

Cuba's governor Diego Velázquez initially approved Cortés's expedition. The terms, or *capitulaciones*, were unacceptably limiting to other aspiring leaders, but Cortés seized the opportunity and was chosen with the support of some prominent supporters. Just prior to the expedition's launching, Velázquez was apparently on the verge of canceling his authorization. Cortés, however, precipitously set sail, leaving for Yucatan on February 10, 1519, with 450 fighting men, fourteen cannon, and sixteen horses. On reaching Mexico's Gulf Coast, the expedition followed the usual practice of exploring the coastline, raiding Indian groups, gathering information, and acquiring provisions. In this early period, Cortés had the good luck to come across a shipwrecked Spaniard, Gerónimo de Aguilar, who spoke Mayan after living for eight years in the region. Also crucial at this early stage was the gift he received from a cacique of a talented, bilingual Indian woman, baptized Marina (she was also called Malinche; confusingly, some Indians apparently called Cortés Malinche as well). Marina spoke Nahuatl and Mayan, while Aguilar spoke Mayan and Spanish. Upon reaching Nahuatl-speaking areas, Marina would translate Nahuatl to Mayan, which Aguilar then translated to Spanish. After Cortés took Marina as his consort, she quickly learned Spanish and made significant contributions as Cortés's cultural as well as linguistic interpreter. Marina played a pivotal role in the subsequent events leading to the conquest of Tenochtitlan.

Early Contacts and the March Inland. After some initial probes in the Maya region, the Spaniards sailed to a Nahuatl-speaking region on the Gulf Coast. In the harbor at San Juan de Ulúa, Cortés's eleven ships were met on April 21, 1519, by men in canoes bringing gifts to the Spaniards as a pretext for making contact and gathering information for Moctezuma. The encounter was important for both sides. Cortés took the opportunity to demonstrate European firepower by firing his cannons, terrifying the Indian emissaries. After waiting for a few days for a response to the report that they sent to the Aztec ruler, the emissaries received a message for the Spaniards instructing them to stay at the coast and not go inland to the capital,

Tenochtitlan. Having seen the Aztecs' gold and other fine goods, Cortés was determined to march inland.

He had first to overcome a legal obstacle, which he did by founding the settlement of Veracruz as a Spanish town and constituting the senior members of the expedition as its cabildo. Cortés then could claim a direct relationship with the Crown and sever his ties to Velázquez. In this way, Cortés sought to dispel the taint of illegitimacy that colored the expedition when he defied Velázquez's authority as well as to position himself as the fully empowered leader. Expedition members who were loyal to Velázquez conspired to return to Cuba. Cortés hanged two of them, cut off the feet of one of the pilots, and stripped the ships of useful equipment and scuttled them. The remaining Spaniards had no alternative but to support Cortés. Leaving a small group of Spaniards at Veracruz, Cortés began marching inland.

The first major Aztec tributary state the Spaniards reached was the Totonac city of Cempoala, ruled by a man known to history only as "The Fat Cacique." Eager to throw off Aztec rule, the Fat Cacique offered to ally with the Spaniards. When tribute collectors from Tenochtitlan appeared in Cempoala, Cortés ordered the Fat Cacique to arrest them. Obviously fearing the consequences but nonetheless seizing the tax collectors, the Fat Cacique appeared to act on his own authority. Cortés then contrived to set two of them free, allowing them to return to Moctezuma with a message of friendship. The Cempoalans, not realizing Cortés's complicity, were appalled that the tribute collectors had escaped. Thinking they would be punished for defying Moctezuma, the Cempoalans rose in rebellion against Tenochtitlan with Cortés's assurances of support. Meanwhile, Cortés had sent word to Moctezuma via the freed tax collectors that the Cempoalans might rebel, setting the stage for establishing friendly relations with the more powerful ruler of Tenochtitlan.

The march toward Tenochtitlan brought Spaniards and their Indian allies to the independent city-state of Tlaxcala. Tlaxcala had maintained its independence from Tenochtitlan despite its closeness to the Aztec capital. With ample opportunity to hone their military skills against the Aztecs, the Tlaxcalans were formidable warriors. Initially, they opposed the Spaniards and their Totonac allies, who were former Aztec tributaries. Tlaxcalan warriors attacked the Spaniards. Under other circumstances, the Tlaxcalans might have forced the Spanish to retreat, but Cortés was not in a position to do so. He had no suitable fallback position, especially since the loyalty of his Totonac allies was fragile at best. Through a combination of defensive tactics using European firepower, entreaties of peace, and attacking and raiding small settlements to obtain supplies, Cortés created conditions whereby the Tlaxcalans reconsidered their opposition. In the end, Tlaxcala allied with Cortés, becoming the largest single Indian group to support the Spaniards against the Aztecs. With Tlaxcalan forces swelling his ranks, Cortés continued the march to Tenochtitlan, moving on to Cholula.

Chronology of the Conquest

1517	Voyage of Hernández de Córdoba
1518	Voyage of Juan de Grijalva
	Authorization of the Hernando Cortés expedition
1519	Gerónimo de Aguilar, shipwrecked bilingual Spaniard, joins Cortés
	Malinche/Doña Marina given to Cortés
	Foundation of Vera Cruz
	Spanish alliance with Totonacs of Cempoala
	Spanish alliance with Tlaxcala
	Cholula massacre
	Spanish enter Tenochtitlan and capture Moctezuma
1520	Pánfilo de Narváez expedition coopted
	Alvarado massacre of Aztec nobles
	Death of Moctezuma
	Retreat of Spaniards on the Noche Triste (June 30, 1520)
	Election of Cuitlahuac as Aztec ruler
	Smallpox epidemic, death of Cuitlahuac
1521	Construction of brigantines
	Siege of Tenochtitlan
	Election of Cuauhtemoc as ruler
	Fall of Tenochtitlan, Spanish capture Cuauhtemoc on August 13, 1521

Cortés's massacre of the people of the city-state of Cholula in September 1519 demonstrated Spanish power as well as his determination to use all means necessary to gain military advantage. Cholula was an important religious center, previously an ally of Tlaxcala but recently incorporated into the Aztec Empire. Although the Cholulans initially met Cortés and his Totonac and Tlaxcalan allies with gestures of friendship, Cortés was alert to possible duplicity. Bernal Díaz credits Doña Marina with tipping off the Spaniards, who turned the tables and attacked the Cholulans, slaughtering as many as six thousand. The city was sacked and burned, particularly the temples, symbolizing a city-state's definitive defeat. The massacre solidified the Spaniards' alliance with the Tlaxcalans. From the Aztec point of view, the alliance of their long-time Tlaxcalan enemies with the unknown foreign force and visible evidence that Aztec tributary states could be toppled meant that Moctezuma faced a force potentially capable of destabilizing the entire empire.

The Spaniards and their Indian allies marched to Tenochtitlan, where on November 8, 1519, Moctezuma himself greeted them. It is likely that since Moctezuma had been unable to prevent the Spaniards' continued penetration of the Aztec heartland, he decided to draw them into the center of power where they could be destroyed. The Spaniards seized Moctezuma a few days after their arrival in Tenochtitlan, however, keeping him prisoner and thereby staving off Aztec retaliation. Moctezuma did not resist capture, and as a prisoner he continued to function as monarch, cooperating with the Spaniards while losing support of his own people. At this point, the Spaniards had some hope that Tenochtitlan would surrender and that the city (and its tributary states) would fall into Spanish hands intact. This was not to be. Very quickly the situation became much more complicated. The result was a protracted, all-out campaign to determine the future of Tenochtitlan.

Aztec Resistance, Spanish Setbacks. As Moctezuma's position as leader eroded in the eyes of the Aztec elites, the Spaniards became increasingly vulnerable to attack. Compounding that, in 1520 a Spanish force led by Pánfilo de Narváez and backed by Diego Velázquez landed on the Gulf Coast with the objective of reining in the Cortés expedition. Reluctantly, Cortés left Tenochtitlan in order to deal with the Spanish threat, leaving Pedro de Alvarado in command. Cortés captured Narváez and persuaded the other Spaniards to join him, marching back to Tenochtitlan with thirteen hundred Spaniards and additional Tlaxcalan allies. In Tenochtitlan, Alvarado allowed the religious celebration of Toxcatl in honor of Huitzilopochtli, in which unarmed noblemen performed sacred dances in an enclosed plaza, to take place. On the pattern of the Cholula massacre, the Spaniards blocked the exits and massacred the flower of the Aztec elite. The Alvarado massacre effectively destroyed any remaining Aztec support for Moctezuma, whom the elites now viewed as nothing more than a puppet of the perfidious invaders. When Cortés returned to Tenochtitlan with the Narváez forces in tow, the Spaniards were besieged. Moctezuma spoke to the warriors from a rooftop, attempting to calm the uprising, and was struck by a stone and killed. Spaniards claimed that Moctezuma's own people were responsible, while some Indian accounts lay the blame on the Spaniards.

Alvarado Massacre

While the Mexican gentlemen were dancing in the temple yard of Huitzilopochtli, Pedro de Alvarado went there, whether of his own notion or following the decision of the rest, I cannot say. Some say he had been warned that the Indian nobles of the city had assembled to plot the mutiny and rebellion which they later carried out; others, that [the Spaniards] went to see them perform this much-praised and famous dance, and seeing them so rich, they coveted the gold the Indians were wearing, so he [Alvarado] blocked the entrances with ten or twelve Spaniards at each one, himself went in with more than fifty, and cruelly and pitilessly stabbed and killed the Indians, and took what they were wearing. Cortés, who must have felt badly about the affair, dissembled his feelings so as not to irritate the [Spanish] perpetrators, for it happened at a time when he had need of them, either against the Indians, or to put down trouble among his own men.

Francisco López de Gómara, *Cortés: The Life of the Conqueror by His Secretary*, trans. Lesley Byrd Simpson (University of California Press, 1964), pp. 207–8.

With Moctezuma's death, the Spaniards' position in Tenochtitlan became completely untenable. The Spaniards had no choice but to flee. On the night of June 30, 1520, known to Spaniards as "La Noche Triste" (the sad night), they attempted to escape from Tenochtitlan. Their retreat turned into a disastrous rout. Spaniards loaded down with Aztec gold fell into the lake and drowned. Cortés's decimated forces took refuge in Tlacopan, eventually making their way to Tlaxcala to recuperate. Six months later, they again took the offensive against Tenochtitlan, securing the support of Texcoco, formerly one of the three powers of the Triple Alliance.

The Siege and Surrender of Tenochtitlan. Spaniards needed to gain control of the central lake system and attack the island capital of Tenochtitlan directly. In February 1521, Cortés ordered construction of thirteen ships capable of navigating the shallow lake waters. Martín López, a shipwright, oversaw the Indian laborers who built the brigantines, which were mounted with cannons. With the ships armed in this fashion towns along the lakeshore became vulnerable to Spanish firepower. Cortés divided his forces between those on board the ships and land-based soldiers who captured the towns where Tenochtitlan's causeways met the lakeshore, Tlacopan, Coyoacan, and Ixtapalapa. Tenochtitlan's sources of food and freshwater were disrupted. Many towns previously loyal to Tenochtitlan went over to the Spanish side.

The final siege of Tenochtitlan was hard fought. The Indians there resisted to the death as a smallpox epidemic ravaged the starved population. Spanish cannons aboard the brigantines bombarded the capital. Tlaxcalan allies were dispatched to pile rubble in canals and other gaps so that Spaniards could use their horses to their advantage. The city fell on August 13, 1519, and Spaniards captured the ruler Cuauhtemoc as he attempted to flee by canoe. Taking revenge on their old enemies, the Tlaxcalans massacred many of the remaining residents of the city.

Explaining the Spanish Conquest

Superior military technology was crucial to the Spaniards' success. Steel weapons did devastating damage to Indians armed with only wooden and stone weapons. Horses were key to controlling warfare on open ground, equivalent to tanks in the modern era. Sitting high on horses with steel swords in their hands, Spanish horsemen were virtually impervious to injury by Indian warriors. Cannons and early long guns called harquebuses did damage by shooting projectiles at a distance and were important psychologically, impressing and frightening Indians. During the siege of the Aztec capital of Tenochtitlan, Spanish naval technology allowed the Europeans to control the whole central lake system. Easily maneuverable brigantines could carry large numbers of Spaniards to any point in the lakes and then served as platforms for firing cannons mounted on the decks.

Disease also played a role in the conquest, with a smallpox epidemic ravaging Indian populations but leaving already immune Spaniards unscathed. Tenochtitlan's natural defenses and stalwart residents were overcome by the Europeans' more advanced technology.

Securing Indian allies was crucial to the Spanish victory, enabling a few hundred Spaniards to conquer the Aztec stronghold. Indian allies fought for their own reasons, usually to achieve autonomy or a privileged position in a new political system. In central Mexico, Tlaxcala became Cortés's main ally, joined by Texcoco, Huejotzingo, and lakeside towns close to Tenochtitlan. Tlaxcala had long maintained its independence from the Triple Alliance. Although Texcoco was a member of the Triple Alliance, under Moctezuma's rule it had been reduced to junior partner status. Thus two important powers had strong reasons to ally with the Spaniards to overthrow Moctezuma. Being on the winning side brought lasting rewards for some indigenous towns, most notably Tlaxcala, which today is a state of modern Mexico largely because it allied with Cortés in 1519 and thereafter constantly reminded the Crown of its role in the conquest.

Conquest-Era Mexico

Mexico City. With the fall of Tenochtitlan in 1521, Cortés immediately moved to consolidate the Spaniards' hold. Despite the damage Tenochtitlan had suffered, Cortés decided to found the Spanish capital of Mexico City on its site, thus appropriating the prestige and power associated with the center of the Aztec Empire. The site of Moctezuma's palace became the seat of Spanish government, and the principal temple became the site for the cathedral. Making Tenochtitlan the Spanish capital meant difficulties. The problem of periodic flooding from the surrounding lakes during the rainy season was not solved until the modern era. It was centrally located, however, defensible on its island stronghold, and it carried enormous symbolic significance.

The Spoils of War. Spanish conquerors expected to reap personal rewards for conquest, while the Crown saw its sovereignty extend over an increasing area, and Spanish friars and priests sought to convert Indians to Christianity. The first twenty years of the Spanish period in Mexico were marked by outward expansion, consolidation of Spanish rule over conquered Indians, and internal Spanish conflicts. New expeditions to areas beyond the Aztec sphere; conflicts between competing factions of encomenderos; struggles between the Crown and the conquerors over the encomienda; the initiation of the "spiritual conquest"; and pressures from later arriving Spaniards for a share of Mexico's wealth all were features of the early Spanish colony. The newly conquered Indian populations provided the economic basis for the new colony, and Spaniards used existing indigenous social and economic structures for their own purposes.

Cortés Awards Encomiendas to Conquerors, 1521

I have likewise informed your Majesty [Charles V] that the natives of these parts are of much greater intelligence than those of the [Caribbean] Islands; they seem to us indeed to possess sufficient intelligence to conduct themselves as average reasonable beings. On this account it seemed to me a very serious matter to compel them to serve the Spaniards in the same way as the natives in the Islands; yet without this service the conquerors and settlers of these parts would not be able to maintain themselves. In order, therefore, not to enslave the Indians at that time, and yet to assist the Spaniards to settle, it seemed to me that your Majesty might order a certain portion of the royal revenues accruing to your Majesty from these parts to be appropriated to the expenses and maintenance of the colonists, as I explained very fully to your Majesty. Since then, however, bearing in mind the many and continued expenses of your Majesty, and the fact that we should seek in every way to increase your Majesty's revenues rather than diminish them and seeing, moreover, the long time that we have spent in fighting against the natives and the hardships and loss which we have been put to on that account, together with the delay which your Majesty might for that reason command above all, on account of the many importunities of your Majesty's officials and all my men, which there was no means of resisting, I found myself practically forced to hand over the rulers and natives of these parts to the Spaniards, taking into consideration when doing so their estate and the services which they have rendered your Majesty in these parts, so that until your Majesty shall make some fresh arrangements or confirm this one, the aforesaid rulers and natives will serve and provide the Spaniards, to whom they were respectively allotted, with whatever they may need to sustain themselves. All this was done with the approval of persons who have great knowledge and experience of the country. No better course could have been taken, nor one which contributes more to both the proper maintenance of the Spaniards, and the conservation and good treatment of the Indians; of all this the procurators now proceeding to your Majesty from New Spain [Mexico] will give your Majesty a long and complete account. Your Majesty's farms and granaries have been placed in the best and most convenient cities and provinces. I beseech your Majesty to approve this and order in what way the royal interests may best be served. Most Catholic Lord: Our Lord God conserve the life, the very royal person and powerful state of your Caesarian Majesty [Charles's title as Holy Roman Emperor], and increase it with many kingdoms and dominions such as your royal heart desires. From the city of Coyoacan, in this New Spain of the Ocean Sea, the 15th of May, in the year 1522, Your Majesty's most humble servant and vassal who kisses your Majesty's royal hands and feet.   Hernando Cortés

Five Letters of Cortés to the Emperor, trans. J. Bayard Morris (New York, 1969), pp. 244–5.

While the new capital was being built, Cortés set up headquarters in the nearby Indian settlement of Coyoacan, proceeding to act as governor even before the Crown confirmed his title. Cortés distributed Indian settlements in encomienda to the successful conquerors, even though the Crown had explicitly prohibited the practice. Not surprisingly, Cortés reserved the richest towns for himself and chose sites with potential for economic development, including big chunks of central Mexico, as well as Tehuantepec in southern Mexico. In addition, in standard fashion he reserved encomiendas for his relatives, some of whom participated in the conquest.

Further Conquests. Once Tenochtitlan fell, Mexico became the prime destination for immigrants, settlers, and potential conquerors of new regions. Some immigrants were relatives of first conquerors and received encomiendas by virtue of their connections. Others came from the Caribbean islands. At the time of the conquest of Mexico, Spaniards did not know whether the Aztec empire was unique or if other similar Indian states existed. The hope that Tenochtitlan was the first of many such fueled Spaniards' dreams to strike it rich.

Both central Mexico and the Caribbean served as staging areas for new expeditions on the mainland. Cortés's right-hand man, Pedro de Alvarado, led an expedition to Guatemala in 1523 and later to Jalisco. Alvarado did not profit as substantially as did Cortés from his participation in the conquest, doubtless the major reason that he pursued further conquests. As a result of his expedition to Guatemala, he became its first governor. There he added to his ruthless reputation, torturing and executing Indian lords while exploiting his encomienda Indians to the fullest. Restless and hearing of the fabulous riches of Peru, Alvarado left Guatemala for Peru, only to find that other conquerors had outflanked him. Returning to Mexico, he went to Nueva Galicia in the west, where he died in the Mixtón War (1541–2) (see Chapter 12). Alvarado never settled down. He always looked toward the next expedition, hoping to increase his wealth from the immediate spoils of war.

From Cuba, Governor Velázquez authorized an expedition led by Nuño de Guzmán to the Huasteca on the northern Gulf Coast, an ill-defined region Spaniards called Pánuco, which had been settled by Nahuatl-speakers and was part of the Aztec Empire. Guzmán was a successful conqueror who built a strong power base as a rival conqueror to Cortés. He was named head of the First Audiencia (high court) while Cortés was pursuing his Honduras expedition in 1524–26. In 1529, Nuño de Guzmán began a bloody campaign in western Mexico, cruel even by standards of the day. Confirmed as governor of the territory called Nueva Galicia, Guzmán held the post until 1533.

Other expeditions included that of Cristóbal de Olid, a close ally of Cortés, who conquered part of Michoacan and then proceeded up the Pacific coast to Colima, where he met resistance. Three men named Francisco Montejo—father, son, and nephew—carried out a long campaign against the Yucatec Maya beginning in 1527, the initial phase of which lasted until 1537. Cortés himself led an ill-fated expedition to Honduras during which the Aztec monarch Cuauhtemoc was executed for supposedly conspiring against the

Gulf of Mexico

PACIFIC
OCEAN

GARAY
CORTES
HUASTECA

Mexico-
Tenochtitlan

JALISCO

GUZMAN
1529

MICHOACAN

OAXACA
CORTES
1522

YUCATAN

MONTEJO
1527

CHIAPAS

ALVARADO
1523

HONDURAS

CORTES 1524
OLID 1522

GUATEMALA

0   250   500 Miles

0   250   500 Kilometers

Further Early Spanish Conquests

Spaniards. Initially Cortés authorized conqueror Cristóbal de Olid to lead the expedition to Honduras, but Olid threw off Cortés's authority and made common cause with Cortes's old enemy, Diego Velázquez. Spanish expeditions to Michoacan, Oaxaca, Chiapas, and Yucatan did not yield the relatively quick success of the earlier conquest of the Aztec Empire, but eventually all those areas were brought under Spanish control.

The Formation of Early New Spain

The Early Economy. Spaniards quickly understood the essential nature of the Aztec Empire and its efficiency in tribute collection. They asked the Indians to record the tribute levies they sent to Tenochtitlan. One of the first Indian books compiled under the Spaniards was *Codex Mendoza*, which enumerated towns under Moctezuma's control and the tribute goods each one rendered. Initially, Spanish encomenderos received tribute in native products, including maize, cacao, chili peppers, turkeys, and lengths of woven cloth, with some encomiendas producing limited amounts of gold in tribute. This tribute-based economy was short-lived. Indian tribute structures were modified only at the top, with the encomendero rather than an indigenous leader receiving the tribute.

Many encomenderos used Indian labor on their landed holdings called *estancias*. Encomenderos sold Indian tribute goods, such as corn and cotton cloaks, in the markets, since there was demand for them among the Indian population. As Spanish immigration increased, an urban market for Spanish crops and animals developed. The immigrants preferred their familiar foods, wheat bread rather than corn tortillas, and beef, mutton, and chicken rather than turkey, dog, and salamanders.

Encomenderos diversified as new opportunities arose. The most prominent example was Cortés, whose enterprises centered in Cuernavaca specialized in sugar, a product requiring large amounts of manpower for cultivation and skilled labor in processing the sugar. Cattle were raised on Cortés's ranches in Tehuantepec, and the meat, hides, and wool were used on his other estates. In addition, he set up a shipyard and became involved in the South Sea trade, to the consternation of the Crown, which worried that Cortés was too powerful and independent. Cortés also initiated silk production, importing mulberry trees and silkworms.

Some encomenderos whose holdings were close to mineral deposits made limited use of their Indians in the mines, although it was illegal to do so. In any case, most of the great deposits of silver that later fueled the colonial economy were found well to the north of the limits of sedentary Indian settlement. Encomenderos did use Indian labor for construction, which boomed as Spaniards built their new capital.

The encomenderos themselves did not deal with day-to-day operations of their holdings. Spanish subordinates, often later-arriving immigrants, sometimes their own kin, managed the business of the encomienda. On site, African slaves often served as labor bosses and developed a reputation for exploiting Indians. In response, colonial legislation banned Africans from living in Indian villages.

Spanish Cities and Indian Towns. As privileged members of the new order, encomenderos lived in Spanish cities. The highest-ranking encomenderos generally lived in Mexico City, while small holders might live in secondary Spanish cities near their labor grants. The early colonial Spanish cities were centers for European settlement and culture. For Spaniards, living in a city meant being in contact with fellow Europeans and living an urban if not urbane life. The countryside was dominated by Indians, with only a few Spaniards, such as encomienda administrators, friars, and a few secular clerics, permanently in residence. Even in the Spanish cities, however, often the majority of residents were Indians.

New cities were established, such as Colima (1524), Antequera (1526, now Oaxaca city), and Guadalajara (1532). Veracruz, the first settlement formally founded in 1519, was the colony's main port on the Gulf Coast, whereas Acapulco, established in 1528, eventually became the terminus of the Manila trade. The Nahua settlement of Quauhnahuac became Cuernavaca and served as the capital of Cortés's holdings. Puebla de los Angeles (1531) was built as a Spanish city midway along the route between Mexico City and the port of Veracruz, protecting nearby Tlaxcala from excessive Spanish presence.

Mérida was founded in 1542 as the Spanish capital of Yucatan, with Valladolid functioning as a secondary city in the Maya interior. A Spanish city with a cabildo provided Spaniards with the legal means to conduct business. Mexico City was Spaniards' preferred place of residence, but secondary cities functioned as the capitals of their respective economic regions. Indian settlements throughout central and southern Mexico received Christian saints' names.

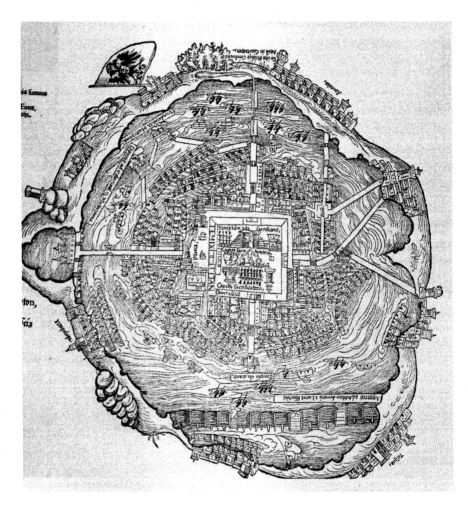

Figure 3-1 **Map of Tenochtitlan, 1524.** This early map of the Aztec island capital shows the causeways to the mainland and central ceremonial plaza. It was widely published in Europe in the early sixteenth century.
From John R. Hebert, ed. *1492: An Ongoing Voyage*. Library of Congress, 1992, p. 143 In Hernando Cortés, *Praeclara Ferdinandi Cortesii de Nova maris* [Norimbergae]. Rosenwald Collection, Rare Book and Special Collections Division, Library of Congress.

In Mesoamerica, existing Indian communities formed the basis for the privately held encomiendas awarded to the conquerors. These Indian towns also were brought under royal authority through the institution of *corregimiento*. The corregimiento was an administrative district with a royal official called the *corregidor*, responsible for establishing and maintaining civil justice. Not surprisingly, many encomenderos viewed the establishment of Spanish administrative districts as a curb on their power, although some encomenderos or their relatives served as corregidors.

Major Indian settlements were constituted as Spanish-style municipalities, with town councils (*cabildo* or *ayuntamiento*) made up of local noblemen, the *principales*. Although Indian towns were held in encomienda by particular Spaniards, the encomendero had no legal standing on the Indian town council. Cabildos became the main instrument by which Indian towns registered their complaints to the Crown about encomenderos. Since encomenderos wanted to maximize their tribute revenue even when Indian populations were decimated by epidemics, Indian cabildos often petitioned the Crown for revised tribute assessments.

Early Colonial Society. Encomenderos and their retinues, royal officials, and religious orders were powerful groups in early colonial Mexico, but a whole range of social types immigrated to the newly conquered land, including Spanish women whose presence reflected and contributed to the rapid consolidation of the colony. In the first five to ten years after the conquest, there were few Spanish women in Mexico, and conquerors formed relationships with Indian women. A small number of high-status Indian women, such as Doña Isabel de Moctezuma, daughter of Moctezuma II and wife of the last Aztec ruler, Cuauhtemoc, married Spanish conquerors and held encomiendas in their own right. Doña Isabel was able to preserve her high status in the early colony. She held encomiendas in her own name, as did her younger sister, Doña Leonor Moctezuma. These Indian noblewomen and their children were part of a very small group that held extensive property and married Spaniards. More commonly Spanish conquerors made informal alliances with Indian women.

Cortés himself fathered a child, Martín, by his interpreter, Doña Marina (Malinche); a daughter, Doña Leonor Cortés Moctezuma, by Doña Isabel de Moctezuma; and children by other Indian and Spanish women. When Cortés's first wife, Catalina Suárez (conspicuously not *doña*), died under suspicious circumstances, he took a second wife, a high-born woman of a Spanish noble house, Doña Juana de Zúñiga. Ties to his second wife's family helped Cortés avoid royal sanctions for insubordination and financial corruption. Their union produced four legitimate children, including his heir, Don Martín Cortés, while his natural son Martín by Doña Marina served his half-brother Don Martín, managing the vast Cortés estate. Cortés's second-in-command in the conquest, Pedro de Alvarado, was married, but he also maintained a long-term relationship with Luisa Xicotencatl, a Tlaxcalan noblewoman with whom he had a child, both of whom accompanied him to Peru.

With increased Spanish immigration to New Spain, men sent for their wives, daughters, unmarried sisters, and other kinswomen. In time first conquerors and wealthy settlers no longer viewed Indian noblewomen as suitable marriage partners, but informal relationships between Spanish men and Indian women remained common. Men who recognized their natural children with Indian women often raised them as Spaniards; children whose fathers did not recognize them were raised as Indians. A small number of racially mixed children retained high status in their Nahua communities, such as Diego Muñoz Camargo of Tlaxcala and Fernando de Alva Ixtlilxochitl of Texcoco, authors of histories of their native towns. Not until a large number of mixed Spanish-Indian offspring emerged in the late sixteenth century did the term *mestizo* come into common usage.

The original conquerors included a range of social types from hidalgos to artisans. Encomenderos, government officials, miners, and merchants played a role disproportionate to their numbers, but a fully developed Hispanic society emerged in Mexico City in the first decade or so after conquest. The arrival of new immigrants with a wide array of skills made Mexico City not just the administrative capital but New Spain's principal urban center. Secondary cities, however, also had artisans who met local demand. Artisans included high-status silver and goldsmiths (*plateros*) and metalworkers such as swordsmiths, armorers, knife and dagger makers as well as the more mundane locksmiths and horse shoers. Leatherworkers included saddle and harness makers, shoemakers, wineskin makers, and tanners. Construction required the skills of masons, stone cutters, carpenters, bricklayers, and street pavers. The realm of health care included many barbers and a few surgeons as well as pharmacists. Printers, booksellers, and musicians contributed to early cultural life in Mexico City. Spaniards' fashion needs were partially met by local tailors, hat and glove makers, and hosiers. By 1550, about 10 percent of Mexico City's Spanish population of approximately eight thousand were artisans.

Evangelization. The possibility and expectation of converting the New World's native peoples provided the justification for Spanish conquest and imperial expansion. As a pious and politic leader, Cortés was interested in promoting conversion of the indigenous population to Christianity. Soon after the conquest of Mexico, Cortés invited mendicant Franciscans and Dominicans rather than the diocesan (or "secular") clergy to evangelize the Indians. Although some mendicants, particularly the Dominicans, criticized encomenderos' treatment of Indians, both mendicants and encomenderos were first-generation interest groups asserting status based on seniority in Mexico. Franciscan Don Juan de Zumárraga arrived in Mexico with the title of "Protector of the Indians" and became the first bishop of Mexico. A leading advocate of the mendicants' role in evangelizing the Indians, he also at times clashed with civil authorities. In colonial Mexico, as in Spain and the rest of Europe, politics often revolved around the differing aims of rulers, bureaucrats, and ecclesiastics, as well as individuals pursuing their private interests and gain.

Politics in Early Mexico. Political conflicts among Spaniards also could reflect a generational factor, with first arrivals holding on to power against later claimants. Conquerors and their kin sought ascendancy over nonconqueror settlers; first arriving mendicant orders sought primacy over later arriving orders and the secular clergy. The Crown attempted to gain control over all the first-generation power groups by directly establishing its authority in both civil and religious spheres, with institutions staffed by royally appointed officials. Even within these institutions, however, there was factionalism and conflict.

The king countered Cortés's political dominance by establishing an *Audiencia* or high court in Mexico City in 1527. The high court was headed by Cortés's political rival, Nuño de Guzmán. Guzmán seized the opportunity to redistribute encomiendas to his own allies and damage Cortés's reputation by accusing him of financial corruption, alleging that he had hidden Aztec treasure and later diverted royal revenues for his own use. The First Audiencia was dissolved and the Second Audiencia established, becoming the legitimate instrument of royal rule.

In 1524, Charles V of Spain established the Council of the Indies with responsibility for Spain's overseas empire, but it became clear that the wealth and importance of New Spain demanded a resident royal administrator. Hernando Cortés expected to be appointed, but during the conquest of Mexico he had demonstrated his inclination to pursue an independent course. In 1535, the crown appointed Don Antonio de Mendoza as viceroy of New Spain. Mendoza was a member of Spain's high nobility, from a family loyal to the Spanish monarch. The office of viceroy invested the full power of the monarchy in the appointee. Given the distance between Spain and New Spain, the viceroy exercised considerable autonomy. Cortés's services could not be ignored, and after a trip to Spain in 1530 he secured the title of Marquis of the Valley of Oaxaca. With the title came twenty-two encomiendas and entailed holdings, providing him a vast income and the legal right to bequeath his estate to his heirs, with the title remaining in his family. A realist, the new marquis initially left the capital to pursue his economic enterprises, which he ran from a magnificent palace he had built in Cuernavaca. In 1540, Cortés again returned to Spain in an unsuccessful attempt to petition the Crown for further privileges as premier conqueror as well as to arrange marriages for his legitimate children. He entered the service of King Charles V in the campaign against Muslims in Tangier but reaped no significant personal reward.

When Cortés died in Spain in 1547, he was a titled and fabulously wealthy man. Denied what he considered his rightful reward, to be viceroy, however, he died an embittered man. Cortés's right-hand man in the conquest of Mexico, Pedro de Alvarado, never settled down, fighting Indians until his death in Jalisco in 1541. Nuño de Guzmán, the President of the discredited First Audiencia of Mexico, rapacious conqueror of Michoacan and Colima, ended his days in Spain, spending twenty years under house arrest. Cortés's son Don Martín became the second marquis of the Valley of Oaxaca and involved himself disastrously in factional politics in Mexico, but the title continued in existence for hundreds of years. Cortés's natural children by Indian noblewomen took their place among the elites of the new colonial society. Pedro de Alvarado and his Spanish wife died childless. Although he had a natural daughter with his lifelong Indian concubine, his encomienda holdings reverted to the Crown. Nuño de Guzmán never married, produced no known children, and had his encomiendas reassigned by the Crown during his long house arrest. These three conquerors' careers lend insight into the possibilities and perils for Spaniards during Mexico's first thirty years.

Glossary

adelantado   leader of an expedition
Audiencia   high court
cabildo   town council
caballero   horseman
cacique   Indian leader
corregimiento   civil jurisdiction, administrative district
entrada   expedition
estancia   Spanish land holding, farm
mestizo/a   person of mixed European-Indian heritage
patronato real   royal power to appoint clerics
quinto   royal fifth of profits

Questions for Discussion

1. What did Spaniards expect when embarking on an expedition of conquest?

2. How did Central Mexican Indians participate in the events of the conquest?

3. How did Spaniards consolidate their conquest of Central Mexico?

4. What was the encomienda?

5.   How did Cortés justify to the king his granting encomiendas to his fol-
      lowers?

Suggested Reading

Primary Sources

Cervantes de Salazar, Francisco. *Life in the Imperial and Loyal City of Mexico in New
     Spain* [1554]. Facsimile with a translation by Minnie Lee Barrett Shepard.
     Westport, Conn.: Greenwood Press, 1953. Early description of the vicere-
     gal capital by one of the first professors at the University of Mexico.
Cortés, Hernando. *Letters from Mexico.* Ed. and trans. by Anthony Pagden.
     New Haven, Conn.: Yale Nota Bene Press, 2001. The conqueror's
     reports to the crown (1519–25).
Zorita, Alonso de. *Life and Labor in Ancient Mexico.* Trans. by Benjamin Keen.
     Norman: University of Oklahoma Press, 1963. Observations by a royal
     judge on indigenous practices with information about the encomienda
     in Mexico.

Secondary Sources

Aiton, Arthur S. *Antonio de Mendoza, First Viceroy of New Spain.* Durham,
     N.C.: Duke University Press, 1927. Biography of a key colonial admin-
     istrator with extensive discussion of institutions of the era.
Altman, Ida. "Spanish Society in Mexico City After the Conquest," *Hispanic
     American Historical Review* (1991) 71(3): 413–45. Careful examination of
     elite and plebeian Spanish society in early Mexico City.
Barrett, Ward. *The Sugar Haciendas of the Marqueses del Valle.* Minneapolis:
     University of Minnesota Press, 1970. Examination of Cortés's estates
     from the 1530s to the twentieth century.
Chipman, Donald. *Nuño de Guzmán and the Province of Pánuco in New Spain,
     1518–1533.* Glendale, Calif.: Arthur A. Clark, 1967. Narrative account of
     the life and career of an important but generally overlooked conqueror.
Foster, George M. *Culture and Conquest: America's Spanish Heritage.* Chicago:
     Quadrangle Books, 1960. Analysis of the transfer of artifacts and prac-
     tices from Spain to Mexico.
Gibson, Charles. *Aztecs under Spanish Rule.* Stanford: Stanford University
     Press, 1964. Monumental and classic study of Nahuas in the Valley of
     Mexico for the entire colonial period.
Himmerich y Valencia, Robert. *The Encomenderos of New Spain, 1521–1555.*
     Austin: University of Texas Press, 1991. A valuable research tool with
     individual and collective biographies of encomenderos.

Liss, Peggy K. *Mexico under Spain, 1521–1556: Society and the Origins of Nationality*. Chicago: University of Chicago Press, 1975. An examination of the formation of a separate identity among the first generation of Spaniards in Mexico.

Riley, G. Micheal. *Fernando Cortés and the Marquesado in Morelos, 1522–1547*. Albuquerque: University of New Mexico Press, 1973. Concise study of the holdings of Cortés.

Sauer, Carl O. *The Early Spanish Main*. Berkeley and Los Angles: University of California Press, 1966. Important study by a historical geographer focusing on the Caribbean phase of the Spanish enterprise.

Thomas, Hugh. *Conquest: Moctezuma, Cortés, and the Fall of Old Mexico*. New York: Simon and Schuster, 1993. Wide-ranging history of the conquest, focusing on the major historical figures.

Vigil, Ralph H. *Alonso de Zorita: Royal Judge and Christian Humanist, 1512–1585*. Norman: University of Oklahoma Press, 1987. Biography of a major administrator of the early period.

Four

Narratives
of Conquest

The Spanish conquest of Mexico was a lengthy process. Relatively quick victories over settled populations in central Mexico brought them under Spanish control, while conflicts with the Indians of the north were more protracted. The Spanish campaign against the Aztecs of Tenochtitlan took two years. In western Mexico, the conquest of the Purepecha of Michoacan was similar to that of central Mexico, while the conquest of the Maya region was lengthier. It took almost a century for Spaniards at least nominally to conquer all of New Spain.

As dramatic and shocking as it was for all the participants, the seizure of Tenochtitlan on August 13, 1521, by Spanish, Tlaxcalan, and Texcocan forces did not represent the fall of a country but rather the collapse of Mexica rule in the Valley of Mexico. Other groups in the region did not necessarily consider the defeat of the Mexica to be a major historical event. No evidence indicates that Nahua groups outside Tenochtitlan considered the city's fall to be calamitous, especially since it meant the end of Mexica political dominance. As conqueror Bernal Díaz del Castillo recalled:

> When the news spread through all these distant provinces that Mexico was destroyed, their Caciques and lords could not believe it. However, they sent chieftains to congratulate Cortés on his victories and yield themselves as vassals to His Majesty, and to see if the city of Mexico, which they had so dreaded, was really razed to the ground. They all carried presents of gold to Cortés, and even brought their small children to show them Mexico, pointing out to them in much the same way that we would say, "Here stood Troy." (Bernal Díaz, *The Conquest of New Spain* [New York, 1963], 413)

For most people in Mesoamerica who had been ruled or threatened by the Mexica the fall of Tenochtitlan was a welcome event. Disappointment would soon replace optimism, however, as the Spaniards did not grant indigenous groups the autonomy they desired.

The conquest of Greater Mexico entailed both a military invasion by Spanish conquerors and a fierce internecine conflict among rival indigenous groups, with multiple ramifications for the internal social order. Totonacs, Tlaxcalans, and Texcocans sided with Spaniards and fought against Mexicas in central Mexico. The Mexicas themselves collaborated with their conquerors after 1521 and fought against other rival groups in western and southern Mexico. At a later time Purepechas, Tlaxcalans, and other central Mexican groups would play active roles as the Spaniards' allies in the colonization and conquest of northern Mexico, helping to create an enduring south to north migratory tradition.

The participation of different actors in this complex process necessarily determined how those historical events were remembered and recorded. The Tlaxcalans, for instance, felt a sense of pride and accomplishment after the fall of Tenochtitlan. Their cooperation with the Spaniards in defeating a rival indigenous group became a source of pride and a pledge of commitment. Nahua writers praised Cortés and celebrated the misfortunes of other indigenous groups, while in Maya accounts caciques affirmed the superiority of Christianity over native beliefs.

A large number of firsthand contemporary or nearly contemporary accounts were written by Spanish conquerors, their indigenous allies, and the vanquished Indians. The conquest of Tenochtitlan is one of the best-documented events in early modern world history. These narratives allow modern readers to see events from multiple perspectives.

The narratives of conquest are diverse and polemical. Each account necessarily incorporates substantial biases that reflect ethnic affiliations, religious partisanship, class interests, local identity, personal achievement, and the desire for recognition and reward. All authors of conquest narratives were male. Women were excluded from political and intellectual pursuits as well as military ones. Some accounts were written by participants, others set down later to present a particular conqueror's or indigenous community's viewpoint. Royal chroniclers crafted dispassionate narratives.

Since prehispanic Mesoamericans had strong oral and written historical traditions, indigenous accounts of the conquest represent an extension into the colonial period of preexisting practices. The Nahuas of central Mexico, the Purepechas of Michoacan and the Yucatec Mayas all produced narratives. These accounts are written in Spanish or indigenous languages— Nahuatl and Mayan—or they are pictorial manuscripts (called codices) either created along with written narratives or subsequently annotated.

Accounts of the Spanish Conquerors

Accounts produced by the European victors range from the letters written during the conquest itself to the king by Hernando Cortés to later petitions submitted to the Crown by Spanish participants who sought rewards— *mercedes*—for their services, usually encomiendas. Conquerors undertook expeditions under royal license but at their own expense. Participants in conquests needed to document their contributions in order to obtain material rewards. The accounts or petitions produced by conquistadores or those who missed the conquest of Tenochtitlan but participated in subsequent campaigns are usually called *probanzas* or *relaciones de méritos y servicios*. They consist of meticulous descriptions of individual contributions to the conquest of a place or people and were intended to secure such rewards as grants of land, tribute or labor services of Indians, or official appointments. The leader of an expedition expected to become governor of the newly conquered area and sought confirmation in office and a noble title.

Not surprisingly, conquerors' accounts exaggerated the deeds and merits of the petitioner and his inner circle and did not hesitate to criticize or refute other conquerors' claims. Accounts stressed loyalty to the Spanish Crown, bravery, honor, and above all an unconditional commitment to Christianity. Conquerors were the heroes of their own narratives, depicting themselves as having played an indispensable role in the extension of Christianity in the New World. Most Spanish narratives underplayed or completely ignored the contributions of native allies.

The Letters of Cortés. Hernando Cortés wrote letters to the Crown during the conquest and its immediate aftermath. He needed to explain his actions and legitimize his independent actions while protesting his loyalty to the Crown. A document sent to the king in July 1519 (often substituted in collections of Cortés's letters for the lost first letter) justifies the transformation of the expedition's purpose from exploration and trade to conquest and settlement by pointing to the benefits that thereby would accrue to the Crown. The document asserts that Cortés's men had demanded that they pursue this course and that he had acceded to their wishes. Thus, Cortés made himself appear to be a reluctant participant rather than the person mainly responsible for drastically modifying the nature and purpose of the expedition, an unlikely scenario since the men involved were directly under his command. The key legal issue was that a unanimous demand made by "good" men constituted grounds to set aside the law. Part of his explanation follows:

> It seemed to us not fitting to our Majesties' service to carry out the orders which Diego Velázquez had given to Hernando Cortés, which were to trade for as much gold as possible and return with it to the island of Fernandina in order that only Diego Velázquez and the captain [Cortés] might enjoy it; and that it seemed to all of us better that a town [Veracruz] with a court of justice be founded and inhabited in Your Royal Highnesses' name so that in this land also You might have sovereignty as You have in Your other kingdoms and dominions. For once the land has been settled by Spaniards, in addition to increasing Your Royal Highnesses' dominions and revenues, You may be so gracious as to grant favors to us and to the settlers who come in the

future. . . . Therefore, [Cortés] disregarded his personal interest in continuing trading, by which he had expected to recover his investment and the great expense of fitting out the fleet together with Diego Velázquez, but rather set all this aside, and was pleased and willing to do all that we requested, for it would greatly benefit the service of Your Royal Highnesses. (Source: Pagden, trans., *Letters from Mexico* [New Haven, 2001], 26)

Cortés sought to shape the Crown's understanding of the conquest even as events unfolded. A literate, articulate, and able politician, Cortés was well aware of the importance of gaining the king's trust and proving his worth to the monarch notwithstanding his insubordination. His letters reveal his pragmatism, military prowess, religious convictions, and social aspirations, as well as his great confidence in the superiority of European and Christian beliefs and institutions and contempt for those of native peoples.

Published and widely read in Europe, Cortés's letters became an instant classic on war and diplomatic history. On gaining advantage in hostile territory, he comments, "When I saw the discord and animosity between these two peoples [of Tlaxcala and Tenochtitlan] I was not a little pleased, for it seemed to further my purpose considerably; consequently I might have the opportunity of subduing them more quickly, for as the saying goes, 'divided they fall'" (Pagden, 69–70). Although he provides relatively little detail about the Indian allies, he does indicate their importance at certain points, such as the final siege of Tenochtitlan, and stresses the allies' ruthlessness. "We had more trouble preventing our allies from killing [women and children] with such cruelty than we had in fighting the enemy. For no race, however savage, has ever practiced such fierce and unnatural cruelty as the natives of these parts" (Pagden, 261–2).

His letters captured the imagination of readers eager for tales of distant and exotic places and word of wealthy lands to exploit. In his second letter to the king, dated October 30, 1520, Cortés emphasized the importance of his find. "From all I have seen and understood touching the similarity between this land and that of Spain, in its fertility and great size . . . and many other things, it seemed to me that the most suitable name for it was New Spain" (Pagden, 159). The Crown concurred and retained the name with all its implications.

Cortés's account contains much detail about military strategy and the brilliance of his leadership. First and foremost, he emphasized his role as premier leader, mentioning other leaders by name on occasion but referring to the Spanish mounted and foot soldiers only in general terms. In the aftermath of conquest, he sought royal approval of the steps he had taken to establish formal political control over central Mexico. Cortés was the master of asking for forgiveness rather than requesting permission, as seen in his decision to distribute Indians in encomiendas.

Because Cortés expected to become governor of New Spain after the conquest, he was not pleased when the king sent Cristóbal de Tapia to assume control of the government. Cortés wrote in honeyed words to the Kings, "I could wish for no better person [than Tapia] to take over the government of these parts by Your Majesty's command." He then proceeded to explain, however, why that could not happen immediately "because the pacification of these lands was not yet so complete as we desired, and any change might arouse the natives." Cortés initiated a series of delaying tactics designed to postpone indefinitely any relinquishing of control. Cortés might well have judged correctly the delicacy of the situation, in which any change might result in rebellion; but he also was determined to maintain his political power. At that juncture he succeeded in doing so, although ultimately he failed.

Shortly after Cortés's death in 1547, a new stage of writing about the conquest began when his secretary in Spain, secular priest Francisco López de Gómara, published the conqueror's authorized biography in 1552. This marked the first major nonconqueror account of the events and instigated immediate controversy. The Dominican Bartolomé de Las Casas persuaded the king to ban the work, which he condemned in 1553, alleging that "Gómara was never in the Indies, and he wrote nothing but what Cortés himself told him to write, fabricated many stories in Cortés's favor which are manifestly false . . ." (quoted in Lesley Byrd Simpson, Introduction to *Cortés*, p. xvi). Dedicated to Cortés's son Don Martín, Gómara's work remained in circulation despite the ban, and later histories written by royal chroniclers incorporated verbatim major sections from it.

Gómara's biography had a signficant impact on many readers. Old conquerors in Mexico City helped to fund a history of the conquest authored by a professor at the new University of Mexico, Francisco Cervantes de Salazar (1515–75), hoping he would write something more favorable to them. In particular, Gómara's book infuriated old conqueror Bernal Díaz del Castillo, who began revising what had begun as a typical conqueror petition into a full-length account of the conquest, provocatively entitled *The True History of the Conquest of Mexico*.

Bernal Díaz del Castillo. Bernal Díaz del Castillo (1496–1584) was a veteran conqueror of the original group led by Cortés. After the conquest of Tenochtitlan he joined Pedro de Alvarado's expedition to Guatemala and was living there as an encomendero when Gómara's biography of Cortés came into his hands. He was incensed not only by that account's failure to acknowledge the importance of his own and other Spanish conquerors' roles but also because Gómara had written a second-hand account.

Bernal Díaz wrote an eyewitness account that is considered indispensable to the study of conquest history, since it was "what I myself saw and the fighting in which I took part." His history is filled with dramatic scenes and telling details even though it was written fifty years after the main events took place. "Those readers who are interested in this history must wonder at the great deeds we did in those days. . . . For what soldiers in the world, numbering only four hundred—and we were even fewer—would have dared to enter a city as strong as Mexico, which is larger than Venice and more than four thousand five hundred miles away from our own Castile, and having seized so great a prince [as Moctezuma] execute his captains before his eyes?" (Cohen, 250). His account was not published until 1632, but it circulated widely in manuscript form before that and was used by later historians, including royal chronicler Antonio de Herrera.

Cortés appears in the narrative as a great commander, "a valiant and enterprising captain." His role is counterbalanced and complemented by the deeds of other participants, the horsemen and soldiers, but Bernal Díaz, like Cortés, downplayed the contributions of the Spaniards' Indian allies. In his view, Spanish military success in central Mexico resulted from a set of decisions taken and carried out as a group by all the conquerors, who were motivated by both religious zeal and personal gain. Divine inspiration enabled them to defeat Mexico-Tenochtitlan. "I believe that we performed [the heroic actions] not out of our own volition but by the guidance of God" (Cohen, 250).

Although understandably much of Bernal Díaz's history deals with military matters, it is also a rich source of information about the Aztecs at contact. His description of the great market in Tlatelolco (see Chapter 1) reflects great admiration for indigenous culture, but he was contemptuous of some aspects and horrified at others, especially the practice of human sacrifice.

Bernal Díaz is a crucial source of information about key participants in the conquest. He wrote extensively about Moctezuma, whom he guarded. His description of the emperor reflects his mixed admiration and repulsion. He praised Moctezuma for his intelligence, refinement, and courtesy, while at the same time he abhorred Moctezuma's horrendous vices, including polygamy, cannibalism, and idolatry. Bernal Díaz is also our main source of information about Doña Marina, whom Cortés mentions but does not name.

Doña Marina's Story
as told by Bernal Díaz del Castillo

I should like to give an account of Doña Marina, who had been a great lady and cacique over towns and vassals since her childhood.

Her father and mother were lords and caciques of a town called Paynala, which had other towns subject to it, and lay about twenty-four miles from the town of Coatzacoalcos. Her father died while she was still very young, and her mother married another cacique, a young man, to whom she bore a son. The mother and father seem to have been very fond of this son, for they agreed that he should succeed to the caciqueship when they were dead. To avoid any

(Continued)

impediment, they gave Doña Marina to some Indians from Xicalango, and this they did by night in order to be unobserved. They then spread the report that the child had died; and as the daughter of one of their Indian slaves happened to die at this time, they gave it out that this was their daughter the heiress. The Indians of Xicalango gave the child to the people of Tabasco, and the Tabascans gave her to Cortés . . .

Doña Marina was a person of great importance and was obeyed without question by all the Indians of New Spain. . . . Doña Marina knew the language of Coatzacoalcos, which is that of Mexico [Nahuatl], and she knew the Tabascan [Mayan] language also. The language is common to Tabasco and Yucatan, and Gerónimo de Aguilar spoke it also. These two understood one another well, and Aguilar translated into Castilian [Spanish] for Cortés.

This was the great beginning of our conquests, and thus, praise be to God, all things prospered with us. I have made a point of telling this story, because without Doña Marina we could not have understood the language of New Spain and Mexico.

Bernal Díaz del Castillo, *The Conquest of New Spain* (abridged edition of *The True History of the Conquest of Mexico*), trans. J. M. Cohen (London, 1963), pp. 85–7.

Other Conquerors' Accounts. Another conqueror who might have been expected to write his version of the conquest, if not in a full-length narrative at least in a petition to the Crown, was Pedro de Alvarado, Cortés's right-hand man. A great deal is known about him from other conquerors' narratives, but there remains little that he wrote. Two of his letters survive, sent to Cortés while Alvarado was in Guatemala. In these he complains that he received insufficient credit for the conquest of Mexico, particularly galling since in 1522 Cortés received honors, titles, and encomiendas that made him the wealthiest and most powerful man in Mexico. Alvarado did not live to the venerable old age of Bernal Díaz, who wrote his *True History* at leisure in his later years of peace and relative poverty in Guatemala. Essentially a man of action rather than letters, he never settled down to administer the regions under his control, much less reflect on earlier expeditions.

Pedro de Alvarado's Complaints

Your Grace [Cortés] favored me with the lieutenancy of Tenochtitlan and I helped take the city, and defended it when I was inside at the risk and danger Your Grace is aware of. Had I gone to Spain, His Majesty [Charles V] would have confirmed the services I have rendered him and would have granted me greater favors. I have been told that His Majesty has issued his decree and I am not surprised, for he knows nothing of me, and no one is to blame for this but Your Grace for failing to report to His Majesty how I have served you: for it is

(Continued)

you who sent me here. I beg Your Grace to inform His Majesty who I am, how I have served him in these parts, where I am, and what new conquests I have made; also my willingness to serve in the future, and how I have received a leg injury in his service, and what small pay these squires and I have earned, and what little benefit we have so far received. May the Lord increase Your Grace's life and excellent condition for a long time to come.

The City of Santiago   Pedro de Alvarado
28 July 1524

Patricia de Fuentes, ed. and trans., "Pedro de Alvarado," in *The Conquistadors: First-Person Accounts of the Conquest of Mexico* (Norman, 1993), p. 196.

Another Spanish conqueror, whose postconquest life took a nonmilitary turn, was Alonso de Aguilar. After the conquest Aguilar received an encomienda and some valuable concessions, such as a license to erect a hostel for travelers between the port of Veracruz and the newly founded Spanish city of Puebla de los Angeles. He tired of his worldly life and became a Dominican friar at age fifty, taking the name Fray Francisco. When he was over eighty, his fellow mendicants persuaded him to write his account of the conquest, which he did succinctly. Like his fellow Dominican Las Casas, Aguilar apparently brooded over the morality of the conquest; but unlike Las Casas, Aguilar chose the contemplative life, avoiding the public sphere. At the end of his narrative he appears to question the success of the conquest that was meant to bring Christianity to the Indians.

Fray Francisco de Aguilar comments on Indian religion

[Before the conquest] all the people, whether noble or plebeian, removed their sandals in the courtyard before they entered to worship their gods; and at the door of the church [temple] they all squatted on their heels and very reverently sobbed and wept, asking forgiveness for their sins. The women brought pies made of poultry. They also brought fruits and paintings done on the native paper. In my opinion they were paintings of their sins. There was such a silence, broken by sobbing and weeping, that I was spellbound with wonder and terror.

And now that they are Christians, and as though in retribution for our sins, most of them come to church by force, and with very little fear and reverence; they gossip and talk, and walk out during the principal part of the Mass and the sermon. In their time, therefore, great strictness was observed in the ceremonies to their gods, but now they feel neither fear nor shame.

Patricia de Fuentes, ed. and trans., "Francisco de Aguilar," in *The Conquistadors: First-Person Accounts of the Conquest of Mexico* (Norman, 1993), p. 164.

Another account, written by Andrés de Tapia, ended abruptly in 1520. Taken together, Spaniards' accounts of the conquest provide the earliest information on Mexico's indigenous peoples, Spanish military strategy and tactics, and the dynamics of political maneuvering in the immediate post-conquest era. They also articulate the conquerors' expectations of material rewards in the aftermath of the conquest.

Indigenous Accounts

Accounts by Indian Allies. Spaniards' indigenous allies wrote lengthy accounts of the conquest, some of them illustrated. They wrote for much the same reasons as did Europeans, in the hopes of gaining political and material rewards based on their services to the Crown. The most prominent Spanish allies were the Tlaxcalans. Local patriot and mestizo historian Diego Muñoz Camargo wrote an extensive account in Spanish of the conquest from

Figure 4-1 **Spaniards on the road to Tenochtitlan.** Doña Marina is shown at the head of the group, with Cortés shown on foot with his hat in his hand, while a black slave holds his horse. This appears to be half of a two-page scene of the first meeting with Moctezuma.
From *Codex Azcatitlan.* Vol. 1. Facsimile. Paris: Bibliothèque Nationale de France, illustration 23.

the Tlaxcalan viewpoint in a report to the Crown (*Relación geográfica*) prepared in 1580. It includes lavish illustrations showing key events of the conquest from the Tlaxcalan perspective such as the interaction between Tlaxcalan lords and Cortés (accompanied by his interpreter, Doña Marina), battles in which the Tlaxcalans fought, and religious aspects of the conquest. The narrative emphasizes the Tlaxcalans' early embrace of Christianity as well as their substantial military contributions. In recognition of their assistance, the Tlaxcalan Indians were not distributed in encomiendas, and Tlaxcalan elites were accorded special rights and privileges throughout the colonial period, including the designation of their polity as a *ciudad*, or city, the highest municipal ranking in the Spanish world. Written in the late sixteenth century, Muñoz Camargo's history is not a firsthand account, but he almost certainly based it on oral history and pictorial records.

Other conquest narratives written by indigenous authors whose families enjoyed high social status before the arrival of the Spaniards show evidence of the struggle to maintain their status in the postconquest era. Their versions of the conquest differ from Spanish accounts in their emphasis on the participation and contributions of native rulers. No other group of writers better expresses the ramifications of the conquest and Christianization of Mexico for different city-states and regions. Native caciques and their descendants were among the first Indians to embrace Christianity, so that by the second half of the sixteenth century they had achieved a degree of acculturation to Spanish values. Tlaxcala's Muñoz Camargo was a mestizo, placing him somewhat apart from other indigenous writers. His writing nonetheless exhibits many characteristics of the genre.

A prime example of this group is Don Fernando de Alva Ixtlilxochitl (ca. 1568–1648), a descendant of the royal family of Texcoco and Nahuatl translator for the viceroy. Although an important ally of Cortés, Texcoco did not gain significant rewards for its contribution to the Spanish effort. In his account Texcocans appear eager to participate in the ruin of the Mexica, their former allies. Their assistance to the Spaniards in defeating the Mexica was crucial, not only in direct combat but also in terms of strategic advice, manpower, and military intelligence. In describing the fall of Tenochtitlan, Alva Ixtlilxochitl echoes Cortés's observation regarding the Tlaxcalans' brutality toward the defeated Mexica, placing the Texcocans in a (contrasting) good light. From Alva Ixtlilxochitl's viewpoint, all his kinsmen's and city's aid to the Spaniards brought Texcocans no material rewards, whereas such service had significantly benefited the Tlaxcalans.

While Alva Ixtlilxochitl's account has been interpreted as presenting an anti-Spanish perspective, it reads much like a standard petition for reward

Fernando de Alva Ixtlilxochitl on Texcoco's Contributions to the Conquest

They say that the best of the army [for the Spaniards] which was taken from Texcoco to go to the places mentioned consisted of more than five thousand soldiers, which Ixtlilxochitl provided as always with everything necessary, both food and clothing, arms and other necessary things, and very good rewards according to ancient custom. In this he spent a great amount of property and treasure belonging to him and his relatives. He also spent all the tributes and royal rents that were in the houses of tribute of his father and grandfather, and those that were brought to him daily by his vassals and the other kingdoms and provinces subject to the three capitals of the empire. Likewise, all the gold and precious stones belonging to him, the other lords and his relatives and friends, he gave to Cortés and the other Christians [Spaniards], who took great care to ask for them in accordance with their hungry envy and avarice. They had greedy eyes, and the more they gave them the more they wanted. They were never satisfied, as clearly appears in the histories written by diverse authors. And even the unfortunate Indians did not merely share their prizes with the Christians but gave them everything to keep them content. The first Christians who came to this land claim for themselves exclusively the triumph of the victory, but the native soldiers were always the first in undertaking every task, as is notorious and appears in the histories. In short, Ixtlilxochitl had very great and excessive expenses in these conquests and the conversion [to Christianity] of this country, which was a small service to God, and to Your Majesty. The King of Texcoco was left without a mantle and without a reward, and nowadays his descendants are without shelter, having only the mercy of God and the clemency of our ruler Philip III.

Fernando de Alva Ixtlilxochitl, *Ally of Cortés: Account 13: Of the coming of the Spaniards and the beginning of evangelical law,* trans. Douglass K. Ballentine (El Paso, 1969), pp. 115–16.

from the Crown for services rendered, together with a condemnation of the Tlaxcalans. Rulers from a town in Texcoco's political orbit, Otumba, claimed that the ruler of Texcoco was "the first who received the Catholic faith with entire devotion and who peacefully received Captain Don Hernando Cortés and the other Spaniards," an implicit criticism of Tlaxcala, which initially had resisted the Spaniards. The lords refer darkly to the suppression of the Texcocan version of the conquest, claiming that "we have given our Accounts to many [historians] and they have never come to light but it seems instead that many sinister accounts have increased" (appendix to Ballentine, trans. Alva Ixtlilxochitl, 131–2). Even Alva Ixtlilxochitl's account did not circulate widely in the colonial era, but it was published in the early

nineteenth century as Mexicans began reinterpreting the conquest to emphasize indigenous resistance to Spaniards.

The integration of Hispanized native rulers into the colonial order was
not confined to central Mexico. The following example from Yucatan reflects
a similar emphasis on the status of a ruling family prior to the conquest,
early and peaceful embrace of Christianity, and loyalty to the Spanish crown
and Christianity:

> And let it be known that I, Nakuk Pech, was ruling when Álvarez, first
> alcalde mayor, came to T-Ho . . . and after that, when the Oidor Don
> Tomás López came, I was also the ruler and my name was Nakuk Pech;
> but when the water fell upon my head and I received baptism, I
> became Don Pablo Pech and ceased to the called Nakuk Pech. The prin-
> cipal chiefs were made hidalgos by the Spanish captains when they set-
> tled here in the region. We were the first in paying tribute to the foreign
> lords. Afterwards, we were invested with power by the Christian God
> and the ruler King. We gave birth to hidalgos and my sons will be
> noble until the sun comes to an end, until the sun is destroyed. And we
> were the principal chiefs in this land when there was no Holy Church
> in this region, when these lands were not ruled by Spaniards. . . . When
> I received the Holy Faith to teach it to those under my authority I was
> the first one in holding the [Spanish] rod of justice to spread the Word
> of God, the word of our Great Prince and King, he who rules. (Agustín
> Yáñez, *Crónicas de la Conquista* [Mexico, 1993], 173)

Mendicant-compiled Accounts from Native Perspectives. Indigenous writings on the conquest of Mexico were not restricted to victors' narratives.
Spanish mendicants solicited accounts of the conquest from the viewpoint of
the conquered Indians, recording their versions of the conquests of
Tenochtitlan, Michoacan, and Yucatan.

In modern times, scholars marvel at what appears to be the mendicants' careful preservation of the narratives by the defeated, since these
accounts differ considerably from the versions of the Spanish victors. The friars, however, were not concerned with historical accuracy or with helping
the Indians to preserve their memories of events. Rather, they sought to
understand the Indians' recollections and beliefs so that Christianization
could proceed. We also must question whether the mendicants' Indian
informants were entirely candid with them. Furthermore, what the Indians
said and how the mendicants interpreted it might well have differed.

The most notable and widely known of these mendicant accounts of
the conquest of central Mexico was compiled by Franciscan Bernardino de
Sahagún, who began collecting information from indigenous participants
around 1555. Book 12 of *The General History of the Things of New Spain*,

known in its manuscript form as the *Florentine Codex* (1576), is written in Nahuatl and Spanish and includes a large number of mainly black-and-white illustrations. Another mendicant working at the same time, Dominican Diego Durán, compiled an account in Spanish entitled *The History of the Indies of New Spain* (1581). It, too, was drawn from native informants and amply illustrated.

When the two friars began collecting information in the 1550s the intellectual climate favored such investigations, but by the time they finished in the 1570s, the Roman Catholic Council of Trent (1545–63) had mandated stricter standards for upholding orthodox doctrine. The intellectual and political climate had become hostile to implicit or explicit native criticism of Spaniards' actions. Probably in an effort to win official approval, Durán included passages lauding Cortés in his *History*. Sahagún went further, producing an entirely new version of the conquest narrative, with several speeches attributed to Cortés and pro-Tlaxcala asides inserted into the largely pro-Tlatelolco text. Today, Sahagún's 1576 conquest narrative is more widely read than the revised account, in part because the 1585 revision reflects a more Spanish viewpoint and is further removed from the native informants. It remains of interest, however, because it provides insight into the shifting Spanish political and intellectual climate of the later sixteenth century.

Florentine Codex Account of Spaniards' Treatment of the Defeated Mexica (1576)

And everywhere on the roads the Spaniards robbed the people. They sought gold. They despised the green stones, the precious feathers, and the turquoise. [The gold] was everywhere in the bosoms, in the skirts of the poor women. And as for us who were men; it was everywhere in their breech clouts, in their mouths. And [the Spaniards] seized, they selected the women—the pretty ones, those whose bodies were yellow: the yellow ones. And some women, when they were to be taken from the people, muddied their faces, and clothed themselves in old clothing, put rags on themselves as a shift. It was all only rags that they put on themselves. And also some were selected from among us men—those who were strong, those soon grown to manhood, and those of whom later as young men they would make messengers. . . . Of some they then burned [branded] the cheeks [as slaves].

Fray Bernardino de Sahagún, *The Florentine Codex*, trans. Arthur J. O. Anderson and Charles Dibble (Salt Lake City, 1975), p. 122.

1585 Revision Account of Spaniards' Treatment of the Defeated Mexica

On the following morning, peace was publicly proclaimed. The [Spaniards] ordered that those who were penned up in the fort should come out safely and freely return to their homes to seek rest and solace. Likewise, they proclaimed a decree to the Spaniards, Tlaxcalans, and all the other Indians that they should not inflict any harm on them, or take any of their possessions, or enslave any men, women, boys, or girls. Having heard the proclamation that had been made, those within the fort emerged and [when they were] arriving at the main road leading to the district called Coyonacazco, some Tlaxcalans attacked, and began to rob and kill some of those who were leaving. Seeing this, the Captain [Cortés] immediately sent Spaniards to protect the Mexicans, and to restrain and imprison those who were harming them.

Fray Bernardino de Sahagún, *The Conquest of New Spain, 1585 Revision*, ed. and trans. Howard F. Cline and Sarah Cline (Salt Lake City, 1989), p. 137.

Some indigenous accounts include descriptions of omens that appeared before the conquest—earthquakes, comets, births of monsters, and other events. This narrative device—the appearance of supernatural wonders foretelling future disaster—was common currency in medieval religious chronicles. Christian writers probably influenced and reshaped indigenous memories of the events preceding the conquest. Omens only appear in accounts of defeated groups compiled by mendicants (Sahagún and Durán) or by the indigenous authors they strongly influenced, such as Tlaxcalan historian Diego Muñoz Camargo.

Accounts in Native Languages. For Indians not directly involved in the events either as allies or vanquished foes, the conquest seemingly merited little attention. In native town annals or other types of records there are references to "when the Christians came" or other relatively neutral indications of a mundane change of power. Such understatement may have been in some cases a cover for native vacillation prior to the Spanish victory. Some towns such as Xochimilco allied with the Spaniards only when Tenochtitlan's destruction was nearly complete. Perhaps for that reason Xochimilcans were reticent about their role.

Early mendicants taught a small number of indigenous men to write their own languages in Latin letters. From the mid-sixteenth century to the end of the colonial era, alphabetic texts in Nahuatl and Mayan, including histories of the conquest, were written for indigenous use. These accounts may have been self-censored so as not to reflect anti-Spanish or anti-Christian attitudes. Spaniards systematically confiscated and destroyed texts antithetical to Christianity. Ethnically aware native intellectuals who had formal training in the preservation of historical memory were among the first casualties of the new colonial order. Native histories produced in the colonial era survived only if they fell within acceptable ideological and religious parameters.

Indigenous accounts appeared by the mid-sixteenth century, with *The Annals of Tlatelolco* dating from perhaps as early as 1528. The *Annals*, written only in Nahuatl, extol Tlatelolco's valor in resisting the Spaniards, asserting that its warriors (and even its women) fought the Spaniards with greater determination than did the men of Tenochtitlan. The Tlatelolcans justify their own actions and attribute their failure either to fate or to turncoat or cowardly allies (or both), assigning themselves a valorous role in the face of all odds. The perspective of these annals is likely that of native priests whose status was collapsing due to Spaniards' Christian zealotry. These priests foresaw no future for themselves in the new colonial order. Many native holy men became leaders of indigenous rebellions against the Spaniards during the colonial era (see Chapter 12).

Primordial titles, a type of document created in Indian communities beginning in the seventeenth century to confirm legal title to land, often include information about a town's role in the conquest. These documents were town histories that included descriptions of the town's territory. Not all the claims advanced in these histories can be taken at face value. They often gloss over any resistance to the Spaniards or in contrast claim to have allied with them, whether or not it was so.

Another indigenous source of information on the conquest is the standard prehispanic genre of annals, year-by-year lists of important events, including natural phenomena such as earthquakes, comets, and droughts. Several annals include the years of the conquest but do not emphasize the defeat of Tenochtitlan. In the *Codex Telleriano-Remensis*, an Aztec pictorial manuscript with Spanish notations that ends in the year 1562, the years covering the conquest have been deleted, a simple and effective technique to suppress unorthodox or subversive interpretations. In some annals, however, the absence of information on the conquest may reflect the insignificance of that event for those Indian towns. The annals written or copied by the seventeenth-century Jesuit-educated Nahua, Chimalpahin, include little information on the conquest. A grandson of Moctezuma, Don Hernando de Alvarado Tezozomoc, wrote an account for a Nahua audience that only briefly mentions the conquest itself. Annals written alphabetically in Mayan also exist.

Pictorial Accounts. The Nahuas and Mayas had a written historical tradition in pictorials before Europeans arrived. Pictorials dealing with the conquest of central Mexico generally reflected a pro-Spanish stance and depicted such events as the march to Tenochtitlan, the meeting between Cortés and Moctezuma, the Alvarado massacre, and the final siege of the Aztec capital. Doña Marina, Cortés's interpreter and consort, appears prominently in several different pictorial sources. The most famous set of pictorials

Figure 4-2 **The lords of Michoacan**. When Spaniards on horseback arrived in western Mexico, the Purepecha (Tarascans) already knew that central Mexico was conquered and had experienced the spreading smallpox epidemic. Dissension amongst the Michoacan noblemen aided Spaniards in subduing the region.

From *The Chronicles of Michoacan*, ed. and trans. Eugene R. Craine and Reginald C. Reindorp (Norman: University of Oklahoma Press, 1970), Plate 18.

is the *Lienzo de Tlaxcala*. The original no longer exists, although copies were made, and pictorials that treat the same subject matter were published in Diego Muñoz Camargo's *Historia de Tlaxcala* and his 1581 *Relación geográfica* of Tlaxcala. Other central Mexican pictorials include the *Codex Telleriano-Remensis* and *Codex Vaticanus A* (two versions of the same sixteenth-century pictorial text), *Codex Aubin,* and *Codex Azcatitlan* (see Figure 4-1). *The Chronicles of Michoacan* (see Figure 4-2), compiled by a Franciscan, deal with the Purepecha peoples of west-central Mexico and illustrate the conquest of Michoacan, among other things. The graphics depict omens as well as Moctezuma's request for help from the Purepecha.

Secondary and Later Accounts

Royal Chroniclers. Royal chroniclers were professional scholars, paid by the Spanish Crown to produce lengthy texts on the acquisition of new lands and peoples for the monarchy. In general, they viewed the conquest of Mexico and Central America as the necessary first step in creating a universal empire to be ruled by the Habsburg dynasty in the name of Catholicism (an objective that became especially important during the religious wars over Protestantism). Royal chronicles provided comprehensive descriptions of the course of Spanish expansion in the New World that established the rights of the Spanish Crown to rule and profit from its empire.

Since the majority of royal chroniclers never visited the places they described, their work relied heavily on reports and petitions submitted by conquerors, including Cortés and Bernal Díaz, as well as Gómara's biography, the work of friars as Franciscans Toribio de Benavente Motolinia and Juan de Zumárraga and the Dominican Las Casas, and documents produced by early colonial officials in Mexico. Their chronicles are filled with inaccuracies, misleading information, and not necessarily insightful digressions about customs, traditions, practices and rituals of the native peoples of the New World. Peter Martyr d'Anghiera (1457–1526), Gonzalo Fernández de Oviedo (1478–1557), Antonio de Herrera y Tordesillas (1549–1625), and Antonio Solís y Rivadeneyra (1610–86) are among the major writers of this group, most of whom never set foot in the Indies.

Conquest and Mexican Identity. The descendants of the first conquerors also left written accounts of the conquest that emphasized its uniqueness. According to Juan Suárez de Peralta, a Spaniard born in Mexico City who was author of *Noticias históricas de la Nueva España*, the conquest of Mexico was a unique event. For the Mexican writers the conquest meant the historic foundation of New Spain as a Christian kingdom. From the perspective of the writers of the second half of the sixteenth century such as Bernardo de Balbuena (*Grandeza Mexicana*), Francisco Cervantes de Salazar (*Crónica de la Nueva España* and *México en 1554*), and Baltasar Dorantes de Carranza

(*Sumaria relación de las cosas de la Nueva España*) the conquest of Mexico provided the basis for a new and distinctive Spanish and Christian identity.

Mexican Spaniards saw Mexico's indigenous past as a source of pride and a worthy alternative to their Spanish heritage. In the independence period and beyond this sense of historic identification with the indigenous past combined with anti-Spanish feelings to produce new views of the conquest. In the early decades after independence Mexican nationalists began publishing works on the conquest with a decidedly anti-European bias. Nationalists glorified indigenous resistance to the Spaniards and denigrated their Indian allies as sellouts. Nationalists promoted Texcocan Alva Ixtlilxochitl's anti-Spanish account, which was widely published in Mexico under various titles, including the *Horrible Cruelties of the Conquerors of Mexico* (1829).

Particularly affected by nationalist revisionism in Mexico were interpretations of the role of Doña Marina, depicted as a traitor to her "own" people. Honored in the colonial period to the extent that her image forms part of the coat of arms of Tabasco, in the nineteenth and twentieth centuries she was reviled, and the term *malinchista* became synonymous with treason and treachery. Today, most scholars regard Doña Marina as a major historical figure forced to make her way in a world that in general offered women few options, and indigenous women even fewer.

Conquest History through Time. After the close of the conquest era in the mid-sixteenth century, the events of the conquest of central Mexico continued to fascinate not only Spaniards in Mexico and elsewhere but Europeans and Anglo-Americans as well.

An English translation of Las Casas's *A Short History of the Destruction of the Indies* appeared as early as 1583 (long before it was published in Spain), fueling English anti-Spanish attitudes, which were strongly rooted in political and religious rivalries, and helping to give rise to the so-called "Black Legend" that emphasized ostensible Spanish cruelty and religious fanaticism. The eighteenth century marked a new period of English interest in the conquest, particularly as they were expanding their American empire. In 1753 an English translation of the history written by royal chronicler Don Antonio de Solís (1610–86), was published. In his preface translator Thomas Townsend called Cortés "the Fortunate Conqueror of the Mexican Empire" and went on to say that the "Discovery and Conquest of that new World have enriched *England* with no small Share of the Wealth of it; which makes it a Point of Gratitude in Behalf of my Country to publish the Actions of this Hero" (Don Antonio de Solís, *The History of the Conquest of Mexico by the Spaniards* [New York, 1973], A2).

In 1767, when the Spanish Crown expelled the Jesuits from its territories, Mexican-born Francisco Clavigero, S.J. was exiled to Italy along with most of his fellow Jesuits. There he wrote (in Italian) a history of Mexico, up," drew more on the account of this ostensibly "common" foot soldier than the "great man" version of the events presented by Cortés. At the end of the twentieth century, even more obscure conquest texts became available in English, such as those from the Yucatan found in *Maya Conquistador.*

The most quoted passage from any of the conquest narratives, however, comes from a Nahuatl manuscript, given the English title *The Annals of Tlatelolco*, written perhaps just seven years after the fall of Tenochtitlan. The English translation by Lysander Kemp is an evocative and haunting lamentation of a lost civilization.

> Broken spears lie in the roads;
> We have torn our hair in our grief.
> The houses are roofless now, and their walls
> are red with blood.
>
> Worms are swarming in the streets and plazas,
> and the walls are splattered with gore.
> The water has turned red, as if it were dyed,
> and when we drink it,
> it has the taste of brine.
>
> We have pounded our hands in despair against the adobe walls,
> for our inheritance, our city, is lost and dead.
> The shields of our warriors were its defense,
> but they could not save it.
> *The Broken Spears, pp. 137–38.*

Glossary

conquistador   Spanish soldier who participated in a military campaign in the Indies

malinchista   a sell-out

merced   reward, grant, favor

relación de meritos y servicios   formal legal petition recording military deeds and services to the Crown

Requerimiento   petition, requirement. Legal statement by which Spanish troops offered Indians peace in exchange for their allegiance to the king of Spain and acceptance of Christianity. A negative response constituted legitimate reason for warfare and conquest

r Discussion

accounts of the conquest of Mexico?

Bernal Díaz del Castillo coincide or

ccounts of the conquest reflect?

Questions for Discussion

1. Why are there so many different accounts of the conquest of Mexico?

2. How did the views of Cortés and Bernal Díaz del Castillo coincide or differ?

3. What kinds of biases did different accounts of the conquest reflect?

4. How did Fray Francisco de Aguilar contrast the Indians' attitude toward their old religion with their feelings about Christianity?

5   How did Sahagún's revised (1585) account of Spanish treatment of the Mexica differ from the original (1576) version?

6. Why did indigenous views of the conquest differ so greatly?

7. What role did religious beliefs and expectations play in shaping conquest histories?

8. How did colonial Mexicans, Mexican nationalists, and people outside the Spanish-speaking world interpret and use the history of the conquest for political and cultural purposes? How have our perceptions of the significance of the conquest changed over time?

Suggested Reading

Primary Sources

Alva Ixtlilxochitl, Fernando de. *Ally of Cortés: Account 13 of the Coming of the Spaniards and the Beginning of Evangelical Law*. Trans. by Douglass K. Ballentine. El Paso: Texas Western Press, 1969. Excerpt from a longer account, focusing on Texcoco's role in the conquest.

Chimalpahin, Don Antonio Muñon. *Codex Chimalpahin* [ca. 1600]. Ed. and trans. by Arthur J. O. Anderson and Susan Schroeder. Norman: University of Oklahoma Press, 1997. Nahuatl texts from the late sixteenth and early seventeenth centuries.

Clavigero, Francisco, S.J. *The History of Mexico* [1787]. New York: Garland Publishing, 1979. Eighteenth-century translation of the exiled Jesuit's conquest history, which devotes considerable attention to indigenous participation.

Codex Azcatitlan [sixteenth century]. Facsimile. Introduction by Michel Graulich, commentary by Robert H. Barlow. Paris: Bibliothèque

National de France and Société des Américanistes, 1995. Late six-teenth-century pictorial history of the Mexica, with depictions of the conquest.

Coruña, Fray Martín de Jesús de la. *The Chronicles of Michoacán* [1541]. Ed. and trans. by Eugene R. Craine and Reginald C. Reindorp. Norman: University of Oklahoma Press, 1970. English translation of the Spanish text with an account of the Purepecha kingdom before the arrival of the Spaniards and the conquest, with many illustrations.

Codex Telleriano-Remensis [1562]. *Ritual Divination, and History in a Pictorial Aztec Manuscript.* Ed. by Eloise Quiñones Keber. Austin: University of Texas Press, 1995. A pictorial manuscript in the annals tradition, with Spanish annotations; unfortunately, the key years of the conquest are not extant.

Cortés, Hernando. *Five Letters to the Emperor.* Trans. and with an introduction by J. Bayard Morris. New York: W.W. Norton, 1969. The premier con-queror's account of the conquest (1522–6).

———. *Letters from Mexico.* Ed. and trans. by Anthony Pagden. New Haven, Conn.: Yale Nota Bene Press, 2001. With a new introduction by the translator/editor.

Díaz del Castillo, Bernal. *True History of the Conquest of Mexico* [various edi-tions]. Vivid account written long after the events by one of Cortés's foot soldiers. Quotations in this text from J. M. Cohen, trans., *The Conquest of New Spain.* London: Penguin Books, 1963.

Durán, Fr. Diego. *The History of the Indies of New Spain* [1581]. Trans., anno-tated, and with an introduction by Doris Heyden. Norman: University of Oklahoma Press, 1994. Dominican friar's history of pre-hispanic and conquest history, based on indigenous sources.

Fuentes, Patricia de. *The Conquistadors: First-person Accounts of the Conquest of Mexico.* Ed. and trans. by Patricia de Fuentes. Norman: University of Oklahoma Press, 1993. Anthology of Spanish conqueror accounts.

Landa, Fray Diego de. *Landa's Relación de las Cosas de Yucatán* [ca. 1566]. Papers of the Peabody Museum of American Archaeology and Ethnology, Harvard University. Cambridge: Peabody Museum, 1941.

———. *Yucatan Before and After the Conquest.* Translated with notes by William Gates. New York: Dover Publications, 1978.

Léon-Portilla, Miguel. *The Broken Spears: The Aztec Accounts of the Conquest of Mexico.* Boston: Beacon Press, 1992. Popular edition of Nahua conquest narratives from both sides of the conflict.

Lockhart, James. *We People Here: Nahuatl Accounts of the Conquest of Mexico.* Ed. and trans. by James Lockhart. Repertorium Columbianum, vol. 1. Berkeley: University of California Press, 1993. New transcriptions and translations of conquest accounts by a leading scholar, with a useful introduction and notes.

López de Gómara, Francisco [1552]. *Cortés: The Life of the Conqueror by His Secretary.* Ed. and trans. by Lesley Byrd Simpson. Berkeley: University of California Press, 1964. Very readable translation of Gómara's biography of Cortés.

Muñoz Camargo, Diego. *Relaciones Geográficas del siglo xvi: Tlaxcala* [1581]. Ed. by René Acuña. Mexico: Universidad Autónoma de México, 1984. Geographical report to the Crown of major significance.

Restall, Matthew, ed. and trans. *Maya Conquistador.* Boston: Beacon Press, 1998. English translations of Maya accounts of the conquest, with helpful introductions to each selection.

Sahagún, Fr. Bernardino de. *Florentine Codex: Book 12—The Conquest of Mexico* [1576]. Trans. by Arthur J. O. Anderson and Charles E. Dibble. Santa Fe, N.M.: The School of American Research and Salt Lake City: University of Utah, 1975. English translation of the Nahuatl text compiled from accounts of Tlatelolcan participants in the conquest.

———. *Códice Florentino* [1576]. MS 218–220 de la colección Palatina de la Biblioteca Medicea Laurenziana. Facsimile edition, three vols. Florence: Giunti Barbera and the Archivo General de la Nación, Mexico, 1979.

———. *The Conquest of New Spain, 1585 Revision.* Trans. by Howard F. Cline, introduction and notes by Sarah Cline. Salt Lake City: University of Utah Press, 1989. Based on materials compiled for the *Historia General*, this version adds pro-Spanish and pro-Tlaxcalan material for political reasons.

Solís, Don Antonio de. *The History of the Conquest of Mexico by the Spaniards* [1753]. Trans. by Thomas Townsend. 3rd edition, two vols. New York: AMS Press, 1973. Seventeenth-century Spanish royal chronicler's history that was translated to English in the eighteenth century.

Vázquez de Tapia, Bernardino. *Relación de méritos y servicios del conquistador* [ca. 1545]. Mexico: Universidad Nacional Autónoma de México, 1972. Typical Spanish conqueror's petition for rewards.

Other Sources

Burrus, Ernest J., S.J. "Religious Chroniclers and Historians: Summary with Annotated Bibliography," in *Guide to Ethnohistorical Sources, Part II.* Ed. by Howard F. Cline, *Handbook of Middle American Indians*, vol. 13, pp. 138–85. Austin: University of Texas Press, 1973.

Glass, John B. "A Survey of Native Middle American Pictorial Manuscripts," in *Guide to Ethnohistorical Sources.* Ed. by Howard F. Cline, associate editors John B. Glass and Charles Gibson. *Handbook of Middle American Indians*, vol. 14 (1975), pp. 3–80. Austin: University of Texas Press.

Prescott, William Hickling. *The Conquest of Mexico* [1843]. New York: Random House, 1998. Modern Library. Popular nineteenth-century retelling of the epic events, based on primary sources.

Warren, J. Benedict. "An Introductory Survey of Secular Writings in the European Tradition on Colonial Middle America, 1503–1818," in *Guide to Ethnohistorical Sources, Part II*. Ed. by Howard F. Cline, *Handbook of Middle American Indians*, vol. 13 (1973), pp. 42–137. Austin: University of Texas Press.

Five

Mexico and the Columbian Exchange

> Great was the stench of death. After our fathers and grandfathers succumbed, half the people fled to the fields. The dogs and vultures devoured the bodies. The mortality was terrible. Your grandfathers died, and with them died the son of the king and his brothers and kinsmen. So it was we became orphans, O my sons! So we became when we were young. We were born to die.
>
> Maya text, *The Book of Chilam Balam de Chumayel*, trans. Ralph Roys (Norman, 1967).

When Europeans and Africans crossed the Atlantic, they unintentionally introduced an array of lethal Old World diseases that had profound social as well as demographic consequences for the peoples of the Americas. The unnamed Maya (above) who lamented the death of so many not only mourned the loss of kin but implicitly longed for the era before disease ravaged the Indians, the time before the coming of the Europeans.

The term "Columbian exchange" has been used to describe the sociobiological consequences of the initiation of sustained contact between Eurasia and Africa, on the one hand, and the Americas, on the other—parts of the world that previously had had virtually no contact for thousands of years. The first fifty years of interaction between Europeans and Indians were critical for this exchange that entailed the contact of previously isolated human populations, ecological zones, languages, technology, flora, and fauna. Processes initiated during this early period would play out over the course of the entire era of Spanish rule. The Columbian exchange created a world system characterized by globalization of diseases and economies and breakdown of the earlier relative isolation of often localized peoples, plants and animals.

The Spread of Disease

The Ecology of Epidemic Diseases. Diseases of Eurasia and Africa played a major role in the Spanish occupation of the Caribbean (1492–1519) and subsequently of Mexico and other parts of the Americas, decimating Indian populations in the early period. They remained a menace throughout the colonial era, but populations began to recover in the seventeenth century. During the twenty thousand years or so of human settlement in the Americas, epidemic disease that could destroy large populations apparently was absent. Scientists once were puzzled by the contrast between disease-ridden Eurasia and Africa and the relatively disease-free environment of the Americas. Many now attribute the difference to the long association of humans with domesticated animals in Eurasia and Africa and the near absence of a connection between humans and domesticated animals in the Americas (with the exception of llamas in the Andean region). Humans who live in close association with animals often exchange pathogens with them. These pathogens retain or sometimes even gain in virulence as they are passed back and forth, often mutating in the process and producing new strains.

When the Bering land bridge submerged around 9000 B.C., the human population of North and South America was cut off from contact with the diseases of Eurasia, which generally developed in relation to domesticated animals. The Americas developed in isolation from Eurasia and Africa and the epidemic diseases that affected those populations. Humans in Europe, Asia, and Africa, by contrast, had long experienced epidemics and shared an array of diseases.

Similar Diseases Found In Humans and Animals

Human Disease	Animal Disease
Smallpox	Cowpox
Influenza	Swine flu/bird flu
Tuberculosis	Bovine tuberculosis
Measles	Cattle (rinderpest)
Whooping cough	Similar disease in pigs, dogs

Based on Jared Diamond, *Guns, Germs, Steel* (New York, 1999), p. 207.

First encounters between Europeans and Indians in the late fifteenth and early sixteenth centuries were more than meetings of representatives of distinct cultures and societies. Eurasian and African microbes found a virgin host population in the Americas, wreaking havoc on native populations. Generally speaking, epidemics occur when a host population lacks immunity from disease agents such as viruses, bacteria, or parasites. In Europe, Asia, and Africa, diseases such as smallpox, mumps, bubonic plague, and measles caused major damage as epidemics. In their wake, however, an immune population remained. These diseases then only attacked a small, new, nonimmune population—children. Children who survived gained immunity for life from such diseases as smallpox, mumps, and measles. Survivors also may have been healthier in general, so diseases mainly carried off the very young, the old, and the weak.

Where diseases take only a small proportion of the population, social systems remain intact. Food production continues unaffected, and adults can care for their sick children, even a large number of them. When children die, sad as that is, surviving adults can go on to have more, since none of the diseases in question affect fertility. When epidemics sweep through whole communities, however, the social fabric is torn. Sixteenth-century Nahua informants of Fray Bernardino de Sahagún articulated these processes when recounting the history of the conquest. "Before the Spaniards had risen against us, first there came to be prevalent a great sickness, a plague. . . . Many indeed died of it. They could no longer walk; they only lay in their homes, in their beds. . . . Many people died of the pustules, and many just died of hunger. . . . There was no one to take care of another" (*Florentine Codex*, Book XII, 83).

Contagious diseases are now understood to be ecological systems, with a relationship between disease agents and their hosts. Until the scientific bases of disease were established, in most parts of the world people believed that illness had supernatural origins, resulting from the wrath of the gods or witchcraft. Men and women believed to have supernatural powers, whether evil or good, were considered capable of inflicting or curing diseases. In seemingly epidemic-free ancient Greater Mexico, beliefs about diseases and their relation to the cosmos and human agents were not well developed. With the arrival of Europeans in the Americas, that situation changed.

In the Americas after the arrival of Europeans, both Indians and Europeans interpreted the epidemics decimating the Indian populations as divine intervention, a belief reinforced by the robust health Europeans enjoyed as Indians sickened and died. The first documented case of smallpox in postconquest Mexico was that of Francisco de Baguia, an African slave owned by Pánfilo de Naváez. In Tenochtitlan, smallpox swept through the population after the retreat of the Spaniards in the Noche Triste, felling the Aztec monarch Cuitlahuac among thousands of other Indians in the city in 1520.

Epidemics helped Spaniards subjugate Indians first by sickening them, making them physically less able to fight, and reducing population sizes, facilitating adaptation to European rule. Science increasingly recognizes the role that spiritual or psychological health plays in the body's immune responses. For many Indians who came into contact with Europeans, the resulting upheaval in their lives exacerbated their vulnerability to disease. The immune system is undermined not only by poor nutrition, overwork, and lack of personal hygiene but also the absence of a social support network, loss of spiritual or religious certainty, and what today we call stress. When Indian states were conquered, they lost their traditional religious and political leaders, and Europeans forced commoners into a regime of work far exceeding anything they had previously experienced. Many Indian women were coerced into unwanted sexual encounters. At the same time, victorious Spaniards who despised indigenous people's religious beliefs and practices actively worked to undermine them. Their normal lives radically disrupted, Indians probably became more vulnerable to illness.

Once Old World diseases were introduced, the environment provided ideal conditions for them to spread. The scale of the demographic disaster resulted from the Indians' lack of immunity together with the breakdown of social mechanisms to care for the ill. With nothing to stop the continuous transmission of disease, not even the intervention of cold weather that would kill bacteria and keep people inside and away from contact with others, entire villages were struck down at once. Adults could not nurse their children or one another; fields went untended; crops failed; and the resulting lack of food further undermined the immune systems of the survivors.

Epidemic Disease and the Colonial Economy. The unintentional introduction of diseases that decimated Indian populations affected the course of Spanish exploration in the Caribbean and their conquest of Mexico. The decline of Indian populations in the Caribbean led Spaniards to undertake further expeditions to enslave Indians in other areas, who were then transported as captives to islands that already had Spanish settlements. During these slaving expeditions, Spaniards, also were on the alert to discover new and more promising areas for European settlement. Spaniards' search for new lands and populations to exploit also spread diseases to other groups of Indians, sometimes in advance of their arrival. As a direct result of the collapse of Indian populations in the Caribbean, Spaniards began to import African slaves to labor for them instead. With their greater resistance to diseases that were endemic in Africa and their ability to work long hours in tropical climates, Africans would supplant Indians as the labor force in the tropical regions of the Americas. In Mexico the coastal and lowland regions, especially the area around Veracruz on the Gulf Coast, eventually would have significant populations of African origin and descent.

The slave trade from Africa introduced more diseases to the Americas, particularly malaria and yellow fever, both transmitted by mosquitoes. Mosquitoes likely were hitchhikers on slave ships that sailed from Africa to the Americas. In Europe, malaria, literally "bad air," was believed to be spread by evil vapors found in damp, tropical areas. Yellow fever, called the "black vomit" because of its characteristic symptom of blood in the vomit, was universally feared once it appeared. Both diseases became endemic in the American tropics. In the nineteenth century, the Mexican government could count on diseases of the Gulf Coast to decimate invading armies in much the way that Russia depended on its winters to defeat foreign aggressors, such as Napoleon and Hitler.

The Impact of Disease. Spaniards saw the smallpox epidemic of 1520–21 as an act of divine intervention in aid of their cause, while Indians may well have seen it as the abandonment of protection by their gods. Smallpox killed the ruler Cuitlahuac, who mounted a resistance to the Spanish invasion after succeeding the vacillating Moctezuma. Infection swept through densely populated Tenochtitlan, which was cut off from fresh water and food supplies. Disease also affected Indians outside Tenochtitlan, but Indian allies and potential allies observed that Spaniards were immune to its ravages, which reinforced the perception of supernatural origins and powers.

How long the initial epidemics lasted is unclear, but there are no major reports of outbreaks for ten years thereafter. Periodic outbreaks occurred throughout the colonial period, with a major one in Mexico City as late as 1779 that killed approximately eighteen thousand people. In 1797, authorities first attempted to vaccinate the capital's population. Although the indigenous population was most vulnerable to disease at the time of the conquest, during the colonial era all sectors of the population were at risk.

In central Mexico, a major epidemic called simply *cocoliztli* (Nahuatl for "sickness" or "plague") sickened and killed Indians in 1545–8. The symptoms were bleeding in nose and eyes, and mortality was high. In the late 1700s, German scientist and traveler Alexander von Humboldt identified the disease as *matlazahuatl*, which may be typhus. Typhus is a rickettsial disease transmitted to humans via lice. Rickettsial diseases are caused by microorganisms intermediate in size between bacteria and viruses that multiply in the cells of their hosts and often are accompanied by rashes and high fever. Typhus is a disease of malnutrition, filth, and overcrowding; Mexico City experienced the full force of an outbreak in 1813, when upward of sixty-five thousand residents contracted it.

Epidemics in Central Mexico

Disease	Symptoms	Transmission	Incidence in Mexico
Smallpox *viruelas*	Vomiting, fever, skin eruption, pustules	Viral, person-to-person	1520–1, 1531, 1532, 1538, 1615–16, 1653, 1663, 1678, 1711, 1734, 1748, 1761–4, 1779

(Continued)

Measles *sarampión*	Skin eruption, high fever	Viral, person-to-person	1531, 1563–4, 1604–7, 1615–16, 1639, 1659, 1692–7, 1727–8, 1768–9, 1779–80 1550, 1595–7
Mumps *paperas*	Glands, inflammation of testes and breasts	Viral, person-to-person	
Influenza *tlatlaciztli*	Coughing, inflammation of respiratory tract, fever	Viral, person-to-person	1590
Typhus *matlazahuatl*	Fever, nervous disorders, weakness, red spots on skin	Rickettsial, lice	1545–8, 1731

Based on Charles Gibson, *Aztecs under Spanish Rule* (Stanford, 1964), pp. 448–511.

Sickness and death reduced the Indian population to a fraction of its prehispanic size. There are scholarly controversies regarding the exact size of the prehispanic population of Mexico and the severity of epidemics in the colonial period. All scholars agree, however, that Indian populations dropped sharply in the sixteenth century and slowly began to rise again in the mid-seventeenth century. In the span of that century or so, major social and economic changes took place in indigenous communities which had an impact on the entire Spanish colonial project.

Until recently syphilis was thought to be a disease that originated in the Western Hemisphere and spread worldwide as a result of the Columbian exchange. The most convincing evidence for the New World origins of the disease was that it reportedly had affected many of the men who had sailed with Columbus on his first voyage. A major outbreak of syphilis occurred in Naples (1494–5) among Spanish soldiers, from whom it spread to French troops; subsequent troop movements spread the disease throughout Europe. Portuguese traders and sailors apparently took syphilis to India, and the disease arrived in China and Japan before Europeans did, in 1505.

At the time, syphilis was considered to be a new, sexually transmitted disease. The spirochete that causes it, however, is indistinguishable from one causing yaws or leprosy, which have a long history in Eurasia and Africa. Recently scientists have found unmistakable evidence of syphilis (which in its advanced form creates deformities in the bones) in Europe, not only in the middle ages but going back to ancient times. Current thinking is that syphilis existed on both sides of the Atlantic in both mild and virulent forms and that the former—a minor skin ailment that conferred immunity to the more serious form of the disease—was predominant in the Americas. By the late fifteenth century, however, the mild form of the disease had become much less prevalent in Europe, making Europeans vulnerable to the serious strain. A hospital dedicated to the treatment of syphilitics was founded in sixteenth-century Mexico City, indicating a sizeable number of affected patients.

Medicine, Disease, and Colonial Society

Medical Treatment in Greater Mexico. Spanish religious personnel and individual benefactors founded hospitals to care for the ill. Hospitals are a European institution that had no counterpart in prehispanic Greater Mexico. People of all races viewed hospitals as places of last resort to which they usually went only on the verge of death. The need for hospitals in the early postconquest era prompted the bishop of Michoacan, Vasco de Quiroga (1470–1565), who was deeply influenced by Thomas Moore's *Utopia*, to found a number of experimental settlements called hospital towns. Santa Fe, founded in 1532 outside Mexico City, was the first. Formal ordinances called for such towns to have large hospitals where the ill could be treated. They would have two separate wards, one for contagious diseases and the other for noncontagious; a dispensary; and offices for the medical staff. As part of his legacy, Hernando Cortés founded the Hospital of Jesus for poor Indians.

Among the earliest information that religious personnel collected from Nahua Indians was material on the medicinal aspects of plants. The first medical text known to have been written in the Western Hemisphere is the *Codex Badianus*, compiled in 1552 by an Aztec physician, Martín de la Cruz, at the Colegio of Santa Cruz Tlatelolco and translated into Latin by another Nahua, Juan Badiano. The lushly illustrated text shows plants in their entirety, from roots to flowers, and provides a precise description of their medical uses. In 1990, Pope Paul II returned the manuscript held by the Vatican Library to the National Library in Mexico. Franciscan Bernardino de Sahagún also included a great deal of information about medical uses of plants in Book XI of his *General History of the Things of New Spain* (1576).

Medical texts were among the first books Spaniards printed in Mexico City. Fray Agustín Farfán's sixteenth-century work, *Brief Treatise on Medicine and All Illnesses* (1592), went through several editions. It drew on the work of the great scientist of Islamic Spain, Avicenna (980–1037), whose empirical study of anatomy foreshadowed modern science. A work by Juan de Barrios, *True Medicine, Surgery, and Astrology* (1607), reflects the mixture of science and magical thought characteristic of the early modern period. A three-volume text, *Medicinal Anthology of All Illnesses . . .* , by Jesuit Juan de Esteyneffer (1712) was the first to combine New World medical knowledge with European traditions for the treatment of illnesses. It was the most important medical publication in the Americas, disseminated throughout the Spanish empire.

Ordinary Spaniards brought to Greater Mexico ancient Greek conceptions about the states of things—wet, dry, cold, hot—and their manifestations in the four humors of bile (hot and dry); blood (hot and wet); phlegm (wet and cold); and melancholy (dry and cold). Illness was generally believed to be caused by a disturbance in the states of things, and the aim of medicine was to bring the humors back into balance.

Treatment of medical conditions often involved purges, to rid the body of poison; bleeding, to bring down fever; application of leeches, to drain wounds; salves and poultices to relieve skin conditions. Some of these have remained in practice to the present. In the colonial period horn of unicorn was especially sought as an antidote for poison, and reports that unicorns grazed on the slopes of Mt. Orizaba excited early interest. Bezoars, a kind of calcification found in the digestive tracts of some mammals, also were greatly valued for their power as an antidote to poison. There is evidence that Spaniards sought these wonder-working stones in the entrails of a type of Mexican deer known in Nahuatl as *teutlalmazames*.

Medical treatment at the local level usually involved unlicensed men and women. Medical doctors were trained at the University of Mexico, but the vast majority of Greater Mexico's population never underwent treatment by a university-trained physician. Although medical practice increasingly was taken over by educated laymen, the founding of hospitals and hospital communities by clerics in early New Spain reflected some of the distinctive characteristics of conquest-era institutions. In the eighteenth century, the Crown established an official medical body, the *Protomedicato*, to promote and regulate public health.

Economic and Social Effects of Population Decline. In the colonial period, the size of indigenous populations was of keen interest to Spaniards, since their own economic welfare initially hinged on the size and productivity of Indian communities. Following prehispanic practices in Mesoamerica, colonial tribute was assessed on towns as a whole, with individual households obligated to provide a certain amount of tribute and labor. Spaniards had records of the amount of tribute that communities owed to Moctezuma. Surviving populations, however, could not possibly meet the old levels of payment. Local indigenous elites who depended on Spanish authority to remain in power found their political and economic positions imperiled as populations decreased. In the mid-sixteenth century, many Indian towns petitioned the Crown for reduction of tribute requirements.

The epidemic diseases of early Greater Mexico brought about massive socioeconomic changes, comparable to those that took place in the wake of the Black Death in Europe (1340s), the Great Famine in Ireland (1840s), or the AIDS epidemic in Africa in more recent times. Epidemic disease destroyed family networks for the care of minor children. The Indians' enthusiastic adoption of ritual godparenthood, or *compadrazgo*, which created new kin ties, bound individuals and families in new networks. Godparents could care for minor children left orphaned. There is strong evidence in Nahuatl testaments of the late sixteenth century that Indians saw this as the explicit function of godparenthood.

Epidemic disease and its resulting mortality often predisposed survivors to move to new localities, where they were welcomed as new tribute payers. Such massive movement was unprecedented in the two hundred years prior to the arrival of the Spaniards. After the conquest many Indians moved, trying their luck elsewhere in similar agricultural communities, migrating to the Spanish cities, or working in Spanish enterprises. Spaniards attempted to counter some of this unfettered movement, by establishing new settlements or congregations (*congregaciones*). Geographical distance between households and communities could work as a buffer and insulator against disease. Congregating survivors of epidemics had the opposite effect, as bringing Indians from different communities together in close contact could retrigger disease.

As the Indian population decreased, indigenous communities had less need to control and cultivate land. In the prehispanic era, men held land almost exclusively. Evidence from late sixteenth-century Nahuatl wills, however, shows that following periods of high mortality Indian women came to own considerable amounts of land in their own names, bequeathing it to a variety of heirs. At the same time, land became private property to be bought and sold outside the community, particularly by Spaniards. The highly dense settlement pattern in which Indians worked every bit of tillable land changed, as large stretches of land lay vacant.

Changes in Environment, Diet, and Lifestyle

Ecological Impact of Spanish Colonial Practices. Spaniards introduced an array of domesticated animals to Mexico, including horses, donkeys, cattle, sheep, goats, pigs, and chickens, that provided both a range of useful products and new sources of power to perform work. The spread of herd animals occurred within the first fifty years, aided in part by Indian depopulation. Vacant land, particularly uplands that previously had not supported intense farming, became grazing land. Cattle herds multiplied unchecked, destroying vegetation. Sheep in particular were a walking environmental disaster. This "plague of sheep" completely destroyed the low growing grasses of some delicate ecological systems, turning many sheep grazing areas into dust bowls. Sheep eat grass down to the roots. In regions where sheep grazed, without grass to hold the soil in place, water ran off the land before it could be absorbed. Animal waste further polluted remaining sources of water.

Mexico's environment changed significantly in the colonial period as a result of deforestation as well as cattle and sheep grazing. Timber was used for construction, industrial processes, and making charcoal for domestic or industrial use. As trees were cut down, the roots that held soil and moisture in place disappeared. Topsoil from uplands eroded during downpours. Central Mexico's climate became drier and droughts more frequent in the colonial era. In 1641–2, illness and death associated with drought appears in the historical record.

Mining likely contributed to environmental degradation, as a result of the contamination of water and soil from the mercury used in the refining process. Mercury attacks the nervous system, making the sufferer "mad as a hatter" (hatmaking also used mercury in processing). The extent to which Mexico's mining districts were affected by mercury contamination remains uninvestigated.

Draining the lake system of the central plateau, a long-term project called the *Desagüe* that was undertaken by Spaniards to control the flooding that periodically submerged large parts of the capital, had some public health benefits and significantly changed the environment of the central plateau. Flooding sent untreated sewage into Mexico City's streets, spreading disease, so controlling the waters meant protection from polluted water. The records of Mexico City's council reported illness of Indians as a secondary effect of flooding in 1627. Draining the lake system also meant destroying the habitat for mosquitoes, also benefiting the human population. Draining the wetlands and the resulting concentration of pollutants in the water, however, destroyed the habitat of a variety of birds, fish, and other water-dwelling creatures. These processes got under way in the early colonial period.

Food and the Columbian Exchange. The Columbian exchange introduced plants and animals from the Americas to Europe and the rest of the world. From Mexico came new foods—Indian corn or maize, tomatoes, chocolate, vanilla, squashes, both sweet and hot peppers, avocados, and kidney beans, plus the native barnyard bird, the turkey; dyestuffs of indigo (blue) and cochineal (red); and tobacco. From other parts of Spain's empire came potatoes, sweet potatoes, allspice, and lima beans. If the Americas failed to provide Europeans the rich spices of East Asia, it nonetheless is difficult to imagine many of the world's cuisines before the Columbian encounter.

Indian corn is Mexico's single most important contribution to the world's diet, adding a major source of carbohydrates to the world's table. In Mexico, corn most commonly was made into tortillas after the kernels were soaked in lime and then finely ground. Prepared and eaten this way, corn is highly nutritious. When corn was introduced to Europe, the Mexican method of processing it was not, often leading to nutritional deficiencies. It was cultivated for animal fodder (and in parts of Europe even today is considered food fit only for pigs), but in many areas it became the food of the poor, since it was easily grown and had high yields. Corn did not revolutionize Europe the way the Andean staple of the potato did, but it became integrated into European farming. It is widely cultivated in Africa and Asia, where it contributed to population growth. In Asia it is cultivated where rice cannot be grown.

Chocolate is Mexico's gift to the world's dessert tray. Cacao or cocoa, named by Linneaus *Theobroma cacao* (Greek for "food of the gods"), grows in tropical regions of southern Mexico. Twenty-foot-high trees produce pods six to ten inches long and about three to four inches in diameter, containing multiple seeds, about an inch long. *Cacahuatl*, the Nahuatl word from which cacao or cocoa derives, was made into a frothy drink called *chocolatl*. Indians also used it as money in the prehispanic and early colonial eras. Cacao beans were fairly uniform in size, small enough to be exchanged for everyday products, and limited in area of production. The prehispanic Aztec code of law had severe penalties for counterfeiting cacao, a crime accomplished by hollowing out the inside of the bean and filling it with dirt. During the early colonial period when Spanish coins were scarce, cacao continued to be used as a medium of exchange.

Moctezuma served chocolate to Cortés and his men, the first Europeans known to drink it. Many Europeans developed an immediate taste for the drink, but its appeal expanded when it was sweetened. It became all the rage among the upper class in early Mexico and found its way to Europe, into coffee, pastries, and candy. Europeans in Mexico added sugar, cinnamon, cloves, anise, almonds, vanilla, and orange-flower water to make a kind of paste, which was then combined with hot water to make hot chocolate.

The transition from exotic food of the Mesoamerican Indians to an essential item of consumption for elites occurred during the first century of Spanish rule. The English Dominican traveler Thomas Gage commented that ladies were unable to sit through Mass without their chocolate. When the bishop of Ciudad Real in Chiapas banned chocolate drinking from the cathedral on pain of excommunication, many elite women challenged the order. "This caused one day such an uproar in the cathedral that many swords were drawn against the priests and prebends, who attempted to take away from the maids the cups of chocolate which they had brought unto their mistresses." The ladies boycotted Mass, and the bishop sickened and died from what his doctor believed was a poisoned cup of chocolate. Gage concludes, "And it became afterwards a proverb that in that country, 'Beware of the chocolate of Chiapas.'" Gage was also well aware of chocolate as a stimulant, and it is now known to contain caffeine. He wrote, "I would take a cup about seven or eight at night, which would keep me waking till around midnight."[1] The eighteenth-century traveler Baron Alexander von Humboldt commented on chocolate's "salutary properties" and its value as a food. "Alike and easy to convey and employ as an aliment [food], it contains a large quantity of nutritive and stimulating particles in a small volume."

[1]Thomas Gage, *Travels in the New World* (Norman, 1959), pp. 143–5.

Pumpkins and squashes are highly adaptable New World vegetables, thriving even in dry areas of northern Mexico. These plants are especially valued for their seeds, which are rich in protein and oils. Some types, such as acorn, butternut, and Hubbard, store well; they harden and can be cooked months after harvesting, particularly appealing in climates that have harsh winters, such as northern Europe.

English Food Words from Nahuatl

chocolatl	chocolate
cacahuatl	cacao, cocoa
tomatl	tomato
chili	chile
ahuacatl	avocado

Spaniards took tomatoes to Spain in 1523. English gardens grew "love apples" as early as the sixteenth century, but only in Italy, from about 1550, did tomatoes become a normal part of the cuisine, used mainly in sauces. Many Europeans believed them to be poisonous, not an entirely absurd notion, because the leaves actually are. Tomatoes are a rich source of vitamin C and cancer-fighting antioxidants, which contributed to the healthy diet of ancient Mexicans.

The avocado did not become a European import. In the tropics, it is known as the "poor man's butter" for its high fat content. But its narrow zone of cultivation, loss of flavor and nutrients almost immediately upon picking, and absence of any process to dry or otherwise preserve it meant Europeans only encountered it in Mexico itself. Its popularity in modern times is recent and to a certain extent remains regional.

Chili peppers were essential to Mexican food, providing a rich source of vitamin C (six to nine times that of tomatoes). Their hot taste added a new dimension to many cuisines, with Hungary's cooks using chili peppers to make paprika. The Indian subcontinent, Asia and the Philippines, also became home to hot peppers. Recent scientific research has been conducted to discover why many people seek out hot food. Findings are that the active ingredient, an alkaloid called capaicin, sets off the body's signals for danger—vertigo and shock. Since the diner knows that there is no real danger, the heat and shock can be a source of pleasure. Hot peppers also stimulate the production of the body's natural opiates, endorphins. A more recent use of hot peppers is in pepper spray to prevent muggers' attacks. Early written and pictorial texts record the Nahuas' practice of holding misbehaving children over pepper-smoke, so the modern use of pepper spray as a crime deterrent is just a new twist on an old practice.

Tobacco was the Indians' ambiguous gift to Europeans. In central and southern Mexico tobacco was widely grown and used extensively in religious rituals. Many Maya murals show lords smoking fat stogies. Bernal Díaz observed Moctezuma smoking tobacco from gold tubes. Tobacco was cultivated in many parts of New Spain, although not on a large scale. Smoking was widespread in colonial Mexico; foreign visitors almost invariably commented on the number of women who smoked cigars in polite company as well as in public. In Mexico, tobacco never became a major cash crop, as it did in Cuba and parts of the English American colonies.

European Contributions to the Columbian Exchange of Foods. Plants cultivated in Europe very soon took root in the Americas, particularly cash crops for the expanding European and Hispanized population of Mexico. One of the first crops to be introduced was sugar. Sugar cane is a member of the grass family, growing twenty feet tall. Europeans first encountered it in the Middle East during the Crusades. It became a valuable commodity in Europe, where tropical sugar cane cannot be grown. Sugar was an exotic item, used in small amounts as spices were. Druggists used sugar to disguise the foul tastes of their concoctions, and it also was used to preserve fruit. Only when sugar was cultivated on a large scale did it become a cheap commodity for all but the destitute. It flavored chocolate, coffee, and tea and was distilled into a potent brandy.

Wheat production began in Mexico in the early sixteenth century, as soon as the European population was large enough to provide a viable market. Europeans preferred wheat to Indian corn. With wheat production came European agricultural technology. Draft animals pulled wooden plows with metal shafts, allowing cultivation of virgin fertile land outside the immediate zone of Mesoamerican agricultural settlements. Introduced with wheat cultivation was the process of milling to produce flour for bread. Highly refined white flour was a status symbol for the wealthy. Wheat production expanded in colonial Mexico as a bread-consuming population grew. Since wheat does not require as much water as corn, Mexico's near north could support large-scale production without disrupting existing Indian agriculture. With some irrigation, yields were even higher. The consumption of wheat bread or wheat tortillas rather than maize tortillas was (and still is) an indicator of a person's status.

Fruits originating in Eurasia appeared in Mexico almost immediately after the conquest. Europeans and Indians alike grew citrus fruits such as oranges and limes, which had been introduced to Spain during the Islamic period, and others such as pears, peaches, apples, apricots, cherries, and figs. An early sixteenth–century Mexican pictorial, the Oztoticpac Lands Map from Texcoco, not only shows European fruit trees being cultivated but also illustrates how fruit trees were grafted. Table grapes and grapes for making wine were not widely planted in early Mexico, although the climate in the central plateau is ideal for them. The royal government also restricted the importation of olive trees. Wine and olive oil were peninsular Spanish products that could be stored and shipped to upscale consumers in the New World. Indians and mixed race people consumed local products—*pulque* and *aguardiente* for alcohol, avocados, and lard from European-introduced pigs for oil.

The European diet put a heavy emphasis on animal protein—beef, pork, mutton, fish, and fowl—with all but fish being domesticated. Ancient Mexico's mainly vegetarian diet developed largely because there were almost no animals large or small that could be easily domesticated and used for food. The narrow land bridge at Panama prevented the diffusion of Andean llamas and guinea pigs from South America to ancient Mesoamerica. The explosion of cattle and sheep herds in early Mexico and the increasingly widespread practice of country dwellers' keeping chickens, ducks, goats, and hogs meant that the mostly vegetarian diet of the prehispanic era expanded to include much more animal protein. Pork was particularly popular among the Nahuas.

The bird known in English as the turkey is the only animal from the Americas to join Eurasia's barnyard animals. Its name in various European languages is of interest: in French *"dinde"* [bird] from India; Portuguese *"peru"* after Peru, the country closest to Portuguese Brazil; and in English *"turkey,"* indicating an exotic bird from a place far away. Turkeys were domesticated in central Mexico, although exactly when is not known. During the Aztec period, both the birds themselves and their eggs were paid as tribute. Given the scarcity of domestic animals and sources of animal protein, turkeys and their eggs played a very important part in Mesoamericans' diet. Turkeys are not as hardy as Eurasian chickens. Young turkeys are especially vulnerable to cold and damp. Even so, by 1530 turkeys were common in Europe. Spaniards were not at all averse to eating turkeys, but tried to get Indians to raise chickens to feed the increasing urban population by imposing a tribute in chickens. The effort failed, but Indians did begin raising chickens for food and eggs.

Animal Power, Sacred and Profane. When Spaniards introduced the horse to Mexico, central Mexican Indians apparently saw it as something more than a beast of burden. During the conquest, Nahua warriors seem to have considered horses as sentient beings with as much agency as the humans who rode them. Later, when Spaniards introduced reenactments of the Christian reconquest of Spain, Indians focused in particular not on Santiago, the Moorslayer, but on his horse. William B. Taylor notes that the seventeenth-century Nahua writer of annals, Chimalpahin, recorded an indigenous tale of Santiago's horse participating in the conquest, "wounding as many of the enemy with his mouth as the saint did with his sword."[2] Throughout the colonial era and into the modern period, Indians believed some animals to be the representation or manifestation of a deity (*nagual*), and the horse may have long continued to have divine associations.

A major result of the Columbian exchange then, was the new availability of animal power for work. Spaniards imported and bred horses, mules, and donkeys for transportation, farming, and industrial enterprises such as mining. Initially, Spaniards tried to restrict Indians' access to horses. In northern Mexico, Indians who formerly hunted and waged war on foot gained an enormous advantage by capturing wild horses that escaped Spanish control or stealing them from Spaniards. Mounted warriors became formidable foes to Spaniards and transformed warfare in the north.

The growth of the colonial Spanish economy and the need to link regions meant the creation of roads for the increased traffic of horses, mules, donkeys, and a variety of wheeled carts and carriages. Huge mule trains traveled the trunklines connecting the mining regions of the north, Mexico City, and the port of Veracruz, moving silver south, food and manufactured goods north, and linking the capital to its main port. Although native porters (*tlameme*) remained a feature of rural life, large-scale commerce necessitated the use of animal power in transportation. Indian traders themselves began to acquire pack animals, mainly mules, as early as the sixteenth century.

The Columbian exchange was generally an informal process. Spaniards brought to Mexico a wide array of plants and animals. They sent back to Europe samples of the flora and fauna of the Americas, such as corn, which subsequently took hold because of its ease of cultivation and high yields. Indians in settled regions of Mexico readily cultivated new crops, adding them to their existing variety. Only in the Spanish missions in Mexico's north, where hunting and gathering bands used to roam freely, were new crops deliberately introduced and the Indians taught to raise them.

Language and the Columbian Exchange. Another area of informal cultural exchange was language. Europeans used many New World products and often retained their indigenous names as well, with such words as "chocolate" and "tomato" eventually entering into English via Spanish. In Mexico, Spanish did absorb many nouns from indigenous languages, the type of word most easily borrowed. The Nahuatl word for market, *tianquiztli*, came into Mexican Spanish as *tianguís* because Europeans depended on Indian markets for fresh produce. These borrowings or loanwords then became part of spoken Spanish without the Spaniards paying much attention to their indigenous origin.

---

[2]William B. Taylor, *Magistrates of the Sacred* (Stanford, 1996), p. 274.

Of Mexico's indigenous languages in the colonial period Nahuatl has been best studied by modern scholars, who have access not only to the dictionaries and other works written by Spanish friars but also to texts written by Nahuas themselves during the colonial era. There is evidence of evolving levels of cultural interaction that had a specifically linguistic impact. Initially Nahuas named new phenomena by expanding the meaning of existing words, so that the previously unknown horse was called a deer (*mazatl*), another large quadruped. With increased contact, Nahuas gradually began using the Spanish word for horse, *caballo* and then embedding the loanword in completely Nahua phrases, such as *nocaballo*, "my horse," *nocaballome*, "my horses." As Nahuatl speakers began to understand Spanish plurals using –s, they made subsequent modifications—*nocaballosme*, "my horses." As more Nahuas became bilingual, there is evidence of changes in the structure of Nahuatl itself. With the cessation of large-scale record keeping in indigenous languages at Independence, it becomes more difficult to trace further changes.

The Columbian exchange marked the integration of Eastern and Western hemispheres. This encounter forever changed the global distribution of plants, animals, diseases, technology, and languages, making it difficult today to imagine the world that existed before the Columbian exchange. It is important to understand the impact each hemisphere had on the other as a result of this complex and mainly unintentional process.

Glossary

cacahuatl   cacao or cocoa; seeds of the cacao or cocoa tree (Nahuatl)

chilli   chili; hot pepper (Nahuatl)

chocolatl   Nahua drink made from cacao beans. English "chocolate"

Columbian exchange   Mutual cultural and biological exchange between the Old World and the New

cochineal   red dye produced by insects living on nopal cacti

cocoliztli   sickness, epidemic (Nahuatl)

congregación   colonial policy of resettling indigenous communities to create new towns

Desagüe   draining of the central lake system of Mexico, radically changing the environment

matlazahuatl   epidemic disease, possibly typhus (Nahuatl)

Protomedicato   colonial governmental body dealing with public health

syphilis   venereal disease producing open sores caused by spirochetes

tianguís   (Nahuatl: *tianquiztli*) market in Mexican Spanish

tomatl   (Nahuatl, lit.: "fat thing") tomato; Spanish: *tomate*

Virgin land epidemic   rapid spread of disease through a population with no previous exposure to a particular disease

Questions for Discussion

1. Why did Old World diseases have such an enormous impact on Indian populations?

2. What were the consequences for Greater Mexico of the introduction of herd animals like cattle and sheep?

3. How did Greater Mexico have an impact on the Old World?

Suggested Reading

Benzoni, Girolamo. *History of the New World*. New York: Hakluyt Society, 1970. Mid-sixteenth-century traveler's account full of acute observations and some illustrations.

Bishko, Charles J. "Cattle Raising and the Peninsular Tradition," *Hispanic American Historical Review* 32:4 (1952), 491–515. Traces development of stockraising to its Iberian origins.

Cook, Noble David. *Born to Die: Disease and New World Conquest, 1492–1650*. Cambridge: Cambridge University Press, 1998. Synthesis of current knowledge of disease outbreaks during the first century and a half of Spanish settlement in the Americas.

Cook, Sherburne F. "The Incidence and Significance of Disease among the Aztecs and Related Tribes," *Hispanic American Historical Review*, 36 (1946), 320–35. Article dealing with the impact of disease by a major demographer.

Cooper, Donald B. *Epidemic Disease in Mexico City, 1761–1813*. Austin: University of Texas Press, 1965. A social and public policy history of Mexico City, focusing on five major epidemics and the Crown's response to them.

Crosby, Alfred W., Jr. *The Columbian Exchange*. Westport, Conn.: Greenwood Press, 1972. Pioneering work on the subject of the impact of the Old and New World on each other.

———. *Ecological Imperialism: The Biological Expansion of Europe, 900–1900*. Cambridge: Cambridge University Press, 1986. An extension of the inquiry initiated earlier.

Denevan, William M. "The Pristine Myth: The Landscape of the Americas in 1492," *Annals of the Association of American Geographers* 82 (1992): 369–85. Argues that humans affected the environment in the Americas and that population decline allowed some fragile ecosystems to recover.

Diamond, Jared. *Guns, Germs, Steel: The Fates of Human Societies*. New York: W.W. Norton, 1999. Bestselling book by a scientist arguing why some societies were able to thrive and dominate and others were not.

Gage, Thomas. *Travels in the New World.* Norman: University of Oklahoma Press, 1958. The vivid travelogue of a renegade English Dominican in seventeenth-century central and southern Mexico.

Gates, William, trans. *An Aztec Herbal: The Classic Codex of 1552.* New York: Dover Publications, 2000. The translated text and illustrations of Codex Badianus, the earliest known work of its type in the New World.

Lockhart, James, *Nahuas after the Conquest.* Stanford: Stanford University Press, 1992. Major work on Nahua history based on native language sources.

———. *Spaniards and Indians: Postconquest Central Mexican History and Philology.* Los Angeles and Stanford: UCLA Latin American Center Publications and Stanford University Press, 1991. A collection of articles dealing with Nahua linguistics and culture based on native language documentation.

McNeill, William H. *Plagues and Peoples.* Garden City, N.Y.: Anchor Books, 1997. Engaging scholarly study of the impact of epidemic disease on world history.

Melville, Elinor G. K. *A Plague of Sheep: Environmental Consequences of the Conquest of Mexico.* Cambridge: Cambridge University Press, 1997. Prize-winning analysis of the effect of grazing on colonial Mexico.

Pilcher, Jeffrey M. *¡Que vivan los tamales! Food and the Making of Mexican Identity.* Albuquerque: University of New Mexico Press, 1998. Delightful investigation of Mexico's cuisine and its cultural context.

Roys, Ralph. *The Book of Chilam Balam of Chumayel.* Norman: University of Oklahoma Press, 1967. English translation of a Maya history with information about Maya perceptions of the coming of the Europeans.

Videos

PBS. *The Syphilis Enigma* (2000). Excellent examination of the question of the origins of syphilis.

PBS. *Food for the Ancestors: The Mexican Celebration of the Day of the Dead* (1999). An in-depth exploration of Mexican food and its cultural significance.

Six

Christianity in Colonial Mexico

Establishment of the Church in Colonial Mexico

The establishment of the Roman Catholic church in the New World was an important and explicit goal of the Spanish Crown. With its churches, monasteries, convents, and clergy, the church was a vital institution of colonial rule present in every city and small village in New Spain. In the Spanish empire, church and state were closely intertwined, two arms of monarchical power that from the time of the conquest onward profoundly shaped life in Greater Mexico. The development of the church as a colonial institution reflected distinct stages that corresponded to broader historical eras in New Spain: the period of the conquest and early consolidation (1521–70), followed by one of midcolonial entrenchment (1570–1770), and, last, an era of late colonial realignments (1770–1821). The late period is discussed in more detail in Chapters 15 and 17.

The Spiritual Conquest

The first fifty years of church activity in Mexico are often called the age of "spiritual conquest," when the mendicant orders (or regular clergy) functioned as virtually the sole effective agents of Catholicism. The regular clergy lived under the religious rule of their orders (Latin *regulum* or rule), taking vows of chastity, obedience, and poverty. In Mexico the most prominent orders were the Franciscans, Dominicans, and Augustinians, who arrived soon after the military conquest of central Mexico to convert the Indians to Christianity.

They were well prepared for the task, as in the late 1400s and early 1500s the Franciscan order in Spain had undergone internal reforms, with the result that the friars were well educated and followed stricter discipline than the diocesan clergy. Many Spanish Franciscans and mendicants from other orders actively engaged in the intellectual ferment of the Renaissance with its interest in classical culture and languages.

In Mexico the mendicants labored to convert the indigenous populations, attempting to stamp out the ancient religions by destroying temples and religious texts and driving priests of the old religions into hiding. The mendicants built churches in Indian settlements and Spanish cities alike and created the early institutional framework of church administration. Normally the mendicant orders did not undertake such tasks, which should have been carried out by the diocesan or "secular" clergy (from *saeculum*, "the world"). At the time of the conquest, however, because of their superior education and organization, the mendicants appeared far better suited for this crucial work than did the secular clergy. The latter frequently were poorly educated, and they acted as free agents, often engaging in business activities since they took no vow of poverty. Mendicants in New Spain received papal permission to perform all the functions of parish priests, including administering the sacraments, a prerogative usually reserved for the secular clergy. During most of the colonial period, however, both the regular and secular clergy enjoyed special legal privileges, collectively called the *fuero eclesiástico*, that allowed all clerics to be judged before canonical (church) courts no matter what the offense.

During the fifty years following the conquest of central Mexico the basic techniques for converting the Indians and creating an active and visible church were developed. Since the military conquest of Greater Mexico took place over an extended period, the spiritual conquest continued as new areas came under Spanish control. The pattern of military conquest followed by mendicant (and later Jesuit) evangelization and eventual assertion of control by the secular clergy was repeated on the northern frontier and in southern Mexico.

The church as a whole fostered and promoted the moral principles, political values, and social behavior that served as the ideal framework for colonial society. It created a community of faith that in principle encompassed all the inhabitants of Greater Mexico. Since the expansion of Christendom was the justification for its overseas conquests, the Spanish Crown took the responsibility of evangelizing the Indians in Mexico quite seriously. Native peoples exhibited a range of responses, from outright hostility to active embrace of the new religion.

Papal grants to the Spanish Crown gave it complete control over the church in its overseas possessions. This power, called the *patronato real* (royal patronage), not only permitted the Crown to appoint clerics but also gave it control over church property and revenue collection, conferring on the monarch full power as head of the church in all matters except religious doctrine. The papal grant of these sweeping powers, made in 1508, was predicated on the evangelization of the pagans living in Spain's new territories. The king's position as effective head of the church infused the monarchy with an aura of holiness and sacred sense of mission.

Although in one sense the church was a unified religious institution, in fact it consisted of many component parts, which could act more as rivals than allies. Furthermore, although the Crown held authority over both church and state, in practice those two branches of royal power were often at odds because the lines of their jurisdictions blurred. In the absence of a viceroy the archbishop served as the king's interim representative; the state collected tithe revenues for the church; and rural clerics often were the only agents of colonial rule in their parishes. Within the church itself the various regular orders (Franciscans, Dominicans, Augustinians) were fairly independent organizations, whereas the diocesan or secular clergy came under the direct control of bishops appointed by the Crown. This situation allowed for the emergence of significant differences across regions and among ethnic groups, religious orders, diocesan clergy, and colonial authorities over such fundamental questions as how Catholic beliefs should be instilled among Mexico's indigenous people and how the church should guide the lives of the faithful.

Evangelizing the Indians. Hernando Cortés was instrumental in establishing Christianity in New Spain during the conquest itself. He tore down pagan altars, had the priests who accompanied the expedition baptize Indian allies, and conquered new territory for the Crown, extending both political sovereignty and Christian hegemony. In the immediate aftermath of conquest, Cortés—in his role as de facto governor—requested that religious personnel "of goodly life and character"—specifically Franciscans and Dominicans, rather than the secular clergy—be sent to evangelize the Indians. The Franciscans and Dominicans appeared to be the ideal agents for evangelizing the Indians as they had worked among Europe's poor. Cortés urged the Crown to send Franciscans and Dominicans with "the most extensive powers Your Majesty is able to obtain" from the pope, the precise course the Crown followed.

When the mendicants arrived in New Spain, they did not have a set plan of action. Once there they worked out techniques for evangelizing populations that did not speak Spanish, a problem they solved by starting to learn Nahuatl, the principal language of central Mexico. They also needed to figure out how to teach Christian doctrine to potential converts whose polytheistic religions were well established. Aiding the mendicants in their task was the expectation of many Indians that they would add the gods of the conquerors to their existing pantheon of deities and provide economic support for the new cults, standard practice in prehispanic Mexico. Mesoamericans probably did not anticipate the thoroughgoing nature of the new Christian religion that tolerated no others.

All the mendicant orders followed the strategy of founding churches in existing Indian settlements, destroying the trappings of local indigenous cults—temples, idols, books—driving out the priests, and then building a church complex with resident clergy. Mendicants undertook their missions in twos and threes, so they were neither the sole agents in their territory nor a large group. The church complex usually consisted of a church proper, a walled patio or atrium that could be used as an enclosed but open-air sacred space, and quarters for resident friars.

Figure 6-1 **Idealized church open chapel (1579)**, showing the Franciscans' vision of evangelization of the Indians, who are baptized, learn the catechism, confess sins, marry, and are buried within its confines. Saint Francis is in the center, carrying the church to the New World.

From Diego de Valadés, *Rhetorica christiana* (1579). Original held by Library of Congress.

Indigenous political organization often underlay the evolving church structure. Large indigenous communities became the headquarters (*doctrinas*) for the mendicant effort, while smaller outlying indigenous settlements became *visitas*, villages visited at intervals by mendicants resident in the doctrina. The conversion of Indians in central Mexico and construction of churches took place as a single, massive effort. Indians themselves built the new churches under the direction of friars who generally were not trained in architecture or engineering. Although some Indians complained about the burden such labor represented, most communities considered a large and impressive church to be a reflection of their town's importance and took justifiable pride in creating a sacred place for divine worship. Many of those early churches crumbled, but hundreds that survived their first few years still stand today.

The mendicant churches reflected the spiritual orientation of the orders that built them. Franciscan churches were often large, designed to accommodate the multitude of Indians to whom they ministered in the most populous centers of central Mexico. The Dominicans often built highly ornamented churches. The Augustinians were known for the opulence and sumptuousness (words used by their critics) of their churches, which were far larger than needed by the congregations and decorated in the most ornate style. However ornate and elaborate, during the first years after the conquest these establishments were fortified structures, a style called "Franciscan militant." In the event of an Indian uprising, the church could serve as a fortress.

The Franciscans. The pattern of first arrivals receiving the greatest rewards in colonial Spanish America held true for the Franciscans. As the first religious order to arrive in Mexico, the Franciscans gained an enormous advantage in subsequent struggles between orders. The first group of twelve Franciscans, a number chosen in emulation of Christ's apostles, landed in Veracruz in 1524. Led by Fray Martín de Valencia, the friars hoped to set an example for the Indians. In striking contrast to the arrogant conquerors, they walked the three hundred miles to the Valley of Mexico barefoot. When they arrived, to the surprise of native witnesses Cortés knelt before Valencia and kissed his robe as a sign of respect and obedience. Notwithstanding this display of piety on the part of the premier conquistador and encomendero, the encomenderos as a group came to see the mendicants as meddlers who sought to protect Indians from their demands for labor.

Franciscans arrived in Mexico with considerable experience in preaching and founding missions across rural Spain and southern Europe, as well as a solid background in working with peasant communities and illiterate populations. Franciscan principles emphasized humility, discipline, and poverty as fundamental Christian values. The friars promoted a nonintellectual approach to the veneration of religious symbols as a means of attracting peasants and commoners to religious life. Together these principles gave the Franciscans a considerable advantage over the Dominicans and Augustinians, who focused more on doctrine.

By the mid-sixteenth century colonial New Spain had more than eighty Franciscan foundations, from Pánuco on the Gulf of Mexico to Zacatecas and Durango in the north-central plateau to Yucatan in the south and Jalisco and Michoacan in the west. In addition Franciscans bore responsibility for Christianizing the entire native population of Mexico City, who were grouped into a parish called San José de los Naturales (St. Joseph of the Natives). Franciscans staked out significant territory in the most populous parts of central Mexico, meaning that later-arriving mendicant orders, the Dominicans (1526) and Augustinians (1533), either had to find areas in central Mexico not already claimed by the Franciscans or go where the Franciscans had not yet initiated their campaign of evangelization, such as Oaxaca and Pánuco.

The Franciscan approach to evangelization entailed the immediate incorporation of Indians into the church through baptism. To forge an indigenous Christian community, the Franciscans relied on public displays of Christian practice in the form of mass baptisms, saints' festivities, and traditional celebrations such as they had used successfully in rural missions in Europe. Franciscans primarily used indigenous languages in teaching, as they wished to reach the Indians immediately. The Franciscans were not alone in using Indian languages, as Dominicans and Augustinians also were committed to their use in teaching and preaching. As part of this effort the Franciscans especially, and other mendicants as well, undertook impressive research on native languages and culture, producing grammars, vocabularies, dictionaries, and confessional manuals in indigenous languages. Among Franciscans of this era whose works remain important are Toribio de Benavente Motolinia, Alonso de Molina, and Bernardino de Sahagún.

In addition to works that the mendicants produced for their brethren who were directly involved in evangelizing the Indians, they also translated or retold in indigenous languages a significant number of religious plays, songs, catechisms, and pious traditions that could be used as aids in converting both adults and children. Plays in indigenous languages promoted Christian values, and the Indians organized and performed these theatrical productions on religious holidays. These presentations blended popular southern European traditions with indigenous religious and artistic styles, and native audiences received them enthusiastically.

Franciscan strategy targeted native children in particular, considering them to be the shock troops of Christianity within their own families. Fray Diego de Landa, the bishop of Yucatan best remembered for destroying a vast number of prehispanic Mayan religious texts, described the friars' reliance on Maya children in the evangelization campaign in the 1560s. Since Yucatan was conquered later than central Mexico, the Franciscans applied the model for conversion developed in central Mexico at a comparable stage in the consolidation of the Spanish presence there.

Franciscan Diego de Landa on Religious Indoctrination of Indians

The method taken for indoctrinating the Indians was by collecting the small children of the lords and leading men, and establishing them around the monasteries in houses, which each town built for that purpose. Here all in each locality were gathered together, and their parents and relatives brought them food. Then among these children they gathered them in for catechism, from which frequent visiting many asked for baptism, with much devotion. The children then, after being taught, informed the friars of the idolatries and orgies; they broke up the idols, even those belonging to their own fathers; they urged the divorced women and any orphans that were enslaved to appeal to the friars. Even when they were threatened by their people they were not deterred, but answered that it was for their honor, since it was for the good of their souls. The admiral and the royal judges always backed up the friars in gathering the Indians to catechism, and in punishing those who returned to their old life. At first the lords gave up their children with ill grace, fearing that they wished to make little slaves of them as the Spaniards had done, so that they gave many young slaves in place of their own children; but when they understood the matter they sent them with good grace. In this way the children made remarkable progress in the schools, and the others in the catechism.

Fray Diego de Landa, *Yucatan Before and After the Conquest* [1566], trans. William Gates (New York, 1978), p. 29.

Franciscans were acting with a sense of urgency rooted in millennialism, an important medieval strain of theology that envisioned the end of the earthly world and its replacement with the heavenly kingdom of Christ. According to this tradition, the final conversion of gentiles (non-Jews) and infidels (Jews and Muslims who rejected Christianity) would bring about a series of events leading to the second arrival of the Messiah, as prophesized in the Book of Revelation. This understanding of their historical and theological mission likely contributed to the Franciscans' highly zealous reaction when they suspected that idolatry was winning the battle for Indians' souls. Fray Diego de Landa, the Franciscan provincial in Yucatan in 1562, used his authority to organize an *auto de fe* in which he proudly burned thousands of Maya "diabolical idols" and dozens of hieroglyphic texts. His actions replicated almost exactly those of the Franciscans in Tlaxcala in the 1520s as described and illustrated in Diego Muñoz Camargo's history.

The Franciscans made an enormous effort to enroll Indian children in Christian schools and instruct them in the basic principles of the Catholic faith. In central Mexico, schools were set up immediately after the conquest, an effort led by Fray Pedro de Gante, who had preceded The Twelve who arrived in 1524. In central Mexico the Franciscans first established a school in

Texcoco and then others in the large Nahua communities of Tlaxcala, Tlatelolco, and Huejotzingo, where they taught Catholic doctrine as well as manual skills, music, and reading and writing alphabetic texts.

The most important school for Indians was the Colegio de Santa Cruz Tlatelolco, founded in 1536 with the patronage of the newly arrived viceroy, Don Antonio de Mendoza. This Franciscan college was intended to educate the sons of Nahua elites in the best humanistic tradition with the ultimate goal of creating a native Christian priesthood. At this point in the early sixteenth century, mendicants and many other Spaniards not only considered Indians to be rational beings but envisioned Indian men as ordained priests. In its heyday, the Colegio trained a generation of literate native Christian scholars trilingual in Nahuatl, Latin, and Spanish, the most prominent of them being Antonio de Valeriano. The school failed utterly to produce a group of indigenous priests, and even the Colegio's most vigorous Franciscan supporters, including Sahagún, concluded that its original purpose should be abandoned and a modest Christian vocational curriculum substituted in its

The Nahua Christian Experiment: Colegio of Santa Cruz Tlatelolco

In the beginning a trial was made of making religious [friars] of them [Indian men], for it seemed to us then that they would be capable in ecclesiastical matters and for the religious life. And so the habit of Saint Francis was given two Indian young men, the most able and unworldly there were at that time, who preached with great fervor on matters of our Catholic Faith to their [fellow] natives. And it appeared to us that if they, clothed in our habit and adorned with the virtues of our holy Franciscan Order, should preach with that fervor with which they were preaching, they would reap the greatest harvest of souls. But when they possessed the habit and made use of it in the affairs of this holy Order, it was discovered through experience that they were not equal to such a calling. And so [the friars] deprived them of their habits and never since has the Indian been received in the Order, nor are they considered capable of the priesthood.

At this time, as even the religious [friars] did not know the language of these natives, they instructed as best they could those Indians who seemed capable and unworldly, that they might preach to the people in the presence of the religious. But after the religious knew the language and began to preach, they relieved [the Indians] of the preaching because of the faults they discovered in them. . . .

And certainly, at the beginning, we were of the opinion that the men would be capable as priests and friars, and the women as nuns and sisters. But our opinion deceived us. From experience, we learned that, at the time they were not capable of such perfection. And so the sisterhoods and convents, which we had planned from the beginning, ceased.

Fray Bernardino de Sahagún, "Author's Account Worthy of Being Noted [1576]" in *The Florentine Codex: Introductory Volume,* trans. Charles Dibble and Arthur J .O. Anderson (Salt Lake City, 1982), pp. 76–85.

stead. The public failure of the Colegio and withdrawal of viceregal patronage ended the most ambitious religious project in early colonial Spanish America, with profound consequences for Indians' place within the church.

The innovative and flexible methods of the Franciscans yielded remarkable successes in native communities with large numbers of Indians brought into Christianity and many churches built. Much of colonial society, including the secular clergy and other religious orders as well as lay people, however, viewed their experiments with suspicion. Elite landowners and encomenderos saw the mendicants as protecting the Indians against civil society's claim to their labor while themselves using it to build church complexes. The secular clergy resented the encroachment of the regular clergy on their traditional jurisdictions and prerogatives, and other mendicant orders envied the Franciscans' primacy in the evangelization project. To a great extent the Indians' conversion to Catholicism in central Mexico was a Franciscan achievement. Their flexible approach to doctrinal matters, promoted the development of a form of Catholicism that retained many older beliefs and practices. The failure of the Franciscan Colegio of Santa Cruz to produce any Indian candidates for ordination, however, also should figure in the assessment of their impact on Mexican Catholicism.

The Dominicans. The Order of St. Dominic arrived in Mexico in 1526, but their evangelization efforts did not get underway seriously until a group of twelve, led by Fray Vicente de Santamaría, came in 1528. With this group the Dominicans began to compete with the Franciscans. They founded monasteries in central Mexico from the highlands of Puebla to the Pacific Ocean in the south, but they were most important in the Zapotec and Mixtec communities of Oaxaca and the Maya communities of highland Chiapas and Guatemala. By 1559 New Spain had about forty Dominican establishments with more than two hundred friars.

Dominicans shared the Franciscans' enthusiasm for the conversion of the Indians but differed considerably as to how it should be accomplished. Rooted in their medieval tradition of combating heresy and popular superstition, the Order of Preachers rejected mass baptism and collective conversion. They relied instead on persuasion, preaching, and teaching, to bring converts into the Christian fold. Because they pursued this intellectual path to conversion, the Dominicans were far less successful in attracting large numbers of converts than the more flexible Franciscans.

The Dominicans played a crucial role in establishing the legal status of Indians as rational beings who merited royal protection from abuse, particularly from encomenderos. In both Spain and the Spanish empire Dominicans used their scholastic background to curb and finally thwart the Spanish settlers' claims to perpetual encomiendas. According to the Dominicans, Indians were free vassals or subjects of the Spanish Crown who required the monarch's protection until they achieved "maturity." Thus Indians were seen as rational but childlike beings. For Dominicans the encomenderos' exploitation of Indian labor for private gain (denounced by

Fray Antonio de Montesinos even before Spaniards reached Mexico, as seen in Chapter 2) was immoral and illegal. Dominican friars articulated and promoted this defense of the Indians from pulpits, in classrooms, and before the royal court itself.

As the wealth of the Spanish empire in Mexico and Peru became apparent, the Crown increasingly favored the Dominicans' arguments against the privileges of the encomendero group, promulgating the New Laws of the Indies in 1542. These laws limited succession to encomiendas to only one generation and terminated the encomenderos' right to the uncompensated labor of Indians under their jurisdiction. Arguably this extension of protection to native communities by the Council of the Indies was a major achievement on the part of the Dominicans, who worked tirelessly on the Indians' behalf. The shift in royal policy, however, also was consistent with the Crown's progressive assertion of authority over its overseas empire.

The most distinguished Dominican was Fray Bartolomé de Las Casas, a former encomendero in Hispaniola and Cuba, the first priest ordained in the Indies (in 1510), and the most vocal opponent of the conqueror faction at the royal court. In 1544 Las Casas became the first bishop of Chiapas, where he fiercely opposed the Audiencia of Guatemala and the conqueror elite on behalf of the Mayas of his diocese. In 1550 Las Casas traveled to the court in Valladolid, Spain, to defend his contention that Christianization should be accomplished through peaceful means by the friars alone. In Castile he composed his *Apologética Historia Sumaria* and other historical writings on the New World.

The Dominican strategy of winning Indian souls by relying on rhetoric and logical principles failed dramatically. Indeed the entire mendicant effort to teach Catholic doctrine to the Indians was doomed from the outset. The central tenets of Christianity did not have precise equivalents in native thought or language. Even the concept of sin itself, central to the Christian understanding of human nature and divine forgiveness, lacked any close equivalent in central Mexican religious thought.

Even where parallels and analogies existed they often fostered misunderstanding. The doctrine of the Trinity, a difficult theological concept even for European laymen and women, could be interpreted as polytheism. For Mesoamericans the crucifixion of Jesus probably was strongly reminiscent of the old practice of human sacrifice. Louise Burkhart's critical reading of Nahuatl texts produced by friars to teach Catholic doctrine shows that friars made a number of strategic compromises in attempting to transmit Christian concepts to Nahua speakers.

By the end of the sixteenth century, European friars had become convinced that true conversion of the Indians would take place only gradually. Well before this, other orders had joined the Franciscans and Dominicans. The Order of St. Augustine arrived in 1533, establishing itself in communities in Michoacan. The Augustinians concentrated along a corridor running from

Teotihuacan, in the Valley of Mexico, northward across the Sierra Madre Oriental. By 1559 they had around forty monasteries. Like the other orders, they became a significant presence in Spanish cities and towns as well.

The Secular Clergy

Secular Clerics and Evangelization. The mendicants dominated the principal organized, sustained campaign to Christianize the Indians. Encomenderos, however, often hired secular priests to instruct encomienda Indians in Christian doctrine to fulfill the legal requirement that they act as agents of evangelization. As the employees of encomenderos, these priests were unlikely to challenge their employers' exploitation of Indian labor.

One secular cleric of the early era stood out from the general venality and mediocrity of his fellow priests. Vasco de Quiroga evangelized the Indians of western Mexico in a spirit more consistent with mendicant practice than that of the secular clergy. Quiroga, a judge of the Second Audiencia, in 1538 was named bishop of the newly created diocese of Michoacan in the Purepecha region. In 1533, even before he became bishop, Quiroga and his followers reorganized Indian communities near Lake Pátzcuaro into *hospitales* on the model of Thomas More's *Utopia.* Supervised by secular clerics, these hospital communities were run by native leaders, held land communally, and practiced collective farming. In addition they set up workshops for crafts and provided health care and Christian schooling. It was hoped that, in such a setting, converts would learn respect for others and appreciate that humility, charity, and love are the most important Christian virtues. A number of modern towns in Michoacan originated with these hospital communities, whose founder is still affectionately called Tata ("Father") Quiroga.

Episcopal Hierarchy and the Secular Clergy. Secular clerics were present in Mexico from the time of the conquest. The Crown established a standard episcopal (bishop-led) church structure, dividing Mexico into districts called dioceses and initially appointing mendicants rather than secular priests as bishops. The first effective diocesan jurisdiction was established not in Mexico City but, rather, in Tlaxcala in 1527, with the appointment of Dominican Fray Julián Garcés as the first bishop in New Spain, in recognition of Tlaxcala's role in the conquest. During the 1540s, however, the seat of the bishopric was moved to the Spanish city of Puebla and the cathedral built there, completed one hundred years later.

The diocese of Mexico, based in Mexico City, was established in 1528 with Franciscan Fray Juan de Zumárraga as the first bishop. Mexico became an archdiocese in 1547, with Bishop Zumárraga elevated to the position of archbishop with authority over the other dioceses. His successor was a Dominican, Fray Alonso de Montúfar (1554–72), who worked aggressively to strengthen the episcopal hierarchy and came into increasing conflict with the mendicant orders.

With the main institutions of both church and state centered in the capital, the archbishop and the viceroy were the two most powerful officials in the realm. Even before the establishment of the viceroyalty in 1535, Zumárraga, the bishop of Mexico, exercised considerable political power, helping to oust the disastrous First Audiencia headed by Nuño de Guzmán. On a number of occasions when the seat of the viceroy was vacant, the archbishop served in that capacity. Jurisdictional quarrels between high royal officials and the episcopal hierarchy often were resolved in favor of the secular clergy, and more than one viceroy in the later colonial era saw his career in Mexico come to an end after he clashed with the archbishop.

In the early 1570s, the structure of religious power within the church changed significantly. As seen, the first two archbishops of Mexico were mendicants. The appointment of secular cleric Pedro Moya y Contreras as archbishop of Mexico in 1572 brought the era of mendicant dominance to an end. The archdiocese encompassed the bishoprics of Tlaxcala-Puebla, Oaxaca (called Antequera in the colonial era), Michoacan, Guadalajara

Figure 6-2 **Mexico City Cathedral**. Built on the site of the Mexica ceremonial center, the cathedral is the oldest and largest in Latin America. This ornate building was begun in 1573 and constructed in stages over the whole colonial period, and exhibits several architectural styles.
Engraving, private collection of Sarah Cline.

(Nueva Galicia), and Durango in the north, with the diocese of Yucatan effectively under control of the Captaincy General of Guatemala.

Elite Mexican families forged close connections with the secular clergy, many training at least one son for a clerical career. A senior family member often endowed a chantry (*capellanía*) for a (usually) younger relative who entered the priesthood, thus guaranteeing his kinsman an income while assuring for himself the benefits of perpetual masses after his death. The church offered an array of privileges (*fueros*) to those who joined its ranks: legal immunity before criminal and civil courts, tax exemptions on income, property and inheritance, life-tenured appointments for some, secure incomes in the form of salary, rents and benefits and social recognition as representatives of the monarchy and church.

Many young men from Spanish families, along with upwardly mobile mestizos and castas trying to cross the racial line, eagerly enrolled in seminaries. Even men with little genuine religious vocation were attracted to the church, often paying little attention to vows of chastity. Colonial society was relatively tolerant of such behavior, although periodically the Crown prohibited priests from baptizing their own children. Clerical absenteeism, particularly in remote Indian parishes, along with poor religious training and disposition, presented chronic challenges to diocesan authorities.

Not all members of the clergy prospered. Priests from elite families had better access to patronage and could draw on family resources in the form of chantries. Many secular clerics failed to secure a parish or any other benefice, or they were assigned to parishes in poor areas that yielded low incomes from sacramental fees. Many priests in the countryside, who were often of marginal racial status, had to supplement their income through other pursuits, sometimes working in the family business if there was one or tilling land along with their parishioners. Elite clerics, in contrast, lived in the major cities where they enjoyed the advantages of their social connections and family wealth.

Abuses by parish priests were common after the initial period of zealous evangelization. Indian communities filed complaints in civil and diocesan courts claiming that priests charged excessive fees for burials and other sacramental services, physically abused them with beatings, whippings, and imprisonment, sexually exploited women, and exacted forced labor service. These complaints sometimes resulted in the replacement of the local cleric.

Despite some bad clerics, many secular priests and mendicants performed important functions in their parishes, serving as models of good Christian behavior and upholding public morals by punishing such irregular sexual behavior as fornication, adultery, and unions not consecrated by marriage. William B. Taylor's magisterial study of the secular clergy shows that clerics played a key role in maintaining control over the vast countryside. Clerics reported to the Crown on such matters as serious crime, local economic conditions, and social and political unrest. Priests often were the sole representatives of Spanish rule in rural communities, meaning that they fulfilled responsibilities in both the religious and the civil spheres. As they usually were conversant in the local indigenous languages, clerics might intercede with civil and religious authorities on behalf of their communities.

Consolidation of the Colonial Church

During the second half of the sixteenth century the church began to emerge as the colony's foremost economic institution. It also took steps to formalize certain practices. Two important new institutions were added in the 1570s, the Jesuits and the Holy Office of the Inquisition.

Church Councils and Reform. In 1555 the First Mexican Provincial Council brought together bishops and most of the ecclesiastical hierarchy to organize governance of the church. In 1561 the Second Mexican Provincial Council unanimously accepted the resolutions of the Council of Trent (1545–63) regarding institutional reform and reaffirmation of Catholic dogma. A third provincial council took place in 1585 which, among other things, mandated the keeping of parish records according to set standards, in effect codifying racial distinctions (see Chapter 13). Together these three episcopal councils in Mexico established a seminary, strengthened and expanded the diocesan jurisdictions, and laid down normative and operational rules for secular parishes.

Holy Office of the Inquisition. In 1571, the Crown established the Holy Office of the Inquisition in New Spain, creating a separate clerical bureaucracy to ensure orthodox Christian practice. Before its establishment bishops had exercised inquisitorial functions in their dioceses. Although important, the Inquisition in New Spain never was as severe as its counterpart in Spain. After a few high-profile trials of Indians, one of which resulted in the execution of a lord of Texcoco, Don Carlos Ometochtzin, Indians were removed from the jurisdiction of the Inquisition. This decision was consistent with the view that Indians were legal minors and neophytes in the Christian religion.

The Inquisition most prominently prosecuted converted Jews who continued to practice their old religion (called *judaizantes* or "Judaizers"), as well as Protestants (whom Spaniards generically called "Lutherans" or *luteranos*). Blasphemers against Catholicism were also prosecuted in the early period. During the sixty years (1580–1640) that the Spanish Crown ruled both Spain and Portugal, Portuguese merchants became active in New Spain and Peru. Many of the most successful of these merchants were converts, and they became targets of both economic resentment and the suspicions of the Inquisition. In the Gran Auto de Fe of 1649, some fifty people, mostly Portuguese, were executed.

After 1650 the Inquisition in Mexico shifted its focus to other infractions of religious norms: bigamy, blasphemy, divination, sorcery, and priestly solicitation of sexual favors from female parishioners. The death penalty, usually reserved for heretics and *judaizantes*, was rarely applied after the auto de fe of 1649. One notable exception was the case of Don Guillén de Lampart, an Irishman who claimed to be the bastard half-brother of the Spanish king. Don Guillén proposed the establishment of an independent kingdom, with himself as monarch, supported by blacks and Indians who would be equal in the new realm. Perhaps mad, he was executed in 1659 after spending seventeen years in the Inquisition prison.

Jesuits. In 1572 the Society of Jesus, a religious association founded by Ignacio de Loyola, a former soldier of Basque origins, arrived in New Spain to join the campaign of evangelization. Technically, the Jesuits were not a monastic order but instead organized themselves along more military lines. Both in Rome and Madrid they enjoyed great influence, which they used to consolidate their presence in the New World. Known as "soldiers of the pope," they took an oath to go where the papacy sent them. They gained a worldwide reputation with their successful missions to India, China, and Japan, and were instrumental in evangelizing Indians in both Spanish and Portuguese America.

The Jesuits quickly established themselves as the premier religious organization in New Spain, replacing the Dominicans as educators of elites and taking the lead in evangelizing new territories in the north, displacing the Franciscans. They attracted wealthy patrons and brought large numbers of Indians into the Christian fold, while building an impressive material base through efficiently run haciendas. In central Mexico the Jesuits founded prominent educational institutions, including an Indian colegio in Mexico City, San Gregorio (where the seventeenth-century Nahua writer Chimalpahin was based). Jesuit educational institutions multiplied in the major cities of New Spain and became centers where elite men could cultivate their intellectual talents. The Society of Jesus produced some of colonial Mexico's greatest intellectuals, such as Francisco Xavier Clavigero, who wrote his history of Mexico in Italian while in exile, and Don Carlos Sigüenza y Góngora, who was educated by Jesuits but became a secular cleric.

Convents for Women. Nunneries were established in New Spain from the mid-sixteenth century onward. They became important institutions, creating religious communities for women seeking an alternative to marriage and an enclosed life based on religious contemplation and prayer. Convents also offered women a degree of autonomy and freedom to pursue their religious and intellectual inclinations and interests.

By the second half of the sixteenth century there were more than enough Spanish women to meet the demand for marriage partners, so convents began to proliferate. Essentially they were institutions for the wealthy, as aspiring nuns could enter only with a substantial dowry, in keeping with the notion that a nun became the bride of Christ. The dowry also provided financial support for the woman and the convent.

Relatively few women entered the most stringent orders such as the Carmelites, which demanded fasting, self-denial, and constant prayer. Most chose orders with laxer rules that allowed nuns to bring their personal helpers into the convent. Because of this practice, the largest numbers of women living in convents were not professed nuns but, rather, their servants and slaves. These *sirvientas* functioned as the personal servants of the nuns and as retainers for the convent, performing much of the heavy labor involved in running a large establishment.

Nuns, or *monjas*, were full members of the order with all privileges. The head of a convent was the abbess. A nonresident priest, usually a member of the secular clergy, was responsible for the spiritual life of the nuns. He played an important role in the religious community but by definition did not belong to it. Lay members of the order, called *beatas*, participated in convent activities but were not full members. Other residents in convents included young girls who lacked dowries and might attract wealthy patrons who would provide them with dowries either to marry or to profess. Some convents operated schools for girls, who lived there as boarders. With the exception of a few convents for Indian noblewomen founded in the eighteenth century, for the most part these institutions were bastions of racial exclusiveness.

Convents were economically self-supporting, offering credit and loans, selling a variety of products manufactured within the convent walls, and investing mainly in urban rental property rather than rural estates. Principally, however, convents were places for spiritual activity, fostering forms of religious piety that often were expressed through mysticism.

The Church and Colonial Society

Secularization of Parishes. In the late sixteenth century the Crown moved against the mendicant orders by insisting that Indian parishes be turned over to the secular clergy in a process known as secularization, formalized in 1574 in Philip II's proclamation of the *Ordenanza del Patronazgo*. Secularization meant placing parishes governed by religious orders under the jurisdiction of the secular clergy, and transferring control of lands, rents, churches, shrines, and religious images to the secular clergy.

In many Indian communities residents resisted the removal of the friars; once underway, however, the process was irreversible. Although secular clerics fought to gain rural parishes, most members of the diocesan clergy much preferred to reside in Spanish cities and to delegate their clerical duties to vicars. The most desirable positions for the secular clergy were positions in the cathedral chapter. For secular clerics of limited means, a salaried position or benefice of any kind was preferable to none, meaning there were willing candidates even for poor parishes and vicarages.

After the mainly Indian parishes in most of central Mexico were secularized, mendicants became more active on the fringes of empire, especially

Mexico's north. Unlike the first heady days of the spiritual conquest, however, by this time friars had few hopes for thoroughgoing conversion and none for creating a native Christian priesthood. In the north many friars became martyrs for their faith. Jesuits and Franciscans maintained their parishes in California, Arizona, Sonora, New Mexico, Nueva Vizcaya, and Texas. When the Jesuits were expelled in 1767 by order of the Bourbon king the Franciscans took over former Jesuit missions in Baja California and founded new missions in Alta California.

The Jesuits' success in missionary work and education and their independence from bishops' supervision aroused the jealousy of the mendicant orders. The Society's autonomy and political influence also angered members of the secular clergy. When the bishop of Puebla Don Juan de Palafox y Mendoza attempted to expel the Jesuits from his lucrative diocese, Palafox was recalled to Spain. The steps that Palafox took to place parishes under diocesan authority and were not repealed, however, and eventually were implemented in all but the frontier regions.

Economic Power and the Church. The church became an extremely powerful economic entity during the colonial era, with each of its component parts amassing wealth for its own use. Its revenue came from agriculture (*diezmos* or tithes, a tax of one-tenth of agricultural production, and *primicias* or first fruits, a tax on first-harvested crops and first-born farm animals); mandatory fees for religious sacraments (baptism, marriage, funeral masses); contributions for religious festivities; and both private and public donations of alms or *limosnas*. From these revenues the diocese paid salaries to parish priests, supported the cathedral chapter in all its pomp and glory, and maintained charitable and educational institutions in the diocese.

They mendicant orders' control over parishes in weathy and populous regions benefited the orders as a whole, but they had no system for redistributing the wealth from rich establishments located amid densely populated Indian communities to poor ones in sparsely settled regions. Only the Jesuits operated integrated enterprises, with the revenues of their efficiently managed rural estates going to support their colegios and missions.

Through direct investments, pious donations, or hostile takeovers as creditor, the church came to possess and exploit a spectrum of assets, generally through intermediaries. By the late eighteenth century royal officials had become critical of the enormous wealth accumulated by the church, and tenants who rented church-owned properties in cities and workers on haciendas resented their economic obligations to the ecclesiastical hierarchy. The colonial church became one of the most important financial corporations in colonial society, extending credit and loans to private citizens and public institutions at prevailing interest rates. In general the church was conservative in its investments, willing to extend loans for mortgages on both rural and urban property but reluctant to fund business enterprises involving more risk. As a result, royal officials and aspiring entrepreneurs saw the church as a stumbling block to economic development and prosperity.

Mexican Devotions and Holy People

Confraternities. Enormously popular in colonial Mexico *cofradías* (confraternities), organized along lines of ethnicity, caste, and occupation, were founded in connection with religious establishments in both rural and urban parishes. The desire of the laity to participate in religious life found an important outlet in the confraternities, which were vital social and cultural organizations dedicated to the celebration of a particular saint or religious idea, such as the Sacred Heart of Jesus or the Immaculate Conception. They had a practical side as well, serving as mutual aid and burial societies.

Cofradías were promoted by the mendicants in indigenous communities, where they fostered community cohesiveness. Cofradías often held land and livestock that supported their activities and were one of the few organizations to which both men and women belonged, although women rarely held office. In the second half of the eighteenth century, under the Bourbons, the confraternities came under attack when the Crown attempted to curb lavish religious displays and gain access to cofradía property, much of which was turned over to the secular clergy.

The Virgin of Guadalupe. Appearances of the Virgin Mary, mother of Jesus, and the cults that developed around these manifestations endowed particular locales with direct connections to the divine. The dark Virgin of Guadalupe eventually became a symbol for Mexico's indigenous population, but devotion to her cult developed gradually during the colonial period.

The story of Guadalupe embodies many of the contradictions of Mexican religious belief and national identity. In 1555 Fray Alonso de Montúfar, the Dominican archbishop of Mexico, decided to promote the veneration of an image of the Virgin Mary placed in a rural shrine on a hill located on the northern outskirts of Mexico City. The image was renowned locally for having performed miracles for Spanish travelers and residents in the city. The hill of Tepeyac (or Tepeyacac) had been an important focus for native religious pilgrimages long before the Spanish conquest and was associated with a female deity known as Tonantzin, "our venerated mother," who had an annual festival and received pilgrims from many places.

Montúfar promoted the cult of the Virgin of Guadalupe among Mexico City's Spanish residents. By the time of his death in 1572, the devotion to Guadalupe had grown locally and was drawing the attention of royal officials, travelers, and clergymen. Following a severe flood in Mexico City in 1629, a solemn procession carried the image of the Virgin to the cathedral, where residents prayed for her intercession to make the waters recede. When the flood

HVEI
TLAMAHVIÇOLTICA
OMONEXITI IN ILHVICAC TLATÓCA
ÇIHVAPILLI
SANTA MARIA
TOTLAÇONANTZIN
GVADALVPE IN NICAN HVEI ALTEPE-
NAHVAC MEXICO ITOCAYÒCAN TEPEYACAC.

Impreſſo con licencia en MEXICO : en la Imprenta de Iuan Ruyz.
Año de 1 6 4 9.

Figure 6-3 **Virgin of Guadalupe, 1649.** Mexico's "dark virgin" is shown in the frontispiece of the earliest known publication in Nahuatl describing her 1531 apparition to Juan Diego. She is a national symbol of Mexico and patron virgin of the Americas. Courtesy of the John Carter Brown Library at Brown University.

waters subsided, diocesan authorities celebrated a thanksgiving Mass dedicated to the Virgin of Guadalupe and escorted her image back to her shrine.

In 1648 Miguel Sánchez, a secular priest from Mexico City, published a book on the Virgin of Guadalupe, whose title translated to English was "Image of the Virgin Mary Mother of God of Guadalupe, Miraculously appeared in the City of Mexico." Many scholars have concluded that Sánchez actually originated the legend of the apparition. Sánchez wrote that in 1531 the Virgin Mary appeared to an Indian from Cuauhtitlan named Juan Diego. He believed that the Mother of God had appeared in New Spain to demonstrate her favor for the land.

A year later Luis Laso de la Vega, vicar of the shrine of Guadalupe, published the *Huey Tlamahuizoltica,* a compilation of different accounts in Nahuatl describing the apparition and subsequent miracles performed for various people. One segment, the *"Nican mopohua"* ("here is recounted, here is told"), presented the story with vivid dialogue between the Virgin and Juan Diego following Nahuatl speech patterns. In Laso de la Vega's account the Virgin appears as the protectress of indigenous populations.

The story goes as follows. Juan Diego was traveling from his village to Tlatelolco, looking for a friar to administer the last rites to his dying uncle. At Tepeyac, Juan Diego saw the Virgin, who instructed him to tell the bishop of Mexico, Fray Juan de Zumárraga, to build a chapel in her honor at that spot. Juan Diego obeyed, but a skeptical Zumárraga demanded evidence of this divine mandate. Once again the Virgin appeared before Juan Diego, giving him the same orders and adding that he should take some flowers that were growing nearby to Zumárraga as proof. When Juan Diego let the flowers fall from his cloak to the floor, the bishop saw the image of the Virgin of Guadalupe imprinted on the Indian's cloak or *tilma.* Marveling and joyous, Zumárraga decided to build a chapel in Tepeyac and placed Juan Diego's miraculous image on the altar, where it remained.

Sánchez's account reflected the narrative tradition relating to miraculous events that had been common in southern Europe since the Middle Ages. In rural Spain numerous Marian images were discovered by or appeared before humble shepherds. One of the most important of these traditions developed around the dark wooden image of the Virgin whose shrine in the town of Guadalupe in southwestern Spain became a major pilgrimage site in the late middle ages.

For Spaniards in New Spain, the apparitions of the Virgin Mary in central Mexico represented a validation of their claims as Spanish imperial subjects, and brought into close conjunction their patriotic feelings as both Spanish Americans and Christians. In the eighteenth century, sermons would further expand on this patriotic theme. For the Indians a dark woman representing the Virgin Mary on the principal altar, at a time when no Indian could become a priest, likely had a powerful appeal. By the end of the late seventeenth century the Indians had refashioned this cult with both Mesoamerican and Spanish roots and adopted it as their own religious icon.

By the eighteenth century, Guadalupe was among the most popular Marian devotions in New Spain. Both the diocesan clergy and mendicants promoted her veneration among all ethnic groups as the Virgin of the land. In 1737 she was credited with protecting the archdiocese against an epidemic of *matlazahuatl* that had devastated New Spain. The Archdiocese and Mexico City declared her patroness of the land. In 1747 she received the title of patroness of all New Spain. Her image appeared on altars in urban and rural churches from Texas and California to Chiapas and Yucatan. Through sermons, pamphlets, books, stamps, prayers, and word of mouth, the diocesan clergy spread word of her fame and miraculous deeds. First along the royal road between Mexico and Zacatecas and then practically everywhere else, her reputation grew exponentially. Soon geographical place names, churches and other religious institutions, rural estates, ships, and ordinary Mexicans were named or renamed for her. The Virgin of Guadalupe had become an important cultural and religious symbol, perhaps the only one with which all Greater Mexico's diverse peoples identified.

Mexican Holy People. Until the nineteenth century no one born in New Spain ever achieved sainthood. The strongest case, pressed by Mexican patriots, was that of Franciscan Felipe de Jesús, who died a martyr in Japan in 1597 and finally was canonized in 1862. In the period after the Council of Trent (1545–63), when many Catholic practices were brought under firm papal control, the church recognized few saints.

Many in New Spain campaigned to have one or another local holy person officially recognized. To support their cases clerics or pious laymen produced spiritual biographies documenting the lives and deeds of holy persons. One such person was a Spaniard, Fray Sebastián de Aparicio (d. 1600), who spent most of his life near Puebla in New Spain, where he worked as a muleteer and later an hacendado. He gained a reputation for holiness in his later years, after contracting two chaste marriages and then joining the Franciscans as a lay brother. He was eventually named a *beato* ("blessed"), the official recognition that precedes canonization as a saint. In modern Mexico, he is the popular patron of truckers and bus drivers.

Another longtime resident of Puebla, a nonwhite woman who was baptized Catarina de San Juan (d. 1688), also achieved a reputation for holiness during her lifetime and became famous as the *China Poblana* (Asian woman of Puebla); the colorful outfit she is said to have designed is considered by many to be the traditional costume not only of Puebla but even of Mexico itself. She apparently was kidnapped somewhere in the Far East and sent to New Spain from the Philippines. In Puebla she worked as a domestic servant and gained a huge local reputation for holiness. Despite her fame during her lifetime and prodigious efforts by her hagiographers and supporters to gain recognition of her sainthood, the church never opened official investigations into the merits of her case.

Other Devotions. Throughout colonial Mexico people venerated religious images thought to have miraculous origins, supernatural powers, or special significance for a particular group of the faithful. Sponsored by local clergy, mendicants, brotherhoods, diocesan authorities, nunneries, or pious associations, these images soon became not only major sources of prestige and revenue for their institutional custodians but, more importantly, powerful cultural symbols of local, regional, and ethnic identity. The Virgin of San Juan de Los Lagos, the Virgin of Zapopan in Nueva Galicia, Nuestra Señora de la Luz in Michoacan, Nuestra Señora del Patrocinio in Zacatecas, the Virgin Conquistadora in New Mexico, the Señor de Mapimí and San Isidro Labrador in Nueva Vizcaya, the Señor de Chalma and the Señor del Cardonal in central Mexico are just a few examples of religious images associated with miraculous powers and particular regions.

Ethnic groups also were associated with particular images. Basques venerated Our Lady of Aranzazu; Galicians were devoted to Santiago (St. James); northern Castilians revered the Christ of Burgos. Guilds and lay brotherhoods (*cofradías*) also had special protectors with their own altars or churches. Masons celebrated the day of the erection of the Holy Cross; students prayed to St. Catherine of Alexandria; secular priests appealed to San Pedro and merchants to St. Martín. Certain saints were believed to exercise particular influence in the domain of disease and natural calamity: St. Lazarus for leprosy; St. Lucy for blindness; St. Ignatius for pregnancy and childbirth; St. Sebastián for plagues; St. Isadore (San Isidro) for droughts.

By the late colonial period, the Catholic church in Mexico reflected many of the contradictions inherent to colonial society and bore little resemblance to the church of the spiritual conquest. Its main focus had become rich congregants in Spanish cities rather than Indians in rural parishes. Mendicant poverty had given way to secular opulence. In the countryside and in the urban *barrios* where mestizos and castas lived many local priests barely eked out a living, while high-ranking ecclesiastics held lifelong appointments and benefices and lived in luxury in the centers of power. Prosperous confraternities celebrated sumptuous annual rituals and functions, while the majority of mutual-aid confraternities could scarcely cover the expenses incurred by epidemic outbreaks or extraordinary taxes. A growing division between rural and urban ministers had developed, along with a significant rivalry among different religious entities and ecclesiastical territories. Catholicism had brought all into the community of faith, but the unity of the church masked deep divisions and fundamental inequalities.

Glossary

auto de fe   penitential religious rite for those prosecuted by the Inquisition

benefice   salaried clerical position

beata/o   layperson who has not taken holy vows; official designation of holiness

capellanía   chantry, private endowment to support a priest

diezmo   tithe, an ecclesiastical tax of one-tenth on agricultural production

doctrina   rural parish of Indians

episcopal hierarchy   religious hierarchy under the control of a bishop

fuero eclesiástico   special privileges of the clergy

limosna   alms, charity

mendicants   members of religious orders taking vows of poverty, chastity, obedience

Jesuits   members of the Society of Jesus, an international religious organization

parroquia   parish, a territorial division of a diocese

primicias   ecclesiastical tax on first-born animals and first-harvested grain

regular clergy   mendicant orders organized under a religious rule

secular clergy   diocesan clergy under the authority of a bishop

visita   Indian settlement with no resident priest, visited at intervals

Questions for Discussion

1.   How was Christianity simultaneously a unifying force in colonial Mexico and a divisive one?

2.   What was the role of the regular orders in Christianizing Mexico's Indians? What were the different approaches used by Franciscans, Dominicans, and Jesuits? How and why did their position in the church change after the era of the "spiritual conquest"?

3.   What was the position of the Indians in the Catholic church?

4.   What role did the secular clergy play in colonial culture?

5.   Why is the Virgin of Guadalupe so important to Mexican history?

Suggested Reading

Baudot, Georges. *Utopia and History in Mexico: The First Chroniclers of Mexican Civilization, 1520–1569.* Niwot: University of Colorado Press, 1995. Analysis of the first Franciscan writers and their texts.

Brading, D. A. *Mexican Phoenix. Our Lady of Guadalupe: Image and Tradition across Five Centuries.* Cambridge and New York: Cambridge University

Press, 2001. Thorough, lucid treatment of the literature and debates on the origins and evolution of the cult.

Burkhart, Louise. *The Slippery Earth: Nahua-Christian Moral Dialogue in Sixteenth-Century Mexico.* Tucson: University of Arizona Press, 1989. Major work analyzing the interaction of Nahuas and mendicants through close reading of mendicant texts.

Cline, Sarah. "The Spiritual Conquest Re-Examined: Baptism and Church Marriage in Early Colonial Mexico," *Hispanic American Historical Review* 73:3 (1993), 453–80. Analysis of Nahua household censuses from the 1530s showing that baptism and church marriage had barely taken hold in many areas.

Costeloe, Michael. *Church Wealth in Mexico: A Study of the Juzgado de Capellanías in the Archbishopric of Mexico, 1800–1856.* Cambridge: Cambridge University Press, 1967. Examination of a key source of endowed wealth supporting the secular clergy.

Cuevas, Mariano, S.J. *Historia de la Iglesia de México.* 5 vols. Mexico: Porrúa, 1921–8. Major work by a Jesuit on the Mexican church, written during a period of anticlericalism in modern Mexico.

Greenleaf, Richard. *The Mexican Inquisition of the Sixteenth Century.* Albuquerque: University of New Mexico Press, 1969. Outline of the institution and its functions.

———. *Zumárraga and the Mexican Inquisition, 1536–1543.* Washington, D.C.: Academy of American Franciscan History, 1962. Brief study of the first bishop of Mexico and the Inquisition, with emphasis on cases of Indian idolatry.

Gruzinski, Serge. *The Conquest of Mexico: The Incorporation of Indian Societies into the Western World 16th–18th Centuries.* Cambridge: Cambridge University Press, 1993. Examination of the conquest that puts particular emphasis on the role of religion in the formation of colonial culture.

Kubler, George. *Mexican Architecture of the Sixteenth Century.* New Haven, Conn.: Yale University Press, 1948. More than strict architectural history, this study delves into the context of the Spanish building projects, especially church architecture.

Morgan, Ronald J. *Spanish American Saints and the Rhetoric of Identity, 1600–1810.* Tucson: University of Arizona Press, 2002. Includes the lives of three Mexican holy people.

Phelan, John Leddy. *The Millennial Kingdom of the Franciscans in the New World.* Berkeley: University of California Press, 1970. Major work examining shifts in Franciscan millennial thought during the sixteenth century and its relevance to Indians.

Pescador, Juan Javier. *De Bautizados a fieles difuntos. Familia y mentalidades en una parroquia urbana: Santa Catarina de México, 1568–1821.* Mexico: El Colegio de México, 1992. Cultural history examining an urban parish based on parochial records.

Poole, Stafford. *Moya de Contreras*. Berkeley: University of California Press, 1987. Life and times of the first secular archbishop of Mexico.

————. *Our Lady of Guadalupe: The Origins and Sources of a Mexican National Symbol, 1531–1797*. Tucson: University of Arizona Press, 1995. Careful examination of the history of the cult.

Ricard, Robert. *The Spiritual Conquest of Mexico: An Essay on the Apostolate and the Evangelizing Methods of the Mendicant Orders in New Spain, 1523–1572*. Trans. by Lesley Byrd Simpson. Berkeley: University of California Press, 1966. Classic work on the mendicant effort, first published in the 1930s but of enduring iimportance.

Schwaller, John Frederick. *Church and Clergy in Sixteenth-century Mexico*. Albuquerque: University of New Mexico Press, 1987. Examination of the structure of the secular clergy.

————. *The Origins of Church Wealth in Mexico*. Albuquerque: University of New Mexico Press, 1985. Analysis of the early economic basis of the secular clergy.

Taylor, William B. *Magistrates of the Sacred*. Stanford: Stanford University Press, 1996. Magisterial study of the secular clergy in Mexico.

Film

The Other Conquest (La Otra Conquista). Mexico, Spanish, and Nahuatl with English subtitles. Film on the conquest of Mexico, emphasizing religious aspects.

Part II

1598–1700

Seven

Mesoamerican Indians under Colonial Rule

Indians constituted the largest racial group in Greater Mexico during the entire colonial period despite the sixteenth-century epidemics that reduced their numbers from as many as twenty-five million to as few as a million. Indigenous communities functioned as conservators of native traditions, despite the changes wrought by the imposition of Spanish rule, accounting for the strong persistence of indigenous culture throughout the colonial period. Since Indians played such a significant role in colonial Mexico despite their subordinate status, understanding their experiences is crucial. This chapter focuses on Central Mexico.

From the time of their earliest contacts with the New World's indigenous populations in the Caribbean, Spaniards grappled with the question of the legal and social status of Indians. Queen Isabel categorically rejected Indian enslavement, considering them to be her subjects and thus endowed with rights and responsibilities. Although rebellious Indians could be enslaved, peaceful Indians were considered free vassals. Finding substantial indigenous populations in Mexico, Spaniards established a major legal distinction between Indians and all others by creating two administrative entities, the "commonwealth of Indians" (*república de indios*) and the "commonwealth of Spaniards" (*república de españoles*). Initially the Crown's intention was to exclude non-Indians from living in Indian towns in order to protect indigenous communities from exploitation as well as the potentially corrupting moral influence of lay Spaniards. Although segregating Indians from New Spain's other residents proved impossible, Indians enjoyed a protected status under colonial law and in many respects were treated as legal minors. They had to pay tribute and perform labor duty but did not pay many other taxes. In the eighteenth century, when the Crown established a standing military, Indians for the most part were not required to serve.

The Crown created uniform institutions to rule Mesoamerican Indians, effectively reconfiguring existing institutions to suit colonial purposes, most importantly the political structure of Indian communities that were ruled by indigenous elites. Central Mexico's densely settled Indian populations initially attracted the Spanish conquerors, but Spaniards' quest for further conquests and precious metals soon took them to northern Mexico. Finding silver in the north they devised new means of bringing the fierce Indians of the region under control (Chapter 9), while expansion of the Northern frontier brought further integration of indigenous people (Chapter 16).

The presence or absence of dense Indian populations and of sources of material wealth directly shaped patterns of Spanish settlement. Spaniards' aversion to living in Indian towns meant that those communities resisted change. As long as Indians remained in their home communities rather than migrating to Spanish cities or mines or taking up residence on Spanish rural estates as permanent workers, they could maintain their indigenous traditions. Indians in cities and on haciendas were more likely to assimilate to Hispanic culture and abandon elements of traditional culture, becoming Hispanized Indians or *ladinos*. Indian towns, therefore, played a crucial role in maintaining indigenous culture, while colonial officials saw them as the key to establishing control over the huge native populations of central and southern Mexico.

Most of Mexico's Indians complied with Spanish demands for labor and taxes, obeyed civil authorities, and accepted Christianity. They were not, however, passive objects of Spanish rule but rather active agents in shaping their own history. Despite their subordinate position in the colonial order, their traditional structures provided a vital framework in which to pursue their own interests.

Mesoamerican Communities under Spanish Rule

The Role of the Indigenous Elite. The key to Spanish rule in Mexico was to establish control over Indian elites, allowing them to maintain their existing positions as community authorities as long as they were loyal to the Crown. The process began with the Spanish conquest. In the immediate aftermath of conquest most Indian polities were given in encomienda to Spanish conquerors. Encomienda grants came to be defined as particular Indian towns with outlying settlements under their existing rulers. By using indigenous rulers as middlemen to collect tribute from and organize the labor of their subjects, encomenderos built up private fortunes for themselves while leaving indigenous structures largely intact. Indigenous rulers retained their privileges, such as having dependent laborers and receiving tribute. With the notable exception of Morelos and Oaxaca, held by Hernando Cortés, in many regions neighboring Indian towns might have different encomenderos, initiating the fragmentation of preconquest political units, a process that continued in different forms throughout the colonial era.

In the first fifty years after the conquest as Mesoamerican rulers and their communities became integrated into colonial institutions, they underwent external transformations while internal structures often continued relatively unchanged and barely perceived by Spaniards. Mesoamerican city-states were reborn as cities, towns, and villages of the Spanish empire. Under colonial rule, Nahua *altepetl*, Maya *cah*, and Mixtec *ñuu* became seats of local government, known in Spanish as *cabeceras* or "head towns." Outlying villages of prehispanic political units, now called *sujetos*, "subject settlements," at first usually remained under the jurisdiction of their old rulers, who were renamed *caciques*, the Taino word for chief that Spaniards used for native rulers throughout their American empire.

Some Indian communities experienced change even before the Crown began to restructure them formally in the mid-1500s. The institution of encomienda affected indigenous entities by detaching many outlying hamlets from their original indigenous communities, especially when more geographically compact units could be created. The process of fragmentation of larger native political units essentially began with the conquest and destruction of the Aztec Empire and would never be reversed in central Mexico. In the later colonial period fragmentation progressed even further as sujetos sought autonomy from their cabeceras, petitioning to become head towns with their own rulers, town councils, and churches. From the Spanish point of view, the fate of indigenous political units mattered less as encomiendas decreased in importance. In the early years after the conquest, however, maintaining indigenous units was important to the establishment of colonial rule.

From the earliest years of the colony Mesoamerican indigenous rulers and their communities pursued their own interests. Indigenous rulers essentially were coopted into the emerging colonial power structure, allowed to retain their privileged positions as long as they acquiesced to Spanish rule. Caciques acted in the interests of their communities within the constraints of their relationship with colonial rulers. They argued for the reduction of their subjects' tribute and labor obligations, particularly in the wake of sixteenth-century epidemics, and led their communities in using Spanish courts to litigate against both Spanish landowners and other Indian communities. Having this avenue for resolving disputes may well have provided a legal outlet for Indian frustrations and resentments that otherwise might have taken more violent form.

Indian nobles adopted some of the markers of high status in Spanish society, using high-sounding Spanish names instead of (or in addition to) important indigenous titles. They used the Spanish honorifics *don* and *doña*, and men in particular dressed in the fashion of Spanish nobles. Many Indian noblemen received exemptions from the ban on Indians' carrying arms and riding horses that Spaniards had imposed because of their fear of armed Indian rebellions. Caciques also created entailed estates called *cacicazgos* on the pattern of Spanish entailments (*mayorazgos*). Cacicazgo lands intended to support the position of the ruler often became the private holdings of the cacique.

Figure 7-1 **Genealogy of the House of Moctezuma**. The Spanish crown recognized Indian noble families as elites with special privileges. Prehispanic nobles are shown in their proper elite regalia, while their colonial descendants wear high status clothing of the new order.
Courtesy of Archivo General de la Nación, Fondo Hermanos Mayo, Concentrados, sobre 363.

Not only caciques but also Indian noblemen maintained their status in the colonial period, forming a ruling group known in Spanish as the *principales*, "principal people." They served as the officials of the new local government that the Crown imposed on Indian communities. Some Indian nobles were in fact mestizos, of mixed Spanish-Indian ancestry, but culturally they were Indians who enjoyed high standing in their communities. The sixteenth-century historians Diego Muñoz Camargo of Tlaxcala and Fernando de Alva Ixtlilxochitl and Juan Bautista de Pomar of Texcoco are prominent examples of such individuals. In the seventeenth century, noblemen of pure Indian ancestry sought to exclude their mestizo rivals from town councils, charging that their opponents' mixed heritage disqualified them from holding office.

Local Government. Because so many encomiendas were distributed in the immediate postconquest period, initially there was no central administrative control over Mexico's Indians. The Crown, however, soon began to counter the encomenderos' unchecked authority over the Indians by establishing administrative districts called corregimientos. At the same time, Indian local government was restructured on the model of Spanish municipalities. The indigenous ruler of a given town became the governor (*gober-*

nador), and each town had an elected town council or *cabildo*. All candidates for office as well as the electorate belonged to the local elite, the *principales*. The main officials of the town council had the same titles and general functions as their Spanish counterparts, with judges (*alcaldes*), town councilors (*regidores*), and an appointed notary (*escribano*) who recorded the proceedings of council meetings. Lower-level officials of town government often had indigenous titles that lacked any equivalent in Spanish civil government.

Indian noblemen serving as town officials received salaries drawn from local taxes collected and deposited in the community treasury (*caja de comunidad* or community chest), a box secured by several locks. The governor earned the highest salary. Local treasury funds also supported community affairs such as fiestas. Spanish officials complained that noblemen squandered the money, but Spanish judge Alonso de Zorita asserted in the late sixteenth century that if the cabildo did not support the fiestas, their communities would "neither hold them in esteem nor obey them."[1]

Studies of Indian town councils in different parts of Mesoamerica indicate that they functioned in fairly uniform fashion, becoming the primary institution for protecting the interests of their communities, litigating in Spanish courts and petitioning the Crown directly for redress of grievances. At the same time, however, the councils played a key role in maintaining Spanish rule over the countryside, mobilizing the organization of labor and collection of tribute in their communities. Thus, Indian nobles and Spanish officials collaborated in exercising control over Indian commoners.

Record keeping. Because Spanish colonial officials were concerned about orderly rule and brought Indians directly into the process of maintaining it, they promoted the use of indigenous languages in official records, such as petitions to the Crown, court testimony, legal descriptions of property transfers, and the like. As a result, Mesoamerican Indians themselves generated considerable documentation in their own languages, written in Latin letters, virtually all of it official in nature. Spaniards initially trained Indian scribes, but literacy soon became a self-replicating tradition in Mesoamerican towns, with one scribe teaching another. A small number of Indian noblemen also became literate.

Records in Mesoamerican languages written in Latin letters appeared very early after the conquest and were maintained until independence in the early nineteenth century. The earliest known documentation in Nahuatl is a set of house-to-house censuses of Hernando Cortés's encomienda towns around Cuernavaca, recorded in the 1530s. These censuses provide considerable information on Nahua family structure, land holding, tribute obligations, and the numbers of people who had been baptized. Native language documentation also exists for other parts of Mesoamerica, particularly the Mixtec and Zapotec areas of Oaxaca and Maya regions of Chiapas, Yucatan,

---

[1]Quoted in Gibson, *Aztecs Under Spanish Rule*, p. 187.

and Guatemala. Many native language documents were prepared for the internal use of indigenous communities, while others found their way into the records of Spanish courts in Mexico and official agencies in Spain.

The Religious Hierarchy. While the political structures of Indian towns were gradually modified in the mid-1500s, the indigenous religious hierarchy felt the immediate impact of Spanish rule. The Spaniards intended to replace indigenous religions with Christianity. Indian priests of the old religion, considered by Spaniards to be among the leading idolaters, were stripped of their status and functions. Spanish friars and priests knew, however, that the active participation of the Indian elite in Christian religious life was crucial to converting their communities, so they had admit Indians to the local religious hierarchy in some fashion. Indian noblemen by design often became the first converts in their communities.

The *fiscal* was the highest Indian religious official in Indian towns, assisting Spanish religious personnel in ritual, organizing community religious celebrations, and overseeing Indian officials who dealt with the day-to-day running of the church. As with the political hierarchy, the religious hierarchy consisted of principales who often alternated between civil and religious offices. The principales helped to oversee religious celebrations such as fiestas dedicated to the town's patron saint, paid for by funds from the *caja de comunidad*. Religion played an important role in reinforcing hierarchy and obedience to authority as well as forging and maintaining community ties.

Resettlement and Migration. Loss of population threatened the viability of many Indian communities as settlements and centers of Christian worship. After the disastrous experience in the Caribbean, where nearly the entire population disappeared within a generation, royal officials hoped to stabilize Mexico's population. They tried to do so through the institution of *congregación*, by which officials attempted to nucleate and resettle Indians in units suitable for evangelization and exploitation of labor. In some cases, congregación merely provided optimal conditions for the rapid spread of disease. Mesoamericans often were reluctant to move away from their home communities and their fields.

In the northwest, particularly Sonora and Sinaloa, Jesuits moved Indians to new settlements called *reducciones*, consolidating traditionally dispersed populations as well as those affected by epidemics and population loss. Spaniards also settled Nahuatl-speaking Tlaxcalans from central Mexico in colonies that thrived in the north. Tlaxcalans served as role models for migratory peoples that were learning to live in settled communities and to cultivate crops.

At the other end of the cultural continuum were Indians who lived in Spanish cities and learned Hispanic ways. Mexico City continued to have a significant indigenous population. The original Nahua city-states of Tenochtitlan and Tlatelolco became cabeceras that exercised jurisdiction over their indigenous residents until nearly the end of the colonial era.

Although there was some separation of Indian and Spanish neighborhoods in Mexico City and other Spanish cities, government measures to enforce strict residential segregation were ineffective. The capital, like most other Spanish cities in Mexico, had a growing racially diverse and residentially mixed population.

In 1560 the Indian population of Mexico City was estimated at eighty thousand. The majority were Nahuas, although there were also Mixtecs and Zapotecs from Oaxaca, Purepechas (Tarascans) from Michoacan, and Chichimecas from the north. Although Nahuas in Mexico City experienced the greatest impact of Spanish culture, the continued existence of indigenous local government with jurisdiction over the capital's Indian residents indicates that Spaniards continued to practice indirect rule, even within the viceregal capital itself.

Indians and the Judicial System. Indians over time proved to be tenacious litigants in Spanish courts. They acted not only as representatives of their corporate communities but also became involved in private lawsuits with other Indians and Spaniards as well. Initially there was no inexpensive, speedy, and effective legal process available to Indians. Under Don Antonio de Mendoza (1535–50), the office of viceroy offered redress for Indians' legal complaints. By the late sixteenth century, Indian communities in central Mexico were experiencing considerable strain as the result of population loss and Spanish exploitation of their labor and acquisition of their land, and the viceroy was unable to afford them sufficient protection. To rectify these problems a new legal institution for Indians was established in 1592.

The General Indian Court was a remarkable institution that, until it was disbanded in 1820, exercised first-instance jurisdiction over lawsuits brought by Indians against other Indians and by Spaniards against Indians. Although in principle suits brought by Indians against Spaniards did not fall within the jurisdiction of the General Indian Court, in fact the court dealt with them. Indians brought cases against Spaniards for illegally requiring personal services or excess tribute and for interfering in Indian municipal elections. They lodged complaints against priests for extortion and other abuses and against non-Indians for taking up residence in Indian towns. Indians litigated with Spaniards and other Indians over rights to water and productive land and disputed boundaries.

Funded by a portion of tribute payments, the purpose of the General Indian Court was to protect Indians by facilitating access to the judicial system. The General Indian Court maintained a corps of lawyers whose legal services were available to Indians at reduced fees or gratis. Effective legal assistance, coupled with the Indians' awareness that Spanish courts could provide them legal redress, unleashed two centuries of Indian litigation. Although Indians by no means always won the suits they brought against Spaniards, they must have experienced sufficient success that they

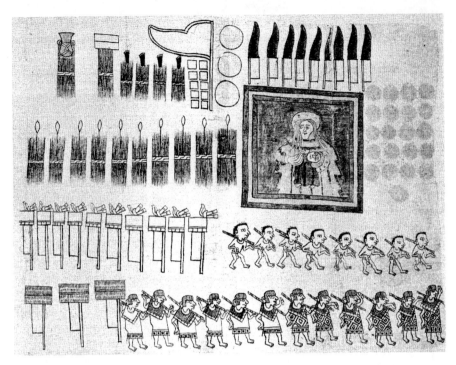

Figure 7-2 **Tribute obligations, Huejotzinco 1531**. Native lords and commoners are shown with Huejotzinco's tribute and the banner of the Madonna and Child that the town made for Nuño de Guzmán's Pánuco campaign. This document was part of a legal case against the First Audiencia for its abuse of Indians.
Courtesy of Library of Congress, Manuscripts Division.

continued to use the courts. The bulk of Indians' legal complaints were economic in nature, dealing with property ownership and taxation. Although Indians framed their legal arguments in terms derived from the Spanish legal system, they also often referred to rights and privileges held "from time immemorial" and advanced arguments based on indigenous legal principles.

Mesoamericans and the Colonial Economy

Labor. Spanish encomenderos relied on Indian lords to mobilize their communities to deliver tribute goods and provide labor. As more Spaniards began to arrive in New Spain and lobby for greater access to Indian labor, the Crown saw an opportunity to undermine the encomendero monopoly on labor by providing the access these newcomers demanded. A new system of labor allotment called *repartimiento* was instituted, still requiring Indians to provide service but now to an expanded group of Spaniards who became eligible for temporary grants of labor. Both Spaniards and Indian lords benefited from the traditional arrangements for taxing commoners and exploiting their labor. For commoners, however, the context in which they provided these services had changed considerably from preconquest times. According to historian Charles Gibson "a major change under Spanish rule was that Indian peoples lost the sense of joyous participation and adopted an attitude of resignation."[2]

Indian labor played a key role in public works in central Mexico. The choice to build the new Spanish capital on the island site of Tenochtitlan meant that seasonal flooding would be a constant problem. In 1555, royal officials ordered thousands of Indians to build dikes, reroute waterways, and implement other emergency measures to stem flooding and prevent its recurrence. Preservation of the viceregal capital from flooding diverted Indian labor from subsistence farming or Spanish agricultural enterprises. Until the late 1770s, long after other types of forced service had been discontinued, the *Desagüe*, or drainage project, continued to require that Indian towns increasingly distant from the Spanish capital furnish manpower.

Indians not only supplied labor for public works but also formed a significant portion of Mexico's artisan population, especially in the capital. At first there was competition between Spanish and nascent Indian artisan guilds, but Spaniards incorporated the latter into their guilds, preventing individual Spaniards from hiring independent Indian artisans. Most colonial guilds were multiracial, recognizing the Indians' skills.

Landholding. Most Mesoamerican Indians lived in the countryside. Indian landholding underwent major shifts in central Mexico as Spaniards acquired land in regions already settled by Indian farmers, whose numbers had been reduced by epidemics. The dramatic drop in the indigenous population during the sixteenth century meant that their communities needed less land. At the same time, more Spaniards were arriving in New Spain and acquiring rural properties where previously only Indians lived and worked.

After the conquest as the market for European staples expanded, Spaniards began acquiring land for wheat production and cattle and sheep ranching, the basis for the agrarian economy in much of Spain. Spanish notions of private ownership of land affected indigenous landholding patterns in Mesoamerica. In many cases caciques and other indigenous elites, including noblewomen, profited from the sale of community land to Spaniards, although some Indians resisted this practice. Spaniards sometimes simply usurped lands. Once these properties left Indian hands, they usually were gone for good. In some cases, however, Indian communities rented land to Spaniards, thus retaining title while earning an income from unused land.

[2]Gibson, *The Aztecs under Spanish Rule*, p. 220.

In the prehispanic period, corporate groups in Mesoamerica held land collectively, although individual families usually worked particular plots of land, producing enough food to feed their households as well as to pay tribute. At least in some places land was retained as long as it was worked. If land was not cultivated, it was reassigned to landless Indians or those needing larger fields. By the end of the sixteenth century, central Mexican Indians treated their fields as if they were private property that could be sold or bequeathed to heirs.

If Indian landholding patterns of the late sixteenth century are an indication of the patterns that obtained earlier in the century, Mesoamericans held scattered plots of land, often with differing agricultural potential (the Spanish pattern of landholding coincidentally was quite similar). Last wills and testaments in Nahuatl and Mayan indicate that individual men and women bequeathed their scattered fields to a variety of relatives. Nahua women's possession of significant amounts of land in the late sixteenth century may have been the result of the abundance of land after the huge population loss. When the numbers of Indians began rising in the seventeenth century, the resulting shortage of available land forced many people to migrate to towns or go to work on Spanish estates.

In the late seventeenth century, in an attempt to ensure adequate amounts of land and water for Indian villages, the Crown established a minimum endowment for Indian communities of six hundred *varas* of land called the *fundo legal*, opening the door to a new wave of lawsuits. Most suits occurred between Indian communities that competed acrimoniously over dwindling resources, but a significant number were brought against Spaniards, as by 1700 the growth of Spanish haciendas had reduced Indian landholding considerably. Indians were able to use the resources of the General Indian Court or administrative authorities outside the Court's jurisdiction to pursue their cases, as claims based on the fundo legal overrode other property rights.

In the seventeenth century the Crown sought to regularize land titles in a process called *composición*. Such a move especially threatened Indian communities that could not produce written titles to land. Starting around 1650 many Nahua communities created documentation in the form of "primordial titles" or *títulos* purporting to prove ownership from "time immemorial." These municipal histories written in Nahuatl usually included a history of the community that sometimes went back to the preconquest period. Whether or not primordial titles are historically accurate, they are an important source for writing Indian history.

For those areas of Mesoamerica where indigenous communities lacked a strong institutional presence and did not litigate regularly in Spanish courts, historians can only sketch out Indian history. Large swaths of western Mexico and the Gulf Coast region had significant Indian populations, but in these areas it is difficult to separate Indians from the larger category of peasants. Around Guadalajara, for example, many Indians worked on haciendas while others were small farmers and ranchers.

Economic Activities. In Oaxaca, which had settled Indian populations but no major mineral deposits, communities and caciques largely retained their lands. Through trade, however, the expansion of the colonial economy could affect even such remote regions. For royal district officials (the *alcaldes mayores* and corregidores) and merchants Oaxaca was a source of raw and woven cotton as well as cochineal. Spanish merchants traded food staples, alcohol, and religious ornaments as well as work animals such as mules and oxen for indigenous products, especially cochineal. There is some debate over the nature of the commercial relationship between Indians and Spaniards. According to many scholars, the terms of trade were far from fair, with merchants charging Indians excessive prices for goods often characterized as frivolous and unwanted, such as silk stockings, fur hats, and other useless items, and undervaluing indigenous products. The practice called *repartimiento de mercancías* ("distribution of merchandise") required Indians to produce goods by growing crops, collecting cochineal bugs, or weaving cotton in order to work off their debts to merchants for goods they did not necessarily want or need.

From another perspective, Indians acquired high value and useful items through credit that royal officials and merchants advanced at some risk. The repartimiento de mercancías allowed Spaniards to acquire products that they would not, or could not, produce themselves, while Indians gained access to desirable goods, such as mules and oxen. In this latter, revisionist view, the repartimiento de mercancías did not force Indians into unwanted arrangements on terms entirely unfavorable to them. Instead, theirs was an advantageous bargaining position, since they produced a valuable commodity, while for their part Spaniards incurred risk by providing high-value goods on credit without any real means to enforce debt repayment.

Although Mesoamericans labored on Spanish haciendas and in mines and were integrated into the colonial economy, Indians continued to produce goods for an almost exclusively indigenous market. These included woven cotton cloaks and other clothing, pots, baskets, and sleeping mats. Regional and local specialization in craft goods catering to Indian tastes has continued into the modern era. Goods produced by and for Indians were exempted from the colonial sales tax (*alcabala*) during the entire colonial period.

Indians also produced for the Spanish market and provided transportation for goods going to Spanish markets. They supplied Mexico City with fruits and vegetables grown on the chinampas in the freshwater area of Lake Texcoco by canoe, a trade that remained exclusively in native hands, as did the chinampas themselves. Xochimilco in particular retained its land and indigenous character, despite its proximity to the capital. Indians living in the northern, saline area of the central lake system supplied salt to consumers in the viceregal capital.

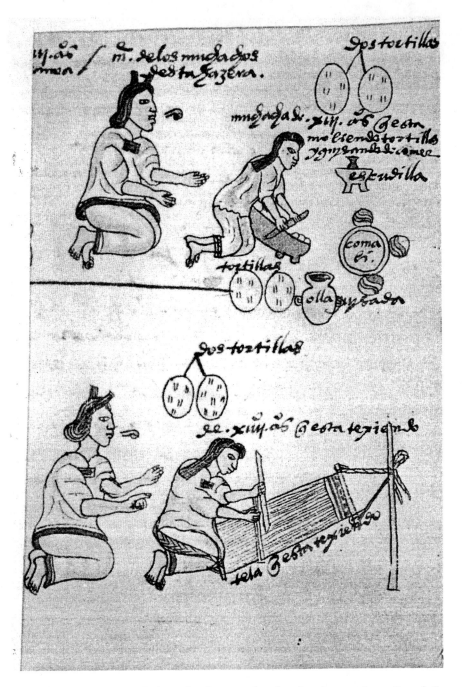

Figure 7-3 **Women's Work.** A mother instructs her daughter in weaving cotton cloth and grinding corn, tasks occupying Mesoamerican women for millennia up to the present era. Cloth was used for tribute payments in the early colonial period.
Permission granted by the Bodleian Library, University of Oxford, for reproduction of MS.Arch. Selden. A. 1, fol. 60r.

154

Indians also became full participants in small-scale trade, becoming muleteers (*arrieros*) and hauling goods locally or regionally. They traveled routes that were established in the prehispanic era but which over time shifted to link major Spanish settlements, especially the ports of Veracruz and Acapulco, with the capital. Indian towns along these routes felt the impact of the traffic of large numbers of mule trains and carts, which could be beneficial as in Tepetlaoztoc, where the Indian population prospered.

The colonial economy brought changes to indigenous economic life. Indians who were entirely dependent on subsistence agriculture fared worse in the new order, while those who filled niches valuable to the Spaniards did better.

Social and Cultural Change

Language Change. Scholars have used texts in Mesoamerican languages, especially Nahuatl in central Mexico, to chart cultural changes in Indian communities. The work of James Lockhart demonstrates that some standard patterns of language change correlated with larger cultural trends. Where Spaniards were few and Indian interactions with them infrequent, indigenous texts were largely unaffected by Spanish. In the immediate postconquest period (1519–45) in central Mexico, indigenous languages reflected few intrusions from the Spanish world. Some early native language documents include words from Spanish or Latin for religious concepts, as early friars in Mexico used nonnative words so that Indians would not confuse Christian concepts with those of their old religions.

A major shift occurred in the mid-1500s, when Indians began to adopt a large number of Spanish nouns, particularly names of objects. Indians used Spanish words for new European items such as tools (knives, saws, axes); clothing (pants, shirts, shoes, socks); household items (boxes, furniture); religious items (saints' images, crucifixes, candles, books); and animals (horses, mules, chickens). As Spaniards reshaped indigenous civil and religious institutions, native speakers began to use Spanish terms for officials. By the late 1500s, Nahuas understood the Spanish concept of marriage and were using Spanish terminology for it. A complex personal naming system developed with the use of Spanish noble titles for the indigenous nobility and Christian given names.

Yet another shift among Nahuatl-speakers seems to have occurred by around 1650, with the development of a bilingual Indian population. The structure of Indian languages changed, with grammar and syntax beginning to reflect influences from Spanish. Fewer texts in indigenous languages were produced in the 1700s. In 1770, the Crown issued an edict ending support for indigenous languages, making linguistic processes beyond that date difficult to trace.

Religious Life. By the end of the sixteenth century, Spaniards' effort to convert Mesoamericans to Christianity resulted in the outward transformation of religious practices and a complicated blending of old beliefs with Christianity. Local religion revolved around the Christian calendar of worship, with celebrations of patron saints' days and high religious occasions. Each Indian town as well as each separate barrio had patron saints, drawing Indian men, women, and children into celebrations that reaffirmed both personal faith and a sense of identification with the community. Indian towns had at least one central place of worship, within which residential wards often maintained their own chapels. Churches featured works of art that might be imported from Europe as well as an organ and choir of singers, all supported by a group of faithful who saw to the church building's upkeep. In many ways the church building became the community's symbol, its size and opulence seen as a reflection of the community's wealth and religious commitment.

In Mesoamerica, the Spanish clergy encouraged the creation of confraternities. There is evidence that among the Nahuas women elders held office in at least one confraternity. In many parts of Mesoamerica, confraternities controlled a considerable amount of land, with revenues from crops or herds supporting the organizations' activities. Members worked on lands that they considered to belong to the saints, perhaps restoring a sacred component to labor that had been lost after the conquest.

The importance of the saints in religious life, at the community and barrio level as patrons and for individuals as intercessors, cannot be overemphasized. This form of spiritual devotion has been called the cult of the saints. Most households had a family altar set in an honored place, usually tended by the women of the household, especially the elders. Most Mesoamerican households had several images of saints, both male and female, that formed the spiritual center of the household. Although at present we do not know when and how this form of devotion began, it almost certainly was encouraged by Catholic clergymen. Indians enthusiastically adopted this practice, perhaps initially as a substitute for the gods of the old religion. Spaniards had introduced the image of Santiago the Moorslayer and his horse, symbolizing their victory, after the conquest (see Figure 2-1). In the middle colonial period Santiago became the patron saint and protector of many Indian villages.

It is difficult to know what individual Mesoamericans believed in the realm of religion. Indians' last wills and testaments in indigenous languages do shed some light on religious devotions and beliefs. In the late sixteenth century, friars encouraged Indians to make final wills, usually (as was the custom among Spaniards also) on the verge of death. Indian notaries wrote the documents, which had formulaic invocations and standard closings. Some formulas were direct translations from Spanish testamentary language and part of a notary's standard repertoire, but others indicate that the testator shaped the language, with special invocations and requests.

Men and women left money for masses for the repose of their own souls and those of their loved ones. Most commonly, individual men and women ordered particular pieces of land or goods sold for masses. Following the practice of well-to-do Spaniards, a few Indian caciques established *capellanías*, endowed funds for perpetual masses. Inventories of Mesoamericans' property included in wills show that men and women owned religious objects of various kinds, such as saints' images, rosaries, and even religious books.

Nahuatl Testament of Angelina Mocel, 1581

Know all who see and read this document that I, Angelina Mocel, of the Culhuacan ward of Santa María Magdalena Tezcacoac, even though I am sick, nonetheless my spirit and soul are undisturbed. And I very truly believe in the Most Holy Trinity, Father, Son, and God the Holy Spirit, just one true God, omnipotent. I place my soul entirely in His hands because He made it and redeemed it with His precious blood. And when I die, let our Lord come to take my spirit and soul. And my body I give to the earth because from earth it came.

—First I declare that my late father Pablo de San Gabriel Huitznahuatl gave me the "woman's house" which faces east; it is to be sold when I die because I have no assets at all with which to be buried. And whatever money should be left of the proceeds from the house will be spent on me, for masses to be said for me. It will belong to me.

—And I give the second house, facing Xochimilco, to my nephew Juan Bautista with all the chinampas that accompany it. And there are seven chinampas in Acatzintitlan by the field of the late Fabián, stone mason. I assign them to my child Nicolás. If he lives, he is to take them. And if he dies, they are to be sold and with the proceeds masses will be said for us. . . .

Sarah Cline and Miguel Léon-Portilla, eds., *The Testaments of Culhuacan* (Los Angeles, 1984), Document 50.

Despite many indications of the successful establishment of Christianity among Mesoamericans, survival of old beliefs continued to concern clergymen. In 1629, the cleric Hernando Ruiz de Alarcón published a collection of Nahua incantations for physical healing that dealt not only with daily activities, such as hunting, sowing, and carrying heavy loads, but also with more occult concerns such as love magic, fortune telling, and spells. Clearly many Indians sought spiritual power and attempted to control many aspects of their lives through alternative means (as did people in Hispanic society as well).

Social Structure. The largest single change in Indian family and community life after the conquest was the massive loss of population from epidemic disease in the early sixteenth century. Since indigenous texts from this period are virtually nonexistent, it is impossible to understand the full impact of these losses. Certainly marriage, family, and kinship networks changed under the influence of the church. Indians in Mesoamerica embraced the Christian institution of godparenthood (*compadrazgo*). Godparents could and did become surrogate parents for orphaned children.

Priests imposed the Christian concept of marriage—a lifelong union with a single spouse—on elite men who were accustomed to taking several wives if they could afford to support them. Once baptism of Mesoamericans had been completed by the second half of the sixteenth century, friars could make more concerted efforts to extirpate the old polygamous marriage practices. In some regions, such as rural Tlaxcala, they have continued clandestinely up until the present. Divorce, which had been a feature of most Mesoamerican societies, no longer was possible under church law except in rare instances. In practice, however, the abandonment of families and formation of common-law unions endowed the system with a degree of flexibility. Spanish terminology for marriage appears in Nahuatl records of the mid 1500s, but it was only a century later that Nahuatl kinship terms for brother and sister, cousins, nieces and nephews, and in-laws conformed to Spanish usage. Nahua inheritance patterns traced through last wills and testaments show that children and grandchildren became the preferred heirs, possibly replacing an older tradition in which testators included brothers and sisters, nieces and nephews among their heirs.

Divisions between the Indian nobility and commoners continued to exist throughout the colonial period, but many elite families in central Mexico became impoverished. By the end of the colonial era the economic circumstances of many nobles might have differed little from those of the common folk. According to William B. Taylor, caciques in Oaxaca retained significant personal wealth although their communities were often impoverished. Although Mesoamericans maintained many basic features of their social structure throughout the colonial period, they also were becoming integrated into wider social and economic networks. Indigenous corporate communities were far from closed. The fewer Spaniards that lived in a given area, the greater was the likelihood that Indian communities would maintain the old ways.

Mesoamericans predominantly lived in the countryside, but the growth of Spanish haciendas meant that many Indians sought work on estates and abandoned their communities. Others migrated to the capital or provincial cities in search of opportunities, living in Indian neighborhoods where they maintained their indigenous identity to a varying degree.

Glossary

altepetl   Nahua city-state
alcalde   judge, member of the city council
cabecera   head town

cacicazgo   entailed estate of a cacique
cah   Maya community
caja de comunidad   community chest or treasury
composición   regularization of land title
Desagüe   central lake drainage project
escribano   notary
fiscal   highest ranking Indian religious official
fundo legal   Indian towns' endowment of land
gobernador   governor, Indian ruler
ladino   Hispanized Indian
ñnu   Mixtec community
principales   Indian noblemen
repartimiento de mercancías   distribution of goods on credit by Spanish
   officials
república de indios legal category of Indians in Spanish law
regidor   city councilman
sujeto   hamlet, subject settlement
títulos   indigenous municipal histories often dealing with land

Questions for Discussion

1. Why were Mesoamerican Indians relatively easily integrated into Spanish colonial rule?

2. What role did the Indian town play in maintaining indigenous culture?

3. How did the Crown protect Indians during the colonial era?

4. How were Spanish political, religious and social structures imposed on Indian communities?

5. How does the will of Angelina Mocel reflect her religious beliefs?

6. What factors undermined indigenous culture?

Suggested Reading

Primary Sources

Anderson, Arthur J. O. and Susan Schroeder, eds. *Codex Chimalpahin*. 2 vols. Norman: University of Oklahoma Press, 1997. Transcription and translation from the writings of the seventeenth-century Nahua annalist.
Cline, Sarah, ed. *The Book of Tributes: Early Nahuatl Censuses from Morelos.* Los Angeles: UCLA Latin American Center Publications, 1993.

Transcription, translation, and analysis of a volume of the 1535 Cuernavaca censuses.

Cline, Sarah and Miguel León-Portilla, eds. *The Testaments of Culhuacan*. Los Angeles: UCLA Latin American Center Publications, 1984. Transcription and translation of the largest group of wills in Nahuatl known to exist for a single town, drawn up largely between 1579–81.

Lockhart, James, Frances Berdan, and Arthur J. O. Anderson. *The Tlaxcalan Actas, A Compendium of the Records of the Cabildo of Tlaxcala (1545–1627)*. Salt Lake City: University of Utah Press, 1986. Transcription, translation, and analysis of the largest extant collection of town council records, particularly important because of Tlaxcala's prominence.

Restall, Matthew, ed. *Life and Death in a Maya Community: The Ixil Testaments of the 1760s*. Labyrinthos, 1995. Transcription and translation of a group of Maya testaments.

Ruiz de Alarcón, Hernando. *Treatise on the Heathen Superstitions that today live among the Indians Native to This New Spain, 1629*. Translated and edited by J. Richard Andrews and Ross Hassig. Norman: University of Oklahoma Press, 1984. Original Nahuatl texts and English translations of a major colonial text showing the persistence of indigenous religious beliefs and practices in the seventeenth century.

Secondary Sources

Baskes, Jeremy. *Indians, Merchants, and Markets: A Reinterpretation of the Repartimiento and Spanish–Indian Economic Relations in Colonial Oaxaca, 1750–1821*. Stanford: Stanford University Press, 2000. Revisionist examination of the *repartimiento de mercancías*.

Borah, Woodrow W. *Justice by Insurance: The General Indian Court: Colonial Mexico and the Legal Aides of the Half-Real*. Berkeley and Los Angeles: University of California Press, 1983. Prize-winning examination of a key colonial institution aiding Indians.

Chance, John. *Conquest of the Sierra: Spaniards and Indians in Colonial Oaxaca*. Norman: University of Oklahoma Press, 1989. Examination of a remote region of Oaxaca that became a major cochineal producing area.

Cline, Sarah. *Colonial Culhuacan, 1580–1600: A Social History of an Aztec Town*. Albuquerque: University of New Mexico Press, 1986. Analysis of the *Testaments of Culhuacan*, particularly focusing on continuities and changes in a single Nahua community, with extensive material on Nahua women.

Farriss, Nancy. *The Maya under Colonial Rule*. Stanford: Stanford University Press, 1984. Important study of the Yucatec Maya, particularly focusing on native communities.

Gibson, Charles. *The Aztecs Under Spanish Rule*. Stanford: Stanford University Press, 1964. Monumental and classic study of the colonial Nahuas, based on Spanish and native sources.

————. *Tlaxcala in the Sixteenth Century*. New Haven, Conn.: Yale University Press, 1952. Path-breaking examination of the early colonial history of Spain's most important ally in the conquest.

Haskett, Robert. *Indigenous Rulers*. Albuquerque: University of New Mexico Press, 1989. A study focusing on internal politics of indigenous communities of the Cuernavaca region.

Horn, Rebecca. *Postconquest Coyoacan: Nahua-Spanish Relations in Central Mexico, 1519–1650*. Stanford: Stanford University Press, 1997. Useful regional study showing ways that Spaniards and Nahuas interacted in a community contiguous to the capital.

Kellogg, Susan. *Law and the Transformation of Aztec Culture, 1500–1700*. Norman: University of Oklahoma Press, 1995. Examination of Nahua culture based on early Mexico City legal cases.

Lockhart, James. *The Nahuas After the Conquest*. Stanford: Stanford University Press, 1992. Monumental study of the major indigenous group of central Mexico by a premier Nahuatl scholar.

Restall, Matthew. *The Maya World: Yucatec Culture and Society, 1550–1850*. Stanford: Stanford University Press, 1977. Important study of the colonial Maya, based on native language sources.

Robertson, Donald. *Mexican Manuscript Painting in the Early Colonial Period*. New Haven, Conn.: Yale University Press, 1959. Classic study of Mexican codices by a major art historian.

Schroeder, Susan. "Jesuits, Nahuas, and the Good Death Society in Mexico City, 1710–1767," *Hispanic American Historical Review* 80:1 (2000), 43–76. Fascinating study of a Nahua confraternity, placing it in its larger cultural context.

Schroeder, Susan, Stephanie Wood, and Robert Haskett, eds. *Indian Women of Early Mexico*. Norman: University of Oklahoma Press, 1997. Important collection of essays on Nahua women, including an especially significant one on Malinche.

Taylor, William B. *Landlord and Peasant in Colonial Oaxaca*. Stanford: Stanford University Press, 1970. Major regional study that revised the view of a uniform domination of Spanish haciendas in the countryside.

Terraciano, Kevin. "The Colonial Mixtec Community," *Hispanic American Historical Review* 80:1 (2000), 1–42. Overview of the largest indigenous group in Oaxaca, based entirely on Mixtec language sources.

Wood, Stephanie. "The Cosmic Conquest: Late-Colonial Views of the Sword and Cross in Central Mexican *Títulos*," *Ethnohistory* 38:2 (Spring 1991), 176–95. Intriguing examination of some Nahua communities' construction of the Spanish military and spiritual conquests.

Eight

Economy and Society
in the Middle Period

By the end of the sixteenth century, a range of demographic, economic, religious and political forces had transformed Mexico in significant ways. Epidemic disease had reduced indigenous populations drastically while the Spanish presence had expanded substantially. Large numbers of African slaves also had arrived. A governmental and administrative framework, extending from the viceregal court in Mexico City to the Audiencias of Mexico City, Guadalajara (Nueva Galicia), and Guatemala to provincial governors, town councils, and other local officials had been established for New Spain, paralleled by an ecclesiastical organization that also encompassed both city and countryside. Some of the primary features of the decades following the conquest, most notably the dominance of the encomienda, proved transitional in face of the rapid growth of the economy and of Spanish society. Nonetheless most of the enduring features of colonial life originated in the immediate postconquest period. The first thirty years following the conquest saw development of an economy based on wealth derived from mining, which in turn fueled transatlantic (and later transpacific) trade; of commercialized agriculture and large scale stockraising; and of Spanish cities that acted as the headquarters for administrative and ecclesiastical institutions and for economic enterprises that drew on the natural and human resources of the countryside.

Over time, the basic patterns that took hold in the postconquest period would be modified and elaborated. In most places encomenderos lost their claim to Indian labor in the mid-sixteenth century, and they came to share their position as the most powerful economic group with other wealthy landowners, miners, and even merchants. Mining shifted from gold to silver and became much more important, heralding a significant reorientation of the economy of central Mexico toward the north beyond the limits of sedentary Indian settlement and giving rise to new towns. Stock raising gradually shifted north as more and more land in the central valleys came under cultivation. Successful merchants made Mexico City, rather than Seville, their main headquarters. While the economic and institutional dominance of Mexico City was not challenged, regional development (in the west, near north, and far south) fostered increasing socioeconomic diversity and breadth. This chapter examines the growth and elaboration of the Spanish economy, focusing mainly on the period from the late sixteenth century through the seventeenth.

The Agrarian Sector

Landholding. Spaniards began to use and acquire land in the countryside from the time of the conquest. The grant of an encomienda did not include rights to land, and generally the sale of the products that an encomendero collected in tribute did not yield a sufficiently substantial income to sustain the European lifestyle to which he aspired. Most encomenderos tried to supplement their income by investing in private enterprises that used the labor of their encomienda Indians. They established farms and ranches, often close to where their encomiendas were located, allowing them to use Indian labor to grow Spanish crops for the urban market.

Given the concentration of Spanish population and hence of the domestic market for agricultural products, not surprisingly Spaniards tended first to take over available land near urban centers. The rate of creation of Spanish farms and ranches, and the amount of land Spanish settlers acquired, varied greatly from one area to another. Where Indian populations were densest, the existence of the landholdings of indigenous communities slowed Spanish land acquisition. The great decline in indigenous population, together with environmental devastation that resulted from the introduction of European livestock, meant that over time in many places more land became available. Some areas, such as parts of the Bajío and the valley of Puebla, had been sparsely populated at the time of the conquest, leaving land open for exploitation by Spaniards. As Spaniards spread into the north, the lack of sedentary Indian population and aridity of the land allowed much of it to be accumulated in the hands of relatively few individuals. Even where indigenous populations were dense, Spaniards nonetheless could claim land that was marginal or unsuitable for indigenous agriculture and use it for stock raising. Although Spaniards for the most part took over unoccupied lands, Indian communities still could experience substantial disruption and loss of property, especially those located closest to the centers of Spanish society.

Encomenderos and officials were by no means the only Spaniards who sought land grants after the conquest, although of course they figured prominently in the early landholding group. On settling in a city, a new *vecino* could petition the municipal council not only for an urban lot on which to construct a house but also for a grant of land in the countryside. Puebla de los Angeles, which was expressly founded in order to create an urban center for Spanish farmers who did not hold encomiendas, attracted a number of settlers who

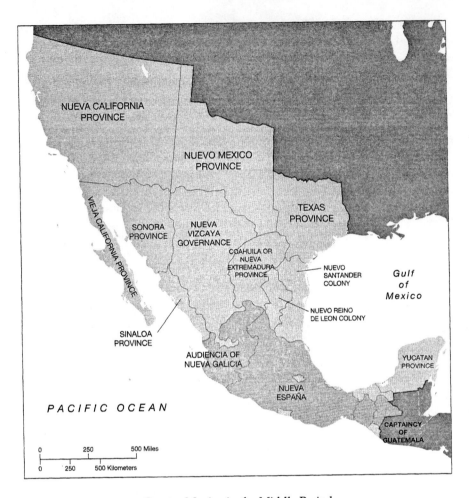

Greater Mexico in the Middle Period

were interested in acquiring land grants in the nearby fertile and temperate valley of Atlixco. Because there was relatively little competition for land as such in the years following the conquest, Spaniards easily acquired farms and ranches throughout New Spain. Through a combination of grants, purchases, and transfers and exchanges of land, some people built up substantial estates that today are usually called *haciendas*. Many Spaniards and other members of Hispanic society, however, continued to hold small or medium-sized farms and ranches (*ranchos* or *estancias*).

Because of the haphazard, sometimes illegal, way that Spaniards occupied lands, the often rapid turnover in ownership as land was bought, sold, and traded, and laws meant to protect Indian communities from the loss of their traditional landholdings, royal authorities eventually required landholders to verify and confirm their titles to land. This process was known as composición. For the most part, if landowners demonstrated that they were using the land and paid the generally modest fees required to clear their titles, they could retain the properties. This could be true even when they lacked title and were squatting, unless someone contested their rights to ownership. The composición process, then, helped landowners consolidate their claims on land to which they previously may not have had any legal right. Indian communities also generated records to assert their primordial claims to land.

By the end of the sixteenth century, the Mexican countryside had become a patchwork of Spanish farms, ranches and mixed estates of varying size interspersed with lands held by Indian communities, including the sometimes sizable estates of Indian rulers and nobles. Some of the latter devoted their holdings to Spanish-type agricultural enterprises, such as cultivating wheat or raising pigs. Access to land was only one of the crucial determinants in the development of estates; the availability of labor and water were equally critical. The location of markets and climatic factors also helped to determine what could be produced profitably and where. The distribution of estates in Yucatan reflects some of these variables. Large estates were located mainly near Mérida and the port of Campeche, with fewer near the interior, smaller city of Valladolid. After 1650 the estates around Mérida occupied an area that extended in a radius of twenty or thirty miles around the city, and estates also developed along the axis from Mérida to Campeche. With the rapid growth of Campeche after the mid-seventeenth century estates near the port began to produce maize to supply the urban population.

Agriculture. Spanish agriculture developed rapidly in New Spain. Wheat, fruit trees, sugar cane, and mulberries for silk cultivation all grew well in various parts of Mexico, and cattle, horses, sheep, goats, and pigs proliferated rapidly. The Spaniards' great success in establishing farming and stock raising meant that flourishing local and regional economies took hold almost from the start, as farms and ranches provided food, wool and leather for consumers and artisans in the towns and the mining centers.

Parallel to this economy that hinged on Spanish agriculture, an indigenous economy continued to thrive. At some points the two economies intersected. Spaniards eventually raised maguey plants, the source of the popular alcoholic beverage called *pulque*, on their commercial estates. Indians in central and southern Mexico produced the highly valued red dye, cochineal, derived from insects that lived on a particular kind of cactus plant, the nopal. Spaniards used cochineal to dye the finer quality woolen cloth they manufactured or they exported it to Spain, hence they became active in the trade in the dye without entering directly into production.

The spread of silk cultivation in Mexico represents one of the more notable cases in which Indians adopted a Spanish-introduced product.

Cortés and other encomenderos were responsible for bringing Indians into participation in silk production, and Spanish farmers planted mulberry trees. In some cases, as in the Mixteca Alta, however, the impetus for involvement seems to have come from the Indians themselves, especially the caciques. Despite an early boom, by the late sixteenth century silk culture was in decline in Mexico, and the manufacture of silk cloth in the colony came to depend on the importation of raw Chinese silk that reached Mexico via the trade with the Philippines.

The Organization of Labor. Just as encomenderos had relied on *mayordomos* (managers or stewards) who managed the operations associated with their encomiendas, large landowners employed managers for their estates. These employees generally contracted their services for a year or two, receiving not only a salary but often some share in what was produced or possibly the right to graze some of their own stock on the estate's lands. Managers and administrators of estates might acquire their own, usually smaller, farms and ranches. Living outside the main Spanish cities, they formed part of a provincial Hispanic society that took shape within many of the leading Indian towns. In the late sixteenth century the Spanish residents of the Indian town of Toluca near Mexico City, for example, included people who owned small pig farms close to town or raised sheep or horses on nearby estancias. Small landholders thus might emulate at a very modest level the lifestyle of larger estate owners, maintaining residences in Indian towns while depending on their overseers, who in these enterprises might be blacks, mulattos, or even Indians, to manage their farms and ranches.

On larger estates such Hispanic, often ethnically mixed or nonwhite, employees performed the skilled or semiskilled and supervisory work, overseeing day-to-day operations. The numbers of these permanent, resident workers (who might include African slaves and Hispanized Indians) generally were fairly small. Unskilled, mostly Indian workers, often recruited and used on a temporary basis, might be much more numerous; Indian men formed the bulk of the labor force for Spanish agriculture throughout the colonial period. In central Mexico at least the increasing use of free wage labor for estates quickly undermined the draft labor system, which did not reliably supply workers. In 1632 the repartimiento for agriculture was abolished.

Whether Indians were drafted for estate labor or worked as wage earners, they mostly provided temporary labor for planting and harvesting, meaning that they generally continued to spend much of their time working their own lands. Their labor was crucial to estate operations, however. As Spanish landholdings expanded, the numbers of Indian workers and the amount of time they devoted to estate work increased as well. Even stock raising enterprises, which most of the year required a relatively small number of skilled and semiskilled workers—shepherds and cowboys—at certain times, such as sheep shearing, needed to supplement the permanent labor force with temporary workers.

The technology involved in sugar production meant that sugar plantations in some respects differed notably from other estates in their labor requirements. Although from the outset sugar plantations used encomienda and later repartimiento Indians, and even Indian slaves in the earliest years, the complex technology of sugar refining demanded workers trained in specialized tasks. The manufacture, use and maintenance of grinding mills, presses, and ovens and other necessary equipment such as copper cauldrons, skimming tools, and drying forms required workers familiar not only with the demanding tasks associated with the process of refining sugar itself but also with blacksmithing, carpentry, and pottery manufacture. Already by 1530 African slaves were being imported into Mexico for this purpose. While sugar estates did use Indian labor for the less skilled tasks associated with sugar production, they also relied on substantial numbers of African slaves. Thus, the levels of capital investment—in labor and equipment—required to establish and operate sugar plantations were much higher than for other agricultural estates.

Haciendas. The development of estates dedicated to cultivating wheat, maize, beans, fruits, and vegetables, or sugar, or to stock raising, or often to some mix of activities, fostered a growing Hispanic presence in the countryside. The core of an hacienda might include housing for the manager and permanent workers, a residence for the *hacendado* (estate owner) and his family, a chapel in which visiting clergy could perform mass, carpenter's and blacksmith's shops, and sheds for storing grain and tools. The hacendado visited his estates from time to time, and he and his family might spend part or even much of the year in residence.

The mix of activities typical of many haciendas—farming, stock raising, processing raw materials—usually served the dual purpose of supplying estate workers with basic food and other material needs as well as yielding a marketable surplus and supporting related enterprises. An estancia devoted to breeding cattle, for example, might include a tannery for treating leather or a shop for building carts that, together with the estate's oxen, formed the basis for a carting business. Sugar estates had complexes (called *ingenios*) for refining sugar, and wheat farms usually included gristmills.

Whereas agricultural estates did not necessarily have to be large to be profitable, stock raising operations often attained enormous proportions. The properties of Don Juan de Saavedra Guzmán in Soconusco in the south included twenty grazing sites and extensive farmland. On his hacienda he grazed a staggering two hundred thousand head of cattle as well as three thousand mares. The entire estate was worth 150,000 pesos. A landowner's properties typically were not contiguous. Don Juan López Mellado, for example, owned farmland as well as numerous ranches and pastures with sixty thousand sheep, valued altogether at 100,000 pesos, located near the towns of Tecamachalco, Nopaluca, Veracruz, Córdoba, and Medellín. It should be pointed out that both these characteristics of estates in New

Spain—the scattered pattern of landholding and the mixed nature of production—had precedents in Castile.

Given the tendency among Spaniards to diversify their economic interests, almost anyone could become a landowner. Convents, monasteries,
cathedral chapters, and individual clergymen all owned rural estates, as did
merchants, professionals, officials, miners, and textile manufacturers. Some
individuals did concentrate exclusively on farming or ranching. The Basque
immigrant Luis Eraso, for example, lived in the pueblo of Tecamachalco and
owned a number of sheep ranches, selling both meat and wool. He rented
cattle from the cacique of Tecamachalco and supplied sheep to the city of
Puebla. By 1600, Eraso owned more than ten thousand sheep and had rented
another twenty thousand head of cattle. Uneducated and illiterate, Eraso
became a wealthy man in Mexico, maintaining close ties with other compatriots from home and paying off the debts on the family homestead in the
Valley of Oiartzun in the Basque country.

Mining

The great majority of people in New Spain made their living directly or indirectly from agriculture. Although Mexico's mines employed many fewer
people than did the agrarian sector, the wealth that they produced had great
significance for the colonial economy. Given that many of the mines were
located in regions where aridity of climate or ruggedness of topography
sharply limited the possibilities for cultivating the soil, agricultural production in much of central, north-central, and western Mexico served in part to
supply the northern mines. The mines required not only a substantial workforce but also foodstuffs and livestock, especially mules, as well. They used
mules for hauling and to operate whims, the huge pulleys that carried ores
to the surface or drained water from mine shafts. Thus the needs of the
mines fostered a large scale of movement of goods and people from central
and western Mexico to the north. Domestically produced staples as well as
iron tools and equipment and mercury, imported from Spain, and other necessary factors of production, all had to be transported to the mines.

By extension, then, even though the mines employed a maximum of
perhaps fifteen thousand workers, the numbers of people involved in activities that directly and indirectly serviced the mining industry and its
employees—farming, stock breeding, trade, transport, making charcoal,
manufacturing woolen cloth—were far greater. Hence, not only was the
wealth of the silver mines the underpinning for long-distance trade across
the Atlantic and Pacific, it also helped to finance a range of activities that
formed the basis for New Spain's local and regional economy. Silver generated profits not just for miners but for others as well—merchants, specula-
tors—as it changed hands. Last, the Spanish Crown received wealth from the

mines in the form of taxes on mining production. Originally one-fifth, by the seventeenth century the Crown's share of mineral production generally had fallen to one-tenth. In addition, the Crown profited from its monopoly on the supply of mercury and collected a percentage of the silver minted in Mexico City.

The Development of Mining in New Spain. The earliest mining activities in New Spain focused on gold, found in small quantities in Oaxaca and Michoacan. Although profits were not great, probably the majority of early encomenderos invested in gold mining, using the tributes they collected to supply work gangs that mainly consisted of Indian slaves. By the late 1520s, Spaniards had begun to work some small silver mines, and gold declined in importance in the 1530s. Nonetheless, because silver ores often contain small amounts of gold, Mexican mines continued to produce some gold.

The discovery in 1534 of silver at Taxco, located southwest of Mexico City and known as a source of copper before the conquest, signaled the real beginning of silver mining as a significant enterprise in New Spain. With the opening in the 1530s and 1540s of mines—some of them substantial—merchants began to invest in mining, new technicians appeared on the scene, and capital investment increased. Spanish miners began to spend at least some of their time at the mines themselves rather than leaving operations in the hands of overseers, as they had done with the gold mines. After the opening of the mines at Taxco, small silver deposits were found elsewhere, and in the 1540s small silver mines were operating near Guadalajara in the west.

With Juan de Tolosa's discovery of major silver deposits well to the north in Zacatecas in 1547, mining reached another stage of development and importance. In subsequent years men fanned out across the north searching for yet other mines. North of Zacatecas (but still fairly close) Francisco de Ibarra and others found silver at San Martín, Chalchihuites, Avino, Sombrerete, and Fresnillo in the 1550s and later at Mazapil, Nieves, and Charcas. Much further to the northwest another mining district began to take shape in the 1560s with the establishment of the first mine in the Parral district at Santa Bárbara, in present-day Chihuahua. Although the yield of the area's mines was unimpressive in the first seventy years, silver strikes in the 1630s resulted in the establishment of the *reales* of San Joseph del Parral and San Diego de Minas Nuevas; in the 1650s gold- and silver-bearing ores were found at San Francisco del Oro, five miles northwest of Santa Bárbara. Eventually important mines developed in the Bajío, at Guanajuato and San Luis Potosí, and elsewhere in central and northern Mexico.

The Spaniards' persistence—and success—in locating silver deposits in Mexico might suggest they had ample experience in mining. With the exception of the iron mines of Asturias and the Basque country in the north, however, actually relatively little mining took place in Spain at the time that Spaniards began to settle the Americas. Fairly early in the sixteenth century, however, silver mines began operating at Guadalcanal in the Sierra Morena, and that mining center would have a direct connection with Mexico's silver mines. In the mid-1530s, Taxco attracted some 150 emigrants from Guadalcanal. They apparently followed a group of ten men who had gone Mexico in 1527 and became involved in mining. Another Spanish mining enterprise also had a direct connection with Mexico. The Almadén mercury mines, controlled in the sixteenth century by the German Fuggers, produced the mercury that would supply the Mexican mines. Germans, who along with northern Italians were the most active miners of medieval Europe, were present in both the Almadén and Guadalcanal mines in Spain. Some also went to Mexico in the early years of the colony, many settling at Sultepec, a mining center northwest of Taxco.

Refining Silver. Both German and Italian miners in Europe contributed to the development of the amalgamation process, by which lower-grade ores are mixed with mercury in order to increase the yield of silver. If this process was not invented by Spaniards, however, miners in New Spain were the first to develop and apply the method extensively; it was in use in Zacatecas as early as 1557. Before then miners relied on smelting, which was cheap and technically fairly simple; it involved fusing silver ore with lead in a blast furnace, heated by wood or charcoal. Smelting, however, was not very effective in treating lower quality ores. It also required large amounts of wood, and most of northern Mexico lacked extensive woodlands. As miners exhausted the richest ores that lay close to the surface and began to dig deeper, they needed an alternative method of refining. Far more technologically complex and capital intensive than smelting, amalgamation largely displaced the latter, although smelting never disappeared altogether.

The amalgamation, or patio, process involved mixing finely crushed ore with water and reagents: mercury, salt, and copper-iron sulphates or pyrites (called *magistral*). The resulting mix was left to stand in piles for weeks, even months, allowing the silver to amalgamate with the mercury; the next step was to wash the mud, then to press the residual into bars which were heated in a small furnace. The increasing importance of this method had significant consequences. The refinery (the *hacienda* or *beneficio de minas*) itself became the real headquarters of the mining enterprise, and miners became dependent on mercury—the supply of which was controlled by the Crown—as an essential element of production.

Salt could be obtained from a number of locales in northern New Spain. After the mid-seventeenth century, miners at Parral were hauling in salt from northern Chihuahua and even New Mexico. Mines also required large quantities of wood, for the construction of refineries, shoring up the mines and making charcoal, which was the principal fuel used in refining and required large amounts of wood. *Haciendas de carbón*, grants of woodland where charcoal could be manufactured, developed around the mines.

Organization of the Mining Industry. Not all requirements for mining and refining could be met by either importing supplies or using what was locally available. The scarcity of rivers and streams in many mining areas led miners to devise methods of recirculating water supplies and using draft animals to power machinery. Teams of six to eight mules or horses provided the power to operate huge whims that could hoist over a ton of ore from deep shafts. The demand for draft animals was substantial in the mines.

The development of the amalgamation process solved the problems involved in working with lower-grade ores, although it also meant that miners became highly dependent on the mercury supplied by the Crown. Interruptions in supply or rising prices could have a substantial impact on production and profits. Mercury seems to have been in short supply in New Spain in the mid-seventeenth century, forcing miners to make a number adjustments. Reportedly more than half the silver in Zacatecas in the years between 1685 and 1705, for example, was produced by smelting rather than amalgamation.

Refining was not the only sector of the mining industry that presented major challenges, however. As silver mines became long-term and permanent sites, miners dug larger and deeper shafts, some of them going one hundred and even up to two hundred meters below the surface by the end of the seventeenth century. Not only was it extremely expensive to cut these shafts, but the greater depths created problems of drainage as they reached to and below the water table. The solution was to build horizontal tunnels known as adits, similarly costly to construct. The increasing concentration of mining claims at many sites in the hands of fewer and bigger miners by the middle of the seventeenth century probably facilitated undertaking such major construction projects. The huge expenses involved in these construction projects, which required substantial investment well in advance of returns, together with the decreasing quality of ores as veins were mined and periodic problems of supply account for the boom-and-bust quality that characterized many mines. Production at Zacatecas, for example, rose sharply in the early decades of the seventeenth century and subsequently fell off just as abruptly in the following decades. Recovery began around 1660, and starting in the early eighteenth century Zacatecas experienced a real boom.

The organization and functioning of the mining industry differed in many respects from that of most agricultural estates. Mining enterprises obviously required a great deal more than agricultural haciendas in the way of skilled labor, technicians, machinery, and construction. They were often highly dependent on outside sources for all kinds of supplies. Some miners did acquire land for farming, stockbreeding, and charcoal manufacture, meaning that they created mixed and integrated enterprises that eased (if they did not entirely eliminate) some of the problems of supply.

The core of the mining enterprise was the refinery rather than the mine itself. A walled compound, the refinery included the stamp mills, washing vats, patios, and machinery needed for amalgamation as well as storerooms, stables for draft animals, and housing for the owner as well as the skilled workers and their families. Although big miners probably maintained a residence in town, they spent much of their time on site.

Labor in the Mines. The recruitment of labor for the mines varied over time and from place to place. Whereas mines in central Mexico to some degree could rely on the draft labor system (*repartimiento*) to provide unskilled workers in the sixteenth and seventeenth centuries, the location of many mining districts well outside the region of sedentary indigenous population meant that miners either had to use slaves, mainly Africans or (in the early years) Indians, or to attract free wage workers. These workers came mainly from the center and south, although the Parral mines also attracted Indians from Sinaloa and Sonora. Over the long run, free workers came to constitute the majority of the labor force in all the Mexican mines.

In the sixteenth century, this wage-earning labor force consisted primarily of Indians, mostly migrants who settled in the mining towns in barrios organized according to their ethnic background. Given the distances that separated them from their communities of origin, however, Indian mine workers were rapidly acculturated to Spanish ways. In general, the workforce became increasingly mixed ethnically and racially. Skilled workers, usually those associated with refining, earned high wages, but even the relatively unskilled workers in the mines earned more than did agricultural laborers. Because of the generally good pay for labor in the mines and the relatively small workforces required, Mexican mines had no real difficulty meeting their labor needs. Whatever shortages existed probably resulted from competition for workers, who in the north were notably mobile, ready to move from one site or town to another in search of better wages or conditions.

Artisanry and Manufacturing

Silver mining constituted the most important and technologically complex industry in New Spain, but manufacturing in the colony was by no means limited to that sector. We have seen that a considerable range of artisans, who were mostly men, were present in Mexico from the time of the conquest, and they established their shops in the cities and mining centers. Many Spanish artisans took advantage of the relative cheapness of labor in New Spain to create establishments considerably larger than the typical artisan shop in Spain, expanding the scope of operations by acquiring and training African slaves and Indian workers. Although Spanish artisans continued to be trained and licensed in their trades and organized guilds in the cities, many of them functioned chiefly as entrepreneurs and managers who oversaw directly or indirectly the activities of their slaves and employees. One of the most important results of this growth in the size of artisanal enterprises was that increasing numbers of Africans, Indians, and people of mixed background acquired the skills associated with Spanish trades and could function independently as artisans in their own right. They thus competed directly with Spanish artisans, leading some guilds to impose not very effective restrictions on the admission of nonwhite tradesmen.

Manufacturing in colonial Mexico chiefly meant the processing of raw materials, either produced locally or imported, mainly for domestic consumption. The huge numbers of sheep in Mexico allowed large scale manufacture of woolen cloth, which mainly supplied the domestic Hispanic market of the cities and mines but also entered into the long-distance intercolonial trade with Guatemala and Peru. Wheat was made into bread for the urban market and biscuit for the fleets. Artisans transformed iron, often imported from Spain in unworked form, into all manner of tools and equipment for domestic and industrial use.

Obrajes. In the sixteenth and seventeenth centuries, the largest manufacturing sector was textile production. Cloth manufacturing shops, or *obrajes,* often were large establishments incorporating every phase of textile production, from washing, combing, and spinning wool to weaving, shearing, dyeing, and finishing cloth. Obrajes could range in size from shops with a few to a dozen or so workers to establishments with a hundred or more men and women. These workers mainly were Indians, although blacks and mulattos, both slave and free, as well as mestizos, almost invariably formed a part of the workforce of the larger obrajes as well. The obraje labor force could include people convicted of crimes or imprisoned for debt. Convicts, however, never constituted more than a minority of workers.

Obrajes developed in a number of locales in New Spain, concentrated principally in towns and cities, both Indian and Spanish, in central Mexico and the Bajío. By the late sixteenth century, Puebla had emerged as the colony's leading textile manufacturer, producing both high quality and coarse cloth and surpassing Mexico City itself in volume of production. Located at the juncture of two rivers that provided the water power needed for fulling, a process that shrank and thickened cloth, Puebla offered nearly ideal conditions for textile manufacturing in the form of cheap supplies of wool and food for workers as well as access to dyes such as cochineal, which was produced in the region, and indigo, imported from Guatemala.

Letter from Juan de Brihuega, in Puebla, to his brother Pedro García, in Brihuega, January 1572

This letter is to let you know that, glory be to God and his blessed mother, I and my wife and children are well, although my wife has been very ill with a pain in the side and at much risk, because she was seven months pregnant. . . . We have three girls and a boy, two children who were born here and Juanico and Marica whom we brought from there, not counting those that died and the one my wife now carries.

(Continued)

As to the rest, glory be to God, all goes well with us. I have an *obraje* with twelve looms and the necessary people. I have four black [slave] men and one woman, and we are well set up to make a living, if it serves God.

I won't go on at length here, because the messenger who will carry this is about to leave. His name is Diego Rodríguez, a citizen of this city and great friend of mine. . . . What in other letters I have written I once again ask in this one, which is that I have great need of you to manage the fulling mill, as a result of having so much business in my house, because here we can hardly find skilled tradesmen. For this reason I beg that you come to this City of the Angels [Puebla de los Angeles] with your wife and children. . . . If you lack the money, on the ship which you find to bring you here if you tell them you have a wealthy brother here, they will cover half the passage and I will pay for everything when you arrive. If you know for certain that you will come, I will send whatever you need.

Please pay my respects to the reverend Juan García Navarro. . . . To the señor Juan Ruiz and all my neighbors pay my respects with all the other gentlemen and friends. . . . Our Lord protect your very noble person as I desire, and may we soon see each other in this City of the Angels.

Archivo General de Indias, Indiferente General legajo 2054, trans. Ida Altman.

The size of obrajes varied. Texcoco, in effect a suburb of Mexico City, had perhaps eight obrajes in the last third of the sixteenth century, the largest with ten to twenty workers and the smallest with just a handful. The Indian town of Tlaxcala had up to twenty obrajes in the early seventeenth century. Although many of the owners were Spaniards and Portuguese, both Indians and mestizos—including the famous Tlaxcalan (mestizo) historian Diego Muñoz Camargo and his brother Juan Muñoz—were active *obrajeros* as well. The workers in the Tlaxcalan shops were almost all local Indians who lived outside the obrajes and generally contracted their services for a year at a time.

The large obrajes of Puebla belonged to Spaniards and their labor forces included both free and confined workers. The latter mainly were Indians who had migrated to Puebla. Their employers believed that these "outsiders" were likely to leave before working off the debt that virtually all employees acquired in the form of an advance on their wages. Many obrajeros tried to employ married men, probably considering them to be more stable than single men or men who were separated from their wives. The practice also allowed them to use the labor of women, almost invariably as spinners. Obraje weavers were male, representing a significant deviation from the indigenous textile tradition in which women monopolized this kind of work.

Official inspections of the obrajes of Puebla and other towns highlighted the poor working and living conditions of workers confined within the obrajes. Workers often testified about physical punishment and mistreatment and various ways in which they were unfairly exploited, such as being forced to work excessive hours or to accept further advances once their accounts were cleared. Nonetheless, many workers continued to contract their services voluntarily, and some worked in the same establishment for many years. By the second and third decades of the seventeenth century, official efforts to prohibit the practice of confining workers in the obrajes had begun to have some impact.

Bakeries. Bakeries—*panaderías*—in which bread and biscuit were prepared in the sixteenth and seventeenth centuries usually were small establishments employing perhaps no more than a handful of individuals. Generally the owner was a Spaniard and the employees Indians or mestizos who contracted their services in return for an advance on their wages. Bakers earned much better wages than did obraje workers, and they seem to have enjoyed better working conditions as well; their contracts frequently stipulated the food (often including chocolate) that would be provided to them in addition to their pay.

Women frequently owned bakeries, probably a reflection of the traditional involvement of women in bread baking in Spain itself. Since bakeries seem to have been fairly small enterprises in this era, it was not uncommon for their owners to be actively involved in other economic pursuits, such as carting and commerce. Women owners, however, were more likely to be involved exclusively in bread and biscuit baking.

Trade and Transport

Trade and transport integrated the colonial economy and connected it with the outside world of markets and supply. The big wholesale merchants based mainly in Mexico City who amassed silver to buy up the wares carried by the fleets from Spain destined for Veracruz or the galleons from the Philippines that docked annually in Acapulco had little in common, perhaps, with merchants involved in the indigo and cacao trade with Guatemala, shopkeepers who specialized in retail sales, or petty traders who on a small scale acted as middlemen between the agricultural producers of the countryside and the markets of the towns and cities. Yet, all these entrepreneurs and traders contributed to—and profited from—the constant flow and exchange of goods and silver that allowed the colonial economy to function.

Notwithstanding the peculiar if tenacious notion that Spaniards disdained commerce and were more interested in pursuing prestige than profits, Spaniards of virtually all social ranks and occupations, from high level officials, ecclesiastics and professionals to landowners, ranchers, artisans, and petty officials, involved themselves directly and indirectly in trade. People in the upper social ranks of society—the descendants of the old conquistador and encomendero group—might scorn the *nouveaux riches* whose wealth from business and commerce allowed them to rise in society. Yet, regardless of whatever qualms the aristocratic class might have had about such upstarts, they readily intermarried and formed business partnerships with them. Over time, the distinctions among upper levels of the entrepreneurial, mercantile, landowning, and professional groups blurred.

The Organization of Trade. Involvement in commerce pervaded Spanish society. At almost all levels of commercial activity the typical mode of organization was the partnership, generally formed for specific, fairly short-term undertakings although often renewed. The terms by which partnerships were contracted varied greatly but usually stipulated that one of the parties would perform, or at least oversee, the actual work involved in the enterprise (traveling to a given destination to trade, operating a retail shop), while the other (or others) would provide the larger share of the investment, in cash or some other form. The advantage of the partnership, or *compañía*, was its flexibility; it permitted people to invest in trade without participating directly and allowed them to maintain a fairly high level of liquidity because of the short-term nature of most investments, which usually brought quick returns. In many cases partners—who might well be relatives, close friends, or *compadres*—reinvested their profits, creating longer-term business associations. As an alternative to the *compañía* merchants also used commission agents, who received a percentage of the profits; the agent might be a merchant in his own right. The hallmarks of commercial and entrepreneurial activity in Mexico were flexibility, quick turnaround, and broad participation.

The sheer volume and complexity of the constant movement and exchange of goods—both raw materials and finished products from the countryside and towns and items imported from Spain and elsewhere in Europe, Asia (via the Philippines), or other places—defy easy description and generalization. Leslie Lewis's study of Texcoco affords insight into the patterns of exchange that supplied local markets and brought profits to a range of traders and middlemen. Texcocans sold produce and livestock to merchants in Mexico City; perhaps surprisingly, petty merchants in the capital supplied Texcoco with maize, selling small quantities to Hispanic traders who in turn sold it to the town's Indians. In addition, Texcocan middlemen bought maize produced on local estates and then sold it in Texcoco.

Over time, Texcocans also came to play an increasingly active role as middlemen in the trade between places like Querétaro, Yucatan, and Guatemala and Mexico City. Traders in Texcoco purchased goods or sold on consignment; they often formed short-term partnerships with Spaniards in the provinces, who might be former residents of Texcoco. Mestizos especially were active in the cacao trade. By 1600, mulatto women from Guatemala also were supplying the Indians of Texcoco with small amounts of cacao.

Texcoco's merchants developed family-based businesses. The head of the family went back and forth to Mexico City and saw to business arrangements there while his wife, who might be a local Indian, took care of the business in Texcoco itself. Sons and sons-in-law traveled between Texcoco and provincial areas. Most traders owned some carts or mules and employed Indians as carters and muleteers.

This brief discussion of trade in sixteenth and seventeenth century Texcoco points to some of the basic patterns in local and regional commerce: the role played by middlemen, the importance of Mexico City as both a market and a source of goods, the tendency of lower-level traders to engage in diverse, often complementary, activities. At this level also people might move in and out of involvement in trade.

The example of Texcocan commerce and its petty traders was not necessarily typical; Texcocan traders both benefitted and suffered from their proximity to Mexico City, which because of the strength of its merchant group and the great concentration of wealth and institutions there tended to dominate the economic life of central New Spain. Merchants who were based in cities located further away from Mexico City or who controlled some particular commodity probably operated with more independence from the capital, or at least exercised greater leverage in dealing with Mexico City's merchants. Merchants in Puebla, for example, despite the city's closeness to Mexico City, were able to take advantage of their location on the trade routes to the south and proximity to both Veracruz and Pacific coast ports (Huatulco and Acapulco) to carve out a strong position in the trade with Guatemala, Peru, and the Philippines; Puebla, not Mexico City, dominated the trade in cochineal in the sixteenth and seventeenth centuries.

Merchants. The wealthiest merchants were based in Mexico City. The structure of transatlantic commerce probably changed over the course of the sixteenth and seventeenth centuries. In the years immediately following the conquest most likely the commercial networks based in Seville that served Spanish colonies in the Caribbean were transferred or extended to include Veracruz and Mexico City. People from northern Castile especially were active in the early Mexican trade.

In the sixteenth century the largest mercantile interests probably had their headquarters in Seville, where the senior partner lived. Junior partners and factors or representatives would live in New Spain, with the most senior probably being based in Mexico City and others spending at least some of their time in Veracruz or in mining towns like Zacatecas. The transitoriness of merchants in the early decades following the conquest, few of whom ever became vecinos of Mexico City, suggests that they tended to spend relatively short periods of time there. Sixteenth-century transatlantic commercial networks in New Spain have not been well studied as yet, so it really is not possible to provide a reliable description of their organization.

A great deal more is known about merchants and commercial organization from the late sixteenth century on. Although the majority of merchants in Mexico City still were Spanish immigrants, many of them members of mercantile families, by the seventeenth century most of the big merchants based themselves in the viceregal capital and functioned independently of commercial interests Seville. They might maintain ties with merchants there, however, in particular acting as commission agents, a practice that apparently became increasingly common in the first half of the seventeenth century.

The establishment of a merchant guild, or *consulado*, in Mexico City at the end of the sixteenth century (approved in 1592, it had come into existence by 1594) reflected the consolidation and autonomy of mercantile interests there. The Consulado performed two important functions: acting as a lobby that represented the merchants' corporate interests, and serving as a court in cases relating to commerce. The Consulado limited its membership to the large wholesale merchants (*mercaderes*) who dealt in long-distance trade and whose assets amounted to at least 28,000 pesos. These wholesalers were not supposed to involve themselves directly in retail trade, although they could (and did) engage in it indirectly.

Although many were immigrants, big wholesale merchants for the most part settled in Mexico City, marrying into wealthy families (often ones with significant commercial ties) and obtaining positions on the city council. They became involved in tax farming and served in midlevel governmental positions, most significantly in connection with the mint, which the Mexico City merchants dominated. They also invested in the local economy, buying urban real estate and to a lesser extent haciendas in the countryside and financing and supplying the mines.

Merchants and Mining. Two kinds of merchants became involved with the mining industry, *aviadores* (suppliers) and *mercaderes de plata* (silver merchants). The aviadores maintained businesses in mining towns, supplying goods, materials and even cash to miners. A few of the aviadores of early-seventeenth-century Zacatecas probably equaled some of the big Mexico City merchants in wealth, but they generally obtained their goods from merchants in Mexico City rather than in Veracruz. Although they avoided direct participation in the ownership or operation of mines, merchants did become involved in refining, buying up the share of ores (the *pepena*) that mine workers received as a supplement to their wages.

In addition to the merchants based in the mining towns, merchants in Mexico City also participated in supplying and financing the mining industry. The wealthiest of these, the *mercaderes de plata* or silver merchants, amassed fortunes through the purchase of unminted silver. They operated on a much larger scale, nearly monopolizing the coining of silver. Not surprisingly the silver merchants were closely connected to the officials of the mint, financing them and sometimes serving in key posts. The silver merchants made their profits by charging a commission known as the discount rate on the bars of silver they purchased. The discount generally amounted to around 12.5 percent, but merchants had to cover such costs as the fees paid at the foundry and mint and the expense of transport and storage. Silver traders also profited from tax evasion and contraband trade. In the mid-seventeenth century, apparently substantial amounts of untaxed silver were being sent to Spain and China.

The Manila Galleon. The trade with China via the Philippines represented another lucrative commercial sector controlled mainly by the merchants of Mexico City. The Philippines essentially had been settled from New Spain. With the establishment of the seat of Spanish government at Manila Bay in 1571, direct trade with Chinese and other Asian ports got underway. The trade between Manila and Acapulco brought raw and finished silk and porcelain from China and later fine cottons from India as well as gold and gemstones, spices from the Moluccas, Java and Ceylon, and slaves (until 1700), all of which were exchanged for Mexican silver. The trade with the Philippines brought not only luxury goods but even such items as iron and copper at prices much lower than those for Spanish imports. By the 1590s, much of the commerce between Mexico and Peru involved the reexport of goods brought to Acapulco by the Manila galleons. When the Crown barred Peru from participating in the transpacific trade in the late sixteenth and early seventeenth centuries, Mexican control grew even stronger.

Long-distance trade, then, placed Mexico at the center of an international network of exchange that brought luxury goods from Asia, textiles and iron from Europe, cacao from Guatemala and later Venezuela and Ecuador, and slaves from Africa and Asia to the colony in return for Mexican silver. The Spanish Crown received revenues from this international trade as it did from silver production, but the trade also helped Mexican merchants, financiers, and miners to build up substantial and even huge fortunes. They reinvested much of their profits in commerce, mining, and landowning, thus underwriting local and regional economic development and trade. A century after the conquest New Spain in many ways little resembled a colony, although royal policy and officials certainly could have an impact on patterns of commerce and other sectors of economic activity.

Transport. Trade routes and systems of transport developed in conjunction with the establishment of the import-export economy. Many of the principal overland routes predated the conquest, especially those that connected central Mexico with the Gulf Coast and the south. With the opening of the mines routes to the north connecting mining centers to Mexico City and Guadalajara quickly developed. Lacking large domesticated animals, the people of preconquest Mexico had relied on human carriers, tlameme, to transport goods. The use of tlameme did not disappear entirely after the conquest, as indigenous traders continued to rely on human power to move their goods. Spaniards, however, quickly switched to animal power, organizing pack trains of mules and, even more significantly, introducing large two-wheeled carts drawn by teams of mules or oxen. Although the owners of mule trains, carts, and oxen might be well-to-do entrepreneurs, the muleteers (*arrieros*) and carters themselves usually were socially and economically quite marginal.

Seaborne commerce for the most part was a postconquest innovation. Veracruz was the major port on the Gulf Coast, providing access to the Caribbean and Atlantic; in the early sixteenth century Huatulco, located close to Antequera in Oaxaca and on the route from Mexico City south to Tehuantepec, Soconusco, and Guatemala, was the most important Pacific coast port for trade and travel between New Spain and Peru. The Mexican-Peruvian trade, which mainly consisted of shipping manufactured goods, dyes, and household items (imported from Spain or produced in Mexico) in return for silver and mercury, peaked in the 1580s, overwhelmed by the expanding trade in goods from China. A royal shipyard at La Navidad, in the jurisdiction of Michoacan, produced ships primarily for the Philippine trade. With the establishment of that trade Acapulco, with its exceptionally fine harbor, became New Spain's main Pacific port.

Urban Development

Spanish cities, Indian towns, ports, and mining centers grew and changed in response to economic development, increased volume of trade with the establishment of the northern mines, and both immigration and internal migration. Spanish communities formed in many of the leading Indian towns, just as Indian *barrios* ringed the centers, or *trazas*, of Spanish cities. This was true even in Puebla, one of the few Spanish cities in central Mexico not established on the site of an existing indigenous town; by the 1540s several indigenous barrios had gained official recognition.

Residential patterns were not everywhere the same. Querétaro, established in the 1530s in the eastern part of the Bajío, about 120 miles northwest of Mexico City, for long lacked the segregated residential pattern of many other Spanish cities. Spaniards, Indians, mestizos, and blacks lived side by side in the seventeenth century, and Indian barrios did not really take shape until the eighteenth century. Nonetheless, despite the common urban pattern of Spanish center and Indian barrios and suburbs, the presence of non-white domestic servants, slaves, and workers in commercial-industrial enterprises meant that residence and work in city centers were never reserved exclusively for Spaniards. Nor were the Indian barrios monopolized by Indians, as not only blacks, mulattos, and mestizos but also poorer Spaniards and other Europeans (often recent immigrants) took up residence in less prestigious neighborhoods.

The growth of local markets in size and complexity and of the commercial-industrial sector in many cities fostered the development of new settlements and urban networks that integrated mining, agricultural, commercial, manufacturing, and administrative centers. A close relationship existed between the mining town of Sichú and the city of Querétaro in the first half of the seventeenth century, as shopkeepers, artisans, agricultural workers, and people who were involved in mining moved back and forth between the two communities. Examination of other regions probably would reveal similar patterns of urban connection and integration.

Supply and regulation of the market were critical to the functioning of urban centers. Town councils appointed special officials to oversee the practice of trades and inspect weights and measures. They also set prices for certain commodities and required some producers and vendors of foodstuffs—bakers, wine sellers—to obtain licenses in order to operate. In most urban centers, meat was supplied through a system called the *abasto*, by which one individual would bid for and receive a contract giving him a monopoly on the town's meat supply for a year. An individual who bid on the meat contract in the bishopric of Puebla had to show that he could supply up to six thousand head of cattle and ten to twelve thousand head of sheep; by the late seventeenth century, the Puebla market consumed as much as two thousand head of cattle and seventeen thousand of sheep annually.[1]

As seen in the production and distribution of other commodities, the *abasto* could reflect the intertwining of Spanish and Indian enterprises. In the case of the Indian town of Tlaxcala, described by David Szewczyk, while the contractor for the abasto invariably was a Spaniard, he had to deliver the cattle to—and come to terms with—the town's butchers, who were Indians. The latter organized themselves into an association that bargained collectively with the contractor.

By the early seventeenth century the centers of Spanish cities usually were physically substantial, with churches, monasteries, convents, city halls, and private residences built of stone. Arcades with shops surrounded the main plazas, and typically the town or city council regulated urban water supply. Despite the symbolism of the concentration of institutional power and private wealth in the Spanish traza, however, the urban milieu was busy and diverse. The characteristic mix of private houses, business establishments, and governmental and religious institutions meant that people of all ethnic groups, ranks, and occupations were physically in close contact, producing friction at times.

New Spain's towns and cities differed significantly from one another. Mining towns generally developed haphazardly, often arising from mining camps hastily assembled after a strike and therefore not exhibiting the typical grid pattern of a planned city. Port cities were physically unimpressive places, other than the fortifications that protected them—San Juan de Ulua at Veracruz, the Castle of San Diego at Acapulco. For most of the year the populations of these ports were fairly small and poor, swelling only with the

---

[1]David J. Weiland, *The Economics of Agriculture: Markets, Production and Finances in the Bishopric of Puebla, 1532–1809* (Ph.D. Diss., University of Cambridge, United Kingdom, 1995), p. 107.

arrival of the fleet from Castile or the galleons from Manila and the merchants or their agents who came to buy. Despite the physical, functional and demographic differences among urban centers, however, they were closely connected through systems of exchange and supply and the notable mobility of the Mexican population.

Glossary

abasto   municipal meat supply
arriero   muleteer
aviador   merchant supplying the mines
barrio   neighborhood
caballería   unit of agricultural land, around one hundred acres
compañía   partnership
composición   legal verification of land titles
consulado   merchants' guild
estancia   medium-sized farm
hacendado   owner of a landed estate
hacienda de minas   refinery
hacienda   large landed estate
ingenio   sugar refinery
mayordomo   steward, manager
mercader   wholesale, long-distance merchant
obraje   workshop, usually for cloth production
obrajero   owner of a textile workshop
panadería   bakery for bread and biscuit
pepena   mineworker's share of ore
rancho   small farm or ranch
real   mining site; also, a coin and unit of monetary value
traza   central district of a Spanish city
vecino   citizen of a Spanish town or city, head of household, neighbor

Questions for Discussion

1.   How did patterns of landholding and land use reflect both Spanish and indigenous traditions and economic priorities? How did Spanish and indigenous agricultural practices conflict or converge?

2.   How did entrepreneurs obtain and organize labor for agriculture, mining, and manufacturing?

3.   What was the role of silver mining in the rapid development of New Spain's regional and international economy?

4.   Why did Spanish immigrants send for their relatives to join them in Mexico?

5.   How and by whom was trade conducted at the local, regional, and international levels?

6.   How did the Spanish urban network develop? What was the relationship between Spanish cities and Indian towns?

Suggested Readings

Altman, Ida. *Transatlantic Ties in the Spanish Empire. Brihuega, Spain and Puebla, Mexico, 1560–1620.* Stanford, Calif.: Stanford University Press, 2000. Examines the experiences of an immigrant group and its economic impact on Puebla.

Altman, Ida and James Lockhart. *Provinces of Early Mexico.* Los Angeles: UCLA Latin American Center, 1976. Regional studies of colonial Mexico.

Bakewell, Peter. *Silver Mining and Society in Colonial Mexico: Zacatecas, 1546–1700.* Cambridge, U.K.: Cambridge University Press, 1971. Socioeconomic study of New Spain's most important mining center.

Borah, Woodrow. *Early Colonial Trade and Navigation between Mexico and Peru.* Berkeley and Los Angeles: University of California Press, 1954. Examines the development of trade between the two main centers of early Spanish America.

———. *Silk Raising in Colonial Mexico.* Berkeley and Los Angeles: University of California Press, 1943. Study of the introduction and spread of silk production in early Mexico.

Brading, D. A. and Harry E. Cross, "Colonial Silver Mining: Mexico and Peru," *Hispanic American Historical Review,* 52:4 (1972): 545–79. Comparison of mining in the two major colonial centers.

Haskett, Robert S. "'Our Suffering with the Taxco Tribute': Involuntary Mine labor and Indigenous Society in Central New Spain," *Hispanic American Historical Review* 71:3 (1991): 447–75. History of the use of indigenous labor in the Taxco mines.

Hoberman, Louisa Schell. *Mexico's Merchant Elite, 1590–1660.* Durham, N.C.: Duke University Press, 1991. Detailed examination of mercantile careers and enterprises.

Salvucci, Richard J. *Textiles and Capitalism in Mexico: An Economic History of the Obrajes, 1539–1840.* Princeton, N.J.: Princeton University Press, 1987. A largely economic study of textile production in colonial Mexico.

Schurz, William Lytle. *The Manila Galleon*. New York: E.P. Dutton & Co., Inc, 1959. Important, detailed examination of the development and impact of trade between the Philippines and Spanish America.

West, Robert C. *The Mining Community in Northern New Spain: The Parral Mining District*. Berkeley and Los Angeles: University of California Press, 1949. Study of the Parral mines emphasizing geography and technology.

Nine

The Northern Frontier

In New Spain, the effort to extend Spanish rule into the lands north of the Tropic of Cancer presented sharp contrasts with previous colonial experiences in central and southern Mexico. Northern New Spain encompassed a vast area that stretched from the present-day states of Tamaulipas and Texas on the Gulf of Mexico to southern Arizona and northern Sonora on the Gulf of California and north to the Upper Río Grande valley in northern New Mexico.

Between 1540 and 1680, a frontier society emerged in northern Mexico with a unique economic, social, and political character that was the product of intense confrontations, adaptations and interactions among Spanish settlers, Mexican Indian immigrants, and native communities. In order to consolidate the Spanish presence in this region colonial structures and Spanish institutions sometimes underwent considerable modification as they responded and were adapted to very different circumstances. The consequences of the imposition of Spanish colonialism for the native populations of northern Mexico also were distinctive.

Indigenous peoples of this region generally shared several traits. The vast majority lived in semi-arid and desert habitats that did not permit the production of agricultural surpluses that could maintain a native or foreign elite. Most communities in northern New Spain were economically self-sufficient entities that lacked organized labor systems such as existed in southern and central Mexico. Although these groups knew and consistently practiced some agriculture, along with hunting and food gathering, they lived in houses or *rancherías* (as Spaniards called them) scattered throughout extensive districts. They occupied and vacated these rancherías according to cyclical (mainly seasonal) migratory patterns. Because of this high degree of annual mobility, colonial explorers and missionaries initially characterized natives as nomads and "desert wanderers," which actually was true of only a small percentage of these populations.

Social organization was based on small communities or bands that had virtually complete autonomy to make war, establish alliances, or flee from external threats. Native communities in northern Mexico engaged in complex but generally circumscribed warfare. At the time the Spaniards arrived in the north none of these groups had been subjugated by large politico-military entities, nor did they have a professional warrior class such as existed in the Aztec and Tarascan (Purépecha) states in central and western Mexico.

Conquest and Conflict in the North

Shipwreck and Survival. In 1531 Nuño Beltrán de Guzmán, governor of Nueva Galicia, and his troops founded San Miguel de Culiacan in central Sinaloa at a site near the present state capital. From Culiacan the rapacious Nuño de Guzmán organized various incursions to the north, west and northwest looking for villages to plunder and people to enslave. His attempts to cross the Sierra Madre Occidental failed, however. In 1536, a band of slave hunters encountered a small group of Indians, among whom they found three Spaniards and one North African slave. These men were survivors of the disastrous expedition of Pánfilo de Narváez, who in 1527 had set sail from Spain to conquer Florida, stopping at Santo Domingo and Cuba and sailing north to Florida in 1528.

The majority of the group led by Narváez—including the man who later would write a famous account of his experiences, Alvar Núñez Cabeza de Vaca—attempted to advance into the interior, planning later to rejoin the ships on the coast; but the rendezvous never occurred. Hungry and vulnerable to the attacks of local Indians, the Spaniards constructed makeshift rafts. The rafts separated and broke up during a tropical storm in the Gulf. Barely alive, a few men managed to land on an island off the coast of east Texas. Often separated from one another for long periods, the survivors spent years living among the indigenous groups of the Gulf Coast region and Texas. Eventually four of them made their way west through the lower Río Grande valley, west Texas, southern New Mexico, and southern Arizona, finally reaching Sonora, from where Indian guides led them south. After some eight years of living as best they could, following Indian trails, adopting indigenous customs, acting as traders, and gaining a reputation as healers, the four survivors reached central Sinaloa.

The North African slave's name was Esteban or Little Esteban (Estebanico); the Spaniards were Alvar Núñez Cabeza de Vaca, Andrés Dorantes, and Alonso del Castillo. Once back in Spanish-controlled territories, the survivors began to spread rumors about great populations living in enormously rich cities to the north.

The Seven Golden Cities. In Mexico City, Cabeza de Vaca's stories captured the attention of colonial authorities, and soon plans for the conquest of the "other Mexico" were underway. Viceroy Don Antonio de Mendoza, in a close race with Guzmán and Hernando Cortés, obtained royal authorization to organize an *entrada* to the north. Meanwhile, as if sent by divine mandate, a Franciscan friar, Fray Marcos de Niza, arrived in Mexico in 1537. With the support of Fray Juan de Zumárraga, the bishop of Mexico and his fellow

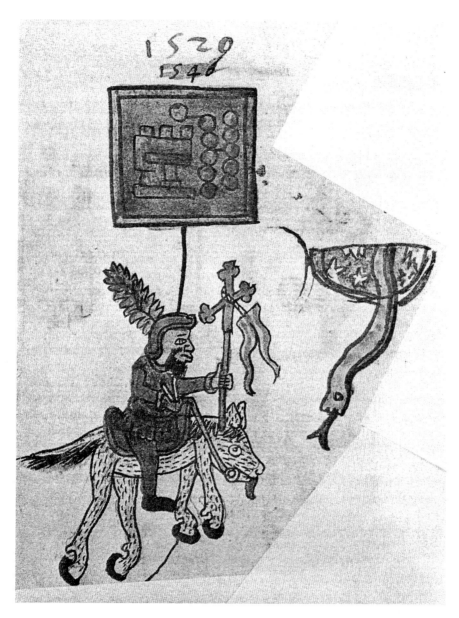

Figure 9-1 **Nuño de Guzmán and the conquest of Nueva Galicia**. A native illustration shows the Spanish conqueror of western Mexico whose reputation for cruelty earned him a special place in Mexican history.
From *Codex Telleriano-Remensis*. Paris: Bibliothèque Nationale de France, folio 44.

187

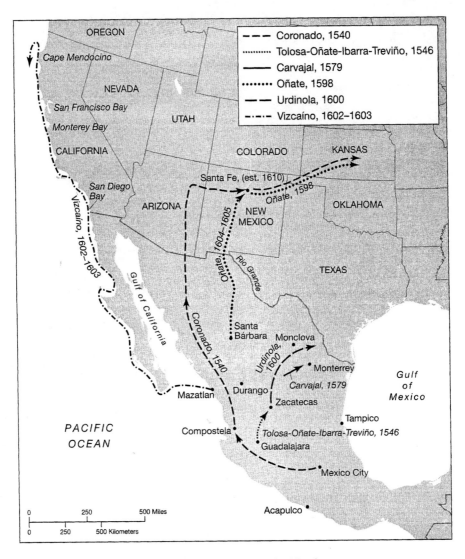

Spanish Expeditions to the North

Franciscan, Niza was commissioned in 1538 to explore the lands north of Culiacan. In March of 1539 Niza, Esteban and a small party ventured forward.

Esteban preceded the group, maintaining contact with the rest of the army led by Niza and sending him secret clues—encoded in crucifixes of various sizes—about the potential riches in native villages. Soon Esteban and his group had significantly outdistanced Niza's band. At the time that they reached Hawikuh, a Zuni community in northwestern New Mexico, Niza was apparently only crossing the Sonora Valley. The Zuni Indians refused to meet Esteban's capricious demands for treasure, food, and women, and decided to kill him, according to his surviving Indian scouts, who escaped to the south and found Niza in the upper Sonora Valley. According to Niza's report:

> I asked that some of them should go with me to Cibola, for to see if any other Indian had escaped and to learn anything new from Estevan, but I could do nothing with them. In the end, seeing me determined, two chiefs said that they would go with me. With these and my own Indians and interpreters, I pursued my journey until within the sight of Cibola, which is situated on a plain at the skirt of a round hill. It has the appearance of a very beautiful town, the best that I have seen in these parts. The houses are of the fashion that the Indians had described to me, all of stone, with their stories and terraces, as it appeared to me from a hill where I was able to view it. The city is bigger than the city of Mexico. At times I was tempted to go to it, because I knew that I ventured only life, which I had offered to God the day I commenced the journey. At the end I feared, considering my danger and that, if I died, I would not be able to make a report of this country, which to me appears to be the greatest and best of the discoveries. (Cleve Hallenbeck, *The Journey of Fray Marcos de Niza* [Westport, Conn., 1973], 33–34)

In truth, Fray Marcos de Niza probably never set a foot beyond the present border between Sonora and Arizona and consequently probably never saw "Cibola" or any other site in either northern Arizona or New Mexico. Once back in Mexico City in 1539, however, Niza reported to viceroy Mendoza on his "findings" and persuaded him to launch immediately a large expedition for the pacification and conquest of the kingdom of Saint Francis, or the Seven Golden Cities.

The Expedition of Vázquez de Coronado. Placing unquestioning trust in friar Niza's account, in 1540 New Spain's civil authorities organized an expedition led by the governor of Nueva Galicia, Francisco Vázquez de Coronado, who set out from Compostela in western Mexico. Vázquez de Coronado's army was made of three hundred Spanish soldiers and eight hundred Indian allies, along with a fleet, led by Hernando Alarcón, that departed from Acapulco and would supply the army until it left the coast.

From the outset, the expedition seemed doomed. Alarcón's ships soon lost contact with the men on land and, after entering the mouth of the Colorado River, turned back to New Spain. On July 7, 1540, Vázquez de Coronado arrived at the Zuni community of Hawikuh and discovered that the Seven Golden Cities were nothing more than seven modest Zuni villages built of adobe. The Spaniards organized small patrols that failed to find a more substantial base for Vázquez de Coronado's army. Garci López de Cárdenas saw the Grand Canyon, Pedro Tovar contacted Hopi villages, and Hernando Alvarado reached the eastern Pueblo towns.

The bulk of the army then turned east and crossed the upper Río Grande, still searching for Niza's golden cities. Once in the eastern Pueblo territory, Vázquez de Coronado met "The Turk," a Cicuye Pueblo Indian who promised to take them to the legendary city of Quivira. Under the Turk's guidance the Spanish expedition ventured northeast into the Great Plains and reached the Arkansas River. In the summer of 1541, after spending months in the area, it became clear to the governor Vázquez de Coronado and his troops that there was no Gran Quivira lying *mas allá* (further on) awaiting them. The Turk was tortured and, before being executed by garrote, confessed he had intentionally misled Spanish troops out of Pueblo lands. In their wandering through the Great Plains the group nearly met up with the equally disastrous expedition led by Hernando de Soto, which had set out with similar objectives from Florida.

Vázquez de Coronado returned to the Río Grande where he faced increasing hostility from the Eastern Pueblo Indians, and by July 1542 his forces had returned to Mexico City. During the trip back to New Spain, Fray Marcos de Niza had to be protected from the angry troops and was forever discredited. Vázquez de Coronado eventually was tried for his misdeeds as commander of the expedition. Although acquitted, he later died from injuries incurred on his way back to Mexico City.

Failed Efforts in the Far North. The massive failure of this expedition kept Spaniards away from Arizona and New Mexico for more than half a century. No less disappointing were expeditions by sea organized in search of the fabulous realm of Queen Calafia and the Strait of Anian, a supposed northwestern passage connecting the South Sea (Pacific Ocean) with the Atlantic waters. Hernando Cortés himself explored the waters of the Gulf of California and financed subsequent expeditions in the 1530s, only to find inhospitable landscapes and hostile Indians. Nonetheless, Spaniards still hoped that wealthy regions like the Aztec empire would be found.

In 1542, the Portuguese pilot Juan Rodríguez de Cabrillo, departing from Navidad in Jalisco, reached the shoreline of present California and founded the present-day bay of San Diego but turned back empty-handed. Decades later, in 1602, New Spain's viceroy Gaspar de Zúñiga, the count of Monterrey, organized a maritime expedition to Alta California. An experienced navigator in Pacific waters, Sebastián Vizcaino, was in charge of the three ships that sailed out of Acapulco in May. On San Diego's day—November 12—they reached a deep bay and port which they christened after the saint. Vizcaino ended his journey at Cape Mendocino, after finding the present Bay of Monterey and naming it for the Viceroy, Mendoza. In 1603, Vizcaino returned to New Spain having mapped out the main entries to California on the Pacific Coast, although he failed to identify the present Bay of San Francisco. In the absence of wealthy empires to conquer, dense Indian cities to subjugate or precious metals to exploit, California native populations would not be affected by Spanish colonization efforts until the mid-eighteenth century.

Settlement of the North

The Silver Cities, 1546–1700. When Hernando Cortés died in Spain in 1547 the Spanish settlements in New Spain had begun to consolidate into three fairly distinct regions: central, western, and southern. Each would become a quasi-independent jurisdiction with its own Audiencia: Nueva Galicia in the west, Mexico at the center and Guatemala to the south.

By the 1540s, the Spaniards not only had replaced the Mexicas as masters of central Mexico but also had expanded their authority to include an area stretching from Honduras and Guatemala in the south to a line that still followed the northern limits of Mesoamerica. Spaniards did not control any populations north of the Province of Pánuco on the Gulf of Mexico nor beyond the area of central Sinaloa on the Pacific Ocean. From there, effective Spanish rule extended southward along the coast to Jalisco and Michoacan, turning toward the center following the line of the Lerma-Santiago rivers and climbing to the highlands surrounding the Valleys of Toluca and Mexico. In the east, Spanish dominions extended to the valleys of Puebla and Tlaxcala, crossing the Sierra Madre Oriental to turn north toward the lands of the Totonaca, Cempoalteca and Huasteca.

Spaniards had been able to extend their dominions to the north from Tepotzotlan in the Valley of Mexico only with the help of Otomi warriors. In 1531, Otomi caciques had founded Querétaro and San Juan del Río on behalf of the Spanish Crown. Beyond the northern limits of Querétaro, Pánuco, and Culiacán lay a vast unknown region that Spaniards renamed the Gran Chichimeca. Spaniards used the generic term "Chichimeca" for all the indigenous groups in the semiarid plateau (Guachichiles, Zacatecos, Pimes) whom they judged to be barbarians by virtue of their lack of centralized government, organized religion, permanent settlements, decent clothing, manners, or respect for property, and for their hostility to Spaniards.

In 1546, four Spanish prospectors (Juan de Tolosa, Cristóbal de Oñate, Diego de Ibarra, and Baltasar Trevino) guided by Indian allies discovered silver ores at a site well to the northeast of Guadalajara, more than nine thousand feet above the sea level. Nuestra Señora de los Zacatecas was founded in 1547 and soon become the richest mining town in North America. Almost immediately, Spanish prospectors discovered other silver lodes nearby. Following the arid eastern flanks of the Sierra Madre Occidental, Spanish miners made astounding discoveries, stimulating a substantial migration from the south to populate the newly created silver cities: Fresnillo in 1554, Sombrerete in 1555, Durango and Santa Bárbara in 1563. To the east more silver lodes were found soon after. By 1590, when San Luis Potosí was established, the north-central plateau indisputably had become the richest region on the continent.

The Chichimeca War. The establishment and development of a *Real y Minas* (mining town) presented enormous challenges. These mining settlements had to import nearly everything. In addition, local tribes strongly resisted the establishment of Spanish towns. In the 1550s Chichimecas attacked and slaughtered a group of Tarascans who were allies of the Spaniards, officially initiating the Chichimeca War. Organized in small bands and increasingly mobile once they had successfully adopted the use of Spanish horses, these Chichimeca warriors launched guerrilla attacks on Spanish settlers and their property, only to disappear into the desert without a trace.

In response, colonial authorities sent military expeditions into Chichimeca territories to punish the attackers and enslave their families. Mining prospectors also organized private raiding parties to retaliate and seize and enslave hostile Indians. Mutual raids, robberies, and murders escalated with the silver booms of the 1560s and 1570s.

Miners and colonial authorities began to provide military escorts to travelers and silver convoys for protection and to deter and repel the raids of hostile Indians. Spanish authorities also created a chain of military forts between Quéretaro and Zacatecas garrisoned by Spanish and Indian ally troops that would protect the silver convoys and stage raids on hostile tribes. Between 1550 and 1600, the Chichimeca War cost the Spaniards more in lives and property than any previous military conflict in Mexico.

Toward the end of the sixteenth century, it had become clear that the military response to Chichimeca depredations had only partially succeeded in securing the region. Although Spanish and ally troops had inflicted heavy casualties among the indigenous population and military garrisons had become permanent settlements along the Camino Real, Chichimeca attacks had not only continued but increased. Loss of human life and cattle and destruction of real property and goods reached a new high.

The failure of military tactics to eliminate the Chichimeca guerrillas forced the Spaniards to adopt a different approach. Religious orders and colonial officials undertook a new policy based on peace and trade. This peace-by-purchase plan promoted the distribution of goods among Chichimecas (clothing, seeds, cattle, tools). Spaniards hoped that hostile Indians would be persuaded by these *dádivas* or gifts to cease their hostilities against Spanish settlers and travelers and become the Spaniards' allies against other, still-hostile, tribes. In the seventeenth century these measures brought peace to the Royal Road and allowed Spanish ranches, haciendas and estancias that stretched between Querétaro and Chihuahua to flourish. Large estates, ranches and missions produced wheat, corn, hides, wax, salt, meat, wine, wood, and other products for consumption in the mines.

Pacification and Development. By this time Zacatecas had become the center of the new region and the economic base for further expeditions into the far north. Francisco de Ibarra, nephew of one of the city's founders, financed the exploration of silver lodes to the northwest in the 1550s. In 1563 he founded Durango at the foot of another mountain rich in minerals, the

Cerro del Mercado. Durango became the capital of a new province, Nueva Vizcaya. From Nombre de Dios, to the south, to the mines in central Chihuahua, to the north, Nueva Vizcaya encompassed a chain of mining and agricultural settlements populated by Spanish entrepreneurs and their Indian, mestizo, and mulatto workers. The haciendas and ranchos of the provinces of Nueva Vizcaya and Nueva Galicia would also become important exporters to other regions.

Francisco de Urdinola, a Basque immigrant and veteran of the Chichimeca War, was a typical northern entrepreneur. He combined investments in mining with long-distance trade activities with Mexico City, Veracruz, and Seville in Spain. On his vast haciendas along the Aguanaval River in Zacatecas and Durango Urdinola grazed European livestock and cultivated crops (mostly wheat and grapes) to be sold in the towns or mines. Urdinola explored the territory northeast of his estates and discovered silver ores in Coahuila, where he founded Saltillo with the assistance of Tlaxcalan immigrants from central Mexico. Years later, in 1603, Urdinola became governor of Nueva Vizcaya. Three generations later, Urdinola's descendants consolidated his properties into an entailment known as the Marquesado de San Miguel de Aguayo.

Throughout the seventeenth century, silver bonanzas would recur on the northern plateau. In 1631, a new chain of silver deposits was discovered near a tributary river of the Conchos, in southern Chihuahua, and the Mineral del Parral was founded by Spanish prospectors. The mining boom in Parral pushed the frontier settlements further north and created overnight a prosperous Spanish town on the boundaries between the Conchos, Tepehuanes, and Tarahumaras, the Indian nations that inhabited those territories.

Naturally, only relatively few mining towns became permanent settlements or prosperous towns. In colonial times, a number of mining towns would go through a cycle from boom to semi-abandonment. These included Sombrerete, Sierra de Pinos, San Martín, Mazapil, and Plateros (in present-day Zacatecas), Mapimí, Guanacevi, Indé, Pánuco, and Cuencamé (in Durango), and Charcas, Matehuala, and Catorce (in San Luis Potosí), among others.

Settlement of the Far North

New Mexico. In 1595, Don Juan de Oñate, the Zacatecas-born son of Cristóbal de Oñate, signed a contract with the viceroy Don Luis de Velasco the younger for the exploration and conquest of New Mexico. Oñate, a wealthy miner in Zacatecas, offered to finance the expedition. The viceroy would assist Oñate's *entrada* by providing six Franciscan friars, four bells, powder, munitions, ten quintals of mercury for assaying silver, and some Indian interpreters. In exchange, Oñate would become governor and *capitán general* of New Mexico with the right to distribute Indian villages in encomiendas among his troops. New Mexico's encomenderos and their descendants would enjoy their villages' labor and fruits for three generations.

In 1597 Oñate gathered his force at Santa Bárbara in southern Chihuahua, and in January 1598 a caravan comprising 129 soldiers, 10 Franciscans, 83 wagons, and 7,000 head of stock headed to the Conchos river, a tributary of the Río Grande. Months later, they forded the Río Grande and named the place El Paso (the ford, the entry). Once in the upper Río Grande, Oñate's expedition established Spanish authority among the Eastern Pueblos, who did not present a unified front against the intruders. After defeating the Acomas and punishing them with mutilation and enslavement, Oñate encountered no further significant resistance.

New Mexico, however, was far from being another Mexico. There were no silver mines to exploit, treasure to loot, or prosperous cities to plunder. From the original Spanish settlement at San Gabriel, Oñate sent out or led further expeditions to the north and west that proved equally unsuccessful. Most of the expedition members started to look for a way out, and Oñate himself, having spent a considerable fortune in the enterprise, resigned as governor in 1607 and left the province.

Convinced by the Franciscan missionaries who reported significant advances in the Christianization of Pueblo villages, in 1608 royal authorities in Mexico City decided to keep New Mexico as a royal colony and appointed a new governor. Don Pedro de Peralta traveled from Mexico City to San Gabriel in 1609 as New Mexico's first royal governor. He decided to relocate the capital to a better site in the south, on a tributary of the Río Grande. Late in 1609 or early in 1610 the new governor and remaining Spanish settlers founded Santa Fe, which became the northernmost Spanish settlement in colonial New Spain until the eighteenth century. Located at the end of the Royal Road that linked Mexico City to Zacatecas, Durango, Parral and El Paso, Santa Fe's residents participated in an active trade, sending south wool, clothing, Indian slaves, wax, blankets, buffalo hides, and pine nuts. In the seventeenth century Santa Fe was the small but prosperous capital of a region based on an economy of sheep raising and small-scale ranching and exploitation of forest products.

Pueblo communities extended throughout the Rio Grande Valley. Unlike the majority of Indians in northern Mexico, the Pueblos had well-developed agriculture based on a sophisticated irrigation system. In the province's sixty-some villages lived more than sixty thousand people, who spoke five different languages. Each compact village was economically self-sufficient, politically autonomous, and militarily independent from the others. Despite linguistic diversity, the Pueblo Indians to a great extent shared a common culture and lifestyle.

Nuevo Léon. Like New Mexico, northeastern New Spain lacked silver mines. Its settlement proceeded along much the same lines as that of New Mexico, orchestrated by authorities in Mexico City.

The Audiencia of Mexico wanted to consolidate its jurisdiction north of Pánuco and protect the upper coastline from corsair intrusions. For that purpose, viceroy Martin Enríquez used the services of Luis de Carvajal, a Portuguese immigrant who had captured some of the English survivors of John Hawkins's disastrous raid on Veracruz in 1568. Appointed *alcalde* of Tampico, Carvajal was to find a road between this port on the Gulf of Mexico and the mining towns of the northern plateau. From there, Carvajal would turn north, reaching the Río Grande and following its course eastward to the coast, then heading south to return to Tampico. Carvajal accomplished the mission, reconnoitering the territories around the Lower Río Grande down to the Gulf of Mexico. He traveled to Spain and obtained a royal concession to colonize the area between Pánuco and present-day south Texas, which he and others erroneously believed bordered on Florida.

With the titles of governor and captain-general of the kingdom of Nuevo León, Carvajal returned to New Spain in 1579 to organize an expedition to settle the area. With a substantial contingent of Portuguese families, Carvajal founded new settlements at Monclova and in the northern fringes of Coahuila and Nuevo León. Soon economic and jurisdictional rivalries developed between Carvajal's party and mining families in Nueva Vizcaya, especially in Coahuila, which both groups claimed rights to settle. Carvajal's rivals brought to light his Jewish ancestry, and the Inquisition of Mexico formally charged him and his relatives as *judaizantes* (Christian converts who had maintained Jewish practices). In 1590 Carvajal was sentenced to six years' exile but died in prison the same year. Nuevo León, however, remained independent of Nueva Vizcaya.

Frontier Society

Between 1546 and 1700 northern New Spain emerged as a frontier society profoundly marked by multiple borders, both internal and external, and stark contrasts.

In the north, Indians were not required to pay tribute. Even if the residents of some villages were not officially exempted, in reality no colonial agency could enforce collection of tribute in the absence of indigenous elites willing to collaborate. Encomiendas were also largely nonexistent in northern Mexico, with the exception of the Upper Río Grande communities in New Mexico. Even there, however, New Mexican encomiendas differed significantly from those in central and southern Mexico, rarely matching the latter in heavy work and brutal exploitation.

Labor in the North. Spanish settlers responded in various ways to the lack of compulsory labor systems in northern Mexico. One means of securing manpower was to stage military raids and enslave "hostile" Indians. Captive Indians were put to work as house servants in Spanish towns, normally for no remuneration other than food and lodging. Some households in Nueva Vizcaya and New Mexico had domestic laborers who had been enslaved in their youth by military raids. Separated from their groups and Hispanized as servants in towns and on ranches, these people, known as *genízaros* in Durango, Chihuahua, and New Mexico, became a significant demographic element in frontier settlements. For these genízaros, the boundaries between slavery and servitude were murky.

A second means of obtaining labor was to transport Indian men and their families from southern and central Mexico as "allies" to be employed as salaried workers in the booming mining industry and the growing cattle and agricultural economy, or to be used as defensive colonizers on the outskirts of mining towns. Tlaxcalans, Mexicas, Tarascans, and Otomíes established several colonies from San Luis Potosí to northern New Mexico and became a significant component of the labor market in the frontier economic system. Families from Chichimeca and other hostile nations also worked for wages in northern mining towns and on ranches and haciendas.

Another important source of labor were Hispanized Indians, migrants who formed a transient labor force that moved from town to town following silver bonanzas. Indians from Jesuit and Franciscan missions, especially in Nueva Vizcaya and Sonora, who abandoned their communities to seek employment with Spanish entrepreneurs, provided an additional source of manpower, along with African slaves used as overseers of Indian workers in mines and haciendas. The results of interracial unions, together with the mestizos and other mixed-race people from central Mexico who joined the expeditions to the north, created another large segment of Spanish-speaking non-Spaniards in the frontier region. They occupied an intermediate space between the Spanish elites and the lower class.

The Composition of Society. The northern mines attracted a mass of immigrant Indians, castas, and mestizos that constituted a labor force not only relatively free from compulsory labor requirements but also dispossessed of the protections and privileges that the Indians of central and southern Mexico enjoyed under Spanish rule. Moreover, for the most part the Indians of the north were unable to use the Spanish legal system to their advantage as did their southern counterparts. Northern Indian corporations, therefore, did not have the presence, authority or influence notable in areas to the south. The legal privileges that Tlaxcalan colonists enjoyed in Saltillo, for example, although significant by northern standards, fell far short of matching the rights they enjoyed in the province of Tlaxcala itself.

Spanish towns in northern New Spain, however, did achieve a greater degree of autonomy from central government and their vecinos engaged in a higher level of civic participation than was true to the south. The strong need for common defense against hostile tribes created a complex network of internal military alliances among the diverse residents of places like Saltillo, Santa

Fe, or Parral. In addition, the Spanish Crown generally provided more, and more easily obtained, land grants and generous municipal benefits to northern settlements, increasing the extent of common lands and public properties as well as collective rights to such resources as water, woodlands, stone, and coal.

Since mining prospectors and colonial entrepreneurs were responsible for the creation of most towns in northern Mexico, the regional origins and internal composition of Spanish communities differed significantly from those of the south. Many northern settlers belonged to families from northern Spain, particularly the Basque country. Basque and Mexican-born Basque entrepreneurs exercised decisive influence over the establishment of several Spanish towns and Reales de Minas in northern Mexico. Basques contributed to the settlement of northern Mexico at rates disproportionate to their actual numbers in Spanish America or the Iberian peninsula.

Basques, Cantabrians, and other Iberians from northern Spain had considerable experience in organizing rural enterprises, especially the production of iron, wood and charcoal. In northern Mexico, as in the mines of Peru, Basques and Cantabrians applied this practical knowledge to the extraction of silver with great success. In addition, the Basques' experience in Spain as merchants, shipbuilders and small-scale entrepreneurs suited them ideally to participate in the mining and ranching economies of northern Mexico. People from Cantabria, Galicia, and Portugal who had a similar economic background also maintained a strong presence in the frontier settlements of New Spain. The significant Basque presence in the Spanish settlements of northern Mexico continued well into the eighteenth century. Families of Basque ancestry such as the Anzas, Vildosolas, and Marqueses de Aguayo played an important role in the history of the Spanish borderlands.

There was considerable internal diversity within the indigenous group as well. Native laborers and immigrants, detribalized Indians (called *nijoras, genízaros,* or *mecos*), former mission Indians and former religious rebels, all worked and lived together in the Spanish towns. Mestizos, mulattos, and castas enjoyed intermediate status as skilled laborers, soldiers, and small entrepreneurs. For those who achieved economic or military success there existed the possibility of ascending the racial scale and redefining their *calidad* (social status) as Spanish, and intermarriage with Spaniards was frequent. Within Spanish society immigrants from Spain, central Mexico, or elsewhere functioned as entrepreneurs or employees.

Frontier life in northern New Spain, then, was characterized by intense interethnic military confrontations, ample economic opportunities (for both laborers and employers), entrepreneurial vision, and a fluid adaptation to local circumstances. Compared to central and southern New Spain, society in the north offered more dynamic channels for social mobility, a more flexible sense of socioethnic identification, a more commercialized labor market, and a more egalitarian perspective on local affairs and government.

The Northern Missions

At the time of the outbreak of the Pueblo Revolt in 1680 Christianization of native populations by the Society of Jesus and the Order of Saint Francis in the north was far from successful. Entire groups, like Seris and Yumas, had no church at all within their territories. Numerous communities not only shunned the missions but relocated in the Sierra Madre Occidental. This was especially true in the Tepehuan and Tarahumara lands but was also notable among the Hopis and Zunis in the north.

Jesuits and Franciscans nonetheless had made significant advances, although these often were followed by drastic setbacks in the vast area north of the Tropic of Cancer. Their missions encompassed significant segments of native nations. Jesuits exerted a degree of control over Mayos, Yaquis, Pimas, Opatas, Tarahumaras, and Tepehuanes in Sinaloa, Sonora, Durango, and Chihuahua, while Franciscans established their missions among the Pueblos and Conchos in New Mexico and Nueva Vizcaya.

Jesuits. In 1590, Jesuits initiated an effort to convert Tepehuanes in the Sierra Madre Occidental and then slowly pushed northward to contact Tarahumaras in Chihuahua in 1607, establishing their first mission in San Pablo Ballesa. The great Tepehuan rebellion (1616–18) led by native religious leaders directed particular violence against the Jesuits and certainly disrupted their missionary work. When the area was again brought under Spanish control, the Jesuits reestablished their missions. In the seventeenth century constant revolts by Tepehuanes and against Christianity and colonial rule produced a fair number of Jesuit martyrs and forced the Jesuits to relocate, and in some cases simply abandon, missions in the area. Despite such setbacks, by the end of the seventeenth century Jesuits had consolidated their presence with a dozen religious foundations between the Río Florido, a Conchos tributary, and the Papigochic River in the Sierra Madre Occidental.

On the other side of the Sierra Madre range Jesuit mission efforts rendered sweeter fruits. Mayos and Yaquis finally signed separate peace agreements with Spanish troops led by Diego Martínez de Hurdaide in 1609. One missionary, Pedro Méndez, started working among Mayos in 1614, and by 1620 three missions were operating in Etchojoa, Camoa and Navojoa. In 1617, Jesuits Tomás Pérez de Ribas and Tomás Basilio began the conversion of the Yaqui, and by 1623 they had established the *rectorado* or mission head at Torim. By the 1640s, Jesuits had founded fifteen permanent settlements along the Mayo and Yaqui rivers.

Jesuits missions also extended into Lower Pima and Opata territories, where the Spanish presence had been eliminated after Indians slaughtered the settlers of Corazones, a town founded by Vázquez de Coronado in 1540. Following the Sonora and Moctezuma rivers, Jesuits established missions in Saguaripa, Bacanora and Matape. In the following decades Jesuits consolidated their mission system and expanded into northern Sonora.

Franciscans. Franciscan missions in the far north formally began with Oñate's entrada to New Mexico in 1598, even though their first contacts with Pueblo communities dated from Fray Marcos de Niza and Coronado's time. Between 1540 and 1590 different expeditions into New Mexico brought friars to the Río Grande Valley with the intention of initiating the process of Christianization. When these missionaries were left behind, however, they were killed by Pueblo Indians or simply disappeared.

With the pacification of New Mexico the Order of Saint Francis embarked on a systematic missionary program along the 350-mile stretch of the Río Grande from Taos to El Paso. Led by Fray Juan de Escalona, the friars established their headquarters at Santo Domingo and divided New Mexico into seven missionary districts. Between 1610 and 1630 Franciscans built some twenty-five missions in the most important Pueblo communities, including Taos and Acoma, traditionally hostile to Christian teachings.

The friars claimed to have baptized thousands of natives and to have erected Christian schools in all the missions during this period. Franciscans reached Zuni villages in 1629 where they established four missions, although by 1640 only Hawikuh and Halona had a permanent missionary. During the same period three churches were raised among the Hopi communities. In 1656 Franciscans from New Mexico started working among Manso Indians on the southern border of the province. In 1659 they founded the mission of Nuestra Señora de Guadalupe on the Río Grande, at the site of present-day Ciudad Juárez and El Paso, where travelers forded the river to and from Nueva Vizcaya. With more than fifty missionaries and increasing economic influence in New Mexico, Franciscans outweighed the power of civil authorities in the province's early years.

By the mid-seventeenth century, there was increasing competition over control and access to Indian labor in New Mexico. The Franciscans used Pueblo laborers to till their fields, build their churches, tend their cattle, and perform domestic chores in the missions, while colonial officials and Spanish settlers tried to force native communities to work on their estates, pay royal tribute and even gather supplies of salt, hides, pine nuts, and other products to export to Nueva Vizcaya. Moreover, the system by which Spanish authorities granted land and encomiendas to Spanish settlers began to undermine Franciscan and Pueblo control over natural resources. In defiance of colonial law, Spanish colonizers settled in Indian communities and encroached upon native rights to water, forests and land. Even worse, epidemics of European diseases took a heavy toll on Indian villages. Altogether the presence of Spanish settlers, Franciscans and colonial authorities severely disrupted Pueblo demographic stability, agriculture, and labor systems.

In the midst of these disputes, Franciscans became increasingly impatient with the Pueblo communities' continued attachment to their ancient religious ways, particularly the public ceremonial dances and collective ceremonies centered on the *kivas* (sacred underground spaces). From the friars' point of view, Pueblos superficially had embraced Christianity but failed to repudiate their traditional religion. Idolatry, they thought, should be confronted with more drastic measures.

In the 1660s, with no support from colonial officials, Franciscan authorities launched a campaign against idolatry aimed at the destruction of traditional Pueblo ceremonies. Kachina dances were prohibited, and missionaries raided the kivas to seize and destroy all the ceremonial objects. This policy was enforced by corporal punishment, especially whipping, a public form of physical abuse strongly resented by the Pueblos.

The Franciscan crusade against Pueblo traditional ceremonies only exacerbated local opposition to Spanish rule in the Rio Grande, already mounting as a result of the profound economic transformations introduced by missions and Spanish settlers. In addition, raiding of Pueblo and Spanish communities by Apaches, Utes, and Comanches increased in response to the introduction of horses, cattle, and other useful goods into the region. Indian raiders, already a threat to Pueblo communities before the arrival of Oñate, became extremely efficient as they adopted the use of horses and began to participate in slave-hunting raids. The arena in which these groups were active expanded considerably in the seventeenth century, and the growing prosperity of the colonial economy provided increased incentives for raiding. By the 1670s, the Spanish presence in New Mexico became extremely vulnerable, marked by internal divisions, external threats and growing native dissatisfaction and opposition. Franciscans would be one of the primary targets in the Pueblo Revolt of 1680.

Mission Life. Spanish missions in northern Mexico achieved varying degrees of success according to the Indians' willingness to adopt new ways of life under the mission system. Both Jesuits and Franciscans introduced new crops, tools, cattle, farm livestock and products from Spain and central Mexico in their settlements. Under the supervision of mission authorities, Indians produced agricultural surpluses to be marketed in the area mining towns. Thus mission Indians participated in the commercial system of the north but not as salaried workers.

The policy of establishing *reducciones,* or resettling Indians who lived in widespread *rancherías* in a more compact pattern centered on the church, was more successful among the Yaquis and Mayos than anywhere else. In northern New Mexico Pueblo Indians already lived in dense settlements, and Franciscans built their churches on the outskirts of Pueblo villages. Christian missions in Tarahumara, Concho, and Tepehuan territories only partially succeeded in realigning former settlements. The policy of amalgamating dispersed native communities into church-centered agricultural units with farm animals, cattle, sheep, and horses was not applied uniformly, even by members of the same religious order in the same ecclesiastical province. In New Mexico, for example, the Franciscan presence among Western Pueblos (Hopis and Zunis) was quite superficial, in part because of the isolation of these communities from the Santa Fe Royal Road and increasingly violent raids by hostile tribes, but above all because of local resistance to the Christian missions. The Hopi (or Moqui as they were called in colonial documents) achieved complete independence from Spanish rule during the Pueblo Revolt. Hopi missions were completely abandoned after 1680 and were never reoccupied by any Spanish religious corporation. The only resettlement that Spaniards accomplished among the Hopi was to inspire them relocate to areas where they could defend themselves better against European attacks.

Piro Pueblos, by contrast, voluntarily joined friars and Spanish settlers when they abandoned New Mexico in 1680. They resettled south of El Paso in new missions established by Franciscan authorities. The missions of Isleta, Socorro, and San Elizario became permanent settlements and successfully combined native and European crops, cattle raising and animal farming.

Mission life in northern Mexico generally provided native populations with a way of life relatively safe from Spanish raids and military expeditions, a certain economic security in terms of housing, food and clothing, and some access to Spanish goods from central Mexico. Mission Indians could participate in internal affairs on a limited basis by electing local alcaldes and town authorities, especially in the Jesuit missions in Sonora and Sinaloa. Mission authorities also delegated some functions to "advanced" natives, that is, already Hispanized and Christianized Indians who were chosen to serve as *temastianes* or missionary-helpers.

Life in the mission, however, also implied the unconditional acceptance of a new set of moral principles, based on Christian values imposed by the Catholic Church. In Jesuit and Franciscan congregations Indians had to comply with rules dictated by authoritarian ecclesiastical officials who allowed for no dissent. Treated as perpetual children by the paternalistic friars, Indians living in missions experienced public humiliation, physical punishment and all sorts of abuses. Friars acted not only as spiritual fathers but also as property owners, assigning labor tasks to the general population without monetary compensation. Mission Indians built the churches, tilled the fields, raised cattle, harvested the crops, performed domestic services and kept the mission running.

Last, and hardly least significant, the policy of amalgamating scattered rancherías into compact pueblos only increased the frequency and virulence of outbreaks of European diseases among native families, especially smallpox, measles and typhus. Mission Indians were more likely to succumb to these diseases than to violence at the hands of other Indians.

Glossary

Camino Real de Tierra Adentro   royal road linking Zacatecas with Durango, Chihuahua, and Santa Fe, New Mexico

Chichimeca generic term for Zacatecos, Guachichiles, Pames, and other Indian groups in Mexico's near north

dádiva gift in exchange for peace

genízaro Hispanized Indian living in the Spanish territories as a servant or slave in Nueva Vizcaya and New Mexico, also called *nijora* in Sonora-Arizona; term derives from the name for Turkish slave soldiers, Janissaries

katsina (kachina) Pueblo ancestral spirits

kiva underground sacred space among the Pueblo Indians

ranchería dispersed agricultural settlement, characteristic of some northern groups

Real y Minas mining town with special privileges granted by the Crown

reducción community in which Indians from scattered settlements were relocated under colonial authorities

seven cities legendary seven golden cities, led by Cibola and Quivira

temastian Indian religious assistant or church custodian in northern Mexican missions

Questions for Discussion

1. Why did Spanish explorations in northern Mexico before 1546 not succeed in creating permanent settlements?

2. What were the main goals of the expeditions of Fray Marcos de Niza and Vázquez de Coronado? How did Niza describe "Cibola"?

3. What were the causes and outcome of the Chichimeca Wars?

4. What contributions did Indian allies from central and western Mexico make to the foundation of Spanish settlements in northern Mexico?

5. What were the socioeconomic functions of missions in northern Mexico?

6. What were the common cultural features of these frontier societies?

Suggested Reading

Bolton, Hebert Eugene, *Coronado, Knight of Pueblos and Plains*. Albuquerque: University of New Mexico Press, 1949. Detailed biography by one of the first scholars of the borderlands region.

———, ed. *Spanish Explorations in the Southwest, 1542–1706*. New York: Barnes and Noble, 1956. Translations of a number of accounts of the exploration and conquest in northern New Spain, with introductions by the editor.

Gerhard, Peter. *The North Frontier of New Spain*. Princeton, N.J.: Princeton University Press, 1982. Essential reference work on geography, towns, missions, Indian groups, population, and historical development in the north.

Officer, James. *Hispanic Arizona, 1536–1856*. Tucson: University of Arizona Press, 1987. A narrative history of Spanish Arizona (including Sonora) under Spain, Mexico, and the United States.

Powell, Philip W. *Soldiers, Indians, and Silver: The Northward Advance of New Spain, 1550–1600*. Berkeley and Los Angeles: University of California Press, 1952. Important study of the expansion of Spanish settlement into the north, the conflict with the Chichimecas, and establishment of missions and fortified settlements.

Sauer, Carl O. *Sixteenth Century North America: The Land and People as Seen by Europeans*. Berkeley: University of California Press, 1971. Traces early Spanish activity in North America from a geographical perspective.

Spicer, Edward H. *Cycles of Conquest. The Impact of Spain, Mexico and the United States on the Indians of the Southwest, 1533–1960*. Tucson: University of Arizona Press, 1962. Major study of the long-term impact of colonialization and socioeconomic and political change on indigenous groups of the borderlands region on both sides of the U.S.-Mexican border.

Weber, David. *The Spanish Frontier in North America*. New Haven, Conn.: Yale University Press, 1992. Important synthesis of the history of the Spanish borderlands in the present-day United States.

Chapter Ten

The African Presence
in New Spain

Africans and people of African descent, both slave and free, were present in New Spain from the time of the Spanish conquest. They accompanied Spaniards to Mexico from the Caribbean and continued to arrive in substantial numbers during the sixteenth and seventeenth centuries, sometimes as voluntary migrants from Spain, Portugal, or the Caribbean islands but far more often conveyed there by the transatlantic slave trade. In Mexico Africans played key economic roles, acting in the early years especially as a crucial extension of the European presence in the colony. Spaniards used their African slaves in the most commercialized and lucrative sectors of the economy—sugar estates, gold and silver mines, and textile manufacture—as well as in domestic occupations. In the first century following the conquest of Mexico virtually any Spanish enterprise or upper-class household would be likely to include at least one or two slaves, and sugar plantations and mines sometimes had large numbers of slaves.

Notwithstanding their economic importance, the position of slaves and of free people of African descent was paradoxical and problematic. Closer to Spaniards culturally than were Mexico's indigenous peoples, Africans nonetheless resembled Europeans physically less than did Indians and mestizos. Furthermore, they bore the stigma of enslaved status, and even free people of African descent often remained closely linked to slaves through marriage, kinship, and occupation. Despite their skills, the high level of demand for African slaves, and the prices they commanded, Africans suffered abuse and mistreatment as well as legal and social discrimination, in some respects enjoying fewer protections under law than did Indians. Unlike Indians, blacks and mulattos, both slave and free, came under the jurisdiction and scrutiny of the Inquisition; unlike mestizos, free people of African descent had to pay a special tribute or tax and were subject to laws (admittedly not always very effective) designed to make them a perpetually servile group. Notwithstanding such constraints, on an individual basis free blacks and mulattos could succeed in forging decent and fairly secure lives for themselves and their families. Even slaves could gain considerable independence, earning money for themselves and seeking out marriage partners who might share their ethnic background. Overall the experience of Africans in Mexico varied greatly.

Establishment of African Slavery in New Spain

The Introduction of African Slaves into Mexico. Slavery was an ancient institution in the Mediterranean world. From classical Greek and Roman times onward almost anyone could end up as a slave through the misfortunes of war, piracy, or economic hard times. Conflicts between Christians and Muslims during the Middle Ages resulted in the enslavement of captives on both sides. The codification of Spanish law promulgated in the thirteenth century—the *Siete Partidas*—specifically provided certain rights and protections for slaves and acknowledged that freedom was the natural state of human beings. Slaves could marry, and married couples and families were not to be separated. Children inherited their mother's status, so a child born to a free woman who was married to a slave would be free. The law code limited a master's power to punish; if he killed his slave, he would be tried for murder. The Siete Partidas also stipulated the conditions by which a slave could gain his or her freedom. Although these laws existed well before the era of the Atlantic slave trade and the establishment of Spanish dominion

Figure 10-1 **Black slave during the conquest**. At the meeting between Cortés and Moctezuma, a black slave holds the conqueror's horse. Blacks were important auxiliaries to the Spanish enterprise of conquest and colonization.
From Fr. Diego Durán, *The History of the Indies of New Spain* (Norman: University of Oklahoma Press, 1994), Plate 58.

in the Americas, later they would provide the legal framework in which African slavery developed in New Spain and elsewhere in the Iberian world. Nonetheless, although these laws were intended to regulate master-slave relations and protect slaves from excessive mistreatment at the hands of their owners, the latter still exercised considerable power, and slaves often were unable to avail themselves of legal protections.

Although some slaves from sub-Saharan Africa reached the Mediterranean region through the North African trade during the Middle Ages, the western trade in African slaves really got underway during the second half of the fifteenth century, when Portuguese traders seeking gold and ivory became active along the coast of West Africa. By the end of the fifteenth century there were substantial numbers of African slaves in Portugal and southern Spain, and the Portuguese were using African labor to cultivate sugar in the islands of the Atlantic and off the African coast. Genoese merchants and financiers contributed to the establishment of the fifteenth-century Portuguese sugar industry, and they also participated in the early economic development of the Spanish Caribbean. They helped to introduce Africans, and sugar cultivation, into Hispaniola early in the sixteenth century.

African slavery, then, was well established in the Caribbean by the time Cortés organized his expedition to conquer Mexico. A member of that group, Juan Garrido, one of the first Africans in Mexico, claimed to have been the first to plant and harvest wheat there. He had lived in Portugal and Spain before crossing the Atlantic to Santo Domingo, apparently as a free man. He participated in the conquest of Puerto Rico before joining the expedition to Mexico, where after the conquest he would engage in a variety of undertakings—gold mining, horticulture, working as the doorkeeper of Mexico City's council—eventually joining Cortés on his expedition to Lower California. Other Africans came to Mexico from the islands, Spain or Portugal in the years after the conquest. Although the majority (unlike Garrido) were slaves, since they had lived among Iberians they often already had learned Spanish or Portuguese and had some familiarity with Catholicism as well as with Spanish economic enterprises. Such Africans were called *ladino*, a word that specifically referred to the ability to speak Spanish but also implied acculturation in a more general sense. A slave coming directly from Africa who lacked previous exposure to Spanish culture was called *bozal*, and people in the process of assimilating Spanish language and culture were often described as being *"entre ladino y bozal"* (between *ladino* and *bozal*).

Because of their origins and background and sometimes prior experience in Spain or the Caribbean, Africans often possessed the knowledge and skills associated with mining, metallurgy, agriculture, and textile manufacture—all of which were well developed in West and Central Africa—that Spaniards needed to organize and develop their economic enterprises. Some African societies mined gold, and others mined and manufactured iron and steel. Some Africans raised cattle and horses, although the disease environment in parts of West Africa made stock raising impossible. Textile production was important in West and Central Africa, and overland and riverine trade and marketing systems flourished there.

In the Caribbean islands Spaniards used Africans in gold mines and on sugar estates, and in Mexico African slaves participated in the same kinds of activities from the outset. In the early postconquest years, when Mexican mining activity focused almost entirely on gold, a typical gold mining enterprise consisted of a Spanish miner, an African slave or two, and a gang of Indian slaves. When mining activity shifted to silver, especially following the discovery of mines in Zacatecas late in 1546, there, too, African slaves played a prominent role in the workforce, particularly in the early years.

In addition to other advantages that African slaves offered to Spaniards in Mexico, the latter also benefited from Africans' exposure to and familiarity with Spanish language, culture, and technology. Originating in an Old World that for millenia had been an arena for the diffusion of diseases as well as technology, Africans and Europeans to a great extent shared relative immunities and resistance to the diseases that proved so lethal to indigenous Americans. Thus, while the prices of African slaves were substantial and increased in the sixteenth century, the investment Spaniards made in this kind of labor brought them much greater returns than did attempts to exploit Indian slave labor, as can be seen in the relative prices of African and Indian slaves in the early postconquest period. Although enslavement of Indians continued in northern New Spain throughout the colonial period, as a result of which there always were small numbers of Indian slaves in central Mexico, for the most part royal prohibitions on the enslavement of peaceful Indians prevailed. Africans quickly became the predominant enslaved group in Mexico in the sixteenth century.

Not only did Africans provide skilled labor on a long-term (which is to say permanent) basis, they also perhaps could be more easily controlled by Spaniards than Indians, being conspicuous and relatively isolated amid the largely indigenous population. That control, however, did not go unchallenged. Africans escaped, sometimes succeeding in maintaining their independence and even forming autonomous communities, and they conspired to revolt. Nonetheless, despite being, like Indians, subject to Spanish domination and exploitation, in general they could not easily make common cause with the Indians, with whom they were often at odds because of the very nature of their occupations. Spaniards frequently used their African slaves and free black and mulatto employees as overseers of Indian laborers. In the textile shops or *obrajes*, for example, the doorkeeper who was responsible for keeping sometimes large numbers of Indian workers literally under lock and key often was black or mulatto, either slave or free. In the countryside, where the rapid proliferation of livestock wrought extensive damage on the unfenced cultivated lands of Indians, the cowboys and shepherds responsible for controlling cattle and sheep often were Africans as well.

Although they were slaves and the Indians with whom they worked technically were free, Africans often despised Indians as a servile and docile group.
On an individual basis, however, Africans and Indians certainly formed
alliances, not least those of a personal nature. The term *mulato* could refer to
people of mixed European and African descent, but in Mexico far more frequently it meant someone whose background was African and Indian.

The Slave Trade and African Origins. Well over one hundred thousand
slaves arrived in Mexico from the time of the conquest until 1640, when
Portugal regained its independence from Spain. During the sixteenth century, the Portuguese dominated the West African slave trade. This virtual
monopoly, together with royal restrictions on the trade, made it difficult for
the residents of New Spain to obtain as many slaves as they wished. The
union of the Portuguese and Spanish crowns under a Spanish monarch during the period from 1580 to 1640 eliminated this problem by opening the
door to direct Portuguese trade with Spanish America. The demand for
slaves and the volume of slave imports in Mexico reached their height at the
end of the sixteenth century and early decades of the seventeenth. According
to Colin Palmer, over fifty thousand slaves arrived in the years 1595 to 1622,
whereas total slave imports for the preceding seventy-five years were 36,500
(Gonzalo Aguirre offers a somewhat higher estimate of an average of two
thousand slaves arriving annually in the period from 1580 to 1650). The slave
trade dwindled considerably in the second half of the seventeenth century,
and in the eighteenth century only around twenty thousand slaves entered
Mexico. Although the slave trade dropped off as the importance of African
slaves diminished, nonetheless the institution of slavery persisted throughout the colonial period. As a result, by the eighteenth century the composition of the slave group had changed substantially, with *criollos*
(American-born people) of African descent coming to predominate. Patrick
J. Carroll has found that in central Veracruz the proportions of criollo and
African-born slaves were roughly equal by 1675; in 1760 only 2 percent of the
slave group he identified were *bozales*. Cheryl Martin shows that *bozales* disappeared from the sugar estates of Michoacan even earlier.

Spaniards usually recorded the origins of slaves, making it possible to
trace changing patterns in the slave trade, which shifted in focus from West
Africa in the sixteenth century to Central Africa in the seventeenth. Most
Africans sent to Mexico in the sixteenth century came from Senegambia and
Guinea-Bissau; in the seventeenth century the great majority arrived from
Congo and Angola. Because the slave trade drew on specific regions, slaves
were likely to work or live with, or at least in proximity to, people who
shared their origins. At the same time, because of the changing focus of the
slave trade and the development of a group of *criollos* or American-born
slaves, slave communities typically were fairly mixed.

Through the early decades of the seventeenth century, then, the market
for African slaves expanded. Not surprisingly, a brisk domestic trade

matched the transatlantic one, although it seems to have been conducted primarily on an individual basis. Locally based merchants and entrepreneurs commonly traded a variety of commodities, which could include slaves bought and sold on their own or others' behalf; but apparently there were few people whose livelihood depended principally on dealing in slaves. As the chief port of entry for New Spain, Veracruz obviously was a key source of slaves for domestic buyers, and cities such as Mexico and Puebla also figured significantly in the domestic trade, mainly because of the volume of demand and numbers of slaves working in the largest urban centers.

The terms by which slaves were sold varied mainly according to the age and skills of the individual. In general young men and women commanded the highest prices, especially if they had particular skills and training, usually selling for around 300 to 400 pesos. In 1609, a couple purchased for their *obraje* seven slaves—five men and two women—from three men for 349 pesos each. Children and older adults generally sold for considerably less. Sale prices for adult women sometimes included their small children, and skilled slaves might be sold with the tools of their trade. Perhaps surprisingly, buyers showed no particular preference for native-born over African-born slaves. Some Spaniards apparently considered mulattos to be less desirable than blacks, perhaps because they were perceived as potentially more difficult to control, but this preference was not invariable.

Ultimately the ascribed value of a slave hinged on his or her skills. In the inventory of the slaves of *obraje* owner Alonso Gómez, the assessed value of two women who worked as housekeepers, from Angola and Bran respectively, was 400 and 450 pesos; Antón, a forty-five-year-old man from Mozambique who was ladino and worked as a cloth shearer, was worth 500 pesos; and a twenty-five-year-old man from Angola named Francisco, also a cloth shearer, was valued at 550 pesos. A *criollo* from Oaxaca, Baltasar, who was the same age as Francisco, was worth 100 pesos less because he had become a cloth shearer only recently. In contrast, however, the worth of another cloth shearer from Mozambique was assessed at only 250 pesos, and a mulatto slave from Mexico City was valued at only 300 pesos "for being a bad spinner." His poor skills might have reflected his unwillingness, rather than inability, to perform the required tasks.

Slaves seldom failed to attract buyers, notwithstanding any undesirable qualities the seller had to disclose. Slaves described as drunkards, thieves, and runaways often sold at prices more or less comparable to those commanded by less troublesome slaves. Even slaves who were in jail or who had escaped and eluded recapture nonetheless found purchasers. All evidence suggests that in the first century or so after the conquest demand for slaves remained high.

It is difficult to be precise about the distribution of African slaves in colonial New Spain. A census of 1570 suggests a great concentration of slaves in Mexico City, which ostensibly was home to eight thousand, making them as numerous as Spanish men. For that year it has been estimated that the archbishopric of Mexico had 10,595 Africans and the bishoprics of Tlaxcala, Nueva Galicia, Michoacan, Oaxaca, and Yucatan 2,958, 2,375, 1,765, 481, and 265 respectively.[1] Concentrated heavily in the Spanish cities, mines, and sugar estates in the sixteenth century, over time the distribution of slaves changed as slavery itself diminished in importance with the increased availability of free, skilled workers. By the eighteenth century, generally the largest numbers of slaves were found working in the sugar plantations of the Gulf Coast region, Morelos, and Michoacan, but by then the considerable growth and diffusion of a free population of African and mixed descent meant that members of this group lived all over New Spain, even in areas where slavery itself had been of little significance.

Conditions of Life and Work

Distribution of Slaves. The explanation for the high level of demand for slaves in the first century or so of the colony lies in the nature of Spanish economic activities in Mexico after the conquest. Africans played a key role in virtually every economic sector—mining, farming, ranching, industry, trade, and transport—even though they seldom constituted the majority of the workforce. When slavery was at its height in New Spain, it is estimated that slaves constituted no more than fifteen percent of the labor force in the mines.

Slaves so commonly formed part of the labor force for estates, mines, and refineries as well as for all manner of artisanal, commercial, and industrial establishments that it is difficult to distinguish consistently between the work experience of slaves and that of other free or coerced laborers. From the far south to the far north of New Spain slaves were ubiquitous, if not always very numerous. Despite low levels of imports—probably averaging no more than 150 a year in the early seventeenth century—the numbers of black and mulatto slaves in Guatemala, both in the city and the surrounding countryside, were large enough that by the eighteenth century a significant group of African and mixed origins existed in the city. The same apparently was true for Yucatan; by the end of the eighteenth century blacks and mulattos were as numerous as whites in the city of Mérida, although by then probably they were mostly free people. Large numbers of mulattos worked on the sugar plantations of Morelos and Michoacan. In Querétaro, north of Mexico City, blacks were about as numerous as Spaniards in the first half of the seventeenth century. They worked in households, artisans' and merchants' shops, and obrajes in the city, and on ranches and farms in the countryside. Over a century later, when slavery had greatly declined in importance in most of New Spain, a handful of African slaves still formed part the labor force of the

[1]Gonzalo Aguirre Beltrán, *La población negra de México* (Mexico, 1972, 2nd ed.), p. 207.

northern estates of the Marqueses de Aguayo; they worked at specialized or supervisory tasks as the overseers of obrajes, weavers, or shoemakers.

Domestic service accounted for sizeable numbers of slaves in urban areas. Not only did most well-to-do households have at least one or two slaves—wealthy ones were likely to have several—ecclesiastical establishments such as monasteries and nunneries also commonly held slaves. It probably is fair to assume that on the whole the conditions for slaves in households or convents were better than for those who worked in mines, obrajes, or sugar plantations. The urban setting could afford opportunities to socialize as well as to earn extra money, and an urban-based slave more likely would be in a position to seek clerical or official protection or intervention if necessary. Yet, even domestic slaves were vulnerable to the whims of their owners and subject to physical discipline and punishment. Nor was domestic service or urban residence any guarantee of stability. Slave owners, especially the less well off, might rent out their slaves, who could end up working for employers little concerned with their welfare. Urban slaves could be sold off to mines or estates if their masters thought they were guilty of misbehavior or criminal acts.

The greatest concentrations of slaves were found in the sugar plantations and the textile obrajes. In both these enterprises, the use of African slave labor seems to have increased in the sixteenth century and peaked in the first half of the seventeenth, owing to several factors. These included the increased volume of slave imports, expanding scale of economic enterprises geared toward a growing domestic market, and official pressure (in the case of the obrajes) to reduce dependence on confined Indian workers in favor of greater reliance on African slaves. In the obrajes of Coyoacan, south of Mexico City, of a total of 372 workers counted in 1660, nearly 60 percent were black and mulatto slaves. The slaves who worked in the obrajes had skills in a range of trades associated with textile manufacture, although some guilds barred blacks and mulattos from entering or achieving the status of master. Nonetheless, slaves might perform all the functions associated with the relevant trades.

Sugar Estates. The sugar industry got an early start in New Spain. Although estates often employed mixed labor forces that included encomienda Indians (in the first part of the sixteenth century) as well as Indian wage laborers, African slaves played a prominent role in sugar production from the outset. Hernando Cortés had Africans working at his sugar mill at San Andrés Tuxtla in southern Veracruz in the 1530s, and the royal accountant Don Rodrigo de Albornoz bought 150 African slaves for a sugar estate he established near Cempoala in 1535. Over one hundred African slaves worked at the Orizaba mill that belonged to the first viceroy, Don Antonio de Mendoza. By the early seventeenth century, the numbers of slaves working on some sugar plantations were even greater. Two hundred Africans worked on the Santísima Trinidad plantation near Jalapa in 1608, and the San José estate, founded in 1599 by a merchant father and son in Mexico City who formed a partnership with a man in Puebla, in 1643 had 220 slaves.

Despite the costs of acquiring and maintaining such large groups of slaves and the continued use on many sugar estates of Indian labor, both temporary and permanent, New Spain's sugar plantations probably represent the main arena in which African slaves performed not only the most skilled tasks, especially those associated with boiling and refining sugar, but much of the most menial and arduous labor as well. In the early seventeenth century at the San José mill, for example, only sixteen slaves, whose assessed worth was 800 pesos each, were considered to be skilled tradesmen, while the rest were described as *"ordinarios de trabajo"* ("ordinary workers").

As the workforce for the sugar plantations grew, over time its composition changed. Patrick Carroll's study shows that in 1620 the Almolonga estate in Jalapa had eighteen slaves, including thirteen men, four women, and one infant, the only one not born in Africa. Of the slaves (thirty-one men, twenty-five women, twelve children) on Almolonga in 1675 only a dozen were African-born. By the end of the seventeenth century, most of the estate's slave community consisted of criollo slave families. Cheryl Martin found that as more Indians went to work on the sugar estates of Morelos, increased mixing between Indians and blacks occurred, resulting in a substantial proportion of mulatos in estate workforces. By 1732, for example, just over 60 percent of the slave group on the hacienda of Atlihuayan were mulattos.

Life as a Slave. Estates devoted to products other than sugar also could have numbers of slaves, although the Jesuit hacienda of Santa Lucía in central Mexico studied by Herman Konrad, which was devoted to farming and raising sheep and goats, probably was unusual in the size of its slave labor force. It had 291 slaves in 1722 and 312 slaves in 1743. In 1722 171 of the slaves worked at the main estate and residence in the textile mill or as domestic laborers or shepherds. Apparently many of the slave women were put to work in the obraje. The other slaves worked on other farms and ranches. Regardless of what an estate produced, where there were substantial numbers of slaves they were likely to live in family groups. Because of the high rate of racial mixing and intermarriage between free and slave workers, Martin suggests that "by the eighteenth century, slavery on the sugar haciendas of Morelos was, quite literally, an accident of birth, a condition inherited from one's mother."[2] Workers of varying race and status shared ties of kinship and compadrazgo.

Because of the diverse working conditions and situations of slaves, their experiences and the treatment they received at the hands of masters varied as well. Martin's evidence from Morelos suggests that in the seventeenth and eighteenth centuries slaves were likely to be well fed, with adults

---

[2]Cheryl English Martin, *Rural Society in Colonial Morelos* (Albuquerque, 1985), p. 135.

receiving six to seven liters of maize a week, in addition to other food; at the hacienda of Atlacomulco, for example, slaves over the age of ten received a weekly ration of 4.6 kilograms of beef in addition to maize. She suggests that in some respects slaves might have enjoyed a relatively secure and privileged existence compared to free hacienda laborers. The skills that slaves acquired and the often high degree of responsibility conferred on them by masters and managers could result in considerable independence. Konrad notes that not only did slaves work in supervisory positions or in trades at the Jesuit hacienda of Santa Lucía, they also were entrusted with the job of conveying supplies and money between Mexico City, Santa Lucía, and the other properties connected with it.

The life of a man named Juan de Morga suggests the wide range of treatment that a slave could experience. Born in Oaxaca around 1627, the son of a priest named Atanasio de Morga and a criollo slave woman, Juan received some basic schooling and in his twenties worked for a public accountant in Mexico City. Most likely his paternal relatives (he had an uncle who was a Dominican friar) helped place him in this position. Despite its advantages, Juan committed some sort of infraction. Anticipating punishment, he contrived to escape and lived some months as a free man before being apprehended. His master pardoned him but following another misadventure decided to send Juan to Zacatecas to find a new master. There his fortunes changed radically for the worse, as he was purchased by a man named Diego de Arratia, an obvious sadist who cruelly beat, tortured, and tormented his new slave and kept him in shackles for months at a time. Morga eventually escaped and attempted to appeal to clerical and civil authorities, finally going voluntarily before the Inquisition to confess his sins in hopes of being removed from his master. The Inquisition officials were sufficiently dismayed at the evidence of Arratia's cruelty that they refused to send Juan back to him, eventually releasing him to a man who claimed to have purchased him from Arratia. Whether Morga lived out his life in happier circumstances is not known.[3]

The actions of Juan de Morga's master in Zacatecas clearly were extreme and probably in some degree aberrant; a carpenter who had worked at Arratia's *hacienda de minas* testified to the desperation and misery of his slaves. Cruelty and violence toward slaves, if not the rule, certainly were not uncommon. Probably the majority of slaves, however, lived and worked in circumstances that much resembled those of other free or semifree laborers and servants. Just as there were cruel and unreasonable masters, there were those who formed bonds of affection with their slaves, as evidenced in bequests made in wills and voluntary manumissions.

---

[3]Solange Alberro, "Juan de Morga and Gertrudis de Escobar: Rebellious Slaves," in David G. Sweet and Gary B. Nash, *Struggle and Survival in Colonial America* (Berkeley and Los Angeles, 1981), pp. 165–76.

Freedom: Manumission, Resistance, and Revolt

Manumission. Manumission was the process by which slaves legally gained their freedom. They could achieve this in several ways, but doubtless the most common was through payment, with either the slave or some other individual paying (or promising to pay) the purchase price. Masters who found themselves more in need of cash than of the services of their slaves were willing to make agreements by which slaves purchased their freedom. While some slaves had the good fortune to accumulate enough money to buy their freedom outright, or someone else (perhaps a parent or other family member) was able to do so, probably the majority of slaves had to borrow money or obligate themselves in some way in order to meet the purchase price. As a result they often began their lives in freedom in debt and under contract to serve someone (sometimes their former owner).

Voluntary manumissions were most frequently found in wills. Such decisions to grant slaves their liberty could reflect ties of affection or even of kinship between master and slave, or they were charitable acts inspired by the perceived nearness of death and concerns for salvation. These manumissions, however, often placed limitations on a former slave's freedom. However achieved, manumission often left former slaves in a situation of what historian Philip Curtin has called "lingering servitude." Not only might they be obligated to work off a debt for their own self-purchase, they might have spouses or other family members who were still enslaved whose purchase price they also hoped to meet. As a result freedmen and women often remained closely bound to former masters and the institution of slavery itself.

Escape. The transition from slavery to freedom entailed time, uncertainty, and often a substantial financial commitment. Given the harsh conditions in which many slaves were forced to live and work, and the impossibility for many of achieving their freedom through legal means, slaves took matters into their own hands by running off. As seen in the case of Juan de Morga, however, escape was one matter, maintaining one's freedom and independence quite another. Runaway slaves could be sold even before they were apprehended precisely because both buyer and seller assumed that in time the truant would be found.

Runaways like Morga who remained well within Spanish society—staying in the cities or traveling the main routes that connected them—in the long run often failed to elude officials or former masters. The most successful runaways, known as *cimarrones*, removed themselves from the orbit of Spanish society and its authorities. They lived in relatively inaccessible areas, often banding together to form groups that collectively not only defied recapture but preyed on colonial society as well. In the sixteenth century, escaped slaves in northern Mexico made common cause with Chichimeca Indians, who were almost constantly in conflict with Spaniards. At the end of December 1572 a missionary in the Huasteca, Fray Pedro de San Luis, wrote that "the Chichimecas . . . had three black slaves of Spaniards who had fled their masters and were acting as captains."[4] Cimarrones joined northern Indians in attacking wagon trains, killing Spaniards, and carrying off property.

Despite official efforts to eradicate them, groups of cimarrones who perfected the arts of guerrilla warfare established themselves all over New Spain, from Nueva Galicia to Veracruz and Oaxaca. Because of the large numbers of slaves working on the sugar plantations, runaways were especially active in the Gulf Coast region, where they established settlements known as *palenques*. One of the most famous of these took shape around 1580 near the city of Córdoba, under the leadership of a man named Yanga. After years of conflict followed by lengthy negotiations, Spanish authorities finally recognized the community's freedom and autonomy. The town of San Lorenzo de Negros came into existence in 1618. Runaway slaves from the Cortés haciendas in Tehuantepec formed a community at Petapa that had been recognized by 1590. Local officials attempted (apparently unsuccessfully) to include the former slaves of Petapa in the labor draft (*repartimiento*) for nearby estates.

Revolt. Legal recognition, however, by no means signaled the end of cimarrón activity or slave rebelliousness. Five serious slave revolts occurred in Córdoba and Orizaba during the eighteenth century, and violence continued until the end of the colonial period. An estimated two thousand slaves took part in the 1735 uprising that lasted some five months and caused damage and losses estimated at over 1 million pesos. Six years later slaves revolted again. In 1769 authorities recognized another community of cimarrones in northeastern Oaxaca as the town of Nuestra Señora de Guadalupe de los Morenos de Amapa.

Slave revolts by no means occurred only in the countryside. As early as 1537 officials in Mexico City took action after receiving reports of an alleged slave conspiracy to kill all the city's Spanish residents. Although the revolt never got underway, a number of slaves were publicly executed in the aftermath of the plot's discovery. Other slave disturbances took place in the capital in the early seventeenth century, the best known in 1611–12. The death of a female slave, apparently the result of excessive punishment on the part of her master, moved some 1500 slaves to take to the streets in protest. After officials arrested and punished the leaders, the city's slaves elected two Angolan slaves as their king and queen. When a planned Christmas uprising had to be postponed and the elected king died, the plotters chose another royal pair, this time a free mulatto and his wife, a mulatto slave, with the intention of rising on Holy Thursday, 1612. Again the plans were aborted when authorities learned of the conpiracy and arrested the leaders of the black religious asociations, the cofradías. More arrests and confessions under torture eventually

---

[4]Quoted in María Luisa Herrera Casasús, "Raíces africanas en la población de Tamaulipas," in Luz María Martínez Montiel, ed., *Presencia africana en México* (Mexico, 1994) p. 489.

led to the execution of twenty-eight men and seven women, who were hanged in Mexico City's plaza mayor, their heads subsequently severed and placed on pikes.

Slave protests and revolts and the hostility of the cimarrones in the Gulf Coast region continued to the end of the colonial period and beyond. During the struggles for independence both Miguel Hidalgo and José María Morelos called for an end to slavery, which brought runaway slaves into rebel ranks in central Veracruz and inspired slave revolts. Even after independence runaway slaves in Córdoba remained in the mountains. In 1829 Vicente Guerrero became president of the new republic and abolished slavery a year later, and over the next decade the cimarrones finally began to enter Mexican society.

Experience of Free Blacks and Mulattos

The difficulties of making the transition from slave to free status and the participation of free people of color in some of the protests and anti-Spanish conspiracies of slaves suggest the close connections that existed between slaves and free blacks and mulattos in colonial Mexico. Not only did free people of African descent suffer from legal and social discrimination, their often uncertain position in colonial society left them vulnerable to exploitation and abuse. The distinction between free and enslaved people of color could be so tenuous that even those born into freedom ran the risk of being reduced to virtual slave status.

Certainly not all free colored people shared close ties with the enslaved. Small numbers of free people of African descent continued to arrive in Mexico as immigrants from Spain, Portugal, or elsewhere. Free blacks and mulattos often seem to be among the least rooted and most transitory members of colonial society, possibly a reflection of the weakness of their ties with either Spaniards or Indians and the disadvantages of associating closely with slaves. Some forged advantageous connections with members of the Spanish group that helped them achieve a measure of upward mobility and respectability. Although many free blacks and mulattos worked in domestic service, all over New Spain they also achieved prominence as artisans, even working in some of the most prestigious trades. They also became merchants and shop owners. By the late colonial period mulattos had made substantial inroads into the medical profession, reflecting the ineffectiveness of ordinances meant to prohibit them from studying at the university. Some free people benefited from the assistance and concern of Spanish fathers, who might provide dowries for daughters, bequeath property to their mixed progeny, arrange apprenticeships, or help set up their sons in business. Lolita Gutiérrez Brockington has shown that by the end of the sixteenth century mulattos almost monopolized supervisory positions on the Cortés haciendas

Figure 10-2 **Black uprising 1537.** Spaniards crushed an early conspiracy by black slaves, hanging many in the main plaza. The event is depicted in an indigenous codex showing important events of the prehispanic and early colonial eras.
From *Codex Telleriano-Remensis*. Paris: Bibliothèque Nationale de France, folio 45.

in Tehuantepec, displacing Spaniards. Most of these mulattos previously had worked as cowboys (*vaqueros*). By the middle of the seventeenth century the majority of the free resident vaqueros also were mulatos.

Excerpts from a list of free blacks and mulatos obligated to pay tribute in Puebla, 1597–1603

Agustín de Xerez, free mulato, single, tailor's apprentice in 1598; by 1601 he is a tailor. Son of Juan de Villafranca, a free black, and his wife Mencía López, a free mulata

Agustin, mulato, shoemaker

Ana de Aguilar, free mulata, widow of Francisco de Valderas Castroverde, a Spaniard

Ana López, free black woman married to Juan Bran, a black slave of the Dominican friars

Ana López, free mulata married to Lorenzo Núñez, free mulato

Andres Diosdado, free black in service in the monastery of St. Agustín, married to Magdalena Sánchez, free mulata

Andrés de la Rosa, mulato married to an Indian woman who lives in the *barrio* of San Francisco

Andrés Ramírez, free mulato married to Mari Pérez, a Spaniard

Antonio González Cordero, mulato, shoemaker. Born in 1577 in Villanueva de Portomar in the Algarve (Portugal), went to Mexico in 1600

Bartolomé Francisco, free mulato, married to Ana Verónica, an Indian from the *barrio* of San Sebastián in Puebla. Was a cloth shearer but started working as a muleteer.

Beatriz de Ribera, free mulata married to Domingo, a black slave belonging to Alonso Gómez, city councilman

Benito Castellano, mulato, single, recently arrived from Castile, sells fruit

Catalina, mulata who serves Bachiller Julián de Ribera, married to Diego de la Isla, a mulato slave on the *estancia* of Doña María Monte

Diego Celado, free mulato, saddler, married to Inés de los Angeles, mestiza

Diego de la Cruz, free black man married to Susana, a black slave woman who belongs to the schoolmaster

Domingo de Anaya, free mulato, shoemaker, married to Antonia Cortés, mulata, a slave woman who belongs to the Dominicans (as of 1601 she is free)

Domingo Díaz, free mulato, single, deals in poultry, recently arrived from Havana

Domingo Fránquez, free black, single, native of Veracruz

Francisco Alemán, free mulato, single, born around 1580, recently arrived in the fleet and now apprenticed to Juan Gómez Melgarejo, carpenter

Francisca Flores, free mulata, widow who was married to Juan Francisco, Spaniard, a carpenter

Francisco Muñoz, free mulato married to Francisca, mulata slave of Alonso Sánchez

(Continued)

Gil Yáñez, free mulato from Portugal, single, recently arrived from Spain, works on the estancia of Rodrigo Hernández

Gonzalo, free mulato, married to María, an Indian woman who is the servant of Salvador Martínez

Gracia Hernández, free black woman, single, who was the slave of Pedro Naranjo, a priest

Isabel Sarmiento, free mulata, daughter of Juan Martín, mulato, married to Pedro, black slave of Juan Domínguez

Josephe de Pérez, free mulato, single, native of Puebla, son of Francisca Hernández, black woman and baker; he is apprenticed to Juan Bautista, tailor

Juan de los Reyes, free mulato, single, native of Seville

Juana, free black woman; city councilman Martín de Mafra Vargas says she is in his house and is old and sick

Lorenzo Núñez, free mulato, native of Puebla, muleteer, married to Ana López, free mulata

Luisa González, free mulata married to Alonso Márquez, mestizo

Magdalena Hernández, free mulata, widow of Juan Bautista, Indian

Manuel de Sosa, free mulato, single, Portuguese who has recently arrived and works as *labrador* for Domingo Hernández

María de León, free black woman, widow of Gonzalo Vázquez, cloth shearer, a Spaniard

Martín de Ballinas, free mulato from Cádiz, works on a farm for Diego Luxan, Spaniard, married to Francisca Rodríguez, mestiza, who works on a farm owned by the Jesuits

Petrona de Benero, black woman, married to a mulato slave belonging to Nicolás de Villanueva

Archivo General de la Nación, Civil, vol. 669, expediente 2, trans. Ida Altman.

In addition to their importance as artisans mulattos also filled another significant niche in colonial society, New Spain's militia units. After the 1692 riot in Mexico City the viceroy specifically ordered that mulattos and mestizos be recruited into the militia, but this action underscored rather than departed from established custom; *pardo* companies already existed in Puebla in the early seventeenth century.

In the eighteenth century, when the Spanish Crown undertook to strengthen colonial military capabilities, *pardo* militia units were created in Mexico City, Puebla, Veracruz, and other cities. Like all military men, the mulattos who belonged to these units enjoyed the *fuero militar* that conferred certain privileges, including exemption from the tribute payment to which they were normally subject. In the late eighteenth century, however, these militia units fell victim to the racial prejudices of Spanish officials and military officers. To the dismay and frustration of their officers, the battalions of free pardos in Mexico City and Puebla were ordered disbanded. Notwithstanding Spanish racial stereotyping of the mulatto militiamen as lazy, undisciplined vagabonds, analysis of 192 men who in 1792 had served in the Mexico City and Puebla battalions for fifteen years shows that nearly all were tradesmen, with weavers, shoemakers, tailors, cigar makers, and ironsmiths the most numerous. The antimulato policy did not extend to Veracruz, however. The *pardo* and *moreno* Fixed Battalions played such a crucial role in the yellow fever–ridden port that without free blacks and mulattos it would have been impossible to maintain an active militia. Yet in contrast to the relative success of the Mexico City and Puebla companies, the Veracruz battalion experienced difficulties in recruiting and retaining local people, who found plenty of other attractive economic opportunities in the thriving port city. By the early nineteenth century, military officers were forcibly conscripting blacks and mulattos for the units.

Africans in Colonial Society

It should be clear that in many senses there existed no sharp distinction between free and unfree people of African descent, or even between slave and free workers. Similarly, blacks and mulattos frequently had close ties to Spaniards, Indians, or mestizos through marriage, kinship, friendship, and work. Racial and ethnic blurring among groups increased as the numbers of Africans entering New Spain fell off sharply in the second half of the seventeenth century and manumissions and intermarriage continued apace. The result was the development of a group of African descent that was increasingly mulatto and criollo and eventually predominantly free. Ultimately these processes that affected Africans in New Spain culminated in the virtual disappearance of an identifiable group of African origin in many parts of the viceroyalty by the time of independence.

Nonetheless, blacks and mulattos, both slave and free, long remained a significant part of colonial society. It probably is fair to say that Spaniards never fully reconciled themselves to the presence of a group that, in principle at least, never should have existed in a society theoretically divided between Spaniards and Indians. Their main response to this dilemma was silence. Although Spaniards depended on African labor in many sectors well into the seventeenth century, real discussion about the morality of enslaving Africans almost never surfaced. In 1560 the archbishop of Mexico, Fray Alonso de Montúfar, spoke out against slavery and the slave trade, and in 1573 a university professor named Bartolomé de Albornoz wrote a treatise directly challenging the legitimacy of enslaving Africans. Such protests were notable for their infrequency and utter lack of impact on Spanish views of slavery and of the people they had brought to New Spain to serve them.

The establishment and subsequent abolition of the *pardo* militias epitomized Spanish ambivalence toward free people of color. Perceived as a rootless, servile group in need of control and discipline—hence, measures taken that required free blacks and mulattos to be in service to someone—paradoxically Spaniards often turned to the same people to act as instruments of control and defense. A similar ambivalence surfaced in the religious realm. Although the clergy seldom made systematic efforts to convert Africans in the same sense they did Indians, nonetheless they apparently expected Africans to convert easily and completely to Christianity.

Africans frequently ran afoul of the Inquisition, which perhaps owed as much to Spaniards' distrust of blacks and mulatos and their embrace of the Holy Office as an instrument of social control as it did to significant religious failings on the part of Africans. The cases brought against them seem to fall mainly into two categories: charges of witchcraft and sorcery, with which black and mulatto women were stereotypically associated, and blasphemy, acts of which frequently occurred when slaves and servants were being punished. Although Inquisition cases generally reveal frustratingly little about the actual beliefs of Africans, the accused usually could recite the catechism and standard prayers, suggesting they were about as Christian in the formal sense as most other members of Hispanic society. The severity of punishments meted out to Africans and the fact that often it was masters who denounced their slaves and servants suggest that the Holy Office served the purposes of social as well as religious discipline and control.

The aspect of religious life which Africans embraced most actively was membership in confraternities, participation in which probably was as much social and even political as it was religious in nature. Slaves and free people of color organized *cofradías* in Mexico well before the end of the sixteenth century, founding the cofradía of San Nicolás Tolentino in 1560 and later the Exaltación de la Cruz de los Negros in the capital. By the end of the sixteenth century, Veracruz had two cofradías for Africans; in Antequera the Cofradía de Nuestra Señora de las Nieves was attached to the Hospital de San Cosme and San Damián. Guadalajara had at least four cofradías of blacks and mulattos in the seventeenth century, and Africans organized the Cofradía de Nuestra Señora de la Soledad in the mines of San Luis Potosí. Similar cofradías came into existence in many towns in Michoacan. Cofradías, such as the one in Antequera, could be associated with hospitals. Mexico City's Hospital Real de la Epifania served blacks and mestizos, and Veracruz's Hospital de Nuestra Señora was intended to serve only Africans, both slave and free.

Given Spaniards' fear of slave conspiracies, not surprisingly officials in the capital especially sometimes viewed these organizations with suspicion. As early as 1572, the viceroy Don Martín Enríquez tried to prohibit members of the black cofradías from congregating publicly, and in 1623 the reformist viceroy Marqués de Gelves again banned them from participating in processions; but clearly, at least outside Mexico City, these associations continued to thrive.

People of African descent in many respects did not differ markedly from other colonial groups in their experiences and activities. In the cities they lived in working-class neighborhoods or as servants in the households of well-to-do Spaniards, and on estates and in mines and refineries they worked side by side with people of all ethnic groups. Both slaves and free people sought marriage partners who most frequently were of the same or similar racial background, but as time went on they increasingly intermarried with other groups. Africans embraced some form of Christianity, joined cofradías, and made charitable contributions to the church. They worked in a variety of trades and occupations. Their eventual disappearance as a distinctive group in most of New Spain reflected their long-term integration into the racially diverse and amorphous Hispanic society of colonial Mexico. In areas such as the Gulf Coast region, where substantial numbers of people of African descent continued to live and work until independence and beyond, however, the genetic and perhaps in some ways the cultural impact of the African presence remains perceptible up to the present.

Glossary

bozal   unacculturated, non-Spanish speaking, African
cimarrón   escaped slave
cofradía   confraternity or lay religious brotherhood
criollo   person born in New Spain
fuero militar   set of privileges enjoyed by members of the military
ladino   person of non-Spanish origin who speaks Spanish
moreno   dark-skinned person of African descent
mulato   person of mixed African and Indian or European background
oficial   artisan
palenque   community of runaway slaves
pardo   light-skinned person of African descent
vaquero   cowboy

Questions for Discussion

1.   Given the size of New Spain's indigenous population, why did Spaniards need African slaves?

2.   How did the role and composition of the African group in Mexico change over time, and what was the nature of their relationship to

Spaniards and Indians? What indications are there that people of African descent increasingly assimilated into Hispanic society?

3. How did colonial and ecclesiastical authorities perceive and treat people of African descent?

4. What were some of the occupations of free blacks and mulattos, according to the Puebla tribute rolls? Whom did they marry?

Suggested Readings

Alberro, Solange. "Juan de Morga and Gertrudis de Escobar: Rebellious Slaves," in David G. Sweet and Gary B. Nash, eds., *Struggle and Survival in Colonial America.* Berkeley and Los Angeles: University of California Press, 1981. Study of the experiences of two individuals of African descent, based on Inquisition records.

Archer, Christon. "Pardos, Indians, and the Army of New Spain: Inter-Relationships and Conflicts, 1780–1810," *Journal of Latin American Studies* 6:2 (1974): 231–55. Examines the controversial role of blacks in the late colonial military.

Carroll, Patrick J. *Blacks in Colonial Veracruz.* Austin: University of Texas Press, 1991. Important study of Africans and their role in the demographic and economic development of the Gulf Coast region.

Davidson, David. "Negro Slave Control and Resistance in Colonial Mexico, 1519–1650," *Hispanic American Historical Review* 46:3 (1966): 237–43. Looks at early revolts and official responses.

Gerhard, Peter. "A Black Conquistador in Mexico," *Hispanic American Historical Review* 58:3 (1978): 451–9. Brief, interesting discussion of what is known about Juan Garrido.

Gutiérrez Brockington, Lolita. *The Leverage of Labor. Managing the Cortés Haciendas in Tehuantepec, 1588–1688.* Durham, N.C., and London: Duke University Press, 1989. A study of the Marquesado estates in southern Mexico with much information on free and slave workers—mainly cowboys—of African descent.

Konrad, Herman W. *A Jesuit Hacienda in Colonial Mexico: Santa Lucía, 1576–1767.* Stanford: Stanford University Press, 1980. A thorough examination of a large Jesuit hacienda in central Mexico, with one chapter devoted to slaves.

Love, Edgar L. "Marriage Patterns of Persons of African Descent in a Colonial Mexico City Parish," *Hispanic American Historical Review* 51:4 (1971): 79–91. Demographic study of Africans in Mexico City.

Lutz, Christopher. *Santiago de Guatemala, 1541–1773: City, Caste, and the Colonial Experience.* Norman: University of Oklahoma Press, 1994.

Study emphasizing demographic and social development and change in the capital of Guatemala.

Martin, Cheryl E. *Rural Society in Colonial Morelos*. Albuquerque: University of New Mexico Press, 1985. A study emphasizing the social and demographic impact of the sugar plantations of Morelos that includes much material on people of African descent and their relationships with other groups.

Palmer, Colin A. *Slaves of the White God. Blacks in Mexico, 1570–1650*. Cambridge, Mass.: Harvard University Press, 1976. Examines the experience of African slaves in Mexico in the first half of the colonial period.

Super, John C. "Miguel Hernández: Master of Mule Trains," in David G. Sweet and Gary B. Nash, eds., *Struggle and Survival in Colonial America*. Berkeley and Los Angeles: University of California Press, 1981. Story of an upwardly mobile, free mulato in sixteenth-century Querétaro.

Eleven

Elite and Popular Culture

Several institutions shaped high culture and intellectual life in early Mexico: the viceregal court, the Roman Catholic church, and the University of Mexico and other schools. In Spain and elsewhere in Western Europe during the early modern period royal courts functioned as patrons to artists, many of whom actually lived at court. Similarly the viceroy, the king's representative and personification in New Spain, supported music, painting, theater, and the writing of poetry. The church promoted sacred music, art, and architecture as well as pious literature. The Pontifical University of Mexico, founded in 1553, employed theologians, learned jurists, and physicians who in turn trained the clerics, lawyers, and medical doctors who formed the core of the professions. Other colleges and universities were established subsequently, helping to create a learned elite who were the main consumers of high culture.

Religious Culture

Religious symbols were everywhere in colonial Mexico. Church bells tolled the hours, warned of danger, and rang in supplication during epidemics and other disasters that seemed heaven-sent to punish sin and transgression. They also rang in celebration, marking such events as the birth of a new heir to the throne and the arrival of a new viceroy or archbishop. Churches and chapels were inextricably connected to the social and cultural life of the city, town, or village where they stood. The households of even the poorest Mexicans usually had a home altar of some kind.

The church played a major role in determining values in colonial Mexico, setting standards of behavior that the clergy in particular reinforced but which were generally accepted and espoused by society as a whole. New Spain was part of Christendom, and Roman Catholicism presupposed the existence of a community bound by common beliefs and ritual practices. Ideally, people were devoted Christians. The biological events of their life cycles—birth, coming of age, sexual union, and death—were marked by the religious sacraments of baptism, confirmation, marriage, last rites, and burial in holy ground. For each event a priest celebrated the appropriate rite and received payment for his services. The poor, however, often could not afford to pay for church marriages or the last rites prescribed by Catholic doctrine.

Fiestas. The annual cycle of feasts and fasts enabled the faithful to participate in a common religious life. Parishioners attended mass, confessed sins, performed penance, and took communion. Pilgrims trekked to holy sites, such as Tepeyac, the site of the apparition of the Virgin of Guadalupe. Processions conducted by church officials and lay confraternities, often featuring floats, religious statuary, musicians and dancers, were community-wide religious celebrations. For the poor and racially marginalized people of New Spain these celebrations broke the monotony of their endless struggle to survive.

The most important Catholic saints were the patrons of rural communities and urban neighborhoods. Each village and neighborhood had a patron saint or virgin who was seen as a protector and represented the community before other villages and saints. The annual celebration of the patron saint was by far the most important religious and civic event in a community. Lay brotherhoods or sodalities took charge of organizing festivities, which usually started at sunset of the previous day and could continue for a week or more. Each brotherhood had a governing board or *mesa*, led by a *mayordomo* or steward, who was elected annually. Stewardships (*mayordomías*) were honorary offices highly regarded in the community. When a board successfully organized the saint's fiesta the members gained prestige, and they would likely be chosen again in the near future to represent the community in other arenas as well.

Mayordomos collected funds, hired musicians, purchased flowers and ornaments to decorate the church, paid the priest's fees for the special masses and other religious ceremonies associated with fiestas, and organized other religious festivities, including dances, pious plays, and children's parades as well as such entertainments as greased pole climbing, bullfights, rodeos, horse races, contests, and fireworks that normally formed part of festivities. Mayordomos provided special food and drinks at their homes and invited as many people as they could afford. Petty merchants and vendors organized public markets or *tianguis* to sell food, alcohol (usually pulque), clothes, and candies. People from nearby communities also attended the local festivities that offered a chance to make or renew friendships or find a mate outside the confines of home villages.

During the age of spiritual conquest the friars consciously organized these festivities along lines familiar to them from Europe. They also were aware that the old indigenous religion included many public religious celebrations and that the new Christian festivities served similar ritual and community functions. Fiestas represented a significant collective expense for poor communities and strained the personal resources of mayordomos. In the late eighteenth century, the Crown attempted to limit the size and number of these enormously popular fiestas.

The diocesan clergy was in charge of organizing the most important civil and religious ceremonies in colonial Mexico and played a decisive role in legitimizing the Spanish monarchy and its colonial authorities. The arrival of a new viceroy, for instance, was carefully planned and celebrated with numerous rituals emphasizing the divine role of royal officials. Royal weddings, births, and deaths were occasions for elaborate ceremonies in the main squares of cities and towns, led in Mexico City by the archbishop of Mexico.

Military expeditions to colonize new territories or to suppress groups of rebels in the countryside or rioters in cities always departed with clerical blessings and prayers. The clergy announced and celebrated Spanish military victories in both Europe and the New World. Bishops and parish priests also organized religious ceremonies in times of collective affliction or disaster, such as droughts, floods, fires, earthquakes, epidemics, bad harvests, hurricanes, plagues of locusts, and civil unrest. Colonial Mexicans believed that natural disasters were divine punishments; priests served as society's intercessors with God. During civil disturbances the appearance of clerics to calm rioters brought to bear religious authority to reinforce obedience to civil authority and submission to God.

Charitable Institutions. Christianity emphasizes care of the poor, and the church promoted the creation and maintenance of charitable institutions. In medieval European theology, the role of the poor was to provide objects of charity for the wealthy. The prosperous had an obligation to aid the poor and helpless and by doing so earned spiritual capital. Virtually all institutions that cared for the sick, orphans, abandoned women, and the mentally disturbed came under the supervision of the episcopal hierarchy. The church controlled hospitals, almshouses, orphanages, and asylums for the insane.

The church encouraged wealthy people to donate or bequeath money to fund the establishment or maintenance of charitable institutions. These donations were known as *obras pías* or pious works. Extraordinarily wealthy individuals could establish new institutions such as the Monte de Piedad ("mount of piety"), endowed by the Count of Regla, which functioned as a pawnshop for Mexico City's poor and is still in operation today. It is estimated that the Count of Regla spent 500,000 pesos on church donations, which represented a substantial portion of the income from his properties.

Wealthy men built churches. José de la Borda was responsible for the construction of the famous church of Santa Prisca in Taxco. Wealthy women sometimes endowed nunneries that they then headed. According to historian Doris Ladd, the eighteenth-century titled nobility was willing to make large donations to the church, but none of them sent their sons into the clergy. It was not only the nobility who used their wealth to support the church. At the end of the sixteenth century, for example, a man named Juan Barranco who made a fortune as a textile manufacturer in Puebla established a convent and school for girls in the city that had made him rich.

The upper class used religious occasions to display their wealth. When a nun from an elite family took her final vows, the ceremony vied a society wedding in opulence. The "bride of Christ" rode to the church in the finest carriage. Marching bands, fireworks, and other public displays often marked the occasion, impressing upon everyone the family's considerable means. Baptisms, weddings, and funerals also were occasions for the elites to show off the extent of their wealth. The procession to the church for baptism of the Count of Regla's child included a hundred hired coaches.

All of these pious acts and public displays reinforced understandings of social and economic divisions in colonial society. It can be argued that by choosing the religious realm to make such displays, the wealthy made genuine contributions to colonial society, creating charitable institutions for the poor as well as beautiful churches. This can be balanced by the counterargument that far too much wealth remained in the hands of the rich, leaving others impoverished and in need of charity.

Education and Literacy

University of Mexico. Formal education in colonial Mexico was in the hands of the church. Although it was a royal institution, the secular clergy controlled the University of Mexico. Higher education was reserved for males who could afford the fees that placed it out of the reach of poor men. The Royal and Pontifical University of Mexico was the first university in the Americas, founded under royal patronage in 1553 (more than eighty years before Harvard). The university's early foundation was part of the Crown's effort to assert control over New Spain by creating an institution that would mold elite attitudes and provide the educated men needed for professional posts, including the church and the lower bureaucracy in Mexico. University students pursued programs in theology, law, and medicine. By the late eighteenth century, there were universities in Guadalajara and Guatemala and colegios and seminaries in most major cities.

The University of Mexico emulated the University of Salamanca, the oldest university in Spain, founded by Alfonso IX of León. The charter of the University of Mexico granted faculty and students the same privileges held by those at the University of Salamanca. Francisco Cervantes de Salazar, one of the first faculty members, wrote about the university in *Life in the Imperial and Loyal City of Mexico* (1554). He complained about his low salary and academic politics, enduring features of scholarly life. Many faculty members were churchmen, mainly secular clerics and a few mendicants. Graduation enabled degree holders to enter the church or to practice law or medicine. Attaining a postsecondary degree of *bachillerato* (bachelor's), *licenciatura* (master's), or *doctorado* (doctorate) allowed the recipient to use his academic degree as a title of address—*bachiller, licenciado,* and *doc-*

tor—which often replaced the man's given name. Since the upper levels of society were keenly aware of the significance of titles as markers of social status, a university education and advanced degrees enhanced a graduate's career opportunities.

The curriculum was that of the medieval university. Written and spoken Latin and Spanish were required for entry. Study and the acquisition of knowledge emphasized memorization of long texts and learning immutable laws and received truths of religious faith and science. This system of education did not encourage students to question either particular aspects of knowledge or the overall structure of the curriculum. At the University of Mexico the establishment of a chair in indigenous languages mandated the teaching of Nahuatl and other languages, especially important for clerics seeking benefices in largely Indian parishes.

Role of the Jesuits. Almost from the time of their arrival in 1572 until their expulsion in 1767 the Society of Jesus played a major and often controversial role in education in New Spain. Jesuits displaced the mendicant Dominicans as premier educators, sparking tension between the two orders. The aggressive and dominant position of Jesuits in education also brought them into conflict with the secular clergy. Elite Mexicans could attend Jesuit *colegio*s located in the major cities of Puebla, Antequera (now Oaxaca City), Valladolid (now Morelia), and Guadalajara and especially in the capital itself. Jesuits also created a few schools for Indian men, including the Colegio de San Gregorio in Mexico City, but none for women. The Colegio Máximo was the most important Jesuit school, but others such as San Ildefonso, San Pedro y San Pablo also were prominent. All were located in the center of Mexico City, within walking distance of the original site of the University of Mexico. Soon after the Colegio Máximo opened its doors, some of its professors were pressured to teach at the University of Mexico. To preserve their autonomy the Jesuits devised an arrangement whereby students could attend lectures at both the Colegio Máximo and the university, while receiving their baccalaureate from their home institution.

The Jesuits' dominant role in education was challenged by the foundation of colegios by the secular clergy, most prominently by the mid-seventeenth-century Bishop of Puebla, Don Juan de Palafox y Mendoza (1642–9), known for challenging the Jesuits at all levels. He used his own funds to endow the colegio-seminaries of San Pablo and San Juan for young men and a school for young women. A reformer who pursued policies that would strengthen the role of the secular clergy and its bonds to the creole elite, Palafox saw education as crucial to these objectives. Palafox called on Spanish Mexican families to enroll their sons in diocesan colegios rather than those of the Jesuits, and many did respond. Palafox's recall to Spain did not end the episcopal hierarchy's struggle with the Jesuits over education. Not until the Crown expelled the Jesuits in 1767, however, did the secular clergy take control of education. Because the Jesuits had educated so many Mexicans, a certain number of whom entered the Society, the expulsion of the Jesuits had a profound impact on creole society.

Education of Indians. Indian education was valued in the early postconquest period, when Franciscan Pedro de Gante established schools for both boys and girls. Under the sponsorship of the first viceroy, Don Antonio de Mendoza, the Franciscan Colegio de Santa Cruz Tlatelolco was founded in 1536 to train Indian men for the Christian priesthood. While the school successfully taught its students to read, write, and compose in Latin, Spanish, and Nahuatl, pessimistic friars came to believe that Indian men did not have the capacity to be ordained. Santa Cruz's students did play a major role as informants and scribes in bringing Bernardino de Sahagún's encyclopedic twelve-volume *General History of the Things of New Spain* (1576) to fruition. Jesuit colegios for Indian men also were important in the writing and preservation of Nahua history. The Colegio de San Gregorio trained and maintained on staff Nahua men who functioned as both copyists and scholars. Most famous of these was Don Antón Muñon Chimalpahin, who recorded events he witnessed in Mexico City, as well as composing a history of his city-state of Chalco Amecameca.

Education of Women. Colonial society for the most part attached little value to higher education for women, even the daughters of wealthy Spanish families. Upper-class girls were, however, expected to learn to read and write so that they could read their devotional manuals and prayer books. Since widows played a significant role in managing the economic affairs of some propertied families, literacy and numeracy could be important for women.

Many convents had schools, with some students going on to become nuns. Portraits of colonial nuns often show their subjects with a book in hand or reading, so there were models for women who aspired to pursue their love of reading and the life of the mind. Nunneries were the only environment in which women were encouraged to read, although the subject matter was mainly religious. Occasionally nuns' confessors urged their charges to write their own spiritual autobiographies, but autobiography and self-consciously reflective writing for the most part were not Spanish genres.

Indian women fared even worse in schooling. Their opportunities for formal education were few and limited. Fray Pedro de Gante's early school for Indian girls was joined by other "patio" schools for teaching Christian catechism. Bishop Juan de Zumárraga founded a few boarding schools for girls. Women became the core group of regular churchgoers, but their religious knowledge was oral. Virtually no Indian women became nuns in the colonial period, more as a result of racial discrimination than because of a lack of religious inclination or ability to pay the required dowry. In effect even elite Indian women generally were excluded from the one environment in which women were encouraged to read. In 1724 the convent of Corpus Christi of the Poor Clares was founded for pure-blooded, elite Indian women of legitimate birth. Those accepted had to be literate in Latin, but it is unclear how its novitiates acquired such knowledge. Even the Real Colegio de Nuestra Señora de Guadalupe de Indias, a model for the education of Indian females, provided little instruction for young women who aspired to intellectual or spiritual development. Its five-person staff taught sewing, embroidery, washing clothes, and grinding chocolate; the curriculum made no mention of reading and writing.

Literacy and Books. Literacy was an important skill in a society in which few could read or write, but the legal system depended on extensive documentation. Professional notaries or scribes drew up legal and municipal documents. Every Indian town in central Mexico had one or more men who recorded the town council's official minutes and drew up wills and legal contracts, just as did their counterparts in the Spanish cities. Most market areas or plazas near municipal offices had freelance scribes, called *evangelistas*, who would write all kinds of documents for the illiterate, including love verses. Travelers to colonial Mexico remarked on them, and they can still be found under the colonial arcades of modern Mexican cities. Notaries and scribes were an enduring feature of urban life, emphasizing the importance of the written word even for the illiterate.

The capital had a significant number of book stores, indicating there were readers to support them. Unlike Protestantism, Roman Catholicism did not encourage lay men and women to read the Bible itself, but devotional works and even light reading matter were readily available. Many households, even those of some Indians, had religious books, particularly books of hours. A significant number of secular works also circulated, including chivalrous romances, poetry and ballads, as well as medical and scientific texts. Light reading material such as novels and romances was openly and widely read. Readers in New Spain had access to Miguel de Cervantes's *Don Quixote* almost as soon as it came off the press in Spain.

Although the Holy Office of the Inquisition acted as official censor, there is considerable evidence that its reach was far from absolute. Not only was there a flourishing book trade, with book dealers selling their inventory from shops, but individual immigrants often brought along volumes from Spain. The Inquisition required that consignments of books unloaded from ships on the Gulf Coast be delivered under seal to the Holy Office for inspection. Inquisitors were particularly concerned about heretical religious writings or philosophical works that might lead the faithful astray. In practice, inquisitorial supervision was not always effective. Not all books were packed in boxes easily identified for inspection; book smugglers hid volumes in large containers designed to transport wine and in barrels containing dried fruit. Even books in the most prohibited category, Protestant religious tracts or Bibles, frequently escaped confiscation.

New Spain's only printing press, established in the 1540s, published a significant number of titles, especially works by mendicants written during the spiritual conquest but also poetry, prose, and even music. Printed by the official press and with the Inquisition close at hand, not surprisingly these works were entirely orthodox. Inquisition files from the eighteenth century preserve erotic poetry, heterodox theology, and other suspect material, but in handwritten form. Ideas circulated and texts were written, but local production of printed works was circumscribed by the existence of only one press and in the seventeenth century by a shortage of paper as well. A long work by seventeenth-century savant Don Carlos Sigüenza y Góngora could not be published for lack of paper.

Colonial Intellectuals

Sor Juana Inés de la Cruz. The most famous intellectual of the Spanish colonial period was a Jeronimite nun, Sor Juana Inés de la Cruz (1648–95). Renowned in her own time, called among other things "The Tenth Muse," and the "Mexican Phoenix," a published poet, playwright, philosopher, and scientist, Sor Juana led an unusual life. She is regarded today as an early feminist intellectual, acerbic and articulate on the condition of women in her day. Modern scholars consider her the most important writer of Latin American Baroque literature. Born Juana Inés de Asbaje y Ramírez de Santillana on an hacienda in the small town of Nepantla, she was one of several natural children her mother bore by different men. Although Sor Juana's origins deviated from Catholic ideals, their irregularity was not an insurmountable barrier to her advancement, first at the viceregal court and later at the convent, for she attracted powerful patrons. Ultimately, however, her gender determined her choices. In her well-known and virtually unique autobiographical essay, "Response to Sor Philotea" (1691), she recounts how she was thwarted from entering the University of Mexico because she was female. She wanted to cut her hair and dress as a man so that she could attend. Somehow brought to the attention of the viceregal court when she was an adolescent, she lived in a milieu of splendor and intellectual stimulation, pursued by many suitors. Most of what is known about Sor Juana's life is drawn from her own autobiographical writings.

Deciding she did not want to marry, she became a novice in the Discalced Carmelite order, noted for its rigorous discipline. She left after a few months, entering a Jeronimite convent in Mexico City that had been founded for elite creole women. Sor Juana lived out most of her years surrounded by books and the musical and scientific instruments of the late seventeenth century, with time to write. Entering a convent required a dowry and proof of unstained lineage. A patron provided Sor Juana's dowry and her illegitimacy was hidden. Although she had taken the veil and made her final vows as a nun, she stayed in close contact with her first patroness, the Marquesa de Mancera, wife of the viceroy, and with another major intellectual, the secular cleric Don Carlos Sigüenza y Góngora. In addition to allowing visitors under cloistered conditions, Sor Juana's convent housed a school for young girls and produced plays for public attendance. She wrote both secular and sacred plays. One of the best known was *El Divino Narciso* (The Divine Narcissus) in which the characters represent aspects of Mexican history and culture: Christian Religion and Zeal from the European side, Occident and America from the New World.

Sor Juana wrote poetry in the baroque style favored in Europe in the mid-seventeenth century, full of plays on words and puns and characterized by a stylized form and deliberate opacity. Much of her writing was religious in nature but decidedly philosophical rather than mystical. Writing when the influence of the literary Don Juan spurred men to womanizing, Sor Juana was acerbic in her observations:

> So where does the greater guilt lie
>   for a passion that should not be:
> with the man who pleads out of baseness
>   or the woman debased by his plea?
> Or which is more to be blamed—
>   though both will have cause for chagrin:
> The woman who sins for money
>   or the man who pays money to sin?
> (*A Sor Juana Anthology*, trans. by Alan S. Trueblood [Cambridge, Mass., 1988], p. 113)

Sor Juana's later years brought a reversal of fortune. Having criticized a sermon of the powerful Brazilian Jesuit, Antonio Vieira, she became embroiled in disputes with her confessor and the church hierarchy; by extension she had criticized the cleric who had published Vieira's sermon. Sor Juana's successful avoidance of official censure came to an end.

Sor Juana bowed to religious discipline, giving away her library and scientific instruments. Her final known written work, a reaffirmation of her religious vows, she signed with her own blood, "I, the worst of all." She died a few years later while caring for her sisters in the convent of Santa Paula during an epidemic. Despite initial attempts to extinguish her name and legacy, Sor Juana found a hagiographer, Jesuit Diego Calleja, who wrote her spiritual autobiography or *vida*, published in Madrid in 1700. By the mid-eighteenth century, Sor Juana's reputation was fully restored. She remains a powerful cultural figure in Mexican life, appearing on paper currency (see Figure 18-1), her verses learned by Mexican school children.

Sigüenza y Góngora. Another major intellectual figure of seventeenth-century Mexico was Don Carlos Sigüenza y Góngora (1645–1700), cleric, savant, poet, and creole patriot. Sigüenza served as professor of mathematics and astrology (astrology was considered to be a science) at the University of Mexico, as well as the chaplain of the Amor de Dios hospital. In the colonial era, clerics dominated intellectual and cultural life, but many promoted ideas that went well beyond the reiteration of dogma and religious piety. Sigüenza, for example, wrote a pamphlet declaring that a comet appearing in 1680 was a natural event, not a religious or supernatural phenomenon foretelling doom. Member of an elite family—his father was secretary to the viceroy—Sigüenza was well placed to play a significant role in the colonial capital. Educated by the Jesuits at Tepozotlan but expelled from the society, he became a secular cleric without a steady income and had to hold a number of positions to support himself. Today he is best remembered for fostering creole nationalism through the study and promotion of Mexican culture and the indigenous past. His identification with Mexico and its culture rather than that of Spain reflected a growing sense of creole identity built on indigenous Mexican origins.

Sigüenza inspired and supported other scholars of his day who worked in the same vein, such as the Franciscan Agustín Vetancurt (1620–1700), author of *Teatro Mexicano*. In his pursuit of the historical underpinnings of a distinctively Mexican creole culture, Don Carlos amassed a significant library of Indian manuscripts or codices. These were both alphabetic and pictorial, such as those of Fernando de Alva Ixtlilxochitl of Texcoco. Sigüenza saw in these indigenous works the foundation for pride in Mexico's past as well as a reason to celebrate its present. He among other intellectuals of the seventeenth century also wrote about the Virgin of Guadalupe, an increasingly creole devotion.

The Lively Arts

Theater. In the sixteenth and seventeenth centuries the theater attracted people of all classes. Early mendicants used religious plays as an integral part of their program to convert the Indians to Christianity. In this context music, dance, and plays were meant not only to entertain but also to teach and reinforce Christian doctrine and create a Christian context for the performance of indigenous music and dance. In this way Catholicism sought to incorporate indigenous traditions without corrupting the message of Christian salvation and orthodox thought. One such late-sixteenth-century Nahuatl play was *Holy Wednesday*, which, drawing on Spanish models, depicted Christ's departure from Mary on the Wednesday before his Good Friday crucifixion. Its unidentified Nahua author, however, altered the European Christian message to fit his own interpretation of aesthetics and understanding of Christianity.

For upper-class urban Spaniards (both peninsular and creole), the literature of Spain's Golden Age provided the basis for Mexican-produced drama. Golden Age drama went beyond strictly religious themes to portray the foibles of human conduct and tragedies of circumstance and action, while pushing language to new heights of lyricism. In Spain Lope de Vega and Calderón de la Barca set the standard, writing in elegant Castilian for a broad audience. In Mexico professional actors and actresses performed in theaters, but convents and hospitals also staged plays, some locally written.

Music. Music formed an essential part of culture in early Mexico. Spanish court and sacred music were highly developed in the sixteenth and seventeenth centuries, and there is abundant evidence that Mexico participated fully in its flowering. European music arrived in Mexico with the Spaniards, and some conquerors were competent musicians. The efforts of early mendicants to use music in their spiritual conquest figured significantly in creating a new Mexican musical culture that broadly disseminated European musical forms. Friars taught central Mexican Indians to sing multipart religious songs, accompanied by European and indigenous musical instruments or *a cappella*. Many of the friars' remarked on the instant appeal of religious music for Indians. They quickly learned not only how to sing the new harmonies but also to compose original pieces themselves. They both made and played European musical instruments.

Fairly soon, however, colonial authorities decided that the Indians' enthusiasm had to be checked. Archbishop Montúfar published regulations from the First Mexican Church Council (1556) mandating that "trumpets shall not be played in churches during divine service. . . . The organ is the correct instrument for use in the church, and we wish its use to become universal in Mexico." The regulations also limited the number of wind instruments that Indian towns could have. Most churches in central Mexico acquired organs, but hand-held instruments continued to be important since they could be used outdoors during fiestas and religious processions. The numbers of Indian men who became musicians alarmed sixteenth-century Spanish officials, in part because they did not pay tribute, a continuation of privileges they had enjoyed in the prehispanic era which as a result were curtailed. Even so, since there were few Spanish singers in the early sixteenth century, most singers even in the cathedrals of Mexico City, Puebla, and Guadalajara were Indian men and boys. This situation partly reflected the low salaries paid to singers; in 1575, when the Archbishop Moya y Contreras of Mexico sought to conduct a competition for singers similar to those held in Spain, no one applied. By the end of the sixteenth century, however, the choir of Puebla's cathedral consisted solely of Mexican Spaniards, and Puebla emerged as a center for creole music.

For all sectors of Mexican society music everywhere played a significant role in religious worship and public celebrations. In the sixteenth century New Spain's printing press published twelve liturgical books containing music, the first music printed in the New World and the only such books produced in the Spanish colonies. During the same period only twenty-nine such books were published in Spain itself. The music of major contemporary Spanish composers, especially those based in Seville or Toledo, which had close connections to the New World, was performed in Mexico. A number of composers worked in early Mexico, some of them immigrants from Spain, such as the chapel master of the cathedral in Mexico City, Hernando Franco. Franco wrote several *Magnificats*, musical treatments of the annunciation to Mary of her pregnancy, a standard sixteenth-century religious theme with a particular musical form. He also wrote two hymns in Nahuatl honoring the Virgin, with standard invocations. One of them, "O Lady, beloved Mother of God, always virgin, intercede for us with Thy believed Son, Jesu Christ, Thou most beloved of the Most High!" was set to a jaunty tune more playful than most liturgical music.

In Puebla de los Angeles the institutional church was particularly strong. Puebla's cathedral rivaled the capital's in opulence and exceeded it in income. Bishop Don Juan de Palafox y Mendoza opted to remain bishop of Puebla rather than become archbishop of Mexico in the mid-seventeenth century. Wealthy, learned, and a patron of the arts, Palafox spent the enormous sum of 14,000 pesos annually on music when he served as bishop. When the cathedral in Puebla was consecrated in 1649 during his term, music was a prominent feature of the festivities.

In 1690, the master of music in the Puebla cathedral, Licenciado Miguel Mateo Dallo y Lana, set several of Sor Juana's *villancicos* to music. Villancicos were a popular form of music in Mexico, originally Christmas or other festival songs, usually joyful religious music although some had secular themes. Sor Juana's were intended to accompany the mass, and hers were in such demand that she produced fifteen collections of them. In the seventeenth century she was the most popular of the many Mexican writers producing villancicos to be set to music. Mexico's early music has been recorded by a number of artistic ensembles in recent years.

Artisans were producing musical instruments in Mexico City by the mid-sixteenth century. As was true for many trades, this one also was officially regulated. An instrument maker had to know how to build an organ, a spinet, a lute, various viols, and a harp and also to be able play them. First promulgated in 1568 and renewed in 1585, the regulations were likely not followed to the letter, but they indicate the existence of a flourishing instrument making industry. Since the regulations only mention instruments made of wood, popular brass wind instruments such as the trumpet, cornet, and trombone may well have been imported. Even so, they were favorite instruments for both sacred and secular music, found even in the majority of small Indian towns.

Dance. Dance was also popular in all sectors of society. The early mendicants incorporated indigenous dances into their repertoire to attract Indians to the church; sacred dance had been an integral part of prehispanic Nahua religious worship. Hernando Cortés took Nahua dancers to perform at the court of Charles V. Although some have suggested that these Mexican dancers introduced the dance known as the pavane to Europe, this is now disputed. Two other dances of the early modern period, however, definitely were of Mexican origin: the sarabande and the chaconne. In the late sixteenth century the sarabande was described as lewd and offensive, with sexually suggestive movements. Its twin was the chaconne, also sexually provocative and accompanied by snapping fingers, castanets, and tambourines. Mexican Spanish creations, both dances later became more stylized and staid. These dances may have reflected African influence, as did dances of the *tierra caliente*, such as the rumba. Although Africans formed only a small proportion of early Mexico's population, they influenced its popular culture. Elite men and women participated in dances at court, but dance also formed part of fiestas that everyone celebrated.

For the gigantic auto de fe of 1649 in Mexico City, in which some fifty people were executed, Indians and blacks performed music and danced as part of the spectacle. A week later, Palafox y Mendoza's consecration of the great cathedral of Puebla took place, also full of musical pomp and circumstance. Since the church hierarchy in Mexico City and Puebla were at odds, the almost coincidental staging of two major religious spectacles was deliberate. Music drew the laity into both events. The auto de fe reinforced the notion of the purity of Christian society, while the participation of blacks and Indians in the ceremonies symbolized Mexico's ethnic diversity under the unity of faith. The consecration of Puebla's cathedral, in contrast, featured a double choir that was exclusively white.

Music and dance in religious processions and celebrations, organized under official auspices, attained great popularity in the first centuries of Spanish rule. In the eighteenth century, however, the Spanish Crown issued a number of edicts intended to check exuberant popular religious expression. Church-sponsored public celebrations now moved into private spaces, particularly the lay charitable gatherings known as *jamaicas*. Clerics and pious lay people denounced the drinking, dancing, and lewd behavior at jamaicas. Although lyrics to naughty songs appear in Inquisition records, there is little evidence that officials acted on complaints. Some dances were of local origin, some imported from Spain, and one came to Mexico by way of Cuba, the *chuchumbé*, a particularly suggestive dance. Another type of party was the *coloquia*, a licensed social gathering open to the paying public. Supposedly alcoholic beverages were not served and the sexes were segregated during these parties held at varying venues, including convents and hospitals. These regulations proved difficult to enforce, provoking more denunciations from the pulpit.

A seasonal and still highly popular religious custom was the reenactment of the search by Joseph and Mary for shelter (*posada*) before Jesus's birth. During the *posadas*, friends and relatives would carry religious images to one or more houses, where food and drink awaited them. The rich also held parties and dances, but their *tertulias* and *saraos* generally were not denounced by the clergy, who often attended. In practice the festivities of the popular classes and elites may have differed but little.

Other Popular Entertainments. Bullfights were not only a popular entertainment but also were staged to celebrate the arrival of a new viceroy, commemorate annually the victory of the Spanish in the conquest of Mexico (August 13), and mark other significant occasions. Like the theater bullfights attracted people of all classes who sat in different areas. Then as now the key distinction was whether one sat in the sun (*sol*) or shade (*sombra*), the sunny seats being cheaper. Elites sat in boxes that belonged to official institutions, so the status of the members of the audience could be gauged by where they were seated. In the eighteenth century shifting peninsular attitudes turned against bullfighting to some degree. But the revenues they generated for the Crown meant that bullfights continued as a popular diversion, although with less pomp and circumstance.

Other popular entertainments included cockfights, dogfights, horseracing, and gambling with cards or dice. With the exception of a state monopoly on playing cards in the late colonial era, most popular entertainments were disapproved by the church but not regulated by the state.

Glossary

bachillerato bachelor's degree
chuchumbé dance with sexual overtones
colegio institute of higher education
coloquia party open to the public with an admission charge
doctorado doctorate degree
evangelista freelance scribe often supplying services to the illiterate
licenciatura licentiate, master's degree
magnificat musical tribute to the Virgin Mary
mayordomía stewardship of an organization
mesa governing board of an organization; lit. "table"
Monte de Piedad national pawnshop
obras pías pious works; charity
posada Christmas-time custom reenacting the search for shelter by the Holy Family
sarao soirée, evening party
sol inexpensive seating at the bullfights, in the sun
sombra expensive seats in the shade at the bullring
tertulia party or gathering; literary salon
tianguís Mexican Spanish word for marketplace (Nahuatl: *tianquiztli*)
vida biography, often of a religious figure
villancicos lively music often for festivals; carols

Questions for Discussion

1. How did the church foster the arts in colonial Mexico?

2. What cultural activities attracted both elites and members of the popular classes?

3. What was the role of formal education in shaping Mexican society?

4. Why were Sor Juana Inés de la Cruz and Don Carlos Sigüenza y Góngora such important figures in Mexican cultural history?

Suggested Reading

Beezley, William H., Cheryl English Martin, and William E. French, eds. *Rituals of Rule, Rituals of Resistance: Public Celebrations and Popular Culture in Mexico*. Wilmington, Del.: Scholarly Resources, 1994. Essays on cultural life in Mexico, including several on the colonial era.

Burkhart, Louise M., editor and translator. *Holy Wednesday: A Nahua Drama from Early Colonial Mexico*. Philadelphia: University of Pennsylvania Press, 1996. An example of sixteenth-century liturgical drama designed to edify Indians.

Cañizares-Esguerra, Jorge. *How to Write the History of the New World*. Stanford: Stanford University Press, 2001. Prize-winning study of how writers treated the question of the origins of the New World, with emphasis on New Spain.

Cervantes, Fernando. *The Devil in the New World: The Impact of Diabolism in New Spain*. New Haven, Conn.: Yale University Press, 1994. Important intellectual history of diabolism in Mexico, giving insight into colonial culture.

Cervantes de Salazar, Francisco. *Life in the Imperial and Loyal City of Mexico in New Spain and the Royal and Pontifical University of Mexico, as described in Dialogues . . .* [1554] Westport, Conn. and London: Greenwood Press Publishers, 1970. Important primary source for the early colonial period.

Cruz, Sor Juana Inés de la. *The Divine Narcissus/El Divino Narciso*. Translated by Patricia Peters and Renée Domeier, O.S.B. Albuquerque: University of New Mexico Press, 1998. Bilingual edition of one of Sor Juana's major works.

———. *Poems, Protest, and a Dream*. Translated by Margaret Sayers-Peden. London: Penguin Books, 1997. Excellent edition of Sor Juana's key works, including her autobiographical essay.

Harris, Max. *Aztecs, Moors and Christians: Festivals of Reconquest in Mexico and Spain.* Austin: University of Texas Press, 2000. Interesting examination of the origin and development of public rituals and festivities in Mexico and Spain before and after the conquest.

Ladd, Doris M. *The Mexican Nobility at Independence, 1780–1826.* Austin: Institute of Latin American Studies, University of Texas, 1976. Prize-winning study of the high nobility in Mexico, with special attention to economic and cultural matters.

Leonard, Irving. *Baroque Times in Old Mexico.* Ann Arbor: University of Michigan Press, 1971. Classic work dealing with cultural and political life during the seventeenth century.

———. *Don Carlos Sigüenza y Góngora, A Mexican Savant of the Seventeenth Century.* Berkeley: University of California Press, 1929. Classic biography of one of the key figures in colonial Mexican intellectual life.

Jacobson, Jerome V., S.J. *Educational Foundations of the Jesuits in Sixteenth-Century New Spain.* Berkeley: University of California Press, 1938. Work chronicling the Jesuit achievement by one of its members.

Merrim, Stephanie, ed. *Feminist Perspectives on Sor Juana Inés de la Cruz.* Detroit, Mich.: Wayne State University Press, 1991. Useful study of recent interpretations of Sor Juana.

Miller, Robert Ryal and William J. Orr, eds. *Daily Life in Colonial Mexico: The Journey of Friar Ilarione da Bergamo, 1761–1768.* Norman: University of Oklahoma Press, 2000. Recently discovered travel account by an Italian Capuchin who observed life in the capital and the mining districts.

Paz, Octavio. *Mexican Poetry: An Anthology.* Trans. by Samuel Beckett. New York: Grove Press, 1985. Anthology that includes a number of colonial poets.

Smith, Bradley. *Mexico: A History in Art.* Garden City, N.Y.: Doubleday Publishers, 1968. Useful publication for the nonspecialist reader that includes a good selection of colonial art.

Stevenson, Robert. *Music in Mexico: A Historical Survey.* New York: Crowell Publishers, 1952. Scholarly examination of music in Mexico accessible to the nonspecialist.

Viqueira Albán, Juan Pedro. *Propriety and Permissiveness in Bourbon Mexico.* Trans. by Sonya Lipsett-Rivera and Sergio Rivera. Wilmington, Del.: Scholarly Resources, 1999. Important essays on the cultural history of the late colonial era.

Discography

The Boston Camarata. *Nueva España: Close Encounters in the New World, 1590–1690.* Erato Disques S.A. 1993. 2292–45977–2 enrigistrement numérique.

Ensemble Elyma. *El Siglo de Oro en el Nuevo Mundo: Villancicos y Oraciones del siglo XVII en Latinoamérica.* Symphonia SY 91S05, 1992.

Ignacio de Jerusalem. *Matins for the Virgin of Guadalupe, 1764.* Performed by Chanticleer. Warner Music Manufacturing, Teldec Classics International, Hamburg, 1998.

San Antonio Vocal Arts Ensemble. *Guadalupe: Virgen de los Indios.* Iago/ Talking Taco Music IAGO CD210, 1998.

Cinema

I, the Worst of All. 1990. Portrayal of the life of Sor Juana, directed by María Luisa Bemberg.

Twelve

Rebellion and Crime

During the *Pax Hispanica*, the colonial peace lasting nearly three hundred years, Spanish rule was never significantly challenged. The Crown established an effective legal system to control crime and civil unrest as well as to provide the framework to adjudicate disputes over property. Despite the long peace, in every century of the colonial era there were large-scale rebellions and riots as well as many smaller ones. On two occasions during the 1600s there were major riots in Mexico City in which broad sectors of the urban populace participated. Crime, riot, and rebellion yield important insights into the racial, economic, and religious tensions of colonial Mexico, but the relative peace during three hundred years is significant as well.

The Imposition of Authority

To explain Spain's long success in maintaining order in a society divided by race and class, historians look to institutional structures and social values that promoted compliance with authority. Sedentary Indians in the central and southern regions of Mexico shared ideas about hierarchy and obedience. In particular the preconquest Nahuas had a highly developed legal system with written law code, established courts, and respected judges. Penalties for legal violations varied by class, but all were subject to the law. Spaniards also had a highly developed legal system, which they transferred to New Spain. In colonial Mesoamerica, the establishment of the Spanish system of justice meant that Indians of the center and south would use Spanish courts to pursue civil lawsuits against Spaniards and Indians alike.

Spanish courts provided a venue for Mesoamerican Indians to air their grievances and obtain justice, but they also petitioned the Crown directly to relieve the burden of tribute, extend privileges, and right wrongs. A number of petitions in Nahuatl directed to the monarch survive (see box). Most are written along the lines of "if the king only knew what was occurring, he would act justly." The Huejotzingo petition below is typical of the genre. Acknowledging the position of the Spanish king as God's "true representative on earth," the writers of the petition assure the monarch that they "have complete confidence" in him and ask for his compassion in the matter of excessively high tribute, the issue that prompted their petition. They urge the king to take action on their behalf before Huejotzingo "completely disappears and crumbles."

Letter in Nahuatl to Philip II from the town council of Huejotzingo, 1560

Our lord sovereign, you the king don Felipe [Philip II] our lord . . . we bow humbly before you; may we deserve your pity, may the very greatly compassionate and merciful God inspire you so that your pity is exercised on us, for we hear, and so it is said to us, that you are very merciful and humane toward all your vassals; and when a vassal of yours appears before you in affliction, so it is said, then you have pity on him with your very revered majesty, and by the grace of omnipotent God you help him. May we now also deserve and attain the same, for every day such poverty and affliction reaches us and is visited on us that we weep and mourn. O unfortunate are we, what is to become of us, we your poor vassals, we of Huejotzingo, we who live in your city? If you were not so far away, many times we would appear before you. . . . But now we are greatly taken aback and very afraid and ask, have we done something wrong, have we behaved badly and ill toward you, our lord sovereign, or have we committed some sin against almighty God? Perhaps you have heard something of our wickedness and for that reason now this very great tribute has fallen upon us, seven times exceeding all we had gone along paying before, the 2,000 pesos. And we declare to you that it will not be long before your city of Huejotzingo completely disappears and crumbles, because our father, grandfathers, and great-grandfathers knew no tribute and gave tribute to no one, but were independent. We nobles who have charge of your subjects are now truly very poor. Nobility is seen among us no longer. Now we resemble commoners: as they eat and dress, so do we. . . . Take pity on us, have compassion with us. May you especially remember those who subsist and live in the wilds, those who move us to tears and pity. Their poverty is before our eyes, we are gazing directly at it, wherefore we speak out before you so that afterwards you will not become angry with us when your subjects have disappeared or dispersed. Here ends this our humble supplication.

James Lockhart, ed. and trans., *We People Here: Nahuatl Accounts of the Conquest of Mexico* (Berkeley and Los Angeles, 1993), pp. 289–97.

The Role of the Church. Religion played a key role in reinforcing colonial obedience to both divine and human law. Confessions to the Spanish clergy provided priests both the opportunity and the obligation to impose penance for sins of disobedience. The exclusively male and preponderantly Spanish (or accepted as Spanish) composition of the priesthood meant that religious doctrine reinforced the power exercised by elite males. In Indian towns *principales* (elite men) held religious positions in which they exerted limited authority, but they could not serve as ordained priests. Parish priests in

Indian towns were often treated as royal officials, the clergy functioning much as did civil authorities in representing and upholding the power of the state. Religious displays greeted new viceroys and other important events, and officials of church and state participated together on the ceremonial dais on other important occasions. The imposition of Christianity on northern Indian populations or crackdowns against Indians' continued practice of their old religion triggered major revolts during the colonial era. In central Mexican parishes abusive behavior on the part of a priest could provoke violent efforts to oust him. For most central Mexican peoples, however, Christianity became a unifying force.

The Inquisition ensured religious orthodoxy; its trials were secret, with the accused never facing their accusers and often remaining ignorant of the charges; but punishment was public. Sometimes the punishment was to be led through the thronged streets of the capital with a public crier announcing to all what sins had been committed. The penitent wore a special robe, the *sanbenito,* and a conical hat. Only in the most extreme cases were penitents executed, usually for repeatedly relapsing into Jewish faith and practices or for refusing to renounce their faith. In these cases the Inquisition turned the prisoners over to civil authorities for execution, since the church had no power to impose the death penalty. Fewer than two hundred men and women were executed in autos de fe in Mexico during the entire colonial period. Inquisition officials did not let the fact that an accused individual was already dead interfere with their investigations, however. In the great auto de fe of 1649 the bones of a number of the condemned were unearthed and burned. The names of these deceased individuals were to be destroyed, their bodies obliterated, and surviving families left to bear the shame.

Civil Justice and Punishment. Public executions for religious crimes or civil insurrection were relatively infrequent during the colonial period. Colonial authorities, however, could move swiftly and drastically to enforce the penalties for transgressing the boundaries set by church and state. Public hangings visibly demonstrated the power of the state.

Urban dwellers especially were frequently reminded of the power of the state, as New Spain's major cities were the headquarters of the main institutions of the colony— royal and municipal government, church, guilds, and other corporate organizations—as well as the residence of Spanish elites. City governments organized police forces that maintained public order; not surprisingly it was the urban poor who most often were prosecuted for crime. Members of the upper class were contemptuous of the disorderly life of the urban poor, largely consisting of Indians and castas. Until the late seventeenth century, however, whites apparently did not fear that the poor would rise up against the established order.

Crime and Punishment in Spanish Cities. Crime was defined by the governing elite who were responsible for promulgating and upholding both civil and canon (church) law. Many crimes, such as murder and assault, were universally viewed as transgressions. Some acts that the elites defined as criminal, such as drinking, common-law marriage, gambling, and petty theft, however, were viewed by the popular classes as acceptable behavior. Sometimes the urban poor were prosecuted for such crimes, reflecting an effort on the part of the *gente decente* (upper classes) to control the public and private behavior of the lower classes. For the urban poor such acts represented normal responses to economic and social problems.

In the early colonial period a small municipal police force patrolled the city streets of the capital. By the late colonial era Mexico City had grown significantly and included a huge poor population. In the eighteenth century, the Crown attempted to institute formal mechanisms to maintain law and order in Mexico City, creating two police forces and nine municipal tribunals. With the creation of an expanded military, barracks were built, providing another reminder of state power in the capital. Other urban improvements, such as the installation of lights in the city's central core, aimed at making the streets safer.

For those arrested, justice was generally swift, with trials taking place within three days after the arrest. Although the poor were jailed in disproportionate numbers, arrest did not automatically result in conviction. Many cases were dismissed for lack of evidence, indicating some fairness in judicial proceedings. Those convicted were often fined or punished moderately. Sentences more often mandated labor on municipal projects or, more rarely, in privately owned *obrajes* (textile workshops).

Many poor people sought solace by drinking in unlicensed taverns, which often led to violations of public order, particularly drunkenness. Authorities arrested publicly intoxicated men and women and tried to limit the number of taverns selling *pulque* (fermented cactus juice) and beer through a licensing system. Petty sellers of alcohol were often prosecuted. These measures were largely ineffective in controlling the sale of alcohol and drinking, not only because of resistance by the popular classes, but also because rich hacienda owners made a substantial profit from alcohol.

Other crimes commonly committed by poor people stemmed from men's inability to support themselves and their families from wage labor alone. Property crimes such as theft, sale of stolen merchandise, gambling, and nonpayment of debts can be seen as survival strategies for breadwinners and those who depended on them. Even so, based on arrest statistics from eighteenth-century Mexico City analyzed by Michael Scardaville, overall these crimes accounted for only a small percentage of arrests. Male heads of household were most often arrested for property crimes. Spaniards were more often arrested for gambling and nonpayment of debts, while Indians and castas were most frequently prosecuted for robbery and sale of stolen goods. Many of those arrested for petty theft were young Indian men who had migrated to the city from the nearby provinces. Although high rates of property crime cannot be linked definitively to bad conditions in the countryside, it is likely that deteriorating rural conditions (such as years of poor harvests) forced more people to seek work in the city. Unemployment and underemployment likely contributed to criminal activity.

Violent crime in eighteenth-century Mexico City, such as murder, assault, rape, and armed robbery, accounted for only a small percentage of arrests. In reality, relatively few arrests took place because for the most part the police did not take the initiative in investigating crimes but, rather, responded if someone filed a complaint. Certainly the urban poor did not look to the police to maintain order or solve crimes in their neighborhoods and not surprisingly filed few complaints.

Crimes in the social sphere, such as domestic conflicts, prostitution, and common-law marriage (in violation of church law) figured in arrest statistics. In this category of arrests women were a significant group, accounting for some 25 percent of those prosecuted in eighteenth-century Mexico City. Families rarely used courts to resolve domestic conflicts. Prostitution was common but seldom prosecuted. Women were sometimes arrested for living in consensual unions rather than sacramental marriages. Common-law marriage reflected the fluidity of life among people who were not much concerned with the possible loss of social status that "living in sin" entailed or with the legitimacy of their offspring, since they had little or no property to divide among heirs. For a married woman abandoned by her legal husband, common-law union with a new partner could provide protection and economic support.

The elite residents of the capital saw the poor as disorderly and contemptible but assumed they could control them by deploying a small police force. In the seventeenth century, however, two major riots in Mexico City demonstrated to royal authorities and colonial elites that the urban poor could threaten not only the public order but even the colonial system itself.

Urban Riots

The Mexico City Riot of 1624. Mexico City experienced a major riot in 1624, a complicated event instigated by upper-class Mexicans who opposed the new reformist viceroy, the Marqués de Gelves. Arriving in New Spain in 1621, Gelves began his term by canceling all the welcoming processions and festivities organized by local elites, calling them a waste of money. Since these events not only served to honor new viceroys but also provided the elites an opportunity to display their wealth and largesse, this was a major affront to the capital's upper class. Supported by the archbishop and the secular clergy, American-born Spaniards mobilized the urban poor to oust Gelves.

Viceroy Gelves was a reformer who expected to make major changes in government and put an end to the blatantly corrupt practices of colonial office holders. These practices included holding multiple offices in defiance of the law and using their offices for personal enrichment to the detriment of royal revenues. The new viceroy broke up a price-fixing racket in corn, thereby benefiting the popular classes. His reform program also targeted freedoms enjoyed by the city's black residents, however, barring them from living together, assembling in groups, or bearing arms. A moral reformer, he banned prostitutes from the streets, closed brothels and gambling houses, and instituted arms control. He had vagrants, thieves, and brigands arrested, filling the jails. Thus, the viceroy's sweeping campaign of reform succeeded in offending the ruling elite of Mexico City, much of the secular clergy, and a significant portion of the urban popular classes.

On January 15, 1624, violence erupted in the Plaza Mayor. Viceroy Gelves was the main object of attack. The crowd shouted "Long live the King! Long live Christ! Death to bad government! Death to the heretic Lutheran [Viceroy Gelves]! Death to the excommunicated heretic! Arrest the viceroy!"[1] The crowd thus affirmed the authority of the monarch and the church, but denounced the viceroy as someone outside the community of the faithful and therefore not a true representative of the Crown, whose authority they still recognized, at least in principle.

Sources do not dispute that Spaniards participated in the riot or *tumulto*, but it is unclear whether rioters included members of the elite. Indians, blacks, and other castas as well as Portuguese foreigners joined the insurrection. At one point, rioters ran to the nearby building that housed the Inquisition, calling on inquisitors to support them. In a show of ceremonial splendor and power, the inquisitors went en masse to the Plaza Mayor holding their crosses high. The crowd fell silent and obeyed the clerics' request that the fires the rioters had set be put out. The viceroy made concessions under pressure, but rioting resumed once the inquisitors left the Plaza. After about seven hours of turmoil, the viceroy fled the palace disguised as a servant and took refuge in a Franciscan priory. Believing him dead, the Audiencia assumed power in his absence, and upper-class gentlemen patrolled the streets, dispersing Indians and castas. Around seventy people died in the rioting, first when the viceroy's guards opened fire on the crowd, and then when royal soldiers positioned on the roof of the archbishop's residence fired on the viceroy's guards.

Although the gates of the viceregal palace were set on fire and the Plaza Mayor suffered damage, no rioters were prosecuted. Mexican elites had helped to foment riot among the popular classes in hopes of ousting the viceroy and restoring power to those who held it before the viceroy's reforms. For the popular classes the departure of the viceroy meant the return to laxer enforcement of laws that affected them negatively. The Crown did not attempt to impose sweeping reforms for another century and a half.

[1] J. I. Israel, *Race, Class, and Politics in Colonial Mexico, 1610–1670* (Oxford, 1975), p. 52.

The Mexico City Riot of 1692. While in the riot of 1624 the elite seems to have manipulated crowds for its own political ends, the *tumulto* of 1692 was quite different. Drought, crop failures of both corn and wheat, and prices for bread that were rising despite the viceroy's efforts to acquire grain from increasingly distant sources created difficult conditions for the urban poor. Two protests occurred in a two-day interval in June 1692, with crowds demanding an explanation for the food shortages from first the archbishop and then the viceroy. The second protest erupted into widespread rioting in the Plaza Mayor and surrounding areas. In this urban insurrection, rather than manipulating the popular classes, the upper class watched in horror as crowds attacked and set fire to the viceregal palace and the residence of the archbishop and looted shops around the plaza and on the nearby streets.

Just what ignited the riot is disputed. Indians testified that they had come to the archbishop's palace bearing the body of a dead Indian woman they claimed had been killed at the royal grain storage facility or *alhóndiga* as a result of the crush of the crowd demanding corn. Spaniards contended that the woman actually was quite alive. Both accounts agree that the archbishop rebuffed the poor's request for aid. The viceroy then denied the poor any possibility of redress by refusing to hear them.

Violence broke out on June 8, 1692. The attack focused on the viceregal palace as well as the town hall, jail, and public granary. Rioters shouted, "Kill the [Creole] Spaniards and the *Gachupines* who eat our corn! We go to war happily! God wants us to finish off the Spaniards! We do not care if we die without confession! Is this not our land?"[2] Rioters with murderous intent directed their wrath at rich whites for the scarcity of corn. They also explicitly rejected the traditional Catholic doctrine concerning confession for the remission of sins. Churchmen carrying crosses could not quell the rioting as they had in 1624.

Although later explanations portrayed the riot as a single continuous event, according to historian R. Douglas Cope it was chaotic and discontinuous. Looting was rampant, with opportunistic thieves making off with merchandise from the upscale shops in the arcades of the plaza and surrounding streets. The looting marked the end of the protest. As rioters turned into looters they took all they could carry. Spaniards' efforts to stop the rioting by persuasion or force were uncoordinated and ineffectual.

In the riot's aftermath Spaniards sought to punish the leaders and find a coherent explanation for the outbreak of violence. The viceroy and his advisors sought immediate solutions to the proximate cause of the riot, the lack of corn. More important from the viceroy's point of view was to reestablish order and reaffirm royal authority, since rioters had effectively challenged both. As the fires burned out, the capital's elite raised a local militia

---

[2]Irving Leonard, *Don Carlos de Sigüenza y Góngora* (Berkeley, 1929), p. 257.

to patrol the central area. Nonwhites found to have looted merchandise were arrested, and they in turn informed on others. The rioters' solidarity evaporated under the pressure of prosecution. Fifteen people were sentenced to death, dozens more to flogging and jail terms of up to ten years. Although the state could be lenient in its treatment of Indians involved in central Mexican village uprisings, usually sentencing them to forced labor rather than death, the 1692 riot was quite different. It represented class warfare that put Spanish authority at risk. Punishment was swift and brutal, and no further riots in the capital challenged the Pax Hispanica.

Revolts in the North

Until the movement for independence in the early nineteenth century, rural rebellions in Mexico were exclusively expressions of Indian discontent. Indian groups rose up in protest against Spanish authority, contesting a colonial order that demanded their labor, encroached on their land, and required them to renounce their old religions. Indians rebelled all over Greater Mexico during the colonial period, but these uprisings had distinct regional characteristics. With the notable exception of the Mixtón War in Nueva Galicia (1541–2), once Spaniards conquered settled Indian populations in central Mexico, indigenous groups did not again significantly challenge colonial rule. The Chichimecas (as the Nahuas named them) or *indios bárbaros*, as the Spanish also called them, resisted conquest and pacification for nearly half a century. Once they were conquered, Spaniards in the north had to deal with a series of rebellions largely set off by efforts to impose Christianity. Violent native uprisings may also have occurred in reaction to their incorporation into the Spanish economic order and disruption of other key aspects of traditional life. The most important of these northern rebellions was the Pueblo Revolt (1680).

The Mixtón War (1541–2). The most serious postconquest Indian uprising in Mexico was the Mixtón War. As in several later major uprisings, native religion played an important role. In most of central Mexico, once Indian groups were conquered they remained pacified. Occurring just twenty years after the conquest of Tenochtitlan, the Mixtón War was so significant for Spaniards that it was called "The Second Conquest of Mexico." Viceroy Mendoza himself led Spanish troops and Indian allies into battle against fifty thousand to one hundred thousand rebellious northern Indians. The revolt occurred in Nueva Galicia (modern Jalisco), a transitional zone between the settled populations of Mesoamerica to the south and the Chichimecas to the north. This region initially was conquered and ruled by Nuño de Guzmán, outstanding even among conquerors for his cruelty. According to the historian Lesley Byrd Simpson, in the aftermath of Guzmán's rule "flourishing provinces were permanently depopulated, and the hatred and despair of the victims mounted to such a pitch that they eventually rose against the Spaniards in the wild rebellion known as the Mixtón War."[3] During the Mixtón War a religious revitalization movement united Indians and galvanized them to expel Spaniards and stamp out Christianity.

As in other settled regions of Mexico, the encomenderos of Nueva Galicia exploited Indian labor and friars brought a portion of the Indian population into the Christian fold. The spark that set off the revolt seems to have been the appearance of charismatic leaders of a revitalized native religion. This religion promised paradise: rich rewards without work, abundant food, turquoise jewelry and feather adornment highly valued in native culture, and magic bows and arrows. For Indians who rejected Christianity, the revitalized traditional religion promised earthly pleasure and immortality. Some contemporary observers believed that the pacified Indians may have rebelled at the instigation of nearby unconquered Chichimecas. Since rebels did not write their own account of the Mixtón War, much of what is known about it is drawn from the official Spanish investigation that followed. The viceroy laid the blame for the uprising on Chichimecas of the mountains of Zacatecas and Tepeque who incited the pacified Indians to renounce Christianity and revolt against Spanish rule. His Spanish opponents blamed Viceroy Mendoza for funding exploratory expeditions to the north (thus undercutting the old system of rewarding conquerors for their services), which they claimed diverted resources from settled Indian communities.

Initial Spanish attempts to pacify rebel Indians through the mediation of the Franciscans and then by military force failed, spurring additional Indian settlements to join the revolt. Viceroy Mendoza called on conqueror Pedro de Alvarado. As other Spaniards considered how best to contain the revolt, the ever-impetuous Alvarado acted. He gathered an army of one hundred horsemen and one hundred Spanish foot soldiers plus five thousand Indian allies from Michoacan to deal with the rebels in summary fashion. His rash decision cost him his life, since the rebel Indians held strategic high ground. Rains turned the flat lands normally ideal for Spanish cavalry charges into a quagmire. Rebel leaders used Spanish blunders to their full advantage. During a disastrous Spanish retreat, Alvarado was thrown into a ravine, his horse landing on top of him. He died ten days later. In the wake of this spectacular battlefield defeat, fifty thousand rebel Indians attacked Guadalajara itself, where defenders holed up in a few major buildings. For Spaniards the hero of the battle was Beatriz Hernández who "fought like an Amazon alongside of the men."[4]

In response to the deteriorating situation Mendoza assembled and led a large fighting force that included Indian allies, notably granted permission for the first time to ride horses but not to use Spanish weapons. Mendoza's

---

[3]Lesley Byrd Simpson, *Many Mexicos* (Berkeley and Los Angeles, 1966), p. 39.
[4]Arthur Scott Aiton, *Antonio de Mendoza: First Viceroy of New Spain* (Durham, N.C., 1927), p. 151.

forces attacked and eventually took Mixtón ("cat's ascent"), the strategic *peñol* that gave the war its name. The high stronghold fell after three weeks, when a defecting defender revealed an alternative route to the Spaniards. Some of the tens of thousands of rebel Indians were enslaved by the victors, taken in "just war" as rebels against royal authority and Christianity, while others were allowed to return to their homes and service to their encomenderos. The defeat of the defenders at Mixtón and their supporters in the region enhanced Mendoza's sterling reputation as a military leader, initially earned fighting Muslims in Granada. Thankful Spaniards believed that the greatest challenge to colonial rule to date had been vanquished. According to Eric Van Young, "the end of the war paved the way for effective Spanish penetration into the Chichimec area, and the resulting discovery of Zacatecas in 1546."[5] Until the Pueblo Revolt in 1680, no large Indian group successfully regained its independence.

Major Conspiracies and Rebellions in Mexico

1541–2	Mixtón War	Jalisco uprising, "Second Conquest"
1550–1606	Chichimeca War	Resistance to Spanish presence in the north
1612	Black conspiracy	Conspiracy to kill whites (Mexico City)
1616	Tepehuan Revolt	Indian revolt in northern Mexico
1624	Mexico City riot	Creole conspiracy against the viceroy
1680–92	Pueblo Revolt	Revolt to expel Spaniards from New Mexico
1692	Mexico City Riot	Indian and casta bread riot
1712	Tzeltal Revolt	Multiethnic revolt in Maya region
1810–11	Hidalgo Revolt	Uprising leading to independence

The Chichimeca War and Aftermath. In northern Mexico the Chichimeca War of 1550–1606 (discussed in Chapter 9) was bloody and long. Northern Indians were difficult to subdue militarily and hostile to conversion to Christianity, but Spaniards' need to secure the trunk lines to the silver-mining areas meant that they had a strong incentive to conquer and control the region. Spaniards adopted a policy of placing garrisons of soldiers to control territory and eventually brought peace to the region by giving gifts of provisions to Indians in exchange for the cessation of hostilities.

Once Indians submitted to Spanish authority, they were subject to Christian evangelization and labor duty. Northern Mexican Indians rebelled in many areas, most often because Spaniards' labor demands far exceeded anything they had experienced previously and because the

[5]Eric Van Young, *Hacienda and Market in Eighteenth-Century Mexico* (Berkeley and Los Angeles, 1981), p. 19.

Franciscans and Jesuits were vigorous in their enforcement of Christian orthodoxy, while Indians resisted conversion. The combination proved deadly, resulting in revolts in 1601 of the Acaxee and of the Xixime in 1609. Tepehuan Indians of Durango revolted in 1616, gaining control over considerable territory and holding out for more than a year. Religion played a significant role in all these rebellions. Christian missionaries became martyrs for their faith, but rebellious Indians targeted Spaniards as a group. From the Indians' point of view they were reasserting their ancient beliefs and autonomy.

The Pueblo Revolt. The most spectacular example of a successful Indian rebellion was the 1680 Pueblo Revolt, which drove Spanish settlers in New Mexico back to El Paso del Norte (modern El Paso, Texas) for ten years. Earlier, scattered revolts in the north and northeast had resulted in the loss of missionary lives and property. In August 1680 a unified rising attacked Spanish missions and settlements. Four hundred twenty-two Spanish friars, soldiers, and settlers were killed or captured and some two thousand colonists, Indian allies, dependents, and slaves expelled. A number of factors contributed to the revolt, including Spanish repression of indigenous religious practices and economic hardship in the region. Just before the revolt an extended drought from 1666 to 1671 caused tremendous suffering. Pueblo herds died and crops failed, bringing starvation and death. Increased raiding by Navahos and Apaches, in which Pueblo Indians sometimes were taken as slaves, also undermined stability.

During the long drought some Pueblos alleged that the foreigners' Christian god had failed to protect them against harm. A revitalization movement developed in which native men led traditional religious ceremonies. Spaniards harshly suppressed the movement, with Governor Juan Francisco Treviño launching a campaign against idolatry in 1675. A number of Indian spiritual leaders were hanged and forty-seven were flogged, acts that set the stage for the regional revolt. Under the leadership of a San Juan Pueblo Indian named Popé, Pueblos united to destroy the Spanish regime that had forced them to embrace Christianity and to perform labor and pay tribute. Around twenty-five Pueblo settlements with seventeen thousand residents rose on August 10, 1680. Pueblos captured and burned Santa Fe, among other Spanish settlements, but allowed some Spaniards and their Indian allies and dependents to flee to El Paso.

Although religious conflict precipitated the rebellion, there is evidence that enslavement of Indians played an important role in mobilizing Pueblos and other Indians to revolt. Spaniards had taken captive Apaches who had received guarantees of safe conduct while visiting Pecos Pueblo and then distributed them as slaves to local Spaniards or miners in Parral (Chihuahua). The Indians of Pecos Pueblo felt betrayed by the Spaniards, and Apaches who hoped to free their captured kin also joined the revolt. Slavery was a long-standing phenomenon in the region, but Spaniards and their Indian auxiliaries (mainly Tlaxcalans from central Mexico) expanded its scope. Some Indians who had been taken as slaves became slave-soldiers (*genízaros*) in the Spanish forces, and they in turn took slaves. The possibility of taking captives may have motivated some rebels.

Pueblo rebels drove all Spaniards from New Mexico within a few weeks, killing an estimated five hundred, targeting the Franciscan missionaries in particular. Pueblos destroyed nearly all Spanish buildings, particularly churches. Popé remained in charge immediately following the revolt and ordered the systematic destruction of all trappings of Christianity; but he was deposed a year later, and factionalism marred the unity of the rebel Pueblos. The destruction of churches, slaying of missionaries, and expulsion of the Spanish residents left the region in Indian hands for over a decade. Pueblos continued to raise Spanish-introduced crops and livestock and to weave wool blankets as Spaniards had taught them. In 1684, Indians in nearby regions also revolted in what some Mexican historians call the Great Northern Revolt, in the region from modern Coahuila west to Sonora.

The Pueblo Revolt had reverberations in other parts of Mexico's north. As Spaniards fled New Mexico, other Indian groups began to consider the possibility of expelling the Spaniards as well. As displaced Spaniards moved elsewhere in the north, they put further pressure on Indian groups. After the disastrous loss of New Mexico, the Crown was determined to lose no more territory and therefore built or reinforced presidios. A prolonged drought, the relative wealth of the new Spanish towns, and Indians' visceral hostility to Christianity meant that Spanish settlements became targets for Indian attacks.

Revolts in the South and Center

The Tzeltal Maya Rebellion. Southern Mexico experienced one major revolt on the scale of the regional uprisings in the north. In 1712 in the southern region of Chiapas a widespread revolt, generally known as the Tzeltal Maya rebellion, erupted. The rebellion involved not only multiple Indian villages but also Indians of different linguistic and ethnic groups, with about equal numbers of Tzeltal and Tzotzil Mayas as well as Chol participating. At the end of the seventeenth century Catholic priests had become frustrated and alarmed that traditional religious beliefs still thrived among the Indians, and priests attempted to stamp them out. Chiapas witnessed four religious movements in the early eighteenth century.

The catalyst for the 1712 revolt was religious, the culmination of long-term Indian conflicts with the Catholic church over recognition of apparitions of the Virgin. Indian claims of sightings of the Virgin Mary were not always rejected, as the case of the Virgin of Guadalupe suggests. The church, however, was wary of lay influence in the religious sphere, requiring lay religious confraternities to be supervised by a priest. The church hierarchy was especially wary of Indian religious autonomy and suppressed independent indigenous cults in several locations. In Chiapas Maya claims to having witnessed miraculous events allowed them to appropriate Catholic symbols and control the cults centered on those symbols.

In 1708, in the Tzotzil town of Zinacantan, a *ladino* (Hispanized Indian) hermit preached to Indians from a hollow tree that the Virgin had descended from heaven to assist Indians. Church officials who investigated the miracle had the tree chopped down and the hermit arrested. On his release Indians built the hermit a chapel, which church officials then burned; but Indians made offerings of food and incense while it still stood. This incident set the pattern for subsequent sightings of the Virgin, who appeared in 1711 in the Tzotzil town of Santa Marta and the following year in the small Tzeltal settlement of Cancuc, near the Spanish provincial center of Ciudad Real. Around the same time Tzotzil residents in the town of Chenalho reported miraculous events in which the image of Saint Sebastian was seen to sweat. Church officials burned the chapel built for the saint, but did not destroy the saint's image.

The cult of the Virgin of Cancuc developed in May 1712, when a young married woman named María de la Candelaria had a vision in which the Virgin told her to build a chapel for her. When the Tzeltal sought permission from the church to build the chapel, the bishop arrested the delegation. A resident of Chenalho involved in the worship of the sweating Saint Sebastian then arrived in Cancuc, where the Virgin was said to have appeared. The man, Sebastián Gómez de la Gloria, said that he had gone to heaven and spoken with key Catholic figures: the Holy Trinity, the Virgin Mary, and Saint Peter. Gómez claimed that Saint Peter had granted him authority to ordain literate Indian men as priests and that Spanish civil authority no longer had jurisdiction over the Indians, either to administer justice or collect taxes. By establishing an indigenous priesthood and declaring Spanish authority null and void, he directly attacked the colonial regime. From Cancuc leaders sent messages purportedly signed by the Blessed Virgin to nearby towns, inviting them to join in a confederation.

Thirty-two Tzeltal-, Tzotzil-, and Chol-speaking towns participated in the uprising. Towns sent their highest religious officials, the fiscales, to Cancuc to be ordained as priests. Highly respected religious figures in their communities, many of these men were literate and already familiar with Catholic ritual. These newly ordained priests were to perform all duties of Spanish clerics, including keeping records of baptisms and marriages, celebrating the sacraments, and preaching sermons. Indian priests wore the clerical robes left behind by fleeing Spanish clerics.

The rebel towns created a parallel Indian civil hierarchy as well, with an Indian audiencia and three Indian kings to replace the Spanish monarch, who was declared dead. The armed forces of the confederation were known as "Soldiers for the Virgin" and were organized in a military hierarchy patterned on the Spanish model. The Virgin's troops marched on Indian towns that initially did not join the confederation.

When Spanish authorities learned of the confederation's existence, they called up men to serve in militia units, especially to defend the Spanish regional center of Ciudad Real. The confederation's forces attacked the smaller towns of Chilon and Ocosingo, massacring Spanish soldiers. They spared Spanish women, however, taking them to Cancuc, where they were forced into sexual unions with Indian men and required to dress as Indian women and perform all the onerous domestic tasks of native women, such as grinding corn and hauling water. For Indian men, the powerful appeal of dominating Spanish women was an important factor in the movement. For Spaniards the capture of their women symbolized Indians' successful defiance of Spanish authority and violation of colonial codes of honor.

By autumn 1712 Spanish troops had initiated a successful offense against the confederation, capturing Cancuc in November. The cult leaders escaped into the mountains for several months. The Cancuc Indians immediately accepted an amnesty that Spaniards offered, infuriating the confederated towns that had vowed to fight on. The viceroy sent a special envoy to pacify the region, and by June 1713 the revolt had ended. According to believers, the Virgin returned to heaven because Indians had lost their faith in her ability to protect them. Although other religiously inspired rebellions would occur in southern Mexico, apparitions of the Virgin were not a factor in those conflicts.

The Tzeltal rebellion's aim was not to reestablish the old Maya religion but rather to break the Spanish monopoly over the Christian priesthood. It also aspired to achieve Indian autonomy from Spanish colonial rule. It briefly succeeded in creating a multiethnic, regional Indian church and state modeled on colonial Spanish religious and civil institutions rather than prehispanic ones. In Mexico's highly racialized social system, Indian men were not on equal footing with Spanish men. Taking Spanish women and forcing them into the position of Indian women represented a significant attack on the Spaniards' racial hierarchy. What happened to the captive Spanish women after Spaniards pacified the region is not known.

Rebellions in the Countryside of Central Mexico. Indian rebellions in central Mexico differed significantly from the large-scale rebellions of northern Mexico or the Tzeltal Revolt in the south. According to William B. Taylor, virtually all uprisings of Indians in central Mexico were spontaneous, brief, and local in character, usually occurring in reaction to outside threats. They did not entail coordinated attacks undertaken over a lengthy period, nor did they seek to overthrow Spanish colonial authority. Typically an entire community would spontaneously rise up, armed with weapons that came easily to hand, such as agricultural tools, but also rocks, burning sticks, and even powdered chili pepper. In central Mexico women participated in the revolts and quite often formed the majority, aggressively leading attacks against outsiders. This pattern contrasts with the north, where women seldom participated in rebellions, perhaps because traditionally northern Indian men were hunters who had and used weapons.

The redrawing of town boundaries by royal officials represented the kind of outside interference that communities in central Mexico might perceive as a threat. Violence aimed at achieving specific, local political objectives, such as ousting a priest or a royal official. Uprisings also typically targeted sites associated with authority, such as the town hall or jail, and usually there was no looting. Since the jail symbolized the state and its power to punish, it is not surprising that Indians often burned it.

The violence usually was short-lived, leaderless, and spontaneous and often achieved its objective, such as the replacement of a hated official. None of these rebellions generated broad coalitions but rather remained localized. Sometimes a successful protest would turn into a village celebration. In general Spanish authorities did not punish entire communities for rebelling but did issue stern warnings. Although some uprisings resulted in deaths of officials, since there seldom were any individually identifiable culprits the justice system could not proceed.

Some colonial rebellions occurred in the immediate aftermath of conquest, as indigenous groups resisted incorporation into the Spanish colony. Once colonial rule was established, Indians protested suppression of their ancient religions or religious autonomy as well as Spaniards' labor demands. Their protests usually remained local but sometimes assumed regional dimensions. Mexico's long history of rebellions meant that during the independence era elites were well aware of the urban popular classes' and rural Indian populations' potential to disrupt and challenge the established order. As long as Mexican-born and peninsular Spaniards remained a basically unified group and were willing to devote substantial resources to maintain military power and colonial authority, that order could prevail. Where whites were few in number, as in the north, or divided along lines of origin or ideology, as they sometimes were during the struggle for independence, rebellion could lead to racial warfare and class conflict.

Glossary

alhóndiga   public granary
gachupines   derogatory term for Spaniards born in the Iberian peninsula
genízaros   Indian slaves
gente decente   white elites
ladino   person of indigenous background but culturally Hispanic
tumulto   riot

Questions for Discussion

1.   How did the Crown maintain the Pax Hispanica and suppress criminal and disorderly behavior?

2.   How did the town council of Huejotzingo portray its circumstances to the king? Why did it appeal directly to the Crown?

3.   What role did religion play in Indian rebellions?

4.   How did rural rebellions differ in central, southern, and northern Mexico?

5.   Why were the Mexico City riots of 1624 and 1692 important to Mexican history?

Suggested Reading

Aiton, Arthur Scott, *Antonio de Mendoza: First Viceroy of New Spain*. Durham, N.C.: Duke University Press, 1927. Traces the career of a key administrator responsible for institutionalizing Crown rule and asserting royal authority in the Mixtón War.

Bancroft, Hubert Howe. *History of Mexico*, vol. II. San Francisco: The History Company Publishers, 1886. Contains a useful account of the Mixtón War.

Bricker, Victoria Reifler. *The Indian Christ, the Indian King: The Historical Substrate of Maya Myth and Ritual*. Austin: University of Texas Press, 1981. A superb work by a cultural anthropologist and ethnohistorian on key events of Tzeltal Maya rebellion, with translations of Maya documents from the era.

Brooks, James. *Captives and Cousins: Slavery, Kinship, and Community in the Southwest Borderlands*. Chapel Hill: Omohundro Institute of Early American History and Culture and University of North Carolina Press, 2002. Major study of interactions between Indians and Europeans in northwestern Mexico.

Cope, R. Douglas. *The Limits of Racial Domination: Plebeian Society in Colonial Mexico City, 1660–1720*. Madison: University of Wisconsin Press, 1994. An examination of the casta system with a detailed analysis of the riot of 1692.

Gradie, Charlotte M. *The Tepehuan Revolt of 1616: Militarism, Evangelism, and Colonialism in Seventeenth-Century Nueva Vizcaya*. Salt Lake City: University of Utah Press, 2000. A careful examination of the factors leading to the revolt with a description of the event and its aftermath.

Hu-DeHart, Evelyn. *Missionaries, Miners, and Indians: Spanish Contact with the Yaqui Nation of Northwestern New Spain, 1533–1820*. Tucson: University of Arizona Press, 1981. Excellent local study of Spanish-Indian relations over the entire colonial period.

Israel, Jonathan I. *Race, Class, and Politics in Colonial Mexico, 1610–1670*. Oxford: Oxford University Press, 1975. Discussion of institutional politics in seventeenth-century Mexico with a lucid analysis of the riot of 1624.

MacLachlan, Colin M. *Criminal Justice in Eighteenth-Century Mexico: A Study of the Tribunal of the Acordada*. Berkeley and Los Angeles: University of California Press, 1974. Study of the viceregal law enforcement agency that could impose and execute sentences.

Scardaville, Michael C. "(Hapsburg) Law and (Bourbon) Order: State Authority, Popular Unrest, and the Criminal Justice System in Bourbon Mexico City, " *The Americas* 50:4 (April 1994): 501–25. A concise study outlining the differences in practice over time.

Sigüenza y Góngora, Don Carlos. "Letter to Admiral Pez Recounting the Incidents of the Corn Riot in Mexico City, June 8, 1692," in *Don Carlos Sigüenza y Góngora* by Irving Leonard. Berkeley: University of California Press, 1929. Primary document dealing with the riot of 1692, an appendix to a biography of the seventeenth-century savant.

Simpson, Lesley Byrd. *Many Mexicos*. 4th ed. Berkeley and Los Angeles: University of California Press, 1966. A classic set of interpretive essays on Mexico, including one on the Mixtón War.

Taylor, William B. *Drinking, Homicide and Rebellion in Colonial Mexican Villages*. Stanford: Stanford University Press, 1979. Brilliant study of three criminal behaviors in late colonial Mexico.

Van Young, Eric. *Hacienda and Market in Eighteenth-Century Mexico*. Berkeley and Los Angeles: University of California Press, 1981.

Weber, David J., ed. *What Caused The Pueblo Revolt of 1680?* Boston and New York: Bedford/St. Martin's, 1999. Contrasting views of the origins of the Pueblo Revolt.

Part III

1700–1824

Thirteen

Race, Class, and Family

Race shaped Mexican society in colonial times, becoming deeply rooted in its social fabric and moral character. Issues related to racial and ethnic identity not only lay at the core of colonial legislation and government but also constituted the primary criteria for social differentiation. Social life in colonial Mexico theoretically was strictly segregated along racial lines. Determination of social status, or *calidad*, was closely connected to hierarchical racial classification, economic position, religious convictions, and gender distinctions.

Early colonial Mexican society hinged on the principle that Spaniards and Indians should live in two completely separate worlds: the *república de españoles*, the commonwealth of Spaniards or *gente de razón* (civilized people), and the *república de indios*, the commonwealth of Indians or *naturales* (native people). The core of this principle was the idea that European blood and Roman Catholicism constituted the main source of moral strength and social virtue. Native American and African ancestries were deemed to be permanently and irredeemably inferior. In theory, no social interaction should take place between Indians and Spaniards other than in working situations. With the exception of the parish priest and colonial officials, in principle Spaniards were not supposed to establish permanent residency within the boundaries of Indian villages. Despite these ideas, a small number of Indian and mestizo elites found a place in the new order.

In reality, the goal of maintaining residential segregation met with as little success as the effort to uphold the ideal of strict social separation of the races. Both the ethnic and racial composition of colonial society and perceptions of race and social status changed over the course of the colonial period. In the postconquest period, three groups accounted for the majority of Mexico's population—Spaniards, Indians, and Africans, with Indians constituting the largest group by far. The continuing arrival of substantial numbers of Spanish immigrants meant that the most crucial differences within the Spanish group hinged more on the precedence and access to resources that conquistadors and earlier arrivals enjoyed than on any meaningful distinction or rivalry between peninsular- and American-born Spaniards. By the middle colonial period, differences between Mexican-born Spaniards (often referred to as creoles) and people who continued to arrive from Spain

261

became more pronounced. Society became more diverse and complex as racial mixture proceeded apace. The late colonial period witnessed increasing rivalry between Mexican-born and peninsular Spaniards and a growing obsession with racial purity and distinctions, even as racially mixed groups made economic gains and carved out a significant niche in society.

A Society of Races

Spaniards. The European group itself encompassed considerable variations in culture, habits, and traditions, although all the members of this group shared values that emphasized racial segregation, social subordination along ethnic lines, and the supremacy of Roman Catholicism. Iberian immigrants from Castile, the Basque country, Portugal, and southern Spain had relatively little in common beyond Catholicism and the privileged position they enjoyed in colonial society by virtue of their European origins. Each group spoke its own language or regional dialect, venerated the traditional religious images associated with their places of origin in the Iberian peninsula, and for the most part developed their economic enterprises by relying on relatives, friends, and associates who shared their background and origins. Intra-Iberian rivalries were not uncommon, at times producing family feuds and open confrontations.

Portuguese immigrants, many descended from Jewish converts, carried the stigma of not being Old Christians. Both despite and because of their economic success as merchants in transatlantic trade, especially the slave trade, Portuguese immigrants were frequently viewed as outsiders within the Spanish-dominated European group.

From around the mid-sixteenth century, a generation of Mexican-born Spaniards emerged as a distinctive group with perspectives forged by their colonial experiences. These Mexican-born Spaniards, or *españoles criollos de la tierra* (called *novohispanos* by some scholars), over time developed a distinct mentality marked by social resentment toward Iberian immigrants and racial contempt for the non-European groups. In the late colonial period, many Mexican Spaniards felt themselves to be disadvantaged by royal policies that favored peninsular Spaniards.

The distance between the two groups should not be exaggerated, however. Few Spanish immigrants returned to Spain; their future, and their interests, lay in New Spain. Those who remained married into Mexican families and therefore had creole children and kin. Closely connected by family ties and common economic goals, creoles and peninsulars together formed the colonial elite. Furthermore, although peninsular Spaniards occupied high positions in the colonial church and government and nearly monopolized transatlantic trade, the majority of Spanish immigrants in the later colonial period were young men who entered Mexican society at a fairly low level. They could spend years trying to establish themselves, and many of them never attained anything like the kind of economic success that would place them in the ranks of the Mexican elite or even the upper middle class. The differences between the two groups did sharpen over time, however, especially in the period of the Bourbon reforms in the eighteenth century when policies favoring the Spanish-born began to affect Mexican interests much more directly. These resentments culminated in an explosion of anti-Spanish feeling and violence during the struggles for independence of the early nineteenth century.

Within a few generations, Mexican-born Spaniards constituted the overwhelming majority of the small European group in colonial New Spain. Mexico, however, remained one of the preferred destinations for Spanish immigrants from the time of the conquest onward, and many communities in the Iberian peninsula developed migratory traditions that continued for centuries. In addition, smaller groups of non-Iberian immigrants, especially Italians, Flemish, Greeks, French, and a few Irish, also went to Mexico, although they generally assimilated into the larger groups.

Despite these significant internal differences, individuals of European ancestry enjoyed privileges that separated them from other groups and guaranteed their collective social preeminence. All Spaniards and their families enjoyed tax exemptions and legal status as *vecinos* or citizens of colonial society. Royal officials, echoing the mindset and expectations of conquistadors and settlers, helped to construct a colonial society based on racial segregation, ethnic discrimination and religious intolerance; not surprisingly, all Spaniards, regardless of region of birth, education, time of arrival, or occupation, adamantly supported this hierarchical system. European men also participated actively in institutions that reflected and enhanced their social status, such as the merchants' *consulado* (guild), and enjoyed special privileges associated with military rank and clerical careers.

Spanish men had precedence in political affairs, social policies, education, defense, land grants, and rights of exploitation. According to law, only Spaniards and their descendants in New Spain could enter institutions of higher learning, hold military rank, governmental appointments, and electoral offices, belong to commercial guilds, and direct mining operations, printing houses, or any other important economic and social activity. Both Spanish men and women could hold noble titles. Colonial legislation granted Spanish men the right to participate in municipal elections in Spanish cities and towns, be elected to municipal office, and serve as royal officials in all branches of government. Furthermore, in theory only Spaniards could wear certain clothes, ride horses, build fortified houses and, most important, bear arms, although these restrictions did not always prevail. Indian nobles, for example, were quite successful in obtaining these same privileges, through special licenses granted by the Crown, and other people simply ignored these restrictions. Colonial legislation decreed that only Spaniards could reside in Spanish parishes and cities, a restriction frequently ignored not only by Spaniards and Indians alike but by royal officials as well.

Indians. The second group that enjoyed legal privileges in New Spain consisted of native rulers and their families who were considered to be allies of the Spanish Crown. As discussed in Chapter 7, this demographically small contingent exercised disproportionate influence in local affairs and played a major role in establishing the foundations for the exploitation of Indian labor. Members of the native ruling group carved out a special niche for themselves in colonial society as providers of Indian manpower for a wide range of economic and military activities. They represented Spanish authority before their Indian subordinates and Indian commoners before the Spanish rulers. As such they collected certain taxes, organized labor gangs inside and outside the village, and governed internal community affairs. In exchange Indian caciques, *gobernadores* (governors) and other officials were entitled to most of the privileges of citizenship granted to colonial Spaniards: they could wear Spanish clothes, bear arms, attend Spanish churches, and in general be treated as noblemen in their communities. Elite Spaniards, however, regarded Indian lords as mere bumpkins with social pretensions.

In the *república de indios* the vast majority enjoyed few legal rights and were exploited by the colonial system, including their own native rulers. Indian commoners had to pay annual tribute to the Crown and provide labor services under different rubrics and for countless purposes. Commoners worked for the encomendero, for the cacique, for the Spanish king, for the secular priest, for the missionaries, for military commanders, and finally for themselves and their families. Such labor services were not remunerated (or if they were, at extremely low levels of pay). Indian commoners lived in villages subject to the authority of both the local indigenous governing group and the Spanish *corregidor de indios,* the administrator in charge of an Indian district.

Despite the legal apparatus that forbade Indians from living in Spanish towns, many resided in urban centers, either as domestic servants in Spanish households or as menial workers living in the indigenous *barrios* of a town's outskirts. Indians from nearby areas provided Spanish towns with charcoal, water, wood, stone, farm animals, and vegetables, and Indians regularly entered the cities on market days and for religious festivities and civic ceremonies.

Africans. The legal and social situation of people of African origin and descent, discussed in detail in Chapter 10, hinged on the close association between Africans and slavery. Although some Africans arrived in New Spain as free individuals, the majority came as slaves, and the stigma of slavery affected even those who were free born. Having brought them to New Spain in large numbers, Spaniards were unwilling to accord Africans and their descendants a full place in Mexican society. By denying them such recognition Spaniards created a marginalized group whom they despised and even feared, as their response to real or imagined conspiracies and indecisiveness about the appropriateness of enrolling people of African descent in military service suggest.

Mestizos, Mulatos, Castas. While royal legislation specifically addressed the legal and social status of Indians and Spaniards, colonial laws regarding the rights and duties of *mestizos* (people of Indian and European ancestry), *mulatos* (people of European and African, or Indian and African, background), and *castas* (a term referring either to all mixed-race people with some African ancestry, or to people of mixed background in general) were scarce and ambiguous. Most Spanish laws that specifically mentioned mestizos and castas restricted or prohibited them from engaging in certain activities, such as living or doing business in Indian towns, dressing like Spaniards, or holding positions in Spanish institutions. For non-Indians and non-Spaniards, colonial society was a legal limbo that deprived them of both Indian and European privileges.

Most mestizos and castas became culturally Hispanic in everything from language to diet, religion and economic activities, yet they occupied a subordinate position. Mestizos and castas had to coexist with the Spanish group within a segregated social hierarchy prescribed and upheld by town ordinances and colonial laws. People of mixed descent could not sit in the front rows of churches; in religious-civic festivities and parades they marched last. Excluded from Spanish religious confraternities, they formed their own brotherhoods, with their devotions relegated to secondary altars. The men could not vote or serve in office at any level of government and were explicitly banned from religious seminaries, universities, guilds, liberal professions, and fine arts—although these, like many other colonial prohibitions, could be manipulated and circumvented.

Although insignificant in number at the dawn of colonial times, the population of mestizos and castas showed high growth rates throughout the sixteenth, seventeenth, and eighteenth centuries. By the end of the colonial period, castas outnumbered the Spanish group and were the most dynamic demographic element in colonial society.

Racial Classification. Spaniards assigned mestizos and castas a variety of racial labels intended to reflect their degree of European, African, or Indian ancestry and to reinforce the distance between the different groups. Such categories often varied significantly according to region, economic position, and other factors. Church and civil records did not use the same system of racial classification, nor did colonial officials use racial designations uniformly. It was not unusual to find individuals and families classified differently in civil, criminal, or tributary records. In parish archives, for example, the only unequivocal categories were those of Spaniard, Indian, and black. Strictly speaking, a mestizo was half Indian and half Spanish, and a mulato was half African and half Spanish or Indian.

Beyond those five primary categories, a variety of labels were used to classify and describe individuals with varying amounts or fractions of Spanish, Indian, or African blood. *Morisco*, for example, usually denoted one-quarter African and three-quarters Spanish ancestry. *Castizo*, similarly, meant one-quarter Indian heritage and three-quarters Spanish. *Coyote* most frequently denoted a mixed Indian and casta background. Regional variations aside, español, indio, negro, mestizo, mulato, castizo, coyote, and morisco were the ethnic terms most commonly used by both church and government officials. People of mixed ancestry, however, were generally called *mestizos y castas*, although the meaning and use of the term casta varied significantly according to the source and context.

Needless to say, the ethnic categories reflected the racial hierarchy and a Eurocentric obsession with "pure" Spanish blood. Certainly not all people of mixed descent were regarded alike. Mestizos, physically more similar to Spaniards than mulatos and lacking the stigma asssociated with African ancestry, generally enjoyed a higher degree of acceptance than people of African descent. Castizos, with a smaller fraction of Indian ancestry than other racially mixed groups, were simply accepted as white in many parts of Mexico.

Notwithstanding these multiple, fine distinctions, essentially three major racial groups existed in colonial Mexico. Indians continued to form the vast majority of the population despite the demographic collapse of the sixteenth century. The numbers of Spaniards, thanks in part to a continuous and increasing migratory flow from Spain but mostly due to the natural increase of the creole population, passed the one million mark in the eighteenth century. The casta group (including mestizos, mulatos, moriscos, castizos, and other people of mixed origin) became the fastest growing group in the eighteenth century, finally outnumbering Spaniards toward the end of the colonial period.

Observations on Race and Class

In a country governed by whites, the families reputed to have the least mixture of *negro* or mulato blood are also naturally the most honored. In Spain it is almost a title of nobility to descend neither from Jews nor Moors. In America the greater or lesser degree of whiteness of skin decides the rank which a man occupies in society. A white who rides barefooted on horseback thinks he belongs to the nobility of the country. Color establishes even a certain equality among men who, as is universally the case where civilization is either little advanced or in a retrograde state, take a particular pleasure in dwelling on the prerogatives of race and origin. When a common man disputes with one of the titled lords of the country, he is frequently heard to say, "Do you think me not so white as yourself?" This may serve to characterize the state and source of the actual aristocracy. It becomes, consequently, a very interesting business for the public vanity to estimate accurately the fractions of European blood which belong to the different castes.

Alexander von Humboldt, *Political Essay on the Kingdom of New Spain* (1804), trans. John Black (New York, 1972)

By the seventeenth century the spatial distribution of these groups in New Spain's territories varied considerably. The vast majority of Spaniards lived in the cities, while the countryside tended to be predominantly Indian. Considerable numbers of Indians, however, lived in Spanish towns and cities as domestic servants and common laborers, while some Spaniards and most of the castas lived on haciendas and ranches and in mining towns. Cities in central, southern, and western Mexico were densely populated, while Spanish settlements in the north seldom had more than ten thousand residents. Mestizos and castas were present in every economic sector as skilled and semiskilled workers and were the predominant demographic group on ranches and haciendas from the Bajío region to the mines and cattle ranches of the north. Indians who migrated to northern areas assimilated to Hispanic society and culture and soon became indistinguishable from mestizos and castas, while light-skinned castas and mestizos acquired the status of Spaniards through military service and economic advancement.

Racial passing (as "white") of individuals and families did occur in colonial times, although this phenomenon did not involve large numbers of people. Economic success and outstanding performance in military campaigns usually constituted grounds for upward racial reclassification. High-ranking Spanish officials, military officers, and prosperous miners, for instance, experienced little difficulty in passing their Spanish status on to their mestizo or castizo children, especially in the absence of Spanish offspring. Here again, however, regional variation was considerable. In northern Mexico racial categories were more fluid, and the lines between Spaniards and mestizos frequently were redrawn to incorporate the latter fully into the community affairs of frontier society. In New Spain economic prosperity and fair skin could enable non-Spaniards to enter the Spanish group, as could paying for a decree of *gracias a sacar* that actually conferred legal status as white. In practical terms, however, these possibilities of passing as white were open mainly to light-skinned castizos and mestizos, much less frequently to mulatos and moriscos, and almost never to Indian commoners, Africans, and dark-skinned castas.

Occasionally mestizos, castas, and Africans were admitted into Indian villages and gained access to community resources, but Indian pueblos largely remained ethnically homogeneous entities, rarely friendly to outsiders. Indian elites, however, engaged in considerable interracial exchange with the Spanish group. Spanish men and, less frequently, women married into Indian cacique households, with expectations of financial security and economic improvement. Elite Indian families placed a positive value on the incorporation of European blood, but they derived their high status from their position within their communities.

Family, Honor, and the Position of Women

After racial hierarchies, patriarchal values were the most important determinants of social and gender distinctions, at least in theory structuring all
human relationships. Respect and obedience were crucial to the patriarchal
structures that shaped, at least nominally, every aspect of human relations.
By virtue of patriarchal constructs women were subordinated to men,
Indians to Spaniards, children to adults, lay people to clerics, settlers to
royal authorities, pupils to teachers, apprentices to artisans, workers to
employers, slaves to masters, artists to sponsors, single people to married,
subjects to rulers, and civilians to soldiers. Hierarchical structures centered
on the patriarch served as the ideal pattern for all social interactions and
human relationships. In every human group, whether ecclesiastic, civilian,
or military, a visible head, usually male, should serve as the source of
authority and respect.

Patriarchalism was present in religion, just as religious beliefs reinforced patriarchalism, although in Roman Catholicism the importance of the
Virgin Mary to some degree mitigated the emphasis on a patriarchal God.
The Holy Family (Jesus, Mary, Joseph, Anne, and Joachim) offered a political
as well as an ethical model. The king of Spain was seen as the father of the
land and his subjects as permanent children, just as his royal functionaries
were expected to love and protect their constituents in exchange for respect
and obedience. From the parish priest to the mine owner or the shopkeeper,
each individual had social obligations and rights in relation to a group of
associates who were linked by social kinship and from whom respect was
expected, in return for protection and economic support.

The father of a family, likewise, was seen as ruler of his household,
with sovereign authority and God-given rights over all aspects of family
affairs. The *padre de familia* was responsible not only for his children's
upbringing, but also for the behavior of his wife and servants. His authority
over his offspring and kin extended well beyond the age of adulthood of
sons and daughters and the boundaries of the house. The patriarch had the
obligation of transmitting moral values and social virtues to his offspring
and turning them into good Christians and loyal subjects.

The combination of patriarchal structures and racial hierarchies produced a complex system where honor and respect could easily be destroyed
and lost. Contradictions inherent to colonial society posed serious challenges
to the functioning of the system. For example, in principle non-Spaniards
owed respect and obedience to Spaniards, as women did to men or children
to adults. But what if an Indian man married a Spanish woman, or a mulato
artisan had a Spanish apprentice? Or if an Indian wet nurse cared for a
Spanish child? Who should be subordinated to whom? Colonial Spanish
elites responded to these dilemmas by reaffirming the primacy of race over
other criteria such as age and gender.

The ramifications of the hegemonic role race came to play are easily imagined. Indians should be considered permanent minors when dealing with Spaniards. Spaniards, even children, were entitled to honor and obedience from non-Spaniards, regardless of age or gender. Indians and all other non-Spanish men should not be granted high or commanding social positions, whether as priests, teachers, or officials, for Spaniards potentially under their direction or authority would be unable to honor and obey them.

Women and Race. The intersections of gender and race in New Spain created the conditions for a wide range of social expectations and practices regarding women in the colonial world. At the top were Spanish women who were subordinate to Spanish men but enjoyed a privileged position vis-à-vis all other groups. Following Iberian legal and customary traditions, Spanish women in colonial Mexico had numerous rights regarding holding and transmitting property as well as family authority. Property could be conveyed to and through women via legacies, dowries, and other legal instruments. Spanish women were entitled to own individual property, which could be sold, leased, or bought according to the same procedures available to men, although a married woman needed her husband's permission to carry out legal transactions.

Daughters could be, and many times were, the main heirs of their parents, especially if they were the eldest (and almost always if they were only children). Once married, women could maintain their properties separately from their husbands and manage them independently if they so desired, and they often named an heir or heiress among their own children. They also had the legal right to defend their individual and family rights before civil, criminal, and ecclesiastic courts. It was not uncommon for Spanish women to manage family estates and to participate actively in the economic sphere.

Inside the household, however, Spanish women were supposed to obey and respect their husbands, feed and care for their children, supervise servants and maintain high standards of moral behavior in the name of honor. Women were responsible for safeguarding the house's social reputation, which depended on the exercise of honorable practices and manners both within the walls of the home and outside them—in the church, the market, and other public places.

Despite their legal autonomy and property rights, however, Spanish women could not participate directly in politics or hold office, exercise leadership in the religious sphere except in nunneries, or, with some exceptions, enjoy full economic independence. At different stages in their life cycles, Spanish women lived under the tutorship and authority of male relatives or husbands. Although many widows were independent and enjoyed certain respectability, Spanish colonial tradition valued remarriage over widowhood, and unmarried women were always perceived with some suspicion.

In the majority of cases only Spanish women were accepted into convents, nunneries, and religious foundations. Together with some mestizas from prosperous families, a few daughters of Indian caciques had a rather limited access to special convents, while other women in colonial Mexico lived in convents only as slaves or servants. The presence of female relatives in convents was a source of prestige for an entire family.

Indian Noblewomen. Elite Indian women held a socioeconomic status in many respects similar to that of Spanish women. Women in cacique or noble families owned property, received dowries and bequests, had access to religious convents, and could inherit and bequeath family property. In many cases, they were designated the principal heirs in their families and enjoyed standards of living even above the average for Spanish women. Women from cacique families intermarried with Spanish conquerors and became members of the emerging colonial aristocracy. In the seventeenth and eighteenth centuries women of this group were more likely to marry colonial bureaucrats, provincial merchants, and landowners. As members of the native ruling class, these women enjoyed all the legal privileges colonial legislation granted to Spanish women, and it was not uncommon for them to appear in civil, criminal, and ecclesiastic records as plaintiffs.

Mestizas, Castas, and Lower Class Indias. In contrast to the situation of upper-class Indian women, Indian women of the commoner group were among the most socially and legally disadvantaged people in colonial society. If single or widowed, they were often denied access to land in their communities when land became scarcer in the seventeenth century and consequently were forced to migrate to haciendas, ranches, and cities to find employment. Once displaced from their rural communities, their experiences were similar to those of women of mixed ancestry.

Women of mixed racial background had remarkably diverse experiences resulting from their varying economic circumstances, place of residence, skin color, upbringing, and marital status. A fair-skinned mestiza born to a prosperous family in the Bajío or the north, or in the cities of New Spain, could easily ascend the racial scale by marrying a Spanish man or by entering a religious institution. In the eighteenth century especially, fair-skinned mestizas and mulatas from wealthy families readily joined the Spanish elites, although they frequently faced hostility once they succeeded in penetrating higher social circles. Spanish families occasionally accused individual women of lacking pure European ancestry in ecclesiastic and civil courts, especially in the eighteenth century.

For the great majority of mixed race women, however, economic advancement and marrying upward were not real options, and they mostly struggled on the margins of colonial society as members of the lower and working classes. Women in the casta group generally worked in the cities, haciendas, and mining towns, usually as food vendors, domestic servants, street peddlers, seamstresses, or wet nurses. Barred from the indigenous world of communally held property and with few possibilities of acquiring private property in Spanish society, mestizas and castas usually were wage laborers or self-employed workers who lived as tenants for their entire lives.

Often lacking communal or familial ties that could offer some measure of economic and personal security, this dynamic group of women was extremely vulnerable to economic hard times and outbreaks of disease. Casta women frequently experienced sexual violence and economic exploitation at the hands of Spanish men. As urban residents these women, together with Indian migrants and impoverished Spaniards, were also the target of colonial policies intended to enforce social control and promote public health; colonial officials frequently incarcerated them in ecclesiastic and civil prisons and other institutions. One such institution was the *recogimiento*, a public house in which single and widowed women were "deposited" and placed under the guardianship of authorities. Recogimientos varied according to social status and private sponsorship. Some were reserved only for Spanish women, while others were merely disguised prisons for prostitutes and common delinquents.

Sex, Marriage, and Children

Illegitimacy and Race Mixture. Given the predominant demographic trends in colonial Mexico and the racial structures that shaped social life, out-of-wedlock births were common. Spanish immigrants were overwhelmingly male. Arriving in New Spain while still young, they frequently entered into informal unions with non-Spanish women, although after achieving a certain level of economic security they preferred to marry Spanish-Mexican women. Large numbers of out-of-wedlock offspring were the result of such unions. Cities had the highest rates of births to single mothers. More than 40 percent of births in the central parish of Guadalajara in the seventeenth century were out of wedlock, and Mexico City, Durango, Puebla, and other cities showed similarly high rates of illegitimacy. Rural areas contrasted sharply with this trend. In predominantly Indian communities fewer than 10 percent of births occurred outside marriage.

Although illegitimacy rates dropped consistently in the eighteenth century, a significant proportion of births outside marriage continued to occur in colonial Mexico. Spanish men frequently engaged in sexual activities with young non-Spanish women who worked as domestic servants in the household, an acceptable practice among colonial elites who considered such involvements to be almost a rite of passage for young Spanish men.

Young female domestic workers were frequently raped by men in the households they served. If they became pregnant as a result, their Spanish mistresses might dismiss them from service. If relations between Spanish men and non-Spanish women usually were exploitative, not all were characterized by violence. In both the city and the countryside, Spanish men formed long-term, stable unions with non-Spanish women, providing their common-law partners with gifts and financial support for them and their children. Both through unpunished sexual violence and consensual informal liaisons, Spanish men and non-Spanish women produced mestizo and mulato children.

Mestizos and castas, more often than not the product of nonmarital unions, also frequently formed families outside the church. Illegitimacy rates among the mestizo and casta population were the highest in colonial Mexico. A variety of possible unions contributed to this pattern, from stable long-term relationships to less formal encounters between single partners, especially in urban settings. Stable mestizo and castizo households often produced children out of wedlock to avoid having to pay the costly fees required for marriage in the church. Underlying this choice was the understanding that the social status accorded to mestizos, mulatos, and moriscos whose parents were married was little higher than if they were not.

Illegitimacy in Indian households varied significantly according to the type of community. Given their precarious circumstances as domestic servants and street peddlers, single Indian women in the cities had considerable numbers of children. In the countryside most Indian children were born of church-sanctioned unions in part because of tighter ecclesiastical control but mostly because of greater economic and residential stability.

Patterns of Marriage. Marriage patterns varied according to racial group, but among all groups these patterns reflected features common to preindustrial societies. In general women married at very young ages in both city and countryside. Men also married young, with the exception of Iberian immigrants who frequently married in their late twenties and even later, when they had achieved some economic stability. Grooms normally were older than their brides and died before their wives did, although childbirth put women at risk. All groups showed high rates of endogamy, that is, the tendency to marry people within the same racial group. In general Spanish women had the highest rates of endogamy and castas the lowest. As was true in any predominantly rural society, most marriages in New Spain took place within the boundaries of the parish, village, or neighborhood.

Within this general trend, each ethnic group had its own characteristics. Indian women tended to marry and have children at younger ages, in their mid-teens, while Spanish women did so in their early twenties. The pattern for mestizas and castas was intermediate between these two. Indians consistently married at the youngest age, while mestizos and castas married later but still at very young ages. Mexican-born Spaniards typically married in their mid-twenties, while Spanish immigrants did so many years later.

Spaniards showed the strongest tendency to marry within the group; their endogamy rates, as can be judged from available documentation, were consistently higher than 80 percent. Indians also practiced endogamy in significant numbers; their likelihood of marrying inside the group oscillated around 70 percent. Mestizos and castas married within their group more often than not; they were, however, the people most likely to marry outside, and they maintained a permanent exchange with both Indians and Spaniards.

Fertility and Mortality. In the absence of effective contraceptives and because of strong ecclesiastical opposition to nonreproductive sexual practices, families in colonial Mexico did not limit their fertility systematically, and married women had numerous pregnancies during their reproductive years. This does not mean, however, that couples necessarily raised large families. Because of extremely high infant mortality rates and frequent epidemics that affected children in particular, many households included only a small number of children. Chronic undernourishment and the debilitating effects of frequent pregnancies in reproductive-aged women and mortality rates among the adult population also limited the numbers of pregnancies and births. Many marriages were interrupted by the death or migration of one of the spouses.

Indian families showed high mortality rates in rural areas, while urban populations also were extremely vulnerable to infectious diseases, especially smallpox, typhus, measles, and others. Infants in both rural and urban areas, even those born to wealthy families, were most likely to succumb to epidemic diseases. In this precarious milieu, life expectancies were extremely low, and only a lucky few reached adult and senior ages.

The Composition of Households. An elite Spanish household normally was home to a nuclear family plus an extended group of relatives, often unmarried kin of both sexes, business partners, employees, and visitors, as well as a much more numerous contingent of domestic servants and slaves (maids, wet nurses, cooks, laundresses), all living under the same roof. Not infrequently, these households included the out-of-wedlock, often mixed, offspring of male members as well as children who were fostered or adopted. As a result elite Spanish households were ethnically quite diverse. Since having a personal helper was a sign of social status, even less well-off Spanish families hired non-Spanish women as domestic servants.

In contrast to these large and complex households, Indians in the countryside often lived in *jacales* or huts in nuclear families with small numbers of children who from an early age helped in the domestic and agricultural chores. Workers of all races who worked for and lived on estates and ranches also lived in modest circumstances, often with their wives and children who also might work for the hacienda in some capacity.

The Evolution of a Multiracial Society

Hispanization. Colonial Mexican society offered non-Spaniards various possibilities for assimilating to Spanish culture. How non-Spaniards adopted some or many aspects of Hispanic culture and lifestyle differed considerably, as did the outcomes of the process.

In the countryside Indian elites became important agents of Spanish acculturation and played a crucial role as middlemen between Indian villages and the colonial government. Indian elites intermarried with the Spanish group. From their point of view the resulting infusion of European blood implied greater refinement and social advancement vis-à-vis both indigenous and Spanish communities.

Indian commoners who stayed in their traditional communities, by contrast, for the most part remained culturally isolated by choice and did not interact on a regular basis with other groups. Other than the parish priest and the sporadic visits of other colonial officials, Indian villagers viewed most with suspicion.

Mestizos, castas and urban Indians experienced a much more direct kind of contact with Spanish culture. Cut off from both the traditional communities of the indigenous world and the protection of the Spanish legal system, these groups experienced considerable influence from Spanish culture in the realm of language, diet, religion, and residential interaction. For most mestizos and castas, Spanish was their principal, if not only, language, although the Spanish they spoke varied considerably by region and even locality and was infused with Indian and African influences.

As members of the colonial Spanish elite whose status at times seemed uncertain or peripheral, Mexican Spaniards constantly challenged the assumption of their inferiority by demonstrating exaggerated loyalty to Spanish institutions and trying to out-Spanish and ridicule the peninsular-born. This hyperperformance of Spanishness among Mexicans did not bring them any closer to the ruling elite but certainly alienated them from non-Spanish groups, who for their part returned their disdain. At the same time Spanish Mexicans looked to Mexico's ancient indigenous civilizations to provide New Spain with a glorious past and classical antiquity in the same sense that pre-Christian Greeks and Romans did for Spain itself. Consequently there evolved among the late colonial Mexican upper class a complex mentality that emphasized loyalty to Spain but antipathy for Iberians, admiration for the indigenous past but contempt for Indians, love for New Spain as the *patria* (fatherland) but hostility toward some colonial institutions.

For peninsular Spaniards Hispanization meant the formation of a colonial elite that would share their goals and interests. From their perspective this elite would bridge the differences between peninsular- and American-born Spaniards, on the one hand, and reconcile Mexicans' grievances without altering their subordinate status within the group, on the other. Peninsular Iberians and their Mexican-born brethren shared the benefits of citizenship and enjoyed the fruits of most of New Spain's economic resources. That privileged position remained at the heart of their alliance for centuries.

Race and the Church. Colonial churches in Mexico were organized along clear racial lines in terms of religious services, internal hierarchies, and even ideals of sainthood. In general Indians were organized into separate parishes called *doctrinas* or *parroquias de naturales*, initially administered by religious orders. A second group of parishes was established for Spaniards, mestizos, and castas, but internally those parishes were strictly segregated by race in terms of religious corporations, fees for services such as masses, sacramental records, burial grounds, and even seating areas inside the temple for hearing mass.

The most formidable racial barrier within colonial churches, however, existed at the altar. The priesthood was strictly reserved for Spaniards (either peninsular or American-born) or other Europeans, although by the eighteenth century some non-Spaniards, especially mestizos and castas, gained access to the priesthood through different strategies. With very few exceptions, Indians were definitively excluded from becoming priests or friars, as were Africans, a practice that would have a profound impact on the nature of Catholicism in colonial Mexico.

The early decision not to ordain Indian men in the colonial church, to create separate churches for them, and to segregate mestizos and castas as second-class parishioners within Spanish churches contributed to ethnic resentment among the groups at the bottom. By excluding non-Spaniards from full participation in the organized church these practices also helped to produce an enormously complex set of popular religious practices among these groups.

Native populations maintained, resorted to and adapted a significant number of ancient religious practices in their lives as Catholics. Native religious practices were reassembled into Catholic rituals, especially in public ceremonies, family gatherings, and community festivities. Religious traditions such as the commemoration of the deceased on November 1 and 2 (Days of the Dead) or the religious dances dedicated to the Virgin of Guadalupe on December 11 and 12 are vivid examples of how native populations intermingled European and Native American elements to create new rituals within the framework of Christianity. Although considerably less is known about the religious beliefs and practices of people of African origin and descent, it probably is safe to assume that they, too, retained aspects of their religious beliefs and practices and combined them with elements of Christianity.

Casta Society in Late Colonial Mexico

No son de fiar:
Indio Barbón,
Español Lampino
Mujer que hable como hombre
Ni Hombre que hable como Niño.

(They are not to be trusted: a bearded Indian, a hairless Spaniard, a woman who speaks like a man, nor a man who speaks like a child.)

This colonial proverb from northern Mexico reflects the concept of social authority based on racial and gender hierarchies and Spaniards' perceived need to enforce clear divisions among opposing groups. Individuals and groups displaying features and traits associated with their opposites or with subordinated groups represented a threat to the entire system: an Indian with Spanish features such as facial hair challenged the distinction between European and native ancestries, just as a manly woman defied the norm of female subordination to men, or a childish man the natural relationship between adults and children.

By the eighteenth century, the emergence of mestizos and castas as a substantial component of the colonial Mexican population and of nontraditional family roles and household structures threatened the traditional moral foundation of New Spain and eroded both racial lines and patriarchal values. Ethnic mixing reached levels that altered the older sociodemographic landscape. Casta and mestizo groups expanded and acquired demographic and economic power, becoming a highly dynamic group in the eighteenth century. They constituted the backbone of the labor force in the Bajío and in western and northern Mexico, New Spain's most economically developed regions. Mestizos and castas formed the largest component of workforces in ranching, cattle raising, and mining; they also contributed to the flourishing of Mexican cities as skilled workers in manufacturing, transportation, and other occupations.

By the eighteenth century mestizos and castas also increasingly embraced some of the values promoted by the Catholic Church regarding marriage, family, and religious life. Illegitimacy rates among castas dropped significantly in this period, and prosperous mestizo and mulatto families adhered more closely to the Spanish patriarchal model. Christian naming patterns among these groups also tended to follow official trends.

Enjoying both economic prosperity and demographic expansion, casta households adopted and reshaped cultural traits from the Spanish group while incorporating elements from the Indian world as well. Varying regionally and locally, mestizos and castas produced a distinctive culture, inspired by but differing from both Spanish and Indian worlds, that began to shape social life in late colonial Mexico. In 1810, castas equaled or outnumbered Spaniards in the intendancies (administrative districts) of Mexico, Puebla, Oaxaca, Sonora, Guadalajara, Michoacan, San Luis Potosí, Tlaxcala, and Guanajuato. In the north, they accounted for at least 30 percent of the general population: 55 percent in Zacatecas, 40 percent in Nuevo Santander, 43 percent in Durango, 40 percent in Coahuila, 35 percent in San Luis Potosí, 32 percent in Texas.

Governmental Response. Colonial authorities responded to this sociodemographic transformation by attempting to reinforce the racial line between the Spanish group and the rest of the population, while acknowledging the blurring of divisions among mestizos, castas, and Indians. In colonial cities the considerable immigration of Indians from the countryside did not mean the transfer of Indian institutions to the urban setting. Royal bureaucrats refused to honor Indian legal privileges within Spanish city limits. Instead, Indian immigrants were treated no differently than other non-whites. Urban Indians were lumped together with castas and mestizos as members of *la plebe* (plebeians, the lowest class). In the archdiocese of Mexico, court records were divided into just two categories: *españoles* and *castas*, the latter including everyone who did not have pure Spanish blood. In the archdiocesan records confraternities also were either "Spanish" or "poor," while parish records in many areas were divided between Spaniards and castas, or Spaniards and *color quebrado* (mixed color).

Colonial Elites. Spanish elites also responded to the socioeconomic transformations that reshaped Mexico in the eighteenth century. Merchants, miners, landowners, and royal bureaucrats benefited substantially from the economic prosperity of late colonial society and amassed significant fortunes. Some acquired noble titles through direct purchase from the Crown; others obtained social distinction by acquiring membership in Spain's prestigious military orders, especially the Order of Saint James (Santiago).

In general, thanks to the success of their entrepreneurial activities in Mexico, Spanish elites were self-confident and optimistic about the future and developed an increasing sense of social refinement based on material culture, public entertainments, and European fashions. Spanish elites espoused European manners, values, and aspirations that were barely in touch with the colonial world. Wealthy families avidly embraced French and Spanish cultural trends in order to reinforce their distance from the general population, giving birth to a colonial Enlightenment.

Society and Race in Art and Literature

Caste Paintings. In the eighteenth century especially, Mexican-Spanish families fostered a new genre in painting, later known as *pinturas de castas* (caste paintings), which portrayed and identified different interracial unions and their offspring in lengthy series. Intended to cover all real and possible racial combinations, the pinturas de castas represented a collective human portrait of colonial Mexican society, portraying people in detailed costumes denoting occupation, residency, and social status. Local products, fruits, animals, and landscapes completed the compositions.

The racial designations on the paintings attempted to identify all potential combinations among Spaniards, Indians, and blacks. Such labels were intended to be picturesque and "humorous" rather than official and scientific. Many of these paintings were sent to Spain, but likely the majority decorated the walls of elite households in Mexico.

The pinturas de castas had no legal value nor were they meant to provide a guide for colonial officials of either church or state. There is no evidence that any court, whether civil, criminal, or ecclesiastic, or municipal government ever used the many ethnic labels displayed in these paintings. Terms used in these paintings, such as *salta-pa-tras* or *ahi-te-estas*, were nothing more than ethnic slurs disguised as racial categories.

The pinturas de castas suggest the growing concern among colonial elite families about maintaining a racially differentiated social structure with clear boundaries. They sought to reinforce the division between the traditionally white elite and upwardly mobile mestizos and mulatos who, thanks to their economic prosperity, had succeeded in crossing the line that previously had separated them from the Spanish group. As racial distinctions to some degree began to blur and were redrawn along more pragmatic lines, especially on the basis of economic wherewithal, Spanish families reacted by ridiculing successful mestizos and mulatos as Spanish "wannabes" or imaginary whites.

Caste paintings not only indicated racial order and classification but also suggested a set of "natural" and occupational hierarchies intimately linked to race. Given their proximity to the Spanish group, the paintings portrayed mestizos as good personal helpers or assistants who were naturally humble, quiet, and simple. Dark-skinned groups were depicted as violent, streetwise, and crude, while unchristianized northern Indians regularly appeared as barbarians—half-naked, defiant, and warlike.

Literature and Race. The eighteenth-century economic expansion also affected members of the Spanish group in negative ways. Many creole families, especially in central Mexico, saw their privileged position deteriorate as their economic status declined. Impoverished creoles joined the masses of poor mestizos and castas in the cities. That social milieu gave birth to *El Periquillo Sarniento* ("the itching parrot"), considered the first Mexican novel, written by José Joaquín Fernández de Lizardi. Set in Mexico City in the middle of the eighteenth century, the novel's hero endures the misfortunes of urban Mexicans, starting with their breast-feeding by non-Spanish women:

> My first wet nurse had an evil temperament, so I turned out malicious, and even more so because not just one gave me her breasts, but today one, tomorrow another, yet another the following day, and each worse than the other. The one who wasn't drunk, was a sweet-tooth; if she didn't have a sweet tooth, she was syphilitic; if she didn't have that illness, she had another, and the healthy one, suddenly ended up pregnant; and this just refers to bodily illness, because those feeble in spirit only rarely would be cured. If mothers would only notice the results of their neglect.[1]

[1] José Joaquín Fernández de Lizardi, *El Periquillo Sarniento* (Mexico City, 1982), p. 49.

Pedro (called Periquillo), the picaresque protagonist of Lizardi's novel, grows up in Mexico City surrounded by negative influences and graduates to a life of vagrancy, delinquency, and excess. Redeemed at a mature age by religious convictions, Periquillo turns his life around, becoming a firm defender of morality, Christian rebirth, and family values. Lizardi consistently places mestizos and castas at the core of social problems. In Lizardi's view, the plebe's natural inclinations can be restrained only through institutional control, discipline, and punishment (prison, exile, military draft). In his perspective, non-Spanish women were at greatest risk and therefore should be the target of specific policies of control, Christian education, and social discipline.

Despite all efforts by both colonial government and elites to diminish and disparage the newfound social prominence of the castas, it is clear that by the end of the colonial era the economic and social achievements of mestizos and mulatos were irreversible; they had reshaped the face of colonial Mexico. Castas had entered the ranks of the military and the lower clergy in the countryside and dominated large sectors of commercial activity. Privileged Spaniards and colonial officials had hoped to promote a moderate degree of upward social mobility through economic success and military service while still reinforcing the old order. Those excluded from this possibility for advancement—the masses of poor Indians, mestizos, castas, and lower-class Spaniards—resented this social realignment that offered them little. Successful mestizos and castas grew impatient with the partially obsolete racial order. By the late colonial period, these groups were preparing to challenge the very foundations of colonial society.

Glossary

calidad   high social status based on racial purity, economic success, and honorable behavior

castas   people of racially mixed heritage

castizo   person of one-fourth Indian and three-fourths Spanish ancestry

coyote   person of mixed African and Indian ancestry or someone of mixed ancestry in general

creole   individual of Spanish ancestry born in Mexico

español/a   person of pure Spanish ancestry born either in Spain or Mexico

gachupín   derogatory term for peninsular-born Spaniards

gente de razón   "civilized" people

hojo/a natural   ecclesiastical term for someone whose parents are neither married nor legally barred from marriage

hijo/a ilegítimo/a   ecclesiastical term for someone whose parents are not married and cannot marry

mestizo/a   person of mixed Spanish and Indian descent
natural   native
pinturas de castas   colonial-era paintings of racially mixed people
plebe   dark-skinned and unmannered masses, the urban lower class
recogida   lay woman placed in the custody of a religious foundation
recogimiento   shelter for women

Questions for Discussion

1.   What were the origins of interracial mixing or *mestizaje* in colonial Mexico?

2.   What were the five predominant socioracial groups in Mexico? How did they differ according to occupation, status, place of residence, and geographical distribution?

3.   What is meant by patriarchalism? What were its implications for the family and social hierarchies in colonial Mexico?

4.   What were the marriage patterns of different racial groups in colonial Mexico? Why were out-of-wedlock births so prevalent among certain groups?

5.   What sociodemographic changes had taken place by the late colonial period and what were their implications for different racial and ethnic groups?

Suggested Reading

Franco, Jean. *Plotting Women: Gender and Representation in Mexico.* New York: Columbia University Press, 1989. Seminal work on history of gender in Mexico, pathbreaking in approach, style, and conclusions, largely based on literary sources.

Gosner, Kevin and Deborah E. Kanter, eds. *Women, Power and Resistance in Colonial Mesoamerica: Ethnohistory* 42 (1995). Special issue with articles by Susan Kellogg, Matthew Restall, Alvis E. Dunn, Deborah E. Kanter, Juan Javier Pescador, and Martha Few.

Gutiérrez, Ramón. *When Jesus Came, the Corn Mothers Went Away: Marriage, Sexuality and Power in New Mexico, 1500–1846.* Stanford: Stanford University Press, 1998. Study of the Pueblo peoples under Spanish rule with particular emphasis on the role of the Franciscans.

Johnson, Lyman L. and Sonya Lipsett-Rivera, eds. *The Faces of Honor: Sex, Shame and Violence in Colonial Latin America.* Albuquerque: University of New Mexico Press, 1998. This volume, organized topically rather than geographically, includes material on Mexico.

Lavrin, Asunción, ed. *Sexuality and Marriage in Colonial Latin America.* Lincoln: University of Nebraska Press, 1989. Includes articles related to Mexico by the editor and other scholars.

Mörner, Magnus. *Race Mixture in the History of Latin America.* Boston: Little, Brown, 1967. Concise basic survey of constructs and implications of racial mixture in Latin America.

Restall, Matthew. *The Maya World: Yucatec Culture and Society, 1550–1850.* Stanford: Stanford University Press, 1997. Sociocultural study of the Mayas of Yucatan, based on native language sources.

Schroeder, Susan, Stephanie Wood, and Robert Haskett, eds. *Indian Women of Early Mexico.* Norman: University of Oklahoma Press, 1997. Articles on aspects of indigenous women's lives before and after the conquest by fourteen scholars.

Seed, Patricia. *To Love, Honor and Obey in Colonial Mexico: Conflicts over Marriage Choice, 1574–1821.* Stanford: Stanford University Press, 1988. Examination of issues of parental authority and free will in marriage choices.

Stern, Steve J. *The Secret History of Gender: Women, Men and Power in Late Colonial Mexico.* Chapel Hill: University of North Carolina Press, 1995. Provocative, controversial study based on criminal cases involving men and women in colonial Mexico.

Fourteen

Economy and Society
in the Late Colonial Period

The eighteenth century was a period of tremendous growth and change in New Spain. The economy essentially based on mining, agriculture, ranching, and some manufacturing continued to develop along the same lines set out in the first two hundred years of the colony's existence. The greater size, diversity, complexity, and regionalization of the Mexican economy, especially from around the middle of the eighteenth century onward, however, meant that in function, organization, and appearance it would differ in some important respects from the earlier colonial period.

The major force driving economic development in the eighteenth century was demographic growth and change. New Spain's population nearly doubled to over six million during the century, due mainly to natural increase. Expansion occurred in all sectors, including the indigenous one. Cities grew as a result of both natural increase and migration from rural areas. By the end of the eighteenth century not only did Mexico City have over 130,000 residents, but other cities boasted substantial populations as well, although none even approached the capital in size. Puebla probably had around sixty thousand people, Guanajuato and surrounding mining villages fifty-five thousand, Querétaro thirty thousand, and Mérida around twenty-seven. In just twenty years Guadalajara's population rose from over twenty-eight thousand, in 1793, to forty thousand in 1813; over the course of the eighteenth century its population increased sixfold.

The growth of urban markets stimulated a steady expansion of commercial agriculture. In many areas estates became larger, as did their workforces, and more land was brought into use. The nature and organization of agricultural production often changed in response to a range of market factors and competition among producers—small, medium, and large, Hispanic and Indian. The growth in regional markets for all kinds of commodities—foodstuffs, manufactured goods—meant that they drew on an expanding area; sheep that grazed on far northern ranches might be sold as far south as Mexico City. At the same time, patterns of production shifted. Puebla, for example, lost out to Querétaro as New Spain's leading producer of woolen cloth, largely because of the latter's greater proximity to the major

Major Cities and Roads in Late Colonial Mexico

sheep raising areas of the north. In compensation, however, Puebla's merchants and entrepreneurs parlayed the city's access to cotton into a successful cotton weaving industry. The mining industry also experienced shifts and growth, with the development of new mines and changes in patterns of ownership and production, although Guanajuato and Zacatecas retained their dominant position.

A key aspect of the commercialization of the eighteenth century economy was the increasingly important role played by merchants at all levels. Merchants became more actively involved in all sectors of the economy, from mining to manufacturing and agriculture, either directly, as investors and owners, or indirectly, financing the activities of local officials who participated in trade and distribution, supplying and sometimes organizing local production of key commodities, and providing miners with cash, goods, and credit. New Spain's merchants more and more provided the means by which local, regional, and even international economic spheres were linked. The establishment of new *consulados* (merchant guilds) in Veracruz and Guadalajara reflected the growth of the merchant class in the late colonial period.

Not all this change represented an unregulated response to the expansion of the domestic market. The policies of the Bourbons (discussed in Chapter 15) certainly had an impact on economic change, encouraging development in certain sectors—mining in particular—and reorganizing others. The creation of the royal tobacco monopoly, for example, fostered significant growth in cigar and cigarette manufacturing while altering tobacco production. External events, such as international conflicts, also played a role affecting economy, especially as warfare periodically disrupted external trade. Domestic manufacturing increased when there was relatively little outside competition, only to suffer when growing quantities of cheaper imported goods—cloth in particular—began to enter the colony.

Questions have been raised as to the implications of economic growth for Mexico's people. Did growth mean general prosperity, or at least some improvement in living standards? For some it did, and perhaps not solely for the wealthy. The establishment of tobacco factories in Mexico City and other cities, for example, provided reasonably secure employment for thousands of urban residents, especially women. At the same time, however, population growth and changing patterns of land ownership and use in the countryside meant more insecurity in rural areas, driving many landless people into the cities where steady employment could be elusive.

Figure 14-1 **Pulque production.** Maguey cacti are the source for this alcoholic drink, popular among Mexico's nonelites. Magueys grow on marginal land and produce a whole array of products, so that they were cultivated on large haciendas and peasant holdings alike because of their high value.
From *Los pintores de la expedición de Alejandro Malaspina*. Madrid: Real Academia de la Historia, 1982.

On the whole, it appears that most of New Spain's residents did not experience an improvement in their standard of living as a result of eighteenth-century economic expansion. Prices of basic commodities rose in the late eighteenth century but wages did not, meaning that the purchasing power of the majority of people actually diminished. It has not proven easy to measure overall economic growth by analyzing data from tithes, treasury receipts, or figures on the volume of trade. Given the variability in patterns of production, land ownership, and the nature of the labor market from one area or sector to another, this chapter will emphasize understanding the nature and implications of regional economic change and development rather than attempting to reach conclusions on the overall scope and significance of eighteenth-century economic development.

The Agrarian Sector

Patterns of Production. As in the first two centuries of the colonial period, the economy of New Spain basically remained agrarian, although there were significant changes in patterns of production, land use, and land ownership. Population growth in the countryside put greater pressure on resources. The steady commercialization of agriculture fostered change, which could take the form of expansion of already established forms of production or the introduction of new ones. Morelos, for example, had produced sugar for the market in Mexico City from the time of Hernando Cortés, but its estates had declined considerably in the seventeenth century.

A new era of expansion began in Morelos after 1760, however, due in large measure to new capital investment (mainly from commercial sources) and the replacement of hydraulic for animal power in the mills. By the 1790s Morelos had thirty-seven sugar mills producing over six thousand tons of sugar valued at nearly one million pesos. This sugar was raised for domestic consumption in New Spain. Less dependent on slave labor than in the sixteenth and early seventeenth centuries, the sugar estates of Morelos employed nearly eleven thousand people—about 12 percent of the area's population—in the late eighteenth century. Assuming that most of these workers supported families, perhaps as much as half of Morelos's population depended on the sugar industry for a livelihood. Although these figures suggest a very high level of economic specialization, the agricultural economy continued to be somewhat diverse, with both small and large growers producing maize and indigo.

In Yucatan, in contrast, sugar production only became important in the second half of the eighteenth century. In the same period, Spanish estate owners, particularly in eastern Yucatan, began to produce more cotton, apparently partially in response to a reduction in indigenous cotton production. Around Campeche estates also began to produce rice, much of it for the market in Mérida but sometimes exporting it to central Mexico or to Cuba, which had close ties to Yucatan.

Whatever form changes in productive patterns took, production generally increased in response to market demand. Historian Eric Van Young has shown that the consumption of maize in Guadalajara doubled while that of wheat quadrupled in the years from 1750 to 1800. Grain cultivation in the region preempted stock raising to the point where the city began to experience difficulties in filling its supply quotas. As prices for beef rose, people appear to have curtailed their consumption, which remained stable as grain sales soared.

While stock raising declined in central Jalisco, forcing municipal officials in Guadalajara to open bidding for the abasto contract to stock raisers as far away as Puebla, Zacatecas, and Mexico City, wheat production flourished as estate owners invested in irrigation works, mills, and storage facilities. By the end of the eighteenth century the large haciendas within a forty- to fifty-mile radius of the city were supplying 60 percent of the urban market, which underwent a seven- to eightfold increase in wheat and flour consumption between 1750 and 1815. This increase reflects the rapid growth of the region's nonindigenous population. Wheat production became concentrated in a smaller number of estates. The failure of urban maize consumption to keep pace with the demand for wheat may have meant that greater amounts of maize were being retained and sold in the countryside as the rural population grew.

Landholding. The tendency toward concentration of landholding, and hence of commercial production, in the hands of small numbers of estate owners who held increasingly large amounts of land became ever more apparent in parts of New Spain, especially toward the end of the eighteenth century. As ranching became more profitable in the north, certain families accumulated vast holdings. The estates and ranches of the family of the Marqueses de Aguayo descended from Francisco de Urdinola, discussed in Chapter 9, for example, eventually encompassed some twenty-two thousand square miles of land in Nuevo León and Coahuila. Although much of this land was arid, and conflicts with hostile Indians at times forced the virtual abandonment of some areas, the Marquesado also included good agricultural land and competed with the area's Hispanic and Indian residents for use of scarce water resources.

The existence of large haciendas, and of individuals and families that sometimes acquired several estates should not disguise the variability of landholding that continued to characterize much of the countryside. The Santiago family of Mexico City, for example, owned the Atengo estates which dominated a stretch of the Valley of Toluca thirty kilometers in length and fifteen in width. The estates shared this area, however, with forty-four Indian communities, five other haciendas, and seventy ranchos. In some regions, like Oaxaca, indigenous landholding remained strong and even predominant, while local Spanish estates tended to be fairly small, about forty-five hundred acres. The distinctive patterns of landholding in Oaxaca reflected the region's relative distance from Mexico City, lack of precious metals to attract a more substantial Spanish presence, and the size and continued strength of traditional indigenous communities.

Even where indigenous landholding was more limited, several factors could make for variability in land ownership, including the nature and location of markets, land values, the type and amount of labor necessary and available, and settlement patterns. Studies of estates and patterns of landholding in the Bajío and Mexico's central valleys suggest the diversity that could characterize different regions.

The Bajío was a very fertile agricultural region lying between the central valleys and drier north. Although at the time of the conquest its indigenous population was fairly sparse, the Spanish encouraged Indians to colonize the area. Communities of Otomí and Tarascan Indians received grants of land there, as did settlers of Spanish towns and cities. A substantial group of small landholders and tenants emerged, as David Brading has documented. Together with Indian villages, they competed fairly successfully with the haciendas, which, like the small producers, also mainly produced maize. In the early nineteenth century in San Luis de la Paz, for example, nearly three-quarters of the maize came from small holders, both independent farmers and tenants. The result was that maize prices remained low through much of the eighteenth century.

After the middle of the eighteenth century, with growth in the rural population, competition for markets increased. Many larger estates stored their grain, selling when harvests were poor (usually because of drought) and prices rose; the rents collected from tenants helped to maintain the estates between maize sales. This practice gave them a competitive advantage over smaller landholders, who lived from harvest to harvest and could not afford to withhold their crops from the market to wait until prices rose. Some estate owners switched to wheat production, investing in irrigation systems and flour mills and growing wheat on the best, irrigated, land. Other haciendas shifted to stock raising.

Probably most large estates combined grain cultivation and stock raising with rentals. One hacienda called Cuerámaro had a flour mill and dam built in the first half of the eighteenth century. With about thirty thousand acres of land, the estate had a permanent staff of fifty agricultural laborers, two shepherds, fourteen cowboys, ten people working in the flour mill, a blacksmith and seven muleteers. The size of the labor force suggests a fairly intensive level of production. In contrast on another hacienda called Juchitlán el Grande, which derived its income from sales of maize, goats, and rents, tenants cultivated four times as much land as did the owners. With nearly eighty *sitios*, the hacienda included some 170,000 acres, but much of the land was unsuitable for agriculture.

In León, in the western Bajío, Brading found that the size of holdings varied considerably, and many small independent farms survived through much of the eighteenth century. The town itself, founded in 1576, originally had about twenty-two thousand acres to be distributed to settlers. Each *vecino* received 370 acres (3½ caballerías). Some people were able to acquire several of these *ranchos*, combining them into holdings called *labores* of between five hundred and fourteen hundred acres. In early eighteenth-century León, there were about thirty of these labores, but a hundred years later many had been subdivided or taken over by larger estates that were expanding in the eighteenth century. New haciendas also appeared, buying up smaller holdings, whose former owners might then become tenants or sharecroppers. Estate ownership was far from stable, however; haciendas were bought and sold frequently. In the 1790s, fifteen out of twenty-seven estates were sold.

In the central valleys of Mexico, Toluca (to the west) and Mezquital (to the north) Indian communities survived alongside Spanish estates and continued to hold and work their own lands. With the growth in population in the eighteenth century, however, more and more Indians worked at least seasonally on the estates, and Indians lacking land worked for longer periods. The elites of these Indian communities, whose landholdings were often substantial, dealt with owners and managers of estates, at times clashing but also bargaining with them, which might allow them to obtain access to hacienda lands in exchange for organizing gangs of Indian workers.

The haciendas of the central valleys grew maize and wheat, both of which were mainly sold in Mexico City. Pig farmers also purchased substantial quantities of maize for fodder. Bakers in Mexico City bought the wheat, and some of them owned haciendas themselves. As in the Bajío small farmers and Indians also supplied the urban market. Some rancheros owned their land, but the majority either leased it from the haciendas or rented it from Indian communities on an annual basis.

Pulque also became an important product on Spanish haciendas in the eighteenth century, when the urban market for the fermented beverage was booming. The source of pulque, the maguey plant, grows well in dry conditions and needs little care although it takes seven years before it begins to produce pulque. Many estate owners in the northeastern Valley of Mexico converted pasture lands to pulque production around the mid-eighteenth century. The Jesuit hacienda of Santa Lucía produced substantial amounts of pulque, by the mid-1750s providing between 12 and nearly 15 percent of the taxed pulque that entered Mexico City every year. The pulque market crashed in the mid-1780s, when a severe famine affected much of central New Spain, but recovered thereafter.

Conditions for Agriculture. As was true in many parts of the world, conditions for agriculture in central and northern New Spain often were difficult and uncertain. The rainy season lasts from May through September, but frequently rainfall is inadequate or begins too early, and severe droughts can be matched by devastating floods. Several significant harvest failures occurred in the eighteenth century, the greatest in the 1780s. A mediocre harvest in 1783 foreshadowed an even poorer one the following year, when the maize yield was only about one-third of the average. In the late summer of 1785, early frosts virtually destroyed the crop. Prices for maize soared from four *reales* per *fanega* in 1782, to twenty-one reales in 1784 and forty-eight reales in 1785. Thousands of people died from starvation or succumbed to disease in late 1785 and through much of 1786. The poor harvests had the most disastrous repercussions in the countryside. Another crisis occurred when frost and drought destroyed much of the 1809 maize harvest and the 1810 harvest failed as well.

Agricultural production and estate ownership were affected by economic and political developments of the late colonial period. Miners and merchants who made fortunes, especially in the late eighteenth century, often invested in haciendas, driving up prices and creating a brisk rural real estate market in some areas. The expulsion of the Jesuits in 1767 meant that their well-managed agricultural estates came up for sale. The Crown's attempt to call in ecclesiastical debts in 1804, although far from uniformly effective, disrupted the most important system for providing capital and credit for Mexican estates. The wars for independence also hurt agriculture in some places.

Labor. Given the changing demographic and economic conditions in the countryside, not surprisingly the situation of labor also was altering in some ways. Often large parts of estates were turned over to tenants and sharecroppers, who might at times work for the estate; an independent farmer or rancher also might do so, or his son or other relatives might be estate employees. The basic organization of estate labor did not change in the eighteenth century; a core of permanent resident workers continued to perform the skilled and ongoing tasks, and estates used temporary labor for planting and harvesting. Nonetheless, as temporary workers became more numerous, often working for longer periods of time, the distinctions between permanent and temporary laborers sometimes became less clear.

John Tutino, who studied the estates of the central valleys, has identified three categories of workers there. The *sirvientes*, mostly Spanish and mestizo, usually occupied permanent skilled and supervisory positions. They earned four pesos a month as well as receiving a guaranteed weekly ration of maize. Typically an estate employed around seven to ten such workers. A special group of sirvientes, almost always Indians, were the *tlachiqueros* who tapped mature maguey plants and made pulque. A second category of resident workers consisted of the *gañanes*, Indians who lived on the estates but earned a daily wage and worked less regularly than the sirvientes. An hacienda in the central valleys might have twenty-five to thirty Indian families in residence. Although they did not receive maize rations, the gañanes were guaranteed an opportunity to buy maize. The last

group that provided estate labor were temporary, part-time workers called
peones, Indians who lived in their own communities, earning two reales a
day for estate work. Labor bosses called *capitanes* organized work gangs in
the Indian villages, supervised the work, and distributed wages. Although
the peones worked irregularly, the evidence suggests that over time they
were employed for increasingly long periods on the estates.

Where populations were sparser, estates could dominate landholding
and labor, as was the case in eastern Querétaro and San Luis Potosí.
Although the highlands remained strongholds for indigenous communities,
in the valleys population concentrated on the haciendas, where people lived
either as employees or tenants. Although administrators were almost invariably Spanish, below that level Spaniards, mestizos, and Indians worked as
supervisors, skilled laborers, herdsmen, and cultivators in roughly equal
numbers. The communities on these haciendas often included extended
families with kinship ties that cut across ethnic lines. Some of these families,
which often combined estate labor with land rentals, maintained long-term
associations with estates.

Through much of the eighteenth century this region's economy was
becoming increasingly commercialized while the population remained low.
The relative shortage of labor worked to the advantage of estate workers, who
received maize rations in addition to their wages. Even temporary laborers did
well in this setting. Indians from the highlands who moved from estate to estate
performing temporary labor received not only wages and maize but even
rations of beans and meat, which the permanent workers had to purchase. Late
in the eighteenth century, however, this optimal situation for labor began to
change, with growth in population and northward migration from the center,
and conditions for both workers and renters became less secure. Fluctuations
in climate that led to poor harvests also might have contributed to the deterio-
ration of the situation of rural residents in the period.

Mining

Expansion and Change. In the eighteenth century mining production soared in
New Spain. Between 1706 and 1798 mintage of silver increased four times,
from 6 to 24 million pesos, and virtually every decade saw a rise in production. Mexican mining output accounted for 67 percent of the total production
of Spanish American mines during the eighteenth century. There were several
reasons for this remarkable expansion. With population growth certainly labor
was abundant. More critical, however, was the increased production of mercury in the Almadén mine in Spain. Together with changes in policies regulating its supply and sale under the Bourbons, this meant the unprecedented
availability of abundant and cheaper mercury in New Spain. The price of mercury was cut by half. Other official policies also helped to reduce the costs of

production. Individuals who were willing to undertake the risks of opening or improving mines received tax cuts or exemptions.

The Bourbons also encouraged professionalization of the mining industry, establishing a privileged guild comparable to the merchants' consulado, with its own central court and representatives in each camp, a mining college to train people in mineralogy and metallurgy, and a finance bank, which was a failure. In 1783 the court published a new mining code which limited liability, conferred patent protection, and defined the terms of contracts with aviadores (the merchants who supplied the miners). These efforts at institutionalization contributed to the industry's growing respectability, although the increasing profitability of mining probably played a much greater role in enhancing the social prestige of miners. Many successful miners purchased titles of nobility.

In terms of technical developments, at some point the use of gunpowder for blasting was introduced and became common in the eighteenth century. Gunpowder became cheaper and more readily available, further reducing mining costs. Although there were no real technical innovations in the eighteenth century, generally techniques of excavation, drainage, and refining all improved. The scale of operations grew. Individual mines might have several shafts, some reaching enormous depths; the shaft of Guanajuato's Valenciana mine was six hundred yards deep. Labor forces grew accordingly; in the early nineteenth century the Valenciana mine had 3,000 workers and the Quebradilla mine in Zacatecas 2,550. Nonetheless, small mines continued to produce silver; although often ephemeral, in the short term, they could be highly profitable.

Some refineries became large industrial complexes in this period; big miners might invest thousands of pesos in these *haciendas de beneficio*. To some extent the refineries were becoming independent of mining operations. The great miners of Guanajuato and Catorce, for example, often sold their ore to independent refiners, and many small miners had no choice but to do so; they sold their ore immediately to refiners in order to meet their operating costs. Integrated mining enterprises, however, still existed.

The increased output of the eighteenth century hinged on both the development of new mines, at both new and long-standing sites, and the refurbishing of older ones. Zacatecas, for example, which had declined in the early eighteenth century, underwent a spectacular revival. José de la Borda, an experienced miner of considerable repute, was exempted from the silver tithe until he recovered his initial investment in a drainage project; he also received a reduction of 50 percent on the tax for the following fifteen years. Taking advantage of unemployment in the area, Borda cut his costs further by reducing wages from six to four reales a day and the worker's share of ore from a fourth to an eighth. At his death in 1779 he had paid off his debts, and his son inherited properties worth a million pesos. Other miners subsequently received similar breaks and incentives, although at two of the most successful sites—Guanajuato and Catorce—such exemptions were never granted.

Despite the importance of official concessions and policies that helped to lower production costs and thus encouraged investment, the availability of capital, from merchants especially, played a crucial role in mining expansion. Mining operations continued to depend on *aviadores*, merchants who supplied miners with iron tools, leather, mules, and food supplies and refiners with salt, lime, and mercury. Traditionally the aviadores preferred to provide supplies and short-term credit rather than to become involved in major long-term investments. The introduction of *comercio libre* (free trade within the Spanish empire) in 1778 to some extent undercut the dominant position of Mexico City's big merchants. One consequence was to increase the amount of mercantile capital available for investment in mining, although some merchants had become directly involved in the productive stages of mining even before 1778. Regardless of the exact timing of the rise in mercantile investment, such investments had become more attractive because of mining's increased profitability, and they were fortuitous because the industry needed capital. Silver merchants, such as those who had operated in the seventeenth century, continued to accumulate great wealth, although in the eighteenth century probably no more than three such individuals functioned in this capacity at any given time.

New Spain's great miners—men such as José de la Borda and Antonio de Bibanco (associated with the Bolaños mine)—made some of the largest fortunes of the eighteenth century. Altogether miners acquired sixteen titles of nobility, many more than did merchants. Big miners could be either immigrants from Spain or native-born Mexican Spaniards. Many of the most successful miners emerged directly from the mining milieu and hence could boast considerable expertise; others started off as merchant-aviadores and silver bankers.

Labor. New Spain's mine workers constituted a mostly free, ethnically mixed, mobile, and well-paid labor force, in some situations functioning as the virtual partners of mine owners. They moved with ease from one mining camp to another, and probably most were fairly skilled. Some camps did continue to use to draft Indian labor, mainly as auxiliary workers, in the eighteenth century. The Count of Regla, for example, obtained a grant for a levy of workers living within a thirty-mile radius of Real del Monte, but he had relatively little success in enforcing the draft.

Mine workers' earnings varied from one place to another. Typically they received a wage of four reales per day (workers on haciendas earned around two reales daily) as well as the *partido*, or share of ore produced. The terms governing the partido varied considerably. In Guanajuato and Real del Monte, once a worker had met the daily quota he divided the remainder from his day's work with the owner; in Zacatecas and other northern mines the workers' share was a fourth. During the early years at the Catorce mines, the partido could be as much as a third or even half, but in situations where the partidos became so large, workers did not earn a wage.

Attempts by mine owners to change or eliminate the partido system could encounter stiff resistance. In 1766, when the Count of Regla tried to reduce both wages (from four to three reales) and the workers' partido, the workers struck in response, closed down one of the mines, and murdered the alcalde mayor. A judge on the Audiencia of Mexico City, a mining expert named Francisco Javier de Gamboa, arbitrated the dispute and essentially restored the traditional system. Elsewhere some mine owners met with greater success in altering customary practice. The partido system was terminated altogether at one of the Guanajuato mines, and José de la Borda lowered both wages and the workers' share when he restored the mines at Zacatecas. In general, however, mine workers managed to maintain their position as the elite of Mexican labor. When partidos were eliminated at the Valenciana mine at the end of the eighteenth century, wages went up; pickmen at the mine were earning 10 reales a day in 1803.

Manufacturing

If not a realm where great fortunes could be made, as in mining, the manufacturing sector nonetheless grew in size and importance in the eighteenth century. The growth in manufacturing responded to the same factors that fueled the expansion of agriculture—rising domestic consumption and increasing availability of labor, especially in urban areas where most manufacturing took place. As in agriculture, manufacturing underwent significant shifts in both the location and the nature of production.

Textiles. In the sixteenth and seventeenth centuries the manufacture of woolen cloth constituted New Spain's main industrial enterprise outside the mining industry, with Puebla the leading producer. By the middle of the seventeenth century, however, Puebla's textile manufacturers had lost their Peruvian outlet with the curtailment of intercolonial trade, and in the eighteenth century they experienced increasing competition from imported Spanish and British textiles. Combined with the displacement of sheep raising to the north and of cochineal production to the south, which raised the costs of basic supplies for woolen cloth manufacture considerably, these changes effectively ruined Puebla's fine woolen textile industry.

In the eighteenth century Querétaro emerged as the leading manufacturer of woolen cloth by far. Querétaro's obraje owners were a diverse group that included merchants, landowners, and public officials as well as people who specialized in cloth manufacture. The labor force for the obrajes was similar to what it had been earlier in the colonial period. African slaves were an important element in the early eighteenth century, but subsequently their numbers decreased, although black slaves still were working in the obrajes in 1810. By the middle of the eighteenth century Querétaro's obrajes were experiencing increased competition for labor from small shops (*trapiches*) and the tobacco industry.

Toward the end of the seventeenth century, Puebla began producing cotton cloth for the local and regional market. Although by the late eighteenth century Oaxaca, Mexico City, Guadalajara, and Valladolid all had important cotton textile industries, Puebla's emerged earlier. Puebla became the principal producer of cotton cloth for much of the eighteenth century, sending cloth as far away as Chihuahua and Coahuila. Puebla's other traditional industries—production of fine glazed pottery (the Talavera style for which Puebla is still famous today), iron working, hat making, tanning—survived. Cotton, however, attracted the greatest amount of commercial capital.

By the 1740s some Veracruz merchants were investing in the cultivation of cotton, and by the end of the century a small group of wholesalers nearly monopolized cotton supply. At the other end of the business merchants became heavily involved in marketing cotton *manta*. Puebla's cotton merchants rivaled the import wholesalers in wealth and prestige. The economic impact of this commercialization was considerable. In 1794 Puebla had nearly twelve hundred looms and Tlaxcala nearly one thousand; according to the 1791 census, in four of Puebla's parishes well over a fifth of the population worked in the textile industry.

Tobacco. Outside of mining, the only other industry to attain a scale and level of concentration comparable to that of the textile industry was tobacco. Tobacco had long been produced in New Spain, mostly by small growers. In 1766 the Bourbon Crown established a monopoly over the manufacture of cigars and cigarettes. The creation of this monopoly concentrated tobacco production in two areas—Orizaba and Córdoba—although contraband was never entirely eliminated, and the factories used some tobacco imported from Yucatan, Cuba, and Louisiana. Planters enjoyed the benefits of interest-free credit and a guaranteed market. The tendency, as with cotton, was toward the control of production by relatively few merchant-planters.

The industry itself was equally concentrated. Six factories were established between 1765 and 1779, in Mexico City, Guadalajara, Oaxaca, Orizaba, Puebla, and Querétaro. At its height in the late 1790s the Mexico City factory employed some nine thousand workers. The Querétaro factory had thirty-seven hundred employees in 1809. The others mostly employed several hundred to around fifteen hundred workers. Factory workers represented a range of social and ethnic groups, performed a variety of tasks, and earned varying wages and salaries. A notable feature was the large number of women workers, many of them single or widowed.

Working conditions in the factories were unhealthy and unsafe. Crowding and high temperatures fostered contagion and fires; the omnipresent tobacco dust contributed to respiratory diseases, some fatal, like tuberculosis. The state-built factory in Mexico City, which provided better lighting and ventilation and more space, did not begin operations until May 1807. The tobacco workers' mutual aid society in Mexico City, the Concordia, to which they contributed half a real a week, helped workers to defray their medical expenses; it also lent them money. In response to the common practice of women bringing their children with them to work for lack of any alternative child care, the administrator of the Mexico City factory proposed using an empty storeroom as a nursery for older children. The working mothers agreed to contribute to the salary of a caretaker from their earnings.

Food Processing and Trades. Apart from large manufacturing establishments, a great deal of semi-industrial activity involving food processing, small-scale manufacturing, and artisanry employed people in towns and cities. The ownership of flour mills and *tocinerías*, which produced tallow and soap as well as pork products for consumption, could be big business. Flour mill owners in Puebla, who usually owned estates and bakeries as well, formed part of the city's elite. The owner-managers of bakeries and tocinerías, by contrast, more likely belonged to the urban middle class.

Guilds became more active in some places in the eighteenth century. By 1730 Puebla had guilds for shoemakers, tailors and hosiers, dyers, saddlers and harness makers, carpenters, broadcloth weavers, silk weavers, potters, hat makers, confectioners, and iron founders, among other trades. Mercantile involvement in crafts, which tended to intensify when external conflict reduced imports, however, often undermined the control that the guilds attempted to maintain over the practice of their trades.

Merchants and Trade

The discussion of agriculture, mining, and manufacturing has underscored the crucial role that merchants played in the eighteenth-century economy. Far from confining themselves to buying and selling, or acting as intermediaries between the countryside and the cities, merchants took an active and often controlling part in all kinds of enterprises. The result was, on the one hand, to blur further the distinctions between various economic sectors and, on the other, to accelerate the commercialization of virtually all forms of production. Merchants' willingness to invest in a variety of endeavors and the liquidity that allowed them to switch readily from one kind of investment to another account in part for both the diversity of economic activity and the sometimes rapid rise and fall in levels of production that characterized some sectors of the economy in eighteenth-century Mexico.

Despite economic growth throughout the colony, a great deal of commercial activity continued to be concentrated in, or organized from, Mexico

City. Most of what John Kicza calls New Spain's "Great Families"—defined as those whose assets amounted to at least 1 million pesos—resided in the capital. Their economic involvements usually were broad, and virtually all of them had mercantile interests of some kind. Many had members who belonged to the merchants' Consulado.

The Consulado had a membership of approximately two hundred merchants officially divided into two parties, Basque and Montañés, which came into existence as the result of long-term conflicts between these groups. From 1742 on all new members had to declare their affiliation with one party or the other, although many merchants were neither Basque nor Montañés in origin. As in the past, the Consulado's members were not all equally wealthy and influential. A small minority garnered most of the wealth and maintained the most extensive operations. Members of this privileged group were most likely to marry into the colonial elite families.

As in earlier periods the majority of big international merchants were immigrants from Spain, but creoles nonetheless figured among them and formed a significant part of the Consulado's membership. Some of the Mexican merchants spent time working in Spain. This would suggest that connections with merchants in Cádiz continued to be important in this period, although the nature of dealings between Mexican merchants and wholesale merchants based in Spain is not entirely clear.

The big wholesale merchants—*almaceneros*—imported goods from Europe and Asia and cacao from elsewhere in Spanish America and exported products like cochineal and sugar, although silver remained colonial Mexico's most valuable export. For much of the eighteenth century, the Spanish port of Cádiz was the major exporter of goods from Europe to New Spain, although many items sent to Mexico were produced in Britain or elsewhere, with Spanish firms acting as middlemen. The Mexican wholesale merchants maintained retail stores in the capital and sent their junior partners or employees to manage retail outlets in the provinces; they also supplied goods to provincial merchants. Some wholesalers maintained more than one store on or near the capital's central plaza which acted as large distribution centers supplying both local and provincial traders.

The introduction of free trade within the Spanish empire in 1778 no doubt affected the big Mexico City merchants, although perhaps not as drastically as once thought. Merchants in Veracruz were able to acquire imported goods on credit and sell them in the provinces; but the Mexico City wholesalers probably maintained a dominant position in provincial trade, although they no longer monopolized it. In response to the altered configuration of trade patterns some of them apparently sent representatives to work in northern Spanish ports.

The big merchants in this period, then, on the whole resembled their seventeenth-century predecessors. Many continued to invest in landed estates, some on a large scale, mainly in the Valley of Mexico and adjacent areas. Kicza has demonstrated that most of the big retailers who were excluded from Consulado membership acquired rural estates. As suggested, mercantile investment and direct involvement in mining increased considerably in the eighteenth century. In the last couple of decades of the century big wholesalers formed consortia that furnished huge amounts of capital for mining operations. With their wealth and permanence—most of the immigrant merchants married into local families—the big merchants were prominent participants in Mexican elite society. They held positions on the city council, became officers in the reformed militia, and twelve of them acquired titles of nobility associated with entailed properties.

The general patterns of trade also largely reflected a continuation of earlier ones, although certainly the dimensions and organization changed. The trade with Asia through Manila continued to be important and lucrative. The cacao trade also was big business, largely controlled by the Mexico City merchants. Despite the continued dominance of the big merchants of the capital, the overall growth in the volume of trade and the complexity of the late colonial economy resulted in the emergence of other merchant groups outside, and at least partly independent of, Mexico City. By the late eighteenth century Veracruz, Guadalajara, and Guatemala City all had their own consulados. The merchants of Guatemala, who controlled the booming export trade in indigo in the eighteenth century, dealt directly with merchants in Cádiz, with whom they maintained close connections.

The Spanish Crown established a trade fair at Jalapa, first held in 1722 and then intermittently through much of the eighteenth century. Intended to take place every two years and last for some three months, between 1736 and 1756 none were held. After the establishment of free trade the fairs ceased to function. In the same era the volume of foreign trade grew notably, and after 1765 British mercantile houses increasingly sent ships directly to Veracruz, bypassing Spanish middlemen.

By the time of independence, a great deal had changed in the New Spanish economy. The introduction of free trade in the empire and other economic reforms, increasing foreign participation in commerce, external conflict and warfare, and the internal upheaval of the decade of struggle that began with the Hidalgo revolt in 1810 all had considerable impact not only on the organization and nature of trade and the merchant class but on other aspects of the economy as well. These questions will be addressed in subsequent chapters that deal with the Bourbon reforms and the coming of independence.

Glossary

abasto   system for regulating municipal supply of meat
almacenero   wholesale merchant
caballería   unit of agricultural land, around one hundred acres
capitán   labor boss
comercio libre   free trade within the Spanish empire
Consulado   merchants' guild

fanega   unit of measure, approximately 1½ bushels
labor   medium-sized rural estate
partido   mine workers' share of ore
peón   unskilled laborer
peso   unit of currency, usually worth eight reales
ranchero   small farmer
sitio   a rural property
tocinería   workshop producing pork products
trapiche   small workshop

Questions for Discussion

1.   What factors contributed to late colonial economic expansion?

2.   What was the impact of royal policy and regulation on the economy in the eighteenth century?

3.   How did the conditions for laborers on haciendas and in mines and factories change by the late colonial period?

4.   What was the role of merchants in organizing New Spain's commercial economy and in mining?

Suggested Reading

Brading, D. A. *Haciendas and Ranchos in the Mexican Bajío: León, 1700–1860.* Cambridge: Cambridge University Press, 1978. Study of patterns of landholding and agrarian production in relationship to silver mining.
———. *Miners and Merchants in Bourbon Mexico, 1763–1810.* Cambridge: Cambridge University Press, 1971. Detailed study of mining, commerce, and government and the interrelationships among, and individuals involved in, these sectors.
———. "Mexican Silver Mining in the Eighteenth Century: The Revival of Zacatecas," *Hispanic American Historical Review* 50:2 (1970): 665-81. Study of the renovation of the Zacatecas mines in the late colonial period.
Deans-Smith, Susan. *Bureaucrats, Planters, and Workers: The Making of the Tobacco Monopoly in Bourbon Mexico.* Austin: University of Texas Press, 1992. Examines the establishment and impact of the tobacco monopoly and growth of the tobacco industry.
Garner, Richard L. with Spiro E. Stefanou. *Economic Growth and Change in Bourbon Mexico.* Gainesville: University of Florida Press, 1993. An effort to assess the dimensions of New Spain's late colonial economy.

Hamnett, Brian R. *Politics and Trade in Southern Mexico, 1750–1812.* Cambridge: Cambridge University Press, 1971. Examination of mercantile and official involvement in the cochineal trade.

Kicza, John E. *Colonial Entrepreneurs: Families and Business in Bourbon Mexico City.* Albuquerque: University of New Mexico Press, 1983. Important study of Mexico City's dominant commercial group in the eighteenth century.

Ladd, Doris M. *The Making of a Strike: Mexican Silver Workers' Struggles in Real del Monte, 1766–1775.* Lincoln: University of Nebraska Press, 1988. Interesting case study of labor conflict in a mining center.

Lockhart, James. "The Merchants of Early Spanish America," in James Lockhart, ed., *Of Things of the Indies.* Stanford: Stanford University Press, 1999. Overview of the development of mercantile networks and practices.

Martin, Cheryl. *Rural Society in Colonial Morelos.* Albuquerque: University of New Mexico Press, 1985. Socioeconomic study mainly focusing on sugar estates and their personnel.

Patch, Robert W. "Agrarian Change in Eighteenth-Century Yucatán," *Hispanic American Historical Review* 65:1 (1985): 21–49. Looks at changing patterns of production and landholding in Yucatan.

Pescador, Juan Javier. "Vanishing Woman: Female Migration and Ethnic Identity in Late-Colonial Mexico City," *Ethnohistory* 42:4 (1995): 617–29. Examination of the experience of working women in a Mexico City parish.

Super, John C. "Querétaro Obrajes: Industry and Society in Provincial Mexico, 1600–1810," *Hispanic American Historical Review* 56 (1976): 197–216. Study of textile production in a leading city of the Bajío.

Taylor, William B. *Landlord and Peasant in Colonial Oaxaca.* Stanford: Stanford University Press, 1979. Detailed study of patterns of land ownership and use in southern New Spain.

Thomson, Guy P. C. *Puebla de los Angeles. Industry and Society in a Mexican City, 1700–1850.* Boulder, Colo.: Westview Press, 1989. Study of manufacturing in Puebla and its relationship to the agrarian sector, tracing developments through the eighteenth century and independence into the early republican period.

Tutino, John. "Life and Labor on North Mexican Haciendas: The Querétaro-San Luis Potosí Region: 1775–1810," in Elsa Cecilia Frost, Michael C. Meyer, and Josefina Zoraida Vázquez, *Labor and Laborers in Mexican History.* Mexico and Tucson: El Colegio de México and University of Arizona Press, 1979. Interesting case study of hacienda communities in the Bajío.

Van Young, Eric. *Hacienda and Market in Eighteenth-Century Mexico: The Rural Economy of the Guadalajara Region, 1675–1820.* Berkeley and Los Angeles: University of California Press, 1981. Examination of the relationship between urban growth and agrarian development in western New Spain.

Fifteen

The Bourbon Era

The economic and demographic expansion of eighteenth-century New Spain contributed to and occurred within a socioeconomic, political, and cultural context that affected nearly every aspect of life there. The transformations that took place during this period both reflected and responded to changes in many arenas. These included new developments in fashions and intellectual life; changing perceptions of the roles of and relationships between the sexes or different social groups, and between state and society; relatively new political concerns in an increasingly complex international context; and the growing wealth of a small but powerful minority that was matched by the increasing impoverishment of a much larger segment of the population. Some of these developments were the product of political and intellectual trends that originated in Spain or elsewhere in Europe. They reached New Spain through various channels as the result of both the adoption and implementation of official policies and the unofficial dissemination and elaboration of new ideas and styles through the activities of an array of individuals and groups. At the same time, however, they were strongly rooted in the changing nature of Mexican society itself.

Many of the developments of the period were associated with the establishment of a new royal dynasty in Spain, the French Bourbons, at the beginning of the eighteenth century. The relationship between the transformations that occurred in Mexican political, social, religious, and economic life in the eighteenth century and the reform program of the Bourbon kings and their advisors was, in many cases, subtle and complex. Influenced by the contemporary political models and thought of France, the Bourbon dynasty, with its French origins and connections, over time undertook an ambitious program of reform that affected governmental administration and personnel, military organization, relations between church and state, the state's role in economic affairs, and even social policy, first in Spain itself and eventually throughout the Spanish empire. Some of the reforms had an impact not only on institutions but on the lives and lifestyles of individuals as well, while others were fairly limited in their effects. Other trends of the period, such as the influence of the ideas of the Enlightenment, bore a relationship to the official program of reform—some of the most important figures associated with the Bourbon reforms both in Spain and New Spain were also strong proponents of Enlightenment thinking—but were not necessarily the product of any deliberate policy or program.

The Bourbon reform program was not the sole impetus for change in the eighteenth century but rather helped to produce substantial transformations in combination with other important socioeconomic and intellectual forces. The extent to which the reforms resulted in significant new directions for Mexican politics, society, and economy continues to be the subject of debate. Some scholars see the Bourbon reforms as effecting a "revolution" in government, a kind of second conquest of the colonies that more rigorously subjected them to the interests of the metropolis. Others suggest that because of the lateness of the reforms they had only a limited impact.

The truth probably lies somewhere between these views. In some respects the reforms accomplished little, while in others they fostered changes that would carry through the independence period and affect Mexico's development as a nation. Recent scholarly work that examines the impact of aspects of the Bourbon program on particular sectors or regions demonstrates substantial persistence of long-standing patterns and attitudes and a complex interplay between older practices and institutions and newer ones. All but inevitably rivalries and disputes arose as new officials began to function alongside existing institutions such as town councils, audiencias, and even the office of the viceroy itself. New cliques and loci of power and influence challenged traditional ones—and vice versa.

Part of the difficulty in identifying and chronicling change stems from the frequently piecemeal and stop-and-start course that implementation of the reforms took. The policy of *comercio libre*, for example, was not fully implemented in New Spain until 1789; but Campeche in Yucatan participated in the new system from 1770, and commercial traffic between New Spain, New Granada, and Peru was permitted in 1774. The effect of the policy was further blurred because during periods of warfare that interrupted Atlantic shipping New Spain's merchants were allowed to trade with neutral countries outside the Spanish empire. The timing of change raises questions about the consequences of the reforms. Given the Bourbons' emphasis on increasing revenues from the colonies and aggressive mercantilist policies, a number of new measures were geared toward fomenting expansion in New Spain's mining sector, as discussed in Chapter 14. Some scholars, however, have concluded that the greatest rise in levels of mining production and output actually occurred in the first half of the eighteenth century, well before the period of significant reform.

Bearing in mind these issues, this chapter will examine the impact of the Bourbon reforms on administration, jurisdictional organization, the church, the military, and society (most of the key reforms affecting the economy were discussed in Chapter 14). It also will consider the ideology associated with the reforms in conjunction with other significant trends that transformed late colonial New Spain.

Enlightenment, Reform, and Society

The ideas of the Enlightenment, an intellectual movement that flourished in eighteenth-century Britain and France and had a significant impact on Spain, are closely linked with the reforms of the Bourbon era. Emphasizing rationality, clarity of thought, efficiency, and scientific inquiry, empiricism and application, these ideas influenced the reformist thinkers and officials who contributed to the formulation of imperial policy as well as the thought and priorities of intellectuals, professionals, and ecclesiastics who had little to do directly with the development or implementation of the reform program.

At the beginning of the eighteenth century, the end of the Habsburg dynasty that had ruled the Spanish kingdoms from the early sixteenth century and consequent dispute over succession to the throne occasioned a war that involved Europe's most powerful states. The treaty of Utrecht (April 1713) settled the conflict and resulted in the establishment of a new dynasty in Spain, the Bourbons. The grandson of Louis XIV of France became Philip V of Spain on the condition that the Spanish Bourbons would be completely independent of the French monarchy. Philip's sons Ferdinand VI and Charles III (the latter succeeded to the throne in 1759 and died in 1788) followed him. The accession of this new dynasty signaled the beginning of a period of intellectual and political change in Spain, which finally was unified politically under Philip V.

In 1726, at the age of fifty, a Benedictine monk and professor of theology at the University of Oviedo in Asturias (in northern Spain), Fray Benito Gerónimo Feyjóo y Montenegro, began publishing what would become the crucial work for the dissemination of Enlightenment thinking in Spain. By 1739, he had published nine volumes of essays in his *Teatro crítico universal* followed over the next twenty years by another five volumes entitled *Cartas eruditas*. Although generally acknowledged not to have been an original thinker, Feyjóo produced a monumental work analyzing critically and elucidating the current state of knowledge in a range of fields, including literature, art, philosophy, science, geography, mathematics, and history. Feyjóo emphasized science and medicine, which he did not believe to be necessarily at odds with religion, and critical thinking rather than rote learning. He also promoted educational reform.

Feyjóo's work fomented considerable controversy but also found a widespread and devoted readership among Spain's educated middle and upper classes. Periodicals emphasizing science and economics appeared in Spain by the 1780s. Groups called "Economic Societies of Friends of the Country" were organized, modeled on a Basque society founded in 1764, focusing on ways of improving the economy. Some of these groups admitted women members and advocated education for women. Other direct outgrowths of the enthusiasm for Enlightenment ideas were curricular reform of Spain's universities, establishment of new medical schools and institutions for scientific research (observatories, botanical gardens, and a museum of natural history), and royal sponsorship of scientific expeditions to the Americas to study natural history and phenomena.

As in other parts of Spanish America, Enlightenment ideas struck a responsive chord in New Spain, especially among educated but nonnoble groups. New periodicals appeared. As in Spain new academic institutions, such as the mining college and the Academy of San Carlos for art, were established; the University of Guadalajara opened in 1792. New Spain's coastlines were explored and mapped and geographical accounts elicited. While foreign observers like Alexander von Humboldt played a prominent role in studying New Spain's geography, economy, society, and cultures, Mexicans were important participants in these projects as well. Mexican intellectuals demonstrated a reinvigorated interest in the country's history. The exile of the Jesuits from the Spanish empire in 1767 was one of the great ironies of the period, as they were advocates of the rationalism that foreshadowed the Enlightenment embrace of Reason and played a key role in introducing new scientific and mathematical ideas in Spanish America in the seventeenth and eighteenth centuries.

The Enlightenment fostered new interest in the position and potential of women. Enlightenment thinkers who emphasized the importance of reason, knowledge, and work in shaping useful citizens increasingly saw women as playing a critical role in instilling these values in their children. Feyjóo himself had argued that women's intellectual abilities were equal to those of men, and the *Semanario Económico de México* advocated the enlightened education of women. Proponents of women's education thought it should encompass Christian doctrine and household skills along with reading, writing, and arithmetic, and new schools began to apply these ideas to the education of women. A teaching order called the Company of Mary established a boarding school in Mexico City known as La Enseñanza in the 1750s and subsequently a second school for the instruction of Indian girls, La Nueva Enseñanza. In 1767 the Colegio de San Ignacio de Loyola, known as Las Vizcaínas after its Basque founders, began operating. With the exception of La Nueva Enseñanza, these schools catered to the daughters of Mexico City's elite families. After 1786, however, the city council ordered parishes and convents to begin providing free primary education, resulting in some broadening of the educational opportunities for girls.

Enlightenment principles could be applied not only to the study and encouragement of scientific inquiry but also to economic, social, and philosophical issues. The growing interest in promoting primary education reflected new ideas about the possibility of "enlightening" the lower classes and incorporating them as functional members of society. Historian Juan Pedro Viqueira Albán has observed that contemporary thinkers believed that the theater had considerable potential for teaching and disseminating the new values associated with the Enlightenment. Not only New Spain's viceroys but the church as well supported the theater in the second half of the eighteenth century, and a new theater built of stone—the New Coliseum—opened in Mexico City in the 1750s. In 1786, Viceroy Bernardo de Gálvez promulgated regulations aimed at professionalizing and upgrading the standards of conduct of actors. Their object, according to Viqueira Albán, was to promote "decency, decorum, and order" in the theater.

Reformers and Enlightenment thinkers attempted in other ways to regulate popular culture and entertainments. Many opposed the sport of bullfighting, which actually was briefly banned in the early nineteenth century under Charles IV. Efforts at social reform could have a dark side. The *recogimiento* of Santa María Magdalena, for example, originally intended to shelter and rehabilitate "fallen" women, by the late eighteenth century had become a prison for female offenders who were obliged to work and were subject to other disciplinary measures. Nonetheless, despite sometimes heavy-handed attempts at social engineering and notwithstanding contradictions in both policy and reality, the most progressive thought of the era pointed the way toward the acceptance of greater social equality. An increasing emphasis on a man's demonstrated competence as the key to holding office, regardless of personal and political connections or social rank, was inherent in the drive to professionalize the expanding bureaucracy of the Bourbon era. One of the most influential political figures in Spain, the Count of Aranda, advocated the appointment of officials regardless of social status or racial origin.

Eighteenth-century viceroys and municipal officials in Mexico City promoted urban beautification and reform, with the objective of creating a clean, safe, attractive, and orderly environment. They named and paved streets, built sidewalks, and numbered houses; installed a thousand oil lamps in 1790 to light potentially dangerous streets at night; cleaned the canals on a more regular basis and established systems for collecting garbage and waste; and planted trees along boulevards and streets. Mexico City's main plaza was transformed along neoclassical lines. Elsewhere local elites and municipal officials undertook similar improvements. The streets of Veracruz were paved with stones in 1786, and houses were assigned numbers. The notoriously unhealthy port city, however, continued to experience problems with sanitation and water supply well into the nineteenth century.

Governmental Reform

In the realm of administration the ideas of eighteenth-century Spanish reformers and Enlightenment thinkers combined with the royal drive to increase revenues and fiscal efficiency to produce a series of changes in governmental structure and practice. Introduced first in Spain itself and then over time throughout most of the Spanish empire, these reforms affected everything from the organization and personnel of government at virtually all levels to tax collection, creation of royal monopolies, and improved record keeping. In Spain itself, the structure of government shifted away from the traditional reliance on councils. The effort to introduce greater efficiency and direct accountability to the Crown led to increasing use of secretaries or ministers, who eventually formed a governing cabinet called the *Junta de Estado* (Council of State), created in 1787. Another administrative innovation—based, like ministerial government, on the model of Louis XIV's France—was the introduction of new provincial officials called intendants endowed with broad responsibility over finance, military matters, administration, and justice. Elimination of the practice of selling offices (at least at the higher levels) in the mid-eighteenth century was intended to foster greater accountability and professionalism and to give the Crown more direct control over appointments. Emphasis on generating higher revenues meant the rapid growth of the fiscal bureaucracy in Spain and the empire.

New Spain did not experience the effects of these reforms all at once. Probably the pivotal episode in determining the timing and nature of reform there was the *visita general*, or general inspection, conducted by José de Gálvez between 1765 and 1771. Gálvez not only had strong notions regarding reform, advocating a reduction in creole political influence; he also, after returning to Spain, occupied a position crucial to the enactment of reforms in Spanish America, serving as Minister of the Indies from 1776 until his death in 1787.

After returning to Spain Gálvez maintained ties to New Spain by appointing to office relatives and compatriots from his native city of Málaga in southern Spain. A brother and a nephew, Matias de Gálvez (1783–4) and his son Bernardo de Gálvez (1785–6), both of whom died in office, served as viceroys of New Spain. The intendants of Puebla and Valladolid (later of Guanajuato) were viceroy Bernardo de Gálvez's in-laws by marriage. While the historian D. A. Brading cites José de Gálvez's "implacable nepotism,"[1] and no doubt favoritism and the opportunity to reward people close to him figured in these and other appointments, the minister's choices probably also hinged on his desire to have in office people who supported his goals and political philosophy. Bernardo de Gálvez was one of the most progressively minded high officials of the era. In an effort to deal with the severe famine of the mid-1780s he summoned a "council of citizens" to discuss possible solutions, and he and his father both attempted to impose measures designed to limit the indebtedness of hacienda workers.

The overall reform program in New Spain can be divided into three stages. The first, underway by the mid-1760s, saw the establishment of royal monopolies, a reformed military and militia, and the expulsion of the Jesuits. The second period, 1776–86, coincided with José de Gálvez's ministry and

---

[1] D. A. Brading, *Miners and Merchants in Bourbon Mexico, 1763–1810* (Cambridge, 1971), p. 37.

included key jurisdictional changes, with the creation of a separate jurisdiction in the north, the *Comandancia General de Provincias Internas* (discussed in Chapter 16), and the implementation of the intendancy system. The third period, after 1787, saw the introduction of comercio libre and marked a phase of retrenchment. Viceroys reasserted their power over the intendants, and some traditional practices associated with lower-level officeholding were permitted to resume with some modifications.

The Intendancy. Although many of the reforms of the era were closely linked and interdependent, perhaps the pivotal one was the establishment of the intendancy system which, despite its importance, was delayed until 1786. Intendancies were large administrative districts, intended to replace the old system of kingdoms and local districts (*corregimientos*). In 1768, José de Gálvez, along with the viceroy, the Marquis de Croix, recommended the introduction of intendants. Subsequent viceroys opposed the program, however. Rising revenues from New Spain, due in large part to more effective collection of the *alcabala* (sales tax), made royal officials reluctant to meddle with a system that appeared to be working well enough in terms of their fiscal expectations. An interim viceroy, the Archbishop Alonso Núñez de Haro, oversaw the establishment of the new administrative system, which entailed the creation of twelve intendancies for Mexico and another four for Guatemala (El Salvador, Chiapas, León, Comayagua). The Mexican intendancies were Arizpe (in the northwest), Durango, San Luis Potosí, Guadalajara, Zacatecas, Guanajuato, Mexico, Puebla, Veracruz, Yucatan, Michoacan, and Oaxaca.

As in Spain, where the Bourbons had introduced the system earlier in the eighteenth century, the intendants exercised power in four areas: *real hacienda* (treasury), *guerra* (war), *policía* (civic order), and *justicia* (justice). Given the general Bourbon prejudice against allowing Mexican Spaniards to serve in high office, not surprisingly most of the intendants—like many other key officials in late-eighteenth-century New Spain—were peninsular in origin, often of military background. As such, they often lacked the legal or financial expertise needed to carry out all their duties. The intendant relied on a legal assistant called an assessor, a lawyer who advised on administrative questions and served temporarily as intendant in the event of the death or absence of that official. Each intendant also worked with a treasurer and an accountant. These officials collectively formed the *junta provincial*. All received a guaranteed salary; intendants earned substantial annual salaries of around 5,000 pesos or more. It was hoped that these salaries would attract able candidates and curb the use of public office for private gain.

Although the intendancy was meant to strengthen royal government in the provinces and hence contribute to greater centralization of authority directly under the Crown, the presence of new officials with extensive powers and responsibilities actually reinforced provincial autonomy and thus contributed to decentralization. In reality, the intendants occupied an ambiguous position. They were subordinate to the viceroy but reported directly to the

ALTA
CALIFORNIA

NUEVO
MEXICO

BAJA CALIFORNIA

TEXAS

SONORA

DURANGO

COAHUILA OR
NUEVA
EXTREMADURA

NUEVO
REINO
DE
LEON

NUEVO
SANTANDER

*Gulf
of
Mexico*

NUEVA
GALICIA

GUANA-
JUATO

VALLADOLID

PUEBLA

YUCATAN

PACIFIC OCEAN

MEXICO

OAXACA

CHIAPAS

GUATEMALA

0   250   500 Miles

0   250   500 Kilometers

Late Colonial Extent of New Spain

Crown. They were intended to be above, and thus free of entanglement with, local society and politics; but like all previous officials they had to work with local interests and officials. At the level of local government many practices of the Habsburg era continued. Some offices still were venal or proprietary and tax farming of some revenues continued as well. New officials had to work directly with already existing institutions to perform some of their duties, and the inevitable result was the perpetuation of some traditional practices. Nor was there always a clear-cut distinction between old and new. The ordinance establishing the intendancy mandated the creation of a *junta municipal* to oversee the management of municipal properties and taxes. While separate in principle, this institution was closely connected with the old *ayuntamiento* (city council), members of which belonged to the junta municipal.

Doubtless the effectiveness of intendants varied considerably depending on a variety of circumstances as well as their own aspirations and interests. Intendants responded in a variety of ways to the responsibilities and opportunities that their positions offered. Michael Polushin, who studied the intendancy in Chiapas, notes that in the interest of career advancement intendants tried to demonstrate their success in introducing reform and upholding royal policy, leading to exaggerated claims or the initiation of ill-conceived projects.[2] Often these officials' best chance at success lay in forming workable connections with local people. Horst Pietschmann notes that intendants and other royal officials forged alliances both with members of the traditional colonial elite and "enlightened" Mexican Spaniards. He mentions that the intendant of Guanajuato associated with enlightened Mexicans, including Father Miguel Hidalgo, who later would be directly involved in the uprising of 1810, while Manuel Flon chose for his assessor a man to whom Puebla's council objected as being a mulato.[3] Conflicts over jurisdiction, authority, and responsibility between old and new governmental agencies and officials continued all through the period of reform.

Because the intendants were assigned to very large units (after independence some intendancies became states and others were divided), the Crown simultaneously created a group of officials called *subdelegados* (subdelegates), with the same powers and responsibilities as the intendants within their smaller districts but under the supervision of the latter. As these lower-level officials were poorly paid, it is commonly thought that at this level local government continued to function much as in the past, with officials attempting to enrich themselves by becoming involved in the local economy. Some subdelegates maintained the practices of the alcaldes mayores and corregidores (whom they for the most part displaced, although not always immediately or entirely), especially the much-criticized and controversial *repartimiento de mercancías*. Yet, like the intendancy, the appointment of subdelegates signaled a new and often stronger governmental presence in areas that previously had experienced relatively little direct official involvement.

Although subdelegates are usually seen as being virtually identical to their predecessors, the alcaldes mayores, in all but name, as individuals the subdelegates often resembled the intendants in terms of background. Many were peninsular Spaniards with military experience, and they aspired to paths of career advancement similar to those of the intendants, if less ambitious. Notwithstanding the qualifications of the individuals appointed to these positions, questions regarding their remuneration and the scope of

[2]Michael A. Polushin, *Bureaucratic Conquest, Bureaucratic Culture: Town and Office in Chiapas, 1780–1832* (Ph.D. diss., Tulane University, 1999), p. 72ff.
[3]Horst Pietschman, "Protoliberalismo, reformas borbónicas y revolución: la Nueva España en el último tercio del siglo XVIII," in Josefina Zoraida Vázquez, coord., *Interpretaciones del siglo XVIII Mexicano: El impacto de las reformas borbónicas* (Mexico, 1991), pp. 33–4, 55.

their authority stubbornly persisted. A number of intendants and viceroys recommended setting fixed salaries; others favored removing the ban on the forced sale of goods. The latter won out. In 1795, subdelegates received the right to provide goods on credit to Indians in their districts and to advance cash against future harvests; in other words they could act as merchants but could not monopolize trade.

Viceroys. The growing fiscal and military concerns of the era, together with adoption of the intendancy system, had a substantial impact on the office of the viceroy itself. Mainly because of new responsibilities in several areas that resulted from the Bourbon reforms—an enlarged military that the viceroy commanded as captain general, new monopolies to be administered, the expropriation of Jesuit properties, the collection of the sales tax—the burden of work associated with the viceroy's office increased enormously. This led to constant efforts on the part of the eighteenth-century viceroys to expand their secretariats in order to deal with the sheer volume of paperwork. The nature of the office itself was threatened by José de Gálvez's efforts to divest the viceroys of many of their traditional prerogatives. In general after the end of the Gálvez era the viceroys of New Spain reestablished in considerable measure their power and ascendancy over all other royally appointed officials.

The Audiencia. The Audiencia also experienced challenges to its position in the second half of the eighteenth century. Traditionally the most powerful governing institution in colonial society after the viceroy, the court's senior members—the *oidores*—acted as civil judges and deliberated on legislative and administrative matters. Their junior colleagues, the *alcaldes de crimen*, heard criminal cases and also acted as senior police officials in the viceregal capital. The typical pattern of advancement for Audiencia members was promotion from alcalde de crimen to oidor. With the Bourbon objective of reducing Mexican Spanish influence in colonial government the membership of the Mexican Audiencia underwent a rapid transformation in the 1770s. In 1769 the dean of the Audiencia, Domingo Valcárcel y Baquerizo, was a peninsular Spaniard, although he had served his entire official career in New Spain; he also had married into a distinguished local family. Six of the seven other oidores were Mexicans, as were at least two out of four alcaldes de crimen. Ten years later only four out of nine oidores were Mexican-born; all the alcaldes de crimen, as well as the dean and the occupant of the new position of regent were peninsular Spaniards. By the late 1780s, there were even fewer Mexicans on the court; the policy of appointing Spaniards to the lower court funneled only peninsular judges into the higher court, fostering resentment on the part of the Mexican upper class.

Furthermore, regardless of their origins—and many of the peninsular judges were, like Valcárcel, thoroughly rooted ("radicado") in local society through long-time residence, marriage, and economic ties—many of the Audiencia ministers resented the progressive reduction of their traditional powers. The growing responsibilities of the expanding fiscal bureaucracy reduced the administrative functions of the court, and the creation of privileged jurisdictions, or *fueros*, as in the case of military officers, undercut their judicial prerogatives. The Audiencia, like the viceroy, remained a powerful institution to the end of the colonial period, but it was no longer the dominant locus of authority it long had been.

The adoption and implementation of all these policies affecting the personnel, organization, and functions of government did not fail to provoke protest and opposition. Antonio Joaquín de Rivadeneira y Barrientos, a native of Mexico City and an Audiencia judge, in 1771 wrote a protest on behalf of the Mexico City council defending the rights of Mexican Spaniards to hold high office. Whereas the composition of the Audiencia hardly concerned the vast majority of New Spain's populace, other measures had far more widespread social and economic consequences. New and increased taxes met with resistance, as did military conscription; in July 1766 around six thousand people attempted to storm the treasury in Guanajuato, shouting "death to bad government!" and protesting new taxes on maize, flour, meat, and wood, the new tobacco monopoly, and plans to enlist local men in a new militia regiment. The following year uprisings in protest of the expulsion of the Jesuits occurred in Guanajuato, Michoacan, and San Luis Potosí and were repressed with great severity by Gálvez.

Bourbon Policy and the Church

Expulsion of the Jesuits. The expulsion of the Jesuits from the Spanish empire was the most notable of the Bourbon measures intended to assert greater royal control over the church. It also arguably was the most successful, in that this decision—in contrast to other Bourbon programs that were delayed or only partially implemented—was carried out quickly and as planned; the order of expulsion arrived in Mexico in May 1767 and was executed within two months. The motivation for the expulsion did not have much to do with Jesuit activities in New Spain itself. Centralizing monarchies in Portugal and France had targeted the Society of Jesus for its internationalism, strong allegiance to the Pope, and autonomous tendencies and had expelled the Society in 1759 and 1764 respectively; the Spanish Crown followed suit. These expulsions effectively suppressed one of the more progressive arms of the Catholic Church in western Europe and the American colonies.

The decision made little sense in terms of the Jesuits' position in New Spain. Far from being an enclave of foreign influence, nearly three-quarters of the 678 members of the Society in Mexico were Mexican-born. Particularly important for their role in education, the Jesuits had strong ties to local society in many parts of New Spain. Despite the protests of many Mexicans, however, the Jesuits themselves obeyed the royal edict.

The expulsion order allowed the viceregal government to expropriate former Jesuit properties, which included some of the most efficiently managed and richest landed estates in New Spain. These haciendas eventually were auctioned off, many of them purchased by the colony's wealthiest citizens. Revenues from sales of the estates went to the royal treasury. The impact of the forced departure of the Jesuits on intellectual life and education can hardly be quantified but must have been considerable, as among the Society's members were some of New Spain's leading intellectuals.

The Attack on Church Wealth. The expulsion of the Jesuits constituted only one facet of the Bourbon program to bring the church more directly under state control. The wealth of the church offered a strong inducement to royal interference in an age in which the preoccupation with revenues loomed so large. The church in New Spain derived its wealth from several sources: the tithe on agricultural production; donations and bequests; and urban and rural property. The confiscation of Jesuit properties benefited the royal treasury, as seen; but the many other entities that constituted the church—cathedral chapters, convents, monasteries—still possessed substantial wealth. The church's total capital in 1805 has been estimated at around 44 million pesos, most of it invested in mortgages and loans on urban and especially rural properties. Most of New Spain's hacendados were heavily in debt, principally to the church, paying 5 percent interest on mortgages and annuities.

The result of this pattern of church lending and private indebtedness was considerable interdependence between the ecclesiastical and landed sectors. Estate owners needed capital and credit, which they obtained from the church, which in return received a guaranteed income from the interest. This income in turn supported the church's charitable works and institutions. Tampering with the complex financial structure of colonial society potentially would have repercussions not only for landowners but also for the entire charitable establishment as well as the clergy and the entities that comprised the church itself.

At the end of 1804 the Spanish Crown, desperate for revenue, enacted the Act of Consolidation—the *Consolidación de Vales Reales*—stipulating that all church funds be turned over to the royal treasury, which would pay the 5 percent interest owed on the principal. The many hacendados as well as merchants and miners who owed money to the church were ordered to pay off their loans in installments over a period not exceeding ten years—the equivalent of a thirty-year mortgage holder being required to pay off the balance of the loan in a third of the anticipated time. The decree met with a clamor of protest from both landowners and clergy who foresaw disastrous effects on New Spain's economy and the church's charitable and educational functions. Some hacendados were expected to pay off virtual fortunes. Nor was it only the wealthy who experienced the impact of the new policy, as smaller landowners were expected to repay their debts as well. Although many did begin the repayment process, the treasury never received the bulk of the money owed. When the Bourbon dynasty abdicated in face of the Napoleonic invasion of 1808, the resulting empire-wide political crisis meant, among other things, that the royal offensive against ecclesiastical and landed wealth in New Spain, greatly resented by Mexican-born and peninsular Spaniards alike, would come to a halt. After independence, however, liberal governments in Mexico would resume the campaign to reduce the wealth and influence of the church.

The Attack on Clerical Privilege. Well before the attempted consolidation of church wealth New Spain's clergy had felt the impact of the Bourbon reform program in less spectacular but nonetheless tangible fashion. In the late eighteenth century, parish priests often found themselves operating at a disadvantage in their dealings with local administrative officials—alcaldes mayores and subdelegates—whose scope of authority was growing and who enjoyed an increasing degree of support in the high courts, as William B. Taylor has demonstrated. For the most part, parish priests and district officials managed to work together without great problems. Nonetheless both the incidence and perhaps the arenas for potential disagreement probably increased in the late eighteenth century as the balance between ecclesiastical and secular authority shifted in favor of the latter. Priests and district governors clashed over such issues as local elections, primary schools, community funds, cofradías, clerical fees, clerical and lay morality and conduct, and the continuing practice of the repartimiento by acaldes mayores and subdelegados.[4]

The changing balance between governmental officials and members of the clergy in part resulted from another key aspect of the Bourbon reform program initiated during the reign of Charles III, which attempted to limit both the personal immunity of the clergy and the church's jurisdiction over lay people. As a result members of the clergy saw their immunity from secular prosecution in both civil and criminal cases substantially reduced, while a series of royal ordinances circumscribed ecclesiastical jurisdiction over crimes committed by the laity. Both aspects of this attack on clerical prerogatives (*fueros*) probably alienated significant elements within the clergy.

One area of attempted regulation that affected the clergy and their parishioners was the publication of a new *arancel* (schedule of fees) for clerical services in 1767. This was not the first time that the church had tried to standardize the fees that priests could charge for performing baptisms, marriages, funerals and in some cases masses, but for the most part local customs regarding payment for services had prevailed. The new arancel continued the earlier practice of dividing parishioners into four categories

[4]William B. Taylor, *Magistrates of the Sacred* (Stanford, 1996), p. 410.

(Spaniards; mestizos, negros and mulatos; Indian estate workers; and Indians living in pueblos) with progressively lower charges.

The adoption of the arancel afforded secular authorities an opportunity to intervene in clerical practices, as it provided a basis for Indians to litigate against parish priests. Audiencia judgments in such disputes made it clear that the courts did not consider the arancel to be subject to negotiation or interpretation. The arancel also offered the courts a means of eliminating the unpaid personal services that priests sometimes exacted from their Indian parishioners. Furthermore, because the ordinance establishing the intendancy specifically stipulated that the clergy should not demand excessive fees from their Indian parishioners, often the complainants in the disputes over the arancel in the 1790s and 1800s were district subdelegates rather than Indian pueblos. Thus the arancel, although a moderate ecclesiastical reform, provided another means by which anticlerical reformers could undercut the prerogatives of New Spain's clergy.

Military Reform

The Spanish Crown's preoccupation with increasing its revenues from the colonies during this period hinged above all on growing military and defensive concerns. The second half of the eighteenth century was an age of conflicts, both internal and international (the Seven Years' War, the American, French, and Haitian Revolutions), many of which involved Spain and its colonies. The Spanish empire reached its greatest extent in the eighteenth century, pushing up into Texas and California and acquiring Louisiana. By this time other European countries, Britain in particular, commanded far greater military and naval power and resources than did Spain. Spanish America attracted increasing British interest because of its resources and markets and the proximity of some of its underpopulated territories (Florida, the Gulf Coast, and Texas) to British America. In 1762–3, during the Seven Years' War, the British occupied Havana for ten months. This episode forcibly brought the inadequacies of imperial defense to the attention of policy makers in Spain. The creation of an effective military presence and renovation of fortifications at key sites like Havana and San Juan de Ulúa (Veracruz) were enormously costly undertakings; these expenses, as well as those associated with the frequent warfare of the period, absorbed a hefty proportion of the revenues the Bourbon reforms helped to generate.

In 1764 the Spanish Crown sent two regiments of troops, led by Juan de Villalba, to serve as the core of a permanent standing army in New Spain; Villalba was also charged with the task of organizing militia units in the colony. In Michoacan, Puebla, and Guanajuato initial attempts to recruit local men for the militias incited riots; yet despite constant problems in organizing and maintaining army and militia units, the royal government

Figure 15-1 **Militiaman 1795**. In response to external threats, the Crown established a military in the eighteenth century, with special privileges, the *fuero militar*. Spain could not provide enough soldiers for its overseas empire so local militias of all races except Indians were created through conscription.
Courtesy of España, Ministerio de Educacíon, Cultura y Deporte, Archivo General de Indias, MP, Uniformes, 73.

could not abandon its objective of providing an effective military for New Spain. By the 1780s Mexico's refurbished military consisted of a small regular army, militia units, and a larger number of reserve units called *compañías sueltas*.

Staffing these new or refurbished regiments and battalions presented a constant challenge. The original intent was that the army units would be led by Spanish officers and include substantial numbers of Spanish soldiers; but whereas in 1790 the balance between Spaniards and Mexicans came close to ideal proportions, ten years later the army had been Mexicanized. Most recruits came from Mexico City and Puebla. The prospect of service overseas or in Veracruz made for problems in recruitment, as did low pay; regular soldiers received 1 1/2 reales a day, the wage earned by the lowest-paid hacienda workers. Coercion became commonplace; Christon Archer mentions the practice of rounding up vagabonds, illegal immigrants, and petty criminals in an effort to fill the ranks of the army.

Militia units drew their members from specified jurisdictions, where censuses identified males between the ages of sixteen and forty who were divided into three categories: single men without families; married men without children; and men with children and other dependents. Normally recruiters targeted those in the first category. Although it was hoped that volunteers would suffice to fill the units, a lottery (*sorteo*) could be conducted if necessary. The system apparently worked somewhat better than did recruitment for the regular army, but there were problems nonetheless. Not only could well-to-do men obtain exemptions through various legal and fraudulent means, entire social and occupational categories received exemptions as well (nobles, government officials, hacendados and tenants on haciendas, priests, students, and mine technicians among others).

The militias were not uniformly unpopular. The mounted regiments of the north were generally successful in maintaining their strength. The appeal of the *fuero militar*, which conferred certain privileges, including the right to be tried in separate military courts, helped to attract some men. Members of the provincial upper classes often were willing to become officers of militia cavalry units because of the prestige and authority such positions could confer. As the viceroyalty's military needs grew, however, so did resistance to militia service. Militiamen especially feared assignment to the garrison at Veracruz, which not only meant leaving home but also exposure to yellow fever, which in 1799 decimated the infantry stationed there.

The growing unpopularity of military service among the men of New Spain's lower classes—who provided the bulk of military manpower—was matched by the racial and ethnic prejudices of royal officials and military officers who feared the implications of having too many nonwhites in arms. With the notable exception of Indians, members of most groups in colonial society were expected to serve, although the initial hope was that whites would predominate. Juan de Villalba felt that many whites would object to

having to associate closely with mixed race men in military units and therefore organized *pardo* battalions in Mexico City and Puebla and companies in
Veracruz and elsewhere. In 1792 viceroy Revillagigedo recommended eliminating the pardo units. His successor Branciforte, however, reinstated most
of them with the exception of the Puebla and Mexico City battalions, and
tried to establish new ones. Given the high mortality rates and demographic
reality of Veracruz, however, there was little choice but to continue to try to
recruit blacks and mulatos for its defense.

Other than in the northern frontier provinces Indians for the most part
were not recruited for service. Nonetheless they experienced the impact of the
expanding military, suffering abuse and exploitation from soldiers stationed
near their villages. The quartering of troops in, and their movement through,
Indian communities created major hardships. In the early nineteenth century,
with ever greater pressures to augment military strength matched by growing
desperation for recruits, Indians were more likely to be forced into service
with little regard for their economic or familial circumstances.

The discussion of Bourbon reforms and policy as applied in New Spain in the
eighteenth century suggests that there was no single coherent program as
such. Although the basic objectives of royal government could be said to have
remained the same—to make administration more rational, accountable, and
efficient and to exact higher revenues—over time there were notable shifts in
methods, expectations, and even underlying ideology. The result was a program that was often fragmented and contradictory both in objective and outcome. The Bourbons tried to reduce the privileges of the church and clergy
while at the same time creating or expanding other enclaves of special privilege, such as the *fuero militar* and new *consulados* and mining guild. The reform
and expansion of the military on the whole did not produce many disciplined
and professional units but instead resulted in the exploitation of the working
classes and fostered corruption, as people bribed officials and clergy to obtain
exemptions. Reformers hoped to create an administrative structure free of
local influence and directly accountable to the Crown but failed to provide the
necessary resources to pay subdelegates adequately, and they inevitably
became enmeshed in the kinds of practices the reformers wanted to eliminate.
Many of the practices and personnel of the Habsburg era persisted, and the
policy of appointing peninsulars rather than creoles to newly created offices
did not always effectively counteract the strength of local tradition. Both officials and military officers sent from Spain to serve in Mexico might live there
long enough to form significant local economic and social ties.

These failures do not mean that the reforms as a whole necessarily
were unsuccessful. Record keeping improved, more accurate censuses were
conducted, royal revenues increased, and in many respects a more professional bureaucratic corps came into existence. Efforts were made to improve
urban life and expand educational opportunities (although paradoxically

the Crown dealt a major blow to higher education when it expelled the Jesuits). Despite some positive outcomes, however, many of the reforms had a disruptive effect on colonial life and society. Mexican Spaniards resented their virtual exclusion from high office and the expulsion of the Jesuits; the church resented interference with its financial affairs and the prerogatives of its clergy; landowners faced the prospect of suddenly repaying huge accumulated debts; workers were forced into disruptive, low-paying, and potentially dangerous military service; Indian communities increasingly lost control over their financial affairs; and many people were paying higher taxes while real wages stagnated.

At the same time some of the concepts rooted in the Enlightenment and the reforms had an enduring impact on Mexican society. After independence, the concepts of civic equality before the law and elimination of special privilege and racial distinctions became part of the Republic's new legal system. Liberal governments and politicians continued to promote anticlerical programs in an effort to reduce the secular and political power and influence of the church. Many of the intendancies survived as states of the new nation. Judging the success or failure of the reforms probably is less important than assessing both their immediate and long-term consequences.

Glossary

alcalde de crimen   criminal judge of the Audiencia
alcalde mayor   presiding local royal official, district governor
arancel   schedule of ecclesiastical fees
colegio   secondary school or seminary
fuero militar   set of special privileges enjoyed by men in the military
intendancy   new administrative district of the Bourbon era
junta   governing council
oidor   civil judge of the Audiencia
real hacienda   royal treasury
residencia   inquiry conducted at the end of an official's term of office
sorteo   military lottery
subdelegado   official in charge of a district within an intendancy
visita   official tour of inspection

Questions for Discussion

1. What was the connection between Bourbon policies and reforms and Enlightenment thinking?

2. How did some of the Bourbon reforms reflect the growth and maturation of society and economy in New Spain?

3.   Why did Bourbon policy makers want to reduce the power and influence of the church and how did they try to do it?

4.   What policies caused resentment among people in New Spain?

Suggested Reading

Archer, Christon I. *The Army in Bourbon Mexico, 1760–1810*. Albuquerque: University of New Mexico Press, 1977. Study of the process and impact of the military reform in late colonial Mexico.

Arnold, Linda. *Bureaucracy and Bureaucrats in Mexico City, 1742–1835*. Tucson: University of Arizona Press, 1988. Examines the evolution of offices and officeholding in late colonial and early republican Mexico City.

Arrom, Silvia Marina. *The Women of Mexico City, 1790–1857*. Stanford: Stanford Univerity Press, 1985. Social and demographic study of women in Mexico City, emphasizing the Spanish group.

Booker, Jackie R. *Veracruz Merchants, 1770–1829: A Mercantile Elite in Late Bourbon and Early Independent Mexico*. Boulder, Colo.: Westview Press, 1993. Study of the Veracruz merchant group.

Brading, D. A. *Miners and Merchants in Bourbon Mexico, 1763–1810*. Cambridge: Cambridge University Press, 1971. Important study of the relationships among mercantile, mining, and bureaucratic sectors.

Chowning, Margaret. "The Consolidación de Vales Reales in the Bishopric of Michoacán," *Hispanic American History Review* 69:3 (1989): 451–78. Detailed consideration of the impact of the early-nineteenth-century consolidation of church wealth in one region.

Costeloe, Michael P. *Church Wealth in Mexico: A Study of the "Juzgado de Capellanías" in the Archbishopric of Mexico, 1800–1856*. Cambridge, Cambridge University Press, 1967. Study of changing royal policy and independence on the church.

Farriss, Nancy. *Crown and Clergy in Colonial Mexico, 1759–1821*. London: Athlone Press, 1968. Examines the impact of late Bourbon policy on the clergy of New Spain.

Herr, Richard. *The Eighteenth-Century Revolution in Spain*. Princeton, N.J.: Princeton University Press, 1958. Standard work on the Bourbon period in Spain, emphasizing intellectual trends and Enlightenment influences.

Lynch, John. *Bourbon Spain, 1700–1808*. Oxford: Basil Blackwell, 1989. Useful basic study of political and economic development in eighteenth-century Spain.

Polushin, Michael A. "Bureaucratic Conquest, Bureaucratic Culture: Town and Office in Chiapas, 1780-1832." Ph.D. diss., Tulane University, 1999.

Detailed consideration of the impact of the Bourbon reforms and socioeconomic context of officeholding in southern Mexico.

Taylor, William B. *Magistrates of the Sacred. Priests and Parishioners in Eighteenth-Century Mexico*. Stanford, Calif.: Stanford University Press, 1996. Major study of the evolving role of the parish priesthood in late colonial Mexico.

Viqueira Albán, Juan Pedro. *Propriety and Permissiveness in Bourbon Mexico*. Trans. Sonya Lipsett-Rivera and Sergio Rivera Ayala. Wilmington, Del.: Scholarly Resources, 1999. A lively treatment of the impact of Enlightenment thought and Bourbon reforms on aspects of popular and elite culture and social behavior.

Sixteen

The Northern Borderlands

Supported by a flourishing mining and ranching economy, significant demographic growth, and a more efficient system to occupy and colonize new territories, between 1690 and 1790 northern New Spain expanded its boundaries to encompass the territory from the Red River in east Texas to the Bay of San Francisco in northern California. Soldiers, friars, and civilian settlers from central Mexico successfully reoccupied New Mexico, colonized Texas, Arizona, and both Baja and "Alta" California, and developed prosperous missions, permanent towns, and strong military outposts. In doing so, colonial authorities and settlers had to adapt and modify colonial institutions and reshape the fluid social patterns that marked life on the northern frontier.

Military reorganization and renewed efforts to settle the north to a great extent hinged on perceived defensive needs. Royal policy reflected concern about the encroachment of other powers on Spanish territory in North America, a threat magnified by the possibility that independent Indian groups would ally with other European powers offering cheaper and more desirable trade goods and better terms of exchange. Thus, Bourbon policies in the late colonial period that aimed at encouraging civilian settlement, strengthening the military presence in the north, and improving relations with such traditionally hostile groups as the Apaches and Comanches in some respects all responded to the perceived need to safeguard Spanish claims to the vast northern region of New Spain.

The Military Frontier

The 1680 Pueblo revolt in New Mexico underscored the vulnerability of Spanish possessions in northern New Spain. Soon after Spanish settlers and their allies were pushed out of the Río Grande basin, Indian nations in northwestern New Spain renewed their efforts to oppose colonial authorities, religious missions, and civilian settlements. Pimas in northern Sonora, Tarahumaras and Tepehuanes in the Sierra Madre Occidental, and Apaches and other tribes in the Chihuahua desert rebelled against Spanish rule, posing a major threat to mines, ranches, and farms in the far frontier region.

The Presidio System. In response to the challenge, Spanish authorities decided to create a chain of military forts throughout northern New Spain to provide protection against rebels and raiders. Staffed by highly mobile and well-armed troops and strategically linked to higher provincial authorities, the garrisons of these forts were prepared to launch combined maneuvers of defense, attack, and retaliation. The northern *presidios* were much larger in scale and better organized than the forts that had been established in the near north during the Chichimeca wars of the sixteenth century. Starting in the late seventeenth century, these *presidios* became one of the most important frontier institutions of northern New Spain, giving rise to a number of important cities in the borderlands region: San Francisco, Monterey, and San Diego in California; Tucson and Hermosillo in Arizona-Sonora; Santa Fe, El Paso, Ojinaga-Presidio in New Mexico–Chihuahua–West Texas; and San Antonio, La Bahía, Monclova, and three settlements named Monterrey, in Texas, Coahuila, and Nuevo León, respectively.

Beginning in the last decades of the seventeenth century the first chain of presidios was established in northern Chihuahua and northeastern Sonora. By the mid-eighteenth century, a strong line of military garrisons stretched from El Paso to Janos, Terrenate, Fronteras, and Tubac. North of El Paso in New Mexico there also was a presidio in Santa Fe, established in 1693. In the eighteenth century presidios grew significantly in influence and expanded to the south in Chihuahua and Sonora and to the east in Coahuila. The presidio system became an indispensable element in the colonization of Texas, Arizona, and

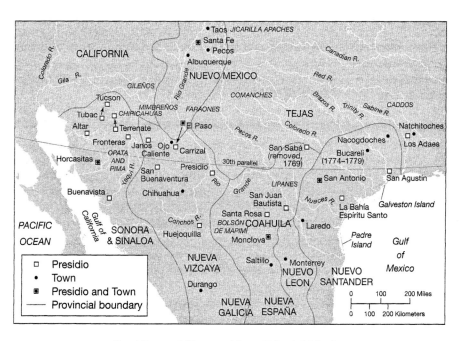

Presidios and Towns of Late Colonial Mexico

California. By the end of Spanish colonial rule in New Spain presidios over-shadowed ecclesiastical missions as the most significant Spanish institution in the borderlands; they extended from the Pacific Ocean in California to the Gulf of Mexico in Texas. Conceived to deter and retaliate against attacks from antagonistic Indians, presidios were only partially successful. Yet their influence was definitive in the foundation and defense of permanent Spanish settlements in present-day northern Mexico and the southwestern United States.

Presidio Life. Presidio residents normally included a few dozen Spanish soldiers, most of mixed ethnic background, together with their families. Their numbers varied considerably, but in general a presidio included between thirty and one hundred men able to fight. Life inside the presidios differed little from that in other northern settlements. Soldiers had to pay for their food and clothing, till the nearby fields, maintain their weapons and horses, and perform other kinds of labor inside the presidio. In return they received fixed salaries and military protection for their families. They also were eligible for land grants and other royal and municipal concessions. Recruiting soldiers for the presidios was not always easy. Some tribunals sentenced criminals to presidio service. Most recruits, however, came from ranches and towns in nearby areas of northern New Spain.

The word presidio referred both to the institution and the actual military structure itself, a solidly built, adobe-walled fortification that enclosed the soldiers' houses, corrals for horses and mules, a small chapel, and garden plots. These forts operated under the authority of a resident commander who was in charge of military actions and administrative functions, such as the punctual payment of soldiers' salaries and distribution of commercial goods among the troops. In reality, presidio commanders were notoriously corrupt and frequently abused their subordinates and allied Indians. Acting as both suppliers and contractors in commercial transactions, presidio commanders imported merchandise to sell to their soldiers at inflated prices. Once their "purchases" were discounted from their salaries, presidio soldiers seldom received any monetary payment.

Presidios also were trading centers providing Indian allies access to goods. Spanish families with business interests in the region and commercial connections in central New Spain tried to place some members as presidio commanders and thus benefit economically. Presidios in Chihuahua and Sonora were in the hands of Basque merchant families that maintained important long-distance trade networks.

Warfare against hostile tribes, however, was the main function of the presidio, both within and outside the boundaries of the settlement. In this intensely confrontational environment mestizos and castas with previous experience as cowboys on cattle haciendas or semiskilled workers in mining towns saw in the presidio an opportunity to join the military and ascend the socioeconomic scale.

New Mexico and Nueva Vizcaya
after the Pueblo Revolt

The Reconquest of New Mexico. In the aftermath of the 1680 Pueblo revolt Spaniards had all but abandoned New Mexico. The task of reoccupation fell to Diego de Vargas, who purchased the governorship of New Mexico for 2,500 pesos in 1688.

Vargas arrived in El Paso in 1691 and the following year ventured north of the Río Grande with only one hundred men. Initially Vargas relied on diplomacy in his dealings with the Indians and tried to exploit the significant internal divisions that had developed among the Pueblos in the aftermath of their victory over the Spanish settlers. During his first trip as governor Vargas crossed New Mexico, reestablishing alliances with some of the Pueblo leaders and managing to win the loyalty of twenty-three communities. His peaceful and successful effort was celebrated in Mexico City with religious ceremonies and court festivities.

In 1693 Vargas returned to New Mexico with troops and settlers who included mestizos, mulatos, Indians, and even Mexican Spaniards from different parts of New Spain, the majority recruited in mining towns and ranches in Zacatecas, Chihuahua and Durango, especially around Cuencamé, Fresnillo, Parral, and Sombrerete. The expedition brought nine hundred head of livestock, two thousand horses, and one thousand mules.

This time Vargas encountered substantial resistance among segments of the native population, who refused to hand over Santa Fe to the Spanish settlers. Spanish troops and their Pueblo allies stormed New Mexico's capital and defeated Tewas and Tanos, executing seventy rebels. Vargas's expedition effectively restored colonial authority to New Mexico but under a different set of rules. The encomienda system was not reestablished, and efforts to bring the Western Pueblos back under Spanish rule met with only partial success among the Zuni and Acoma and complete failure among the Hopi. Franciscans resumed their activities in their missions along the Upper Río Grande, attributing the reconquest of New Mexico to the divine intercession of a statue of the Virgin Mary, renamed Nuestra Señora de la Conquista, or *La Conquistadora* Pueblo Indians, however, soon rebelled again. In 1696 insurgents killed five Franciscans and burned their missions to the ground but suffered defeat at the hands of Spanish troops shortly thereafter.

The reconquest of New Mexico also involved a considerable effort to settle Christian families from central New Spain in the region and consolidate colonial rule by founding civilian settlements similar to Santa Fe. An expedition consisting of people recruited in Mexico City and Puebla, led by Fray Francisco Farfán, founded the Villa Nueva de Santa Cruz de los Españoles Mexicanos (present-day Santa Cruz de La Cañada). In 1706 Spanish settlers founded another town on the Río Grande, south of Santa Fe, which they

Figure 16-1 *La conquistadora,* **Santa Fe**. This statue of the Virgin Mary was taken by Spaniards fleeing the 1680 Pueblo Revolt and brought back to New Mexico when Europeans retook the region in 1693. It remains a powerful image in New Mexican history.
Photo by Robert H. Martin. Courtesy Museum of New Mexico, Neg. No. 41984.

named La Villa de Albuquerque in honor of New Spain's current viceroy, Francisco de la Cueva Enríquez, duke of Albuquerque.

Economy and Society. In the second half of the eighteenth century, New Mexico and Nueva Vizcaya experienced remarkable economic prosperity and population growth among non-Indian groups. The opening of a signifi-cant number of silver mines in Chihuahua promoted commercial expansion along the Camino Real between Durango and Santa Fe. Moreover, the con-solidation of a military front consisting of several presidios that ran from Arizona-Sonora to east Texas generated permanent demand for some locally manufactured goods and agricultural products. In New Mexico Spanish authorities established an alliance with Comanches in 1785, and a few years later governor Juan Bautista Anza's troops defeated the Comanche leader Cuerno Verde. As colonial New Mexicans had to face common threats from Ute, Apache, and Navaho raiders, Pueblo Indians and Spanish vecinos alike set aside their historical animosity and collaborated in trade, agriculture, and defense.

The mining boom in Chihuahua oriented the New Mexican economy to the Chihuahua Trail and stimulated the production of textiles, wool, and blankets to be sold in southern markets. The Spanish population reached more than five thousand in the 1750s and ten thousand in the 1780s, out-numbering the native Pueblo sector for the first time in New Mexico's his-tory. By 1820 the province had a Hispanic population of more than twenty-five thousand. Part of a long-distance trade network connecting New Mexico with Nueva Vizcaya, Spanish settlers in the Upper Río Grande found an outlet for their exports in the prosperous population centers to the south. Spanish merchants in Chihuahua City, Durango, Parral, and El Paso acquired New Mexican products—especially hides, blankets, and clothing—to resell on the local market. In the 1790s the expansion of Spanish popula-tion north of Santa Fe resulted in the establishment of new villages along the Colorado River and in the Chama Valley.

Nueva Vizcaya, situated at the heart of the Spanish borderlands, was by far the most prosperous and densely populated province of northern Mexico, with nearly fifty thousand Spanish inhabitants, most of them mesti-zos, mulatos, and castas. The foundation of the Real de San Felipe de Chihuahua near the Franciscan mission of San Francisco de Cuéllar in 1709 initiated a new cycle of economic growth in the region. New discoveries at old mining sites followed. By the mid-eighteenth century, the Spanish pres-ence in the lower Conchos had been consolidated with the establishment of a set of presidios along the Conchos and Río Grande, such as Huejoquilla, Presidio la Junta de los Ríos, and Presidio del Norte. In this period the Camino Real de Tierra Adentro (Royal Road of the Interior) could be traveled between Durango and Santa Fe with less risk, and the volume of traffic reached new levels. Nevertheless Comanche and Apache depredations continued to exact a heavy toll in human lives, livestock, and property in Nueva Vizcaya through the eighteenth century and beyond.

Northeastern New Spain: The Colonization of Coahuila, Texas, and Nuevo Santander

With the expulsion of Spanish and non-Pueblo settlers from New Mexico in the 1680s the mission of El Paso became not only the northernmost Spanish outpost but also the area's economic, social, and political center. El Paso played a crucial role in the reconquest of New Mexico and expansion of Spanish settlements into present-day Texas. In 1684 the governor of New Mexico, Domingo Jironza Petris de Cruzate, formally established a presidio at El Paso named Nuestra Señora del Pilar y San José. A year later Juan Domínguez de Mendoza, a prominent soldier from a wealthy New Mexican family in exile, departed from El Paso on an expedition to Jumano lands. Following the Río Grande downstream to its junction with the Conchos River (La Junta de los Ríos, present-day Ojinaga-Presidio), Domínguez de Mendoza turned northeast and crossed the Pecos, Conchos (Texas), and Colorado (Texas) rivers, claiming those territories for the province of New Mexico. After establishing Franciscan missions to Christianize the Jumano natives, Capt. Domínguez de Mendoza traveled to Mexico City and lobbied for financing a larger expedition to create permanent Spanish settlements in the area. Colonial authorities, however, did not support the plan, and only the Franciscan missions remained.

The French Challenge. In this same period various French explorers from New France in Canada were competing with one another to find the Gulf of California, which they erroneously believed lay at the mouth of the Mississippi River. After explorations by the Jesuit Jacques Marquette and Louis Joliet in 1673 that reached the Arkansas River, Rene Robert Cavalier de La Salle, a self-made entrepreneur, obtained support from the governor of New France to navigate the Mississippi from Quebec in 1682. French colonial settlers were hoping to find new commercial routes to Asia as well as to encroach on New Spain's mining centers. La Salle found that the Mississippi emptied into the Gulf of Mexico, between Spanish Florida and New Spain. After taking possession of the land and naming the province Louisiana after Louis XIV, La Salle returned to Canada. In 1683 the king of France received La Salle, who presented a formal proposal for the colonization of Louisiana on the Gulf of Mexico.

La Salle departed from La Rochelle on July 1684, sailing to Santo Domingo, where he made his final preparations. By this time the French had effectively occupied the western part of Hispaniola in the Caribbean (later the French colony of St. Dominque), although Spain had not yet formally ceded it to them. In Santo Domingo La Salle lost one of his ships to Spanish forces, and some of his men deserted. He departed with the remaining vessels, but his efforts to reach the Mississippi Delta were completely unsuccessful. Instead, he landed at present-day Matagorda Bay in East Texas in 1685.

Ravaged by disease and suffering deep internal divisions, La Salle's expedition barely managed to establish a settlement named Fort Saint Louis. In the meantime, some of La Salle's defectors had joined a French raid of Yucatan led by Michel de Grammont. Unfortunately for La Salle's colony, New Spain's fleet had captured some of these men in two French vessels off Campeche. Spanish authorities soon learned of the existence of Fort Saint Louis and launched two expeditions to destroy the new French colony. The first departed from Havana in 1686 but could not find the settlement, ending up in Veracruz months later. The second one, led by Alonso de León, departed from Monterrey and Cadereyta in Nuevo León.

De León, a Mexican-born Spaniard, was an entrepreneur with various business interests in the area, in particular some salt deposits near the San Juan River, a tributary of the Río Grande. Following orders, de León took fifty men to the mouth of the Río Grande and then turned south to Las Palmas but found no trace of the French. In a second expedition, in 1687, de León's forces reached present-day Baffin Bay, near Kingsville, with the same negative results. Meanwhile, New Spanish authorities in late 1686 organized a second expedition by sea, departing this time from Veracruz, headed by Martín de Rivas and Pedro de Iriarte. Navigating north along the shore, the Rivas-Iriarte forces crossed the Río Grande and followed the entire Texas coast, where they found debris from vessels and other evidence of the French settlers. Iriarte and Rivas continued to the Mississippi Delta and Florida, returning from there to Veracruz.

A third maritime expedition departed from Tampico in 1687 under the command of Andrés de Pez and Francisco de Gamarra, who followed the same itinerary as Rivas-Iriarte and mapped out the harbors on the coastline, identifying the sites of present-day Corpus Christi, Matagorda, and Galveston bays. Yet one more maritime search patrol navigated the Río Grande upstream from its mouth to present-day Roma, Texas, with no results. In July 1687, Alonso de León became the first governor of Coahuila, a new province formed from territory formerly part of Nueva Vizcaya and Nuevo León, and was ordered to organize a final search. Recruiting soldiers from Nueva Vizcaya, Coahuila, and Nuevo León, de León used Jean Gery, a French immigrant captured the previous year, as his guide. De León departed on March 1689 with more than one hundred men, and one month later finally found the ruins of Fort Saint Louis, which had been sacked and destroyed by Karankawa Indians. De León learned from French survivors that La Salle had died at the hands of his own men near the Trinity River while trying to return to Canada.

Missionary Efforts. De León's expeditions established contact with Caddo-speaking groups that occupied the woodland areas between the

Trinity and Red Rivers in present-day eastern Texas and western Louisiana. The Spanish called these groups the Tejas Indians, noting that they culti- vated corn, squash, and beans, lived in scattered residences, and belonged to larger political entities or confederacies: Hasinai, Kadohadacho, and Natchitoches. In 1690 De León crossed the Río Grande one more time with the purpose of creating a Spanish outpost and mission among the Tejas. With Franciscan friars from Querétaro, led by Damian Massanet, de León entered the Caddo lands and near the Neches River erected the missions of San Francisco de Los Tejas and Santísimo Nombre de María. Leaving the Franciscans in charge and without the military protection they had demanded, de León returned to Monclova. In 1691 the Spanish authorities appointed Domingo Terán first governor of Texas. The first missions in East Texas did not survive long, as the natives soon became hostile to the Spanish presence in the area. A severe smallpox outbreak had accompanied the Franciscans to the missions. In 1693 native authorities told Massanet and his friars to leave the area. Choosing retreat over martyrdom, Massanet buried the mission bells and set the churches on fire before heading back to Monclova.

Despite their initial fiasco in East Texas, Franciscans from the Colegio de Santa Cruz de Querétaro continued to push their chain of missions in Coahuila northward. In 1699 their settlements reached the Río Grande near present Eagle Pass–Piedras Negras. Fray Francisco Hidalgo, Fray Antonio Olivares, and Fray Marcos Guerena founded the mission of San Juan Bautista. In 1700–02 two more missions were founded with Coahuiltecan Indians, and in 1703 the establishment of a military garrison consolidated the Spanish presence in the area. San Juan Bautista would become the gate- way into Texas from Coahuila and the seed of future missions.

Settlement of the Northeast. The French-Spanish alliance during the War of Spanish Succession (1700–14) created a more favorable climate for the formation and survival of a French colony in Louisiana, an effort resumed in 1699 by Pierre Lemoyne d'Iberville. In 1716 Spaniards also resumed their attempts to colonize East Texas, when Capt. Domingo Ramón departed from Saltillo and San Juan Bautista, Coahuila, with soldiers and ten Franciscans. Ramón built a presidio, San Francisco de Dolores, among the Hasinai and two more missions to the west of the French settlement at Natchitoches: San Miguel de los Adaes and Dolores de los Aiz. Meanwhile a second Spanish expedition led by Martín Alarcón was ordered to create a new settlement halfway between the Río Grande and the East Texas missions. As governor of Texas Alarcón marched across the Río Grande and in 1718 established the presidio of San Antonio de Béjar, the mission of San Antonio de Valero, and the town of San Antonio.

Despite being the only settlement with the rank of town or *villa*, San Antonio did not become the capital of Texas; Spanish authorities instead choose San Miguel de los Adaes. In 1719 French soldiers from Louisiana attacked the Spanish settlers in East Texas and forced them out of their missions and military forts. Once again the Franciscans had to abandon their missionary activities and relocate in San Antonio.

In Coahuila, a Spanish immigrant who had married Doña Ignacia Xaviera de Echeverz, the great-great-granddaughter of Francisco de Urdinola and sole heiress to the family's immense possessions in northern Mexico, thus becoming the second Marqués de San Miguel de Aguayo, offered to reconquer East Texas at his own expense. As the new governor of both Coahuila and Texas, Aguayo organized a force of five hundred men and crossed the Río Grande with the goal of recovering East Texas from the French. Aguayo's opponents put up no resistance and in 1721 agreed to leave the area. A new presidio, Nuestra Señora del Pilar, was established in Los Adaes with one hundred soldiers, and the missions were reoccupied and expanded.

Aguayo returned to Coahuila in 1722 having finally consolidated the Spanish presence in Texas. Given its location between New Spain and East Texas, San Antonio soon became an important agricultural and commercial center, with seven missions along the San Antonio River. In 1731 a group of fifty-five Spanish immigrants from the Canary Islands arrived at San Antonio as part of a larger project to bring "industrious" Spanish families to the northern frontier. Sponsored by the Crown, these Isleño families received free land and noble status and were authorized to establish the town of San Fernando de Béxar in 1731.

With the consolidation of Spanish colonies in East Texas and along the San Antonio, Guadalupe and Colorado Rivers, colonial authorities in New Spain made efforts to colonize the area between the Nueces River and the Río Las Palmas in present-day Soto La Marina, Tamaulipas. After considering proposals made by various private entrepreneurs in the 1730s, in 1746 the Spanish Crown chose José de Escandón y Elguera, Count of la Sierra Gorda, for the project. With considerable military experience in the pacification of the Sierra Gorda, a mountain range that runs north from Querétaro into the Huasteca area, Escandón planned to settle the area with several expeditions sent simultaneously from Texas, Tampico, and Coahuila. By 1755, twenty-four villages had been founded and a new province, Nuevo Santander, had emerged between Texas, Nuevo León, and New Spain. One of these settlements was the town of Laredo, established by José Vázquez Borrego, a rancher from Coahuila, on the north bank of the Río Grande. Other settlements included Reynosa, Camargo, and Mier on the Río Grande's southern shore. As a result of Escandón's expeditions, colonial settlements dedicated to agriculture and cattle raising flourished along the Lower Río Grande.

By the mid-eighteenth century Spanish efforts to colonize Texas and deter similar efforts by other colonial European powers had become a reality; Spanish settlements extended from the Red River in East Texas to Laredo in the Lower Río Grande Valley. The Tejano economy was primarily based on cattle ranching, and most long-distance trade was conducted through Saltillo and Monclova. Interracial marriages and immigration from Coahuila and other places created a largely mestizo population in East Texas.

The Northwest: Sonora and Arizona

At the close of the seventeenth century the Spanish presence in Sonora consisted primarily of Jesuit missions and military outposts. Besides Alamos, whose founding in 1684 had triggered the first major mining boom in Sonora, no more than a few mining centers had developed into permanent civilian settlements: the Reales de Minas in Nuestra Señora del Rosario Nacozari, San Miguel, San Ildefonso, Bacanuche, and San Juan Bautista. Small ranches and estancias for cattle raising dotted the countryside. Presidios such as Santa Rosa Corodeguachi (later renamed Fronteras) barely held out against marauding Apaches and other rebels. Indian raids caused many Spanish settlements in northern Sonora to be relocated or simply abandoned.

Jesuit Missions. In contrast to the very limited nature of civilian settlement, the Jesuits established a strong presence in the northwest. Encouraged by the success of their missions among Mayos, Yaquis, and Opatas, the Jesuit project expanded rapidly. The Compañía de Jesus increased its personnel in northern New Spain by bringing in priests from Catholic countries other than Spain, sidestepping Spanish colonial restrictions on the presence of foreign clergy.

One of these non-Spaniards, a Tyrolese named Eusebio Kino, received the assignment of expanding the Jesuit missions into the lands of the Upper Pimas, or Pimería Alta, in 1687. In the next decades Kino extended the Jesuit missions among Upper Pimas, Papagos (O'odham), and Yumas, occupying significant areas along the Magdalena, Santa Cruz, San Pedro, and Colorado-Gila Rivers. By the 1700s, the Jesuit line of settlements also included missions among Sobaipurus, Maricopas, and Cocomaricopas. Soon impressive ecclesiastical buildings emerged in places like San Xavier del Bac, Santa María de Magdalena, Caborca, and Altar in northern Sonora and southern Arizona. When Father Kino died in 1711 his body was buried in Magdalena, where his tomb became the object of local veneration by both Jesuits and Indians.

Settlement and Confrontation. In 1734, royal authorities detached the territories of Sonora and Sinaloa from Nueva Vizcaya, creating an independent province with its capital at the presidio of Horcasitas. A significant stage in the region's development commenced in 1736 with the discovery of Arizonac, a silver-mining site in the Altar Valley, which triggered a population rush to the north. The consequent demand for a native labor force to work in Arizonac inevitably exacerbated Indian unrest in the area. Upper

Pima groups revolted in 1737 and Apache raids intensified, inflicting heavy casualties on the Spanish population. In response colonial officials created two more presidios in 1741-2, in Pitiquin or Pitic (present-day Hermosillo) and Terrenate, near the mining town of Arizonac, to prevent future Pima revolts and retaliate against depredations by Seris in western Sonora and Apaches to the north.

In 1740 the Yaqui revolt began, with fatal consequences for the entire region. Spanish troops and Indian allies, led by Captain Agustín Vildosola, defeated Yaqui rebels at Tecoripa, Cerro del Tambor, and Otamcahui. By the end of the year more than five thousand rebels had perished, together with over a thousand Spaniards. After suppressing the rebellion colonial authorities severely punished the leaders and their families, executing, deporting, or enslaving many. Yaqui communities responded by abandoning the area in massive numbers. They migrated to Durango and Chihuahua on the other side of the Sierra Madre or joined hostile tribes in the Sonora-Arizona desert to the north.

In 1748 Seris protested the invasion of their recently assigned lands in Populo. Spanish officials, hoping to avoid another violent conflict, took drastic measures against the rebels, arresting many with their families and deporting them to Guatemala and other places in southern New Spain. A 1750 expedition to subdue the independent Seris on Tiburón Island resulted in failure. In coalition with Upper Pima rebels in 1751, rebel Seris and anti-Spanish Pimas congregated in Cerro Prieto (between Guaymas and Hermosillo). From there they launched an all-out war against Spaniards, destroying Guaymas in 1756 and taking control of the lower Sonora river.

Although the marauding activities of the Seris constituted less of a threat after the 1790s, the community at Cerro Prieto remained completely independent of colonial rule, despite several military campaigns and violent attacks by Sonora governors in the 1760s and 1770s. Tiburón Island managed to maintain its autonomy well beyond the end of the colonial period. While Sinaloa had around thirty thousand inhabitants, in the 1760s the Spanish population of Sonora did not exceed two thousand residents who lived in scattered mining towns, military camps, and civilian settlements such as Ures, Arizpe, and Alamos. Present-day Tucson, Arizona became a permanent settlement when Spanish authorities decided to relocate Tubac to the north in 1775.

Despite frequent conflicts with Pimas, Seris, and Yaquis, the Sonora mining settlements prospered in the eighteenth century. The growth in the province's silver production convinced colonial authorities to establish a Caja Real (Royal Treasury) in Alamos in 1766. Spanish immigrants played a major role in expanding trade and commercial agriculture. The development of the local economy, however, was hampered by the almost irreconcilable interests and perspectives of Spanish settlers and anticolonial native groups, opposition that would continue well into the nineteenth century. As a result Spanish settlements in Sonora and Arizona had not yet consolidated in this era, and the northwest constituted the most vulnerable part of the frontier region.

Baja and Alta California

The Spanish effort to colonize California in the second half of the eighteenth century shared many characteristics with the earlier settlement of Texas. Hoping again to prevent other powers, in this case Russia and Great Britain, from establishing colonies near the prosperous mining centers of northern Mexico, authorities in New Spain decided to occupy the lands identified by Sebastián Vizcaino in 1602.

Baja California. Toward the end of the seventeenth century Jesuits based in northwestern New Spain managed to establish permanent missions in the Baja California peninsula. Between 1697 and 1767 the Jesuits had exclusive control over sparsely populated Baja California, their jurisdiction extending even to civil and military affairs. The few Spanish troops stationed in the region came under Jesuit authority.

In the first decades of the eighteenth century missionaries in Baja California, led by the Italian Juan María Salvatierra, met with cooperation and sympathy from local tribes and created the missions of Nuestra Señora de Loreto, San José del Cabo, and Pilar de La Paz, among others. With economic support from the provinces of Sonora, Sinaloa, and Ostimuri, Jesuits in Baja California introduced agriculture and cattle and other farm animals in their missions. In 1734, Pericues Indians revolted against the priests, but after two years of fighting they surrendered to the punitive expedition launched from Sinaloa by the governor Manuel Huidobro. Jesuit territories expanded to the north in the 1750s with the creation of the missions of San Francisco de Borja, Santa Gertrudis, and Santa María de Kabujakamaang. After the expulsion of the Jesuits from New Spain—carried out in 1768 in Baja California— Franciscans and later Dominicans took over these missions but were never as successful as the Black Robes.

Alta California. In 1769 colonial authorities organized an expedition led by Gaspar de Portolá, governor of Baja California, and Fray Junipero Serra, the Franciscan guardian of the Baja California missions recently assigned to the Order of Saint Francis. Portolá and Serra departed by sea, while an overland military column led by Fernando de Rivera y Moncada ventured north from Baja California. Soldiers, Franciscans, and Baja California Indians founded the first permanent Spanish settlements in San Diego and Monterey Bay, initially as presidios.

In the following years Franciscans from the Colegio de San Fernando in Mexico City created a chain of missionary settlements along the coastline:

San Diego (1769), San Carlos Borromeo in Monterey (1770), San Gabriel (1771), San Luis Obispo (1772), San Juan Capistrano (1775), San Francisco (1776), Santa Clara (1777), San Buenaventura (1782), and Santa Bárbara (1786). By 1800 the Order of Saint Francis had established more than twenty-five missions in Alta California. Thanks to Indian labor and a mild Mediterranean climate—unusually benign by borderlands standards—these missions experienced great success, comparable only to that of the Jesuit missions in the Sonora-Arizona lands. From the perspective of the native population of California, however, the ramifications of Spanish settlement of the area, whether in the form of towns, presidios, or missions, were devastating. As was true virtually everywhere in northern New Spain, the arrival of soldiers, missionaries, and settlers unleashed severe epidemics resulting in high rates of mortality. Native populations in California started a vertiginous decline, reaching drastically low numbers in the nineteenth century.

Alta California soon replaced the Baja peninsula as the area's most important economic center, and colonial authorities moved the provincial capital from Loreto to Monterey in 1777. The same year Felipe de Neve, governor of California, founded the first civilian settlement, naming it San José de Guadalupe (present San José). In 1781 the colonial government promulgated the "Regulations for the Governance of California," a set of laws and regulations drafted by Neve that became California's first constitutional corpus.

In 1774 Capt. Juan Bautista Anza established a land route from Tubac in southern Arizona to the missions in Alta California. Anza's party met Yuma leaders at the junction of the Gila and Colorado Rivers and signed a peace agreement that would allow subsequent expeditions to cross Yuma territory. The next year Anza guided nearly two hundred and fifty colonists to northern California.

In 1779 viceroy Antonio Bucareli commissioned Rivera y Moncada to recruit families and soldiers for two civilian settlements in Alta California. Rivera y Moncada made the initial arrangements in Arizpe, Sonora and traveled south to Sinaloa, Nayarit, and Jalisco to enlist potential settlers. In 1781 Rivera y Moncada's expedition departed from Alamos and headed north in two groups. One would cross the Gulf of California and march north from Loreto; the second would cross the Altar desert with livestock and supplies.

In the summer of 1781 the first contingent arrived at their destination and founded the town of Nuestra Señora la Reina de Los Angeles, present-day Los Angeles. Meanwhile the overland party had been attacked by Yuma Indians who slaughtered the livestock, took women and children captive, and killed Capt. Rivera y Moncada. Only a few survivors reached Los Angeles. In the same year, 1781, the presidio of Santa Bárbara was built to protect civilian and religious settlements in the area. The original settlers of Los Angeles were mestizos, mulatos, and Indians from northwestern Mexico, especially Sonora and Sinaloa. The city's first *alcalde mayor* was José de Vanegas, an Indian from the mining town of Bolaños in northern Jalisco.

The Apache Corridor

The Apache Threat. Of all the Indian tribes in the Spanish borderlands the Athapaskan-speaking groups, collectively labeled Apaches by colonial settlers, played the most important role in shaping frontier life and institutions in the eighteenth century. Although Apaches were far from being the only group antagonistic to Spanish rule, they were the main target of the various reforms that Bourbon authorities implemented on the frontier.

Apache depredations did not begin with the establishment of Spanish rule in northern New Spain, but their mastery of horsemanship and adoption of Spanish tools, together with the strong appeal of colonial goods (livestock, clothing, alcohol, slaves), turned the Apaches into highly efficient marauders. Spanish horses significantly increased the scope of Apache activity, and the economic prosperity created in northern Mexico by ranches and mines enhanced the profits from each raid. The agricultural productivity of more sedentary Indian groups, especially the Pueblos and Opatas, similarly increased the incentives for Apache bands to plunder the area.

By the end of the seventeenth century, Athapaskan peoples were divided into many different groups (Jicarilla, Mescalero, Chiricahua, Lipan, Faraon, among others) and occupied a vast territory known as the Apache Corridor. It stretched from northern Sonora and Arizona to southern and western New Mexico, Chihuahua, northern Coahuila, and west Texas. Apache bands constituted a permanent threat to any Spanish or Indian ranch, hacienda, mine, town, mission, or village located between San Antonio and Sonora and between southern Chihuahua and northern New Mexico.

Attempts at Pacification. Spanish settlers and authorities tried different means to counter the Apaches' continuous plundering. The *cordón de presidios* (defensive line of forts) was fully implemented in the eighteenth century primarily as a response to the Apaches. Military expeditions that were organized in Chihuahua, Santa Fe, Monclova, El Paso, and northern Sonora inflicted heavy casualties on Apache groups and seized children and women to be enslaved. Partial truces and peace agreements also formed part of the Spanish response. When violence escalated, which was not unusual, mutual raiding led to extreme behavior on both sides, resulting in the loss of innocent lives and deportation of entire families of *"indios bárbaros"* to southern New Spain.

By the end of the eighteenth century, Bourbon officials decided to adopt a more diplomatic strategy by which Apache bands would receive trade goods (clothing, alcohol, tools) in exchange for temporary peace agreements. The tactic of turning enemy Indians into colonial consumers had been used with some success in dealing with Chichimeca tribes in north-central Mexico in previous centuries. In the case of the Apaches, it seemed to decrease the frequency of their depredations and curb their violent attacks

Figure 16-2 **Leather-jacketed soldier, ca. 1803.** Frontier soldiers dressed in distinctive leather coats defended the northern frontier. Troops were named for these thick coats (*"soldados de cuera"*), which were designed to deflect Indian arrows, protecting soldiers' lives while constricting their movements.
Courtesy of España, Ministerio de Educacíon, Cultura y Deporte, Archivo General de Indias, MP, Uniformes, 71.

on noncombatants. Bartering for peace with trade goods, however, failed to achieve the much-desired permanent settling of the Apaches.

Missionary efforts to Christianize the Apaches were rare, with both Franciscans and Jesuits failing in their attempts. In only one instance did Franciscans manage to create a mission for Apaches, in 1756 on the San Saba River in Texas. Led by Fray Alonso de Terreros, Franciscans from Querétaro began working with Lipan Apaches. They made no progress toward converting the Indians, and enemy Comanches attacked and destroyed the mission of Santa Cruz de San Saba in 1758. The Franciscans added more names to their list of martyrs in northern Mexico.

Apaches remained entirely free from Spanish rule for the rest of the colonial period, but their way of life nonetheless underwent significant transformations as a result of their interactions with settlers from New Spain. Consequently, like every other Indian nation in colonial Mexico, Apaches also became colonial Apaches although not subordinate to Spaniards.

The Spanish Frontier in the Late Colonial Period

Regional Articulation. The process of colonizing the Spanish borderlands over time entailed a distinctive kind of development reflected in the formation of several corridors that were closely integrated from south to north but more loosely linked from east to west. Combined with the particular character of Spanish-Indian relations in each microregion, this historical process decisively influenced the economic, ethnic, and cultural configuration of the northern regions of colonial Mexico.

The first of these corridors integrated Sonora and Sinaloa with Arizona and the Californias, while a second one linked Zacatecas with Durango, Chihuahua, and New Mexico, with the Camino Real de Tierra Adentro acting as both an economic and cultural backbone. A third corridor connected Coahuila and Nuevo León with the Lower Río Grande Valley and the Texas settlements. Although clearly divided by the Bolsón de Mapimí—even today an inhospitable region—and the permanent threat posed by Apaches and Comanches, more interaction occurred between the second and third areas than between any other two regions in the borderlands.

Secondary roads linked Chihuahua and El Paso to San Antonio and Zacatecas to Coahuila, while the Sierra Madre Occidental, along with extremely hostile Apaches, Yumas, Navahos, and Utes, prevented normal trade and contact between Nueva Vizcaya, New Mexico, and the regions of the Pacific corridor. In 1780, Juan Bautista Anza and José Antonio Vildosola unsuccessfully tried to open a safe route between Santa Fe, New Mexico and Arizpe, Sonora, in the midst of Apache Mimbreño and Chiricahua territories. California had no connections with New Mexico, and Indian depredations frequently disrupted interchange between Sonora and Arizona and the central corridor. This south-north pattern of historical development in the borderlands would persist long after colonial times.

Jurisdictional Reorganization. Colonial Bourbon officials tried to develop a more efficient system to govern these colonial territories, hoping to defend Spanish possessions at a lower cost to the royal treasury and to generate higher revenues as well. For the most part ignoring existing interregional connections, Bourbon officials created the *Comandancia General de Provincias Internas* in 1776, putting all the northern provinces under a single centralized governing authority. The first governor was Teodoro de Croix, a recent arrival from Spain who had gained some experience in colonial government when his uncle served as New Spain's viceroy (1776–81). In 1778, Croix, along with the governors of New Mexico, Coahuila, Nueva Vizcaya, and Sonora, tried to forge an alliance with Comanches and some smaller Apache groups against the majority of Apaches. The next year Croix made Arizpe his headquarters.

Croix reorganized the line of presidios, closing down some, relocating others, and promoting the use of *compañías volantes*, mobile companies that would patrol the borderlands and aid local troops against marauding Indians. In 1786 the borderlands were divided into two independent commands: the Eastern, which included Coahuila, Nuevo León, Nuevo Santander, and Texas; and the Western, encompassing the Californias, Sonora, Nueva Vizcaya, and New Mexico. This apparently more functional division disappeared in 1793 when colonial officials in Spain decided to reunify the Provincias Internas under one authority and exclude Nuevo León, Nuevo Santander, and the Californias from the comandante general's jurisdiction.

The War of Independence. Toward the end of Spanish rule in colonial Mexico, the northern provinces already had initiated an intense process of interaction and exchange with Anglo-American traders and settlers, particularly in Texas, where Anglo colonizers played a significant role in the Mexican War of Independence (1810–21). The military and political confrontation that shook central and western Mexico between 1810 and 1821 went practically unnoticed in northern territories like California and New Mexico. Colonial troops from Sonora and Sinaloa did join the royalists and moved south to confront the insurgent army led by Villaescusa, but the majority of settlers in the region simply sat out the conflict. In contrast the populations of Durango, Chihuahua, Coahuila, and Texas participated actively on both sides and consequently affected, and were affected by, the wars for independence.

Late Colonial Borderlands Society. Christianization efforts in the Spanish borderlands produced uneven results because of the differing responses of native groups. The mission system did bring Christianity to northern Mexico and offered Indians a life-style based on sedentary agriculture and ranching as well as protection from the predations of other Indians. The price that native groups had to pay for these benefits in the eighteenth century—abandonment of their old religion and communal traditions, greater exposure to disease, subjection to the friars' authority—was, however, too high for many northern Indians.

Many groups in the borderlands repudiated the missions altogether and managed to evade colonial rule. Missionizing efforts among Seris, Yumas, Hopis, Apaches, Utes, Comanches, and Karankawas ended in notable failure. In East Texas and both Californias Spanish missions met with only partial success, as had been the case with Tarahumaras and Tepehuanes in the Sierra Madre Occidental in the seventeenth century. As the revolts organized by Pericues (1734–7), Yaquis (1740), Seris (1750–90), and Yumas (1781) abundantly proved, Spanish rule in the borderlands required a strong military presence as well as the mission system in order to survive.

Although throughout the eighteenth century a significant number of exclusively civilian towns emerged in the Spanish borderlands (Los Angeles, San José, Albuquerque, Santa Cruz de la Cañada, San Fernando, Nacogdoches, Laredo), in reality it was the presidio that became the primary institution for the colonization of northern Mexico. The vast majority of Spanish towns featured a substantial military presence.

Compared with southern and central New Spain, frontier populations in colonial Mexico had smaller proportions of native Indians; instead, the majority of residents and workers in presidios, mining towns, ranches, estancias and haciendas were people of mixed racial origins. This predominance of non-Indians was equally true both in older towns such as Durango, El Paso, Monclova, and San Antonio and in smaller and more recent settlements such as Los Angeles, Arizpe, Nacogdoches, or Reynosa. The majority of residents in the north were culturally Hispanic. Virtually all were Spanish speakers, retaining few if any vestiges of native languages or practices. As the result of generations of colonial rule, linguistic change, racial intermarriage, and life on the frontier, the people of the north had lost their particular ethnic identities and acquired new ones as colonial Hispanics of mixed blood.

The Spanish borderlands were also distinctive in that Hispanic settlers often maintained close contacts, and in many cases lived side by side, with French and Anglo settlers and traders. The Hispanic population also had regular contacts with Indian nations that were completely independent of colonial rule.

Glossary

Apache   general term for Athapaskan-speaking groups

Apache Corridor   territory stretching from San Antonio in Texas to Tucson in Arizona, and from Santa Fe in New Mexico to Chihuahua and Durango in Nueva Vizcaya, where Apaches represented a serious threat to Spanish settlements

Caja Real   royal treasury

California   mythic prosperous island ruled by the legendary Queen Calafia

compañía volante   mobile military squadron

cordón de presidios   defensive line of forts

indios bárbaros   unpacified, nomadic Indians

presidio   fortified and enclosed military garrison and settlement

Tejas   land of the Tejas Indians, the term coined for Caddoans, Karankawas, and other Indian groups in present-day east Texas and western Louisiana.

Questions for Discussion

1. What role did presidios play in the Spanish Borderlands?

2. What external threats triggered the colonization of Texas?

3. Why were New Mexico and Nueva Vizcaya more prosperous than other parts of the north?

4. Which Indian nations remained independent of Spanish rule and why?

5. How would you characterize Christianization efforts in the borderlands?

Suggested Reading

Bannon, John Francis. *The Spanish Borderlands Frontier: 1513–1821.* Albuquerque: University of New Mexico Press, 1974. Standard, influential synthesis of the literature on the borderlands.

Castañeda, Carlos E. *Our Catholic Heritage in Texas.* Austin: Von Boeckmann-Jones, 7 vols. 1936–58 (reprinted New York: Arno Press, 1976). Detailed multivolume history of Texas into the mid-twentieth century; emphasizes the role of missions during the colonial period.

Chipman, Donald E. *Spanish Texas: 1519–1821.* Austin: University of Texas Press, 1992. Solid history of Texas during the Spanish period.

Crosby, Harry W. *Antigua California. Mission and Colony on the Peninsular Frontier, 1697–1768.* Albuquerque: University of New Mexico Press, 1994. Detailed examination of the Jesuit enterprise in California.

Cutter, Charles R. *The Legal Culture of Northern New Spain, 1700–1810.* Albuquerque: University of New Mexico Press, 1995. Study of judicial procedure in New Mexico and Texas in the eighteenth century.

Forbes, Jack D. *Apache, Navaho and Spaniard.* Norman: University of Oklahoma Press, 1960. Examination of the changing relationships among Apache, Navaho, and Pueblo Indians and Spaniards in the sixteenth and seventeenth centuries.

Jackson, Robert H. *Indian Population Decline: The Missions of Northwestern New Spain, 1687–1840.* Albuquerque: University of New Mexico Press, 1994. Demographic study of the decline of the northwestern mission.

Radding Murrieta, Cynthia. *Wandering Peoples. Colonialism, Ethnic Spaces and Ecological Frontiers in Northwestern Mexico, 1700–1850.* Durham, N.C.: Duke University Press, 1997. Ethnohistorical study of the indigenous peoples of Sonora during the late colonial period and early republican Mexico.

Swann, Michael M. *Migrants in the Mexican North. Mobility, Economy, and Society in a Colonial World.* Boulder, Colo.: Westview Press, 1989. Examination of the impact of migration to northern Mexico in the eighteenth century and the connections between places forged by mobility and migration.

West, Robert C. *The Mining Community in Northern New Spain: The Parral Mining District.* Berkeley: University of California Press, 1949. Detailed study of the development of the Parral mines.

Seventeen

The Struggle
for Independence

The more than decade-long conflict that resulted in the creation of an independent Mexico was a complex phenomenon. Like the revolution that would occur in Mexico a hundred years later, the struggle for independence was regional and encompassed a range of ideas and objectives as well as participants whose circumstances and aspirations sometimes were at odds or only superficially related. Social, economic, and even cultural discontent that lay at the heart of popular protest and participation did not necessarily dovetail with the political ambitions of the colony's middle and upper classes. Resentment of peninsular-born Spaniards (often called *gachupines*) and their prerogatives frequently made them targets for violent attack, but from almost anyone's point of view the lines dividing upper-class peninsulars from well-to-do Mexican Spaniards were far from clear. Substantial Mexican support for the royalist cause for many years proved critical to maintaining imperial control over New Spain. As Spain itself lurched from foreign domination under the Bonapartes to liberal constitutionalism to absolute monarchy with the return of the displaced Bourbon king Ferdinand VII to a brief restoration of constitutional monarchism, Mexican ambitions for autonomy grew. Somewhat ironically they coalesced around the desire to affirm and protect the reforms guaranteed in the liberal Spanish Constitution of 1812.

The story of the struggle for independence embraces three fairly distinct but closely interrelated sets of issues and developments. One of these consisted of the series of political changes that took place in Spain, beginning with the Napoleonic invasion of the Iberian Peninsula in 1807–8 and extending through the restoration of Ferdinand VII in 1814 and the liberal revolt of 1820. All the political developments in Spain during that period had direct and significant repercussions throughout the Spanish empire and hence in New Spain as well, stimulating and shaping political responses and changes that were welcomed by some and rejected by others. A second set of developments hinged on creole actions and ambitions, on the one hand, and overt, often sustained and violent expressions of popular resentment and discontent on the other; at times they intersected and at others did not. Like the twentieth-century revolution, the struggle for independence in Mexico in many senses was not a single, coherent phenomenon but, rather, an aggregate of locally and regionally based movements that took place in the same period but often were tenuously connected at best. The third aspect of conflict was the progress and prosecution of the war itself—the organization and maintenance of rebel forces and of guerrilla warfare, on the one hand, and the viceregal response to insurrection and political challenges, on the other.

Much of the complexity of the struggle, which has been called a revolutionary civil war, stemmed from the complicated interplay of these sets of forces, which sometimes ran parallel and at other times clashed or converged. This chapter will begin with a discussion of the pivotal events that shaped the course of the conflict and then examine in more detail some of the most important aspects of this turbulent era.

The Struggle for Independence: An Overview

In 1807 Napoleon Bonaparte obtained permission to enter Spain with the ostensible objective of attacking Portugal, which was closely allied to France's chief rival, Britain. Napoleon's ambitions, however, extended to Spain as well. Prince Ferdinand led a revolt against his father's minister, Manuel Godoy, as a result of which the king, Charles IV, abdicated in favor of his son, who became Ferdinand VII. At this point Napoleon intervened and forced them both into exile in France in 1808, placing his brother Joseph Bonaparte on the Spanish throne. Despite, or even in part because of, the considerable French influence that had penetrated the royal court—especially in the person of the king's minister Godoy—and also had affected many other educated Spaniards, the Napoleonic coup ignited a Spanish War of Independence.

Governing councils, or *juntas*, quickly took shape in Spain. Finally a Junta Central that claimed the right to govern in the absence of the legitimate monarch emerged in the south, eventually establishing itself in the southern port city of Cádiz which was safe from the threat of French attack. There the Junta convened an assembly or *Cortes* to undertake the task of organizing a new government. Although ostensibly representing all of Spain as well as its overseas colonies, because of the French occupation of much of the country and the distances that colonial representatives had to travel, delegates to the Cortes of Cádiz were heavily representative of the south and distinctly liberal in their political thinking. The Spanish Cortes deliberated for more than three years and adopted a number of liberal measures, culminating in the promulgation of the liberal Constitution of 1812.

The Napoleonic invasion and displacement of the Bourbon monarchy raised the same crucial questions in Spain's overseas territories as in Spain itself. With an alien usurper on the throne, where did sovereignty lie and what individual or collective body could legitimately claim to govern? Despite the liberalism of the junta and assembly at Cádiz and their efforts to incorporate colonial representatives, in broad terms they retained an unaltered view of the metropolitan-colonial relationship: the overseas territories were Spanish possessions to be ruled from Spain. All over Spanish America, however, creoles repudiated this formulation. In Mexico many Mexican Spaniards (and perhaps some sympathetic peninsular Spaniards as well) rejected the claim that New Spain was a colony, insisting that it had always been one of several kingdoms of the Spanish Crown. They believed that with the abdication of the Bourbon monarchs sovereignty had reverted to, and now lay with, "the people." Mexican elites argued that, as the bodies most representative of the people, city councils could claim sovereignty and the right to organize a government in place of the monarchy. They pressured the viceroy, José de Iturrigaray (1803–8), to summon a junta to determine the best response to the imperial political crisis.

The removal of the Bourbon monarchy by Napoleon created what has been called a vacuum of legitimacy rather than of power per se. In New Spain in a sense nothing had changed; institutions representing the Crown—the viceroy, intendants, audiencias—still existed. But did they exercise legitimate authority in the absence of the king? Iturrigaray, sympathetic to the arguments of Mexicans who held that sovereignty lay in New Spain itself or hoping to shore up his own increasingly precarious position, agreed to demands that he call an assembly representing the city councils. The Audiencia of Mexico City, most of whose members were peninsular Spaniards, opposed the plan. The viceroy nonetheless convened a junta representing the principal corporations of New Spain. Basically it drew its representatives from the traditional establishment; the participants were wealthy landowners, miners, merchants, ecclesiastics, academics, bureaucrats, and ayuntamiento members. The junta met several times in August and September 1808, but the attendees failed to reach an agreement on how to proceed.

This attempt to reach a political solution to the pressing questions of sovereignty and legitimacy ended abruptly in mid-September when Gabriel de Yermo, a peninsular landowner and merchant, arrested Iturrigaray and a number of the leading creoles of the capital. Supported by the Audiencia, the archbishop, and Yermo's fellow merchants of the Consulado, the coup polarized antagonisms between creoles who aspired to greater political control and self-rule and peninsulars who looked to the Junta Central in Spain as the source of legitimate authority. The coup ended the process of political evolution toward greater autonomy, at least in the short term, and pushed resentful creoles to consider alternative and extralegal means of achieving their political aspirations.

All told the coup accomplished little that was positive. Not only did it exacerbate tensions and frustrations, it also failed to restore effective authority to the office of the viceroy, and a period of fairly inept government followed. The two years after the coup brought a wave of conspiracies and protests, most of which never produced much beyond discussion and the formation of clandestine groups in the cities. One of these conspiracies, organized in the city of Querétaro in the Bajío, however, spawned the first mass popular revolt in New Spain. In mid-September of 1810, exactly two years after Yermo's coup and two days after the arrival in Mexico of a new viceroy, Francisco Javier Venegas, the parish priest of Dolores, Miguel Hidalgo y Costilla, called on the people to rise up—against Spanish government but in the name of the absent monarch Ferdinand VII. Hidalgo took as his symbol and protector the Virgin of Guadalupe, who had particular appeal for Mexico's dark-skinned groups.

Within days the revolt attracted the support of thousands of rural workers who, armed mainly with knives, machetes, and stones, quickly captured the towns of San Miguel el Grande (modern San Miguel de Allende) and Celaya in the Bajío and took revenge on upper-class whites by looting the haciendas of the wealthy. On September 23, nearly twenty-five thousand people converged on the rich mining center of Guanajuato and slaughtered the loyalists (including the intendant) who had taken refuge in the city's granary, the Alhóndiga; more than three hundred Spaniards died there. By early October the rebels, whose ranks had swollen to some sixty thousand and now included many mine workers as well as estate tenants and laborers, had occupied the city of Valladolid (today Morelia) in Michoacan. In the wake of these successes the insurrection attracted many thousands of additional participants. The explosiveness and scale of the revolt were unprecedented in New Spain's history.

The conspirators of Querétaro most likely had not imagined that the insurrection they helped to launch would become a powerful vehicle for the violent expression of the social and economic frustrations and resentments rampant among the Bajío's lower classes. The plotters came principally from the Bajío's secondary provincial elite. These men could boast some degree of status and influence in provincial society, but in a real sense they were about as far removed from New Spain's wealthiest circles of great landowners, miners, and high officials as they were from the estate workers, peasants, and mine workers who responded to Hidalgo's call for revolt. Several key figures—Ignacio Allende, Juan de Aldama, Mariano Abasolo—were militia officers who brought to the revolt their experience in military leadership and organization. No doubt these men had recruited Father Miguel Hidalgo because of the popularity he enjoyed among his parishioners, an obvious bid to enlarge their base of support. Although many of the creole participants in the revolt later may have regretted their choice to involve Hidalgo, in some ways he resembled the other conspirators in background.

Territorial Extent of the Independence Struggle

Miguel Hidalgo was born in 1753 on a hacienda southwest of Guanajuato, where his father was the administrator. He received an education from the Jesuits and after their expulsion studied at the Colegio de San Nicolás in Valladolid, where he subsequently taught and served as rector. Ordained as a priest at the age of twenty-six, he was a brilliant intellectual but an unorthodox clergyman. On the whole his principal interests were more secular than religious, running toward art, literature, and politics, and his private life was far from exemplary for a cleric. Although he was popular among his parishioners, he was known to be a gambler and a womanizer.

Hidalgo did not become a parish priest until 1792, when he lost his position at the seminary. In 1803, at the age of fifty, he was assigned the mostly Indian parish of Dolores, the equivalent of exile for such an accomplished intellectual. Once there, however, he applied himself to the challenges of a poor parish. He became involved in efforts to promote small-scale industry by establishing artisan workshops, probably hoping both to help his parishioners and improve his own financial situation. Influenced by Enlightenment thought, Hidalgo was a long-time friend of the Spanish cleric Manuel Abad y Queipo, an advocate of liberal political and economic ideas who in 1810 became bishop-elect of Michoacan. Although Hidalgo's participation in the rebellion created an irreconcilable rift between the two clerics, nonetheless Abad y Queipo's denunciation of the inequities of New Spanish society and his advocacy of the abolition of tribute and of land reform probably influenced Hidalgo. Hidalgo never developed or pursued a very coherent program for socioeconomic and political reform.

Despite initial disarray in face of the uprising, perhaps understandable given the rapidity of events, the viceregal government soon was able to produce an effective military response, reviving the system of local militias. Viceroy Venegas placed an experienced officer, Félix María Calleja del Rey, in command of the army of the center. Calleja's disciplined forces eventually inflicted a series of defeats on the mostly unorganized and untrained men they faced.

The rebels led by Hidalgo and Allende had moved south from the Bajío toward Mexico City but were unable or unwilling to take the capital, possibly because they found little support for the revolt among the residents of the central valley or the city itself. Farther west in Jalisco, however, the insurrection attracted thousands of new recruits, and rebel numbers reached at least eighty thousand once again. At its maximum the insurgency might have involved as many as one hundred thousand. By this time the rebels' violent actions and pillaging had thoroughly alienated much of the creole middle and upper class; the elites of Guadalajara, for example, sent their militia out to combat the revolt. Early in 1811 the rebels suffered a key defeat at Puente de Calderón at the hands of Calleja and Puebla's Intendant Manuel de Flon. Late in March Hidalgo was captured and subsequently tried, stripped of his priestly status, and executed, along with his chief officers, at the end of June. Their heads were displayed in cages on the walls of the Guanajuato granary, earlier the scene of such shocking carnage, a grisly warning to others that was typical of the Spanish mode of exemplary justice. They remained there until 1821, when Mexico achieved its independence.

The end of the Hidalgo revolt as such hardly meant the pacification of the country. A second major movement developed in the south under the leadership of José María Morelos, another diocesan priest who had studied with Hidalgo at the seminary in Valladolid. A dark-skinned mestizo of relatively humble origins and native of Michoacan, Morelos had at one time worked as a muleteer. Even after being ordained he continued to struggle to make a decent living. Morelos began recruiting men in the Costa Grande area of the modern state of Guerrero early in November 1810, attracting some three thousand by the end of the month. Emerging as the major leader of the insurrection in the south, Morelos proved to be a capable and efficient military organizer who also provided a more coherent political program than Hidalgo ever had tried, or wanted, to advance.

The Hidalgo rebellion, as seen, quickly took on strong overtones of class and ethnic warfare. Although Hidalgo over time increasingly spoke of independence from Spain and called for the abolition of slavery, on the whole his movement failed to develop an ideology that went much beyond the initial proclamation of loyalty to the king and the Virgin of Guadalupe and repudiation of Spain. In contrast Morelos not only recruited successfully among all classes in the hot country of the Pacific lowlands, he also advanced a political program meant to attract and retain a broad base of support. Along with Ignacio López Rayón, one of Hidalgo's lieutenants who had eluded capture and continued the struggle in the Bajío, Morelos took steps to organize a government. In 1813, a congress convened in Chilpancingo in present-day Guerrero, which was Morelos's principal base of action and support. It remained for the most part under insurgent control until 1815.

The Supremo Congreso Nacional Americano declared independence on November 6, 1813 and, despite military defeats the movement began to suffer, continued its work in Apatzingan in the summer of 1814. There they drafted a constitution that provided for indirect election of a congress and a three-man executive based on universal male suffrage. Local government remained strong, probably reinforced to some degree by the militia system that Morelos had devised that was based on village communities. The Congress called for the abolition of tribute and slavery and an end to ethnic and social discrimination, provisions that particularly appealed to the heavily mulato population of the hot country. Indeed Morelos declared that the Constitution and new government were for all "*Americanos,*" whom he defined as all those born or living in Mexico. Equally important, Roman Catholicism would remain the only permissible religion.

José María Morelos, "Sentiments of the Nation," presented to the Chilpancingo Congress, September 14, 1813 (excerpt)

1. That America is free and independent of Spain and every other nation, government, or monarchy, and thus it shall be proclaimed, informing the world why.
2. That the Catholic religion shall be the only one, without tolerance for any other.
3. That the ministers of the Church shall live only from the tithes and first fruits, and the people shall not be required to pay for services. . . .
5. That sovereignty flows directly from the people, and they wish it to be lodged only in the Supremo Congreso Nacional Americano, composed of representatives of the provinces in equal numbers.

(Continued)

6. That the legislative, executive, and judicial powers shall be divided among those bodies that are established to exercise them. . . .

9. Government posts shall be held only by Americans.

10. Foreigners shall not be allowed to enter the country unless they are artisans who can instruct others and are free of all suspicion.

11. States alter the customs of the people; therefore, the Fatherland will not be completely free and ours until the government is reformed, replacing the tyrannical with the liberal, and also expelling from our soil the enemy Spaniard who so greatly opposed our Fatherland.

12. Since the good law is superior to any man, those [laws] that our Congreso issues shall be so, and shall promote constancy and patriotism, and moderate opulence and poverty so that the daily wage of the poor man is raised, his customs improved, and ignorance, preying upon others, and thievery removed.

13. That the general laws shall apply to everyone, including privileged corporations except as applies directly to their duties. . . .

15. Slavery shall be forever forbidden, as shall caste distinctions, leaving everyone equal. . . .

17. The property of every individual shall be protected, and their homes respected as if they were a sacred asylum.

18. That the new legislation shall not allow torture.

19. That the new legislation shall establish by constitutional law the celebration of December 12 in every community of the land in honor of Our Most Holy Lady of Guadalupe, patroness of our liberty, and every community is to practice monthly devotions to her. . . .

Appended:

23. That September 16 also shall be solemnized each year as the anniversary of the beginning of our struggle for Independence and our holy Freedom, for on that date the Nation spoke, demanding its rights with sword in hand so as to be heard. Thus the distinction of the great hero, Señor Don Miguel Hidalgo, and his companion, Don Ignacio Allende, will be remembered forever.

Kenneth Mills and William B. Taylor, eds., *Colonial Spanish America: A Documentary History* (Wilmington, Del. 1998), pp. 342–4.

In November 1815 Morelos was captured and sent to Mexico City, where, like Hidalgo, he was defrocked and executed. After his death Vicente Guerrero continued to lead the remnants of the rebellion in the highlands of the *tierra caliente* until 1821, when he agreed to an alliance with the royalist commander of the south, Agustín de Iturbide, under the Plan of Iguala, which established Mexico's independence. Although by the middle of the decade large-scale insurrection for the most part had ended, guerrilla warfare, usually involving small groups of perhaps several hundred to a thousand men, continued to plague parts of New Spain and defy viceregal efforts to achieve complete pacification. At times nearly indistinguishable from bands of highway robbers and cattle rustlers (*gavillas*) that had become active in some regions during the late eighteenth century (and with whom they might have cooperated at times), guerrilla fighters hid in inaccessible mountainous areas, attacked and harried royalist troops and supply lines, and over time put a considerable strain on royalist fiscal and military capabilities. If the guerrillas could not achieve outright military victory, they nonetheless created a constant drain on viceregal resources and stymied the royalist drive to reestablish uncontested authority. Royalist counterinsurgency efforts took a variety of forms and became more effective over time.

In response to the Hidalgo revolt, Viceroy Venegas organized New Spain under twelve regional military commands. He also called for donations and loans to pay for the war effort. Up until 1812 the viceregal treasury did indeed receive substantial contributions from both peninsular and Mexican Spaniards but after that time increasingly had to impose special taxes and extort forced loans.

Over time, the burden of supporting the royalist war effort with money, supplies, and manpower became increasingly intolerable. Mining production and import-export trade declined, and civilian populations grew weary of the disruptions caused by military conscription and taxation. Civilians suffered abuse at the hands of the military as it became more and more difficult to maintain military discipline. Mexicans persisted in demanding the political prerogatives guaranteed in the Constitution of 1812, which had been suspended but then reinstated by the liberal revolt in Spain in 1820. The royalist army faced bankruptcy, and royalist officers—many of them creoles or men who had lived for years in New Spain—began to consider the

Figure 17-1 **José María Morelos (1765–1815).** Mestizo secular cleric Morelos continued the struggle for independence following Hidalgo's execution. Morelos helped to formulate a political plan for independence before his execution.
Mexican banknote, courtesy Sarah Cline.

advantages of bringing the conflict to an end by changing sides and opting for independence.

The Plan of Iguala, written by Agustín de Iturbide and accepted by rebel leader Vicente Guerrero, was proclaimed on February 24, 1821. Iturbide, a creole and son of a peninsular immigrant, was a long-term royalist officer who had been made commander of the army of the south in 1820 by Viceroy Apodaca. Ambitious, ruthless, and conservative, Iturbide nonetheless recognized the need to forge a broad coalition and consensus that would bring royalists and insurgents together and put an end to the war, and he had the circle of contacts necessary to do so. Exhausted by the unending hardships and expense of warfare, the people of New Spain were eager to support Iturbide and his program of "Independence, Religion, and Union," protected by the so-called Army of the Three Guarantees (*Ejército Trigarante*). The Plan, although conservative, represented a political compromise, endorsing the Spanish Constitution of 1812, which remained in force until December 1822, and providing for a constitutional monarchy. It also proposed the abolition of slavery and the extension of full citizenship to all (going well beyond the liberal Spanish Cortes, which had disenfranchised blacks and castas) and eliminated racial classification for all official purposes but did not enfranchise women of any race or class.

At the end of September Iturbide entered Mexico City as the head of government. Since no member of the Bourbon dynasty would agree to take the throne of the new "Mexican Empire," the Mexican Congress made Iturbide the emperor Agustín I, its constitutional monarch. The old titled nobility became his court. After Iturbide dismissed Congress in October 1822 a revolt began under Guadalupe Victoria (soon to become first president of the Republic) and Antonio López de Santa Anna, who would figure prominently in independent Mexico's turbulent politics for the next forty years. The opposition coalesced around Santa Anna's Plan de Casa Mata, which called for election of a new congress and establishment of a federalist system. Iturbide abdicated and left the country, then returned in July 1824 after a year's exile, ostensibly to defend Mexico from outside intervention. He was captured and executed.

Political Aspirations and Frustrations

The first overt act of the independence struggle in New Spain, as seen, was Yermo's coup of September 1808 which succeeded in temporarily neutralizing, if not eliminating, Mexican ambitions for greater autonomy and control. The coup drew support from two significant sectors, the upper echelons of the church and army officers.

The popular classes' violence against members of the white upper classes, whether *gachupín* or creole, during the Hidalgo revolt further pushed many creoles into tacit, if often reluctant, support of the royalist regime. Wealthy Mexicans helped to organize urban militia units for the royalist cause and mobilized the manpower and resources of their haciendas. Given the nature of the conflict, however, Mexican Spaniards' decisions about whom to support often had less to do with ideology and loyalties than with intimidation, coercion, or accommodation. Wealthy individuals might end up contributing men, money and supplies to either or both sides, just as people from the humbler classes could find themselves forced into military service or support of one side or the other, depending on circumstances. Men granted amnesties would switch sides, or revert to their original allegiance once they were free to do so.

Despite real and perceived limitations on their freedom of action, Mexicans nonetheless found unanticipated new political opportunities as a result of the work of the Spanish Cortes, which governed from September 1810 until King Ferdinand VII's return in May 1814. The reforms adopted by this assembly, intended to be applied throughout the empire, included the abolition of tribute and of the Inquisition, equal status for all men within the empire, and freedom of the press. The new Constitution, promulgated in March 1812, was proclaimed in New Spain in September 1812. The Constitution, which established a constitutional monarchy with the Cortes as the legislative branch, also provided for several levels of political representation in the colonies: Provincial Deputations that would share power with the governor or viceroy (now designated the *Jefe Político*), town councils (*Ayuntamientos Constitucionales*), and deputies to the Cortes itself, all to be chosen through indirect elections.

The implementation of the political and other reforms of the Cortes and Constitution followed an erratic course in New Spain. Mexico sent deputies chosen by the municipal councils of the leading cities to the Cortes where some of them participated actively in the drafting of legislation and of the Constitution itself. Some of the key reforms demanded by American and Asian delegates failed to be enacted, however, including proportional representation in the Cortes and free foreign trade. People of African descent were denied citizenship over the protests of the Mexican deputies, who hoped to increase the numbers of Mexican delegates if members of the casta group were declared citizens. A number of the men who served as deputies to the Cortes, both during the period the Constitution was being drafted and later in 1820-1 after the liberal revolt forced its reinstatement, would become important figures in Mexican political life after independence.

Both Venegas and Calleja, who served as viceroy from 1813 to 1816, implemented only some of the reforms proclaimed by the Spanish Cortes, and both suspended or intervened in elections, especially those in Mexico City itself. The election procedures adopted by the Cortes were complicated as well as indirect. The new constitutional ayuntamientos were elected in a two-step process that involved the selection of parish electors who then chose the municipal officials. Elections to the provincial deputations and to the Cortes entailed selection at three levels—parish, district, and province. Notwithstanding their complexity and viceregal intervention, the elections nonetheless were significant in at least two respects. First, virtually all elections that were allowed to proceed resulted in victories of creoles, most of whom were firmly committed to the liberal reforms of the era. Virginia Guedea has demonstrated that members of the so-called Guadalupes, a secret society in Mexico City that sympathized with and supported the insurgency, figured prominently both in preelectoral activities and as electors. Second, despite the indirect procedures and exclusion of the castas, the elections meant much broader participation in the political process than ever had been the case before.

In March 1814 the French released Ferdinand VII, who returned to Spain and revoked the Constitution and all acts of the Cortes of Cádiz. The king abolished all elected bodies in the empire and restored the former powers of the audiencia (which had lost its nonjudicial functions under the liberal Cortes) and viceroy. The constitutional system would not be restored until 1820.

Along with the provisions for elections, another key reform of the Cortes of Cádiz was the Law of Freedom of the Press, similarly resisted by the viceroys of New Spain. Although the law was enacted in November 1810, Viceroy Venegas did not proclaim it in New Spain. With the adoption of the Constitution, which incorporated the provision for freedom of the press, and its official promulgation in September 1812 Venegas could no longer delay implementing the law. The creole response in Mexico was immediate, if short lived. Such prominent figures as Carlos María Bustamante and José Joaquín Fernández de Lizardi launched publications (*El Juguetillo* and *El Pensador Mejicano*) sharply critical of the viceregal government. The *Diario de México* printed the entire text of the law as well as a Spanish translation of the U.S. Constitution and Bill of Rights. In December of the same year Venegas suspended freedom of the press. Bustamante went into hiding and Fernández de Lizardi was jailed. The suspension forced the genie of liberal political expression back into the bottle but could not seal it up entirely. Since a free press continued to exist in Spain until 1814, publications and news from Spain and elsewhere continued to arrive and circulate in Mexico.

The experience of participating in the elections during the years 1810–14 and enjoying freedom of the press in 1812, while truncated and ephemeral, nonetheless established a precedent that Mexicans certainly would not forget. When the liberal revolt in Spain in 1820 forced the king to restore the Constitution of 1812 and liberals returned to power in Madrid in March, Mexicans were quick to respond to the changed circumstances. A group of creole and peninsular Liberals forced the viceroy to promulgate the Constitution in Mexico City at the end of May resulting in the restoration of freedom of the press and abolition of the Inquisition. The next month an Ayuntamiento Constitucional was elected in Mexico City, and elections to the Cortes, the provincial deputations, and other municipal councils took place as well. Viceroy Juan Ruiz de Apodaca, who had followed a concilia- tory policy that included offering amnesty to thousands of rebels, cooper- ated in implementing provisions of the Constitution.

If Mexicans were eager to take advantage of the revived opportunity for political participation, however, they soon found themselves frustrated by the imperialist outlook of the Spanish Cortes, which as before continued to ignore American demands for free trade and self-government. Even for many conservatives, the time had arrived to take the next step toward achieving control over Mexico's political and economic affairs. With the ter- mination of financial support for the royalist military effort (Mexicans inter- preted the reinstated Constitution of 1812 to mean the termination of local taxation to support the military, resulting in the elimination of militia units), the political disaffection of Mexico's upper classes combined with the popu- lace's exhaustion from war to produce a workable compromise. The result was Iturbide's nearly bloodless coup and the Plan of Iguala.

Whether a broad political consensus had emerged is debatable. By this time probably most politically minded Mexicans agreed on the liberal prin- ciples of separation of powers, political representation proportional to pop- ulation, and equality of men of all races and classes before the law. Some of the more radical proposals advocated by Morelos and others, such as land redistribution, however, had disappeared entirely from the political agenda.

Dissent and Insurgency

Motivation for Rebellion. The lack of an identifiable, coherent ideology or political program in the great Hidalgo revolt, the increasing localization of the insurgency, the variability in patterns of participation, not only from region to region but even from village to village, the overwhelmingly rural character of rebellion and seeming lack of a corresponding urban compo- nent, all confound efforts to formulate simple generalizations about the insurgency. Although after the early stages of the Hidalgo revolt most of the Mexican upper class withheld support for the insurgency, certainly there were exceptions. If urban residents did not engage in overt or violent protest in conjunction with or in response to rural uprisings, nonetheless most of the leading liberals and critics of the royalist regime were based in the cities, and their secret societies provided insurgents with men, supplies, and information. And if the upper echelons of the ecclesiastical hierarchy stood firmly aligned against the insurgency, many lower-level priests not only lent support but assumed leadership roles, as did Hidalgo and Morelos.

By 1816 rebel forces mainly were small and confined to relatively isolated regions, leading some scholars to conclude that by then viceregal military efforts essentially had achieved complete military pacification. Others
argue that the survival of remnants of the insurgency up to the time of
Iturbide's 1821 coup is evidence of the failure of counterinsurgency efforts to
achieve the kind of order and stability that would have permitted effective
reestablishment of Spanish rule.

The insurgency encompassed a range of motivations and interests and
reflected an array of grievances and hopes. One of its apparent paradoxes
was that while the majority of insurgents were rural people, and Morelos
and others called for land redistribution, the quest for land does not seem to
have been an important objective for most rebels. The great question, then,
is why did so many rebel, so suddenly and almost spontaneously? Although
we have seen that revolts were hardly uncommon during the colonial
period, they were almost invariably limited in scale and scope. The Bajío, the
cradle of the insurgency, had long been an economically diverse and prosperous region that had not previously produced rebellions.

In the Bajío the grievances of estate workers whose wages had
decreased or failed to keep pace with price increases, of mine workers who
suffered from unemployment and diminishing compensation, and of tenants
and sharecroppers who were becoming increasingly insecure were the product of the late years of the eighteenth century and first decade of the nineteenth. Furthermore, the objects of their resentment—tax collectors, estate
owners and administrators, merchants—were close at hand. The hardships
occasioned by the severe drought and famine of 1809 and 1810 further exacerbated resentments and frustrations. By 1810, the apparent sympathy of at
least some members of the creole group and evident split within New
Spain's upper class, as reflected by the Querétaro conspiracy and Hidalgo's
call for rebellion, seemed to offer Mexico's working classes the chance to
redress their grievances.[1] Unpredictably, the summer of 1810 brought ample
rain, promising a substantial harvest and the assurance of a reliable subsistence base for the Bajío's insurgents.

The lack of response to the revolt among the residents of the mostly
Indian communities of Mexico's central valleys has been explained by the
differences in their situation compared to that of the people of the Bajío. The
more traditional communities of the center certainly had experienced strains
as a result of growth in population, greater pressure on resources, and
Bourbon policies that undercut aspects of local autonomy and control.
Nonetheless for the most part they had retained their lands and social structure, often because of colonial legislation intended to protect the integrity of
Indian communities. As a result, they possibly were more inclined to view
colonial officials and courts as guarantors of their survival than as agents of

---

[1]John Tutino, *From Insurrection to Revolution in Mexico* (Princeton N.J., 1986), p. 181.

exploitation. Nonetheless, in areas where tensions between villagers and landed elites were marked, as in Jalisco, large numbers of villagers joined estate workers in supporting the rebellion.

Even at the local level, as might be expected, unanimity did not prevail. In the Mixteca region of Oaxaca the insurgency apparently attracted wealthier members of Indian communities, while more traditional and poorer Indians remained uninvolved or even actively supported the royalist side. Peter Guardino writes that around Taxco the rebellion divided some villages and sometimes fostered internal "revolutions" in which one faction drove another out. By contrast, Van Young has suggested that internal tensions within traditional communities resulting from increasing differentiation along social and economic lines at times might have been displaced toward outsiders, allowing them outwardly to maintain a common front even as internal consensus frayed. There were, in other words, no hard and fast rules about who would be likely to join the rebellion and who would not. Lucas Alamán, who lived through the insurrection in the Bajío, later wrote that many of the insurgent officers were estate managers and overseers, while cowboys formed the cavalry and estate laborers filled the ranks of the foot soldiers. Guardino notes that on the Costa Grande of the modern state of Guerrero militia units readily gave their support to Morelos, and officials and landowners often joined mulato sharecroppers in the insurgency; but the mulato sharecroppers of the Costa Chica demonstrated consistent loyalty to the royalist side.[2]

The extent to which the rebels and others supporters of the insurrection responded to or developed any unifying ideology is debatable. Some of the difficulty in discerning similarities and differences in elite and popular ideology stems from the fact that "different aims were not expressed in radically different ways."[3] Furthermore elite participants and supporters generally were far more articulate about their goals and aspirations than were lower-class insurgents. Because they organized societies in the cities and published articles and books, their views are often much better known than those of the relatively silent majority of rebels

Religion, Revolt, and the Clergy. Many writers have noted the revolt's religious and even mystical dimension. Religious belief and symbolism manifested themselves in a variety of forms: Hidalgo's raising the banner of the Virgin of Guadalupe, the active participation of clergymen, biblical references to rebellions favored by God, and—strangest of all—messianic expectations that frequently centered on the figure of the captive Bourbon king Ferdinand, "el Deseado," rumors of whose actual presence in Mexico circulated in 1810–11. Even those who did not believe that the king was in Mexico apparently considered him to be the symbol of justice and righteous

---

[2]Peter F. Guardino, "The War of Independence in Guerrero, New Spain, 1808–1821," in Christon I. Archer, ed., *The Wars of Independence in Spanish America* (Wilmington, Del., 2000), pp. 102–3.
[3]Guardino, "The War of Independence in Guerrero," p. 107.

retribution against rapacious *gachupines* who frequently were the targets of popular violence. Thus, while it rightly has been argued that religion served as the great unifier of social and ethnic groups in New Spain and therefore could hardly *not* have figured in the insurgency, clearly all groups did not share the same religious convictions or practices.

The prominence of some diocesan priests in the insurrection has led many—both contemporary observers and later historians—to assume that the majority of the clergy supported the rebellion, but probably only a substantial minority, heavily concentrated in the Bajío and highlands of Jalisco and Michoacan and in the *tierra caliente* of Michoacan, Guerrero, and Puebla, participated actively. As was true for many people caught up in the turmoil of the independence struggle, there was no sure way to predict where a priest's loyalties would lie. Some of the most active insurgent priests were highly educated men like Hidalgo, while some of the clergy who had embraced Enlightenment ideas most enthusiastically remained royalist. Taylor suggests that probably the majority of priests tried to remain neutral, concerned principally with ensuring their own safety and that of their parishioners and avoiding overt political commitments. Their very neutrality, however, probably undermined the royalist cause.

Regardless of the actual numbers of priests who supported the insurgency—historian Nancy Farriss compiled a list of 401 clergymen (244 seculars and 157 regulars) who were active participants—the larger issue of the impact of royal policy toward the church on the struggle for independence must be considered as well. The Bourbon attack on ecclesiastical immunity, only partially implemented (and to almost no one's satisfaction) during the late years of the colony, gave way with the outbreak of the Hidalgo revolt to extremely harsh treatment of priests accused of rebelling. The viceregal *bando* or decree of 1812 authorizing military officers to order the summary execution of captives included priests.

The application of the policy of summary execution to the clergy—repudiated by the reinstated Council of the Indies after the restoration of Ferdinand VII and in any case no longer implemented after 1816, when the country appeared to have been largely pacified—had the further effect of identifying the royalist cause with persecution of the clergy, while in contrast for the most part the insurgents respected the clergy and eschewed violence against priests or churches identified with the royalist side. By alienating and even persecuting at least some of the diocesan clergy, who exercised considerable social influence in New Spain, royal and viceregal policy may have estranged many Mexicans.

Many members of the lower clergy as well as of the regular orders suffered financially from the Crown's attack on church wealth, creating discontent and perhaps predisposing them to rebel or at least sympathize with the insurgency. Farriss judges royal policy toward the church to have been an important contributing factor to the demise of the colonial regime. "This new policy of antagonism to the Church . . . whose purpose was to weaken the influence and the authority of the Church, must ultimately be judged a failure as far as Mexico was concerned. In all three phases of its development—Bourbon absolutism, military expedience, and liberal anticlericalism—the policy helped to weaken the colonial régime and in the end contributed to its destruction, while leaving the Church and the clergy in a stronger position than ever."[4]

The withdrawal of church support for the royalist cause and nearly unanimous ecclesiastical endorsement of Iturbide's Plan de Iguala surely helped to ensure its acceptance. The embrace of the "Three Guarantees" by members of the upper echelons of the church probably hinged on their desire once again to defend clerical privilege in face of new anticlerical measures adopted after the liberal revolt in Spain in 1820. Regardless of the clergy's motivation in supporting Iturbide, however, the Spanish government's efforts to control and restrict the church ultimately undermined the royal effort to retain the Crown's richest American possession, New Spain.

Counterinsurgency and War

At the time of the outbreak of the Hidalgo revolt the military capacities of the viceregal government seemed virtually nonexistent. It did not take long, however, for the viceroy to organize a system of provincial brigades. Calleja's regulations of 1811 required generals to name commanders responsible for local defense in major cities and towns; big hacendados were obligated to organize companies of 150 men. Military and civilian officials had to maintain surveillance over roads in their districts and arrest suspicious individuals.

When Calleja became viceroy in March 1813 he reorganized the military command structure. At the time the army was divided into small units. Many of them were inadequately armed, and the pay for soldiers often was months in arrears. Desertion rates were high, even among recently arrived Spanish expeditionary troops. Calleja's plan was to establish strong regional commands that would bring royalist divisions in one region under a military chief who also would be governor. The result, according to Christon I. Archer, was to divide the country "into a series of semiautonomous and autonomous military satrapies" in which military authority quickly eclipsed civilian rule.[5]

Militiamen became professional soldiers who looked to their commanders for rewards and promotion; an officer who offered leadership and security could gain and retain the support of his troops. Following varying policies, some military officers emptied provincial treasures, confiscated

[4]N. M. Farriss, *Crown and Clergy in Colonial Mexico, 1759–1821* (London, 1968), p. 237.
[5]Christon I. Archer, "Politicization of the Army of New Spain during the War of Independence, 1810–1821," in Jaime E. Rodríguez O., ed., *The Origins of Mexican National Politics, 1808–1847* (Wilmington, Del., 1997), pp. 12, 14, 15, 20.

whatever they chose to label as "insurgent" properties, and rewarded their men with booty. Some royalist commanders held their posts long enough to become involved in business enterprises and corrupt practices, including engaging in contraband trade with the enemy. Officers extorted and stole money from miners and exacted inflated taxes from merchants. Some, however, remained honest and loyal to the viceregal regime and campaigned against contraband and other illegal practices.

The daunting task of suppressing the rebellion, especially as it fragmented into guerrilla warfare, called forth a range of responses and techniques. Both sides committed atrocities. Morelos's men massacred Spanish troops who were imprisoned in a church near Acapulco. While he was a royalist commander Iturbide executed hundreds of rebels. Calleja had towns burned, and royalist forces terrorized the countryside. The very conduct of the counterinsurgency effort itself could exacerbate hostilities and polarize populations.

In conventional battles royalist troops generally had the advantage over the insurgents, but pursuing and suppressing elusive guerrilla units was frustrating and exhausting. Expensive counterinsurgency campaigns were wasted if permanent garrisons were not established to consolidate royalist control. For the most part the royalists were able to retain (or regain, in the case of places that fell early on to the rebels) control over the major towns and cities. Because of the crucial importance of maintaining trade and production as a basis for supply and taxation, convoys were organized to protect travelers and merchants on the major routes for commerce and transportation.

Some insurgents traveled to the United States or were in contact with sympathizers there. Although it is unlikely that much aid reached rebels from that source, the very possibility of U.S. support for the insurgency alarmed the royalists. At the end of March 1818, Viceroy Apodaca reported on the activities of "Anglo-Americans" in his account of the current military situation in Mexico. He mentioned the capture of Javier Mina, a Spaniard who took up the cause of Mexican independence and organized an expedition in the United States that landed in Mexico in 1817. Royalist forces captured him in October of that year, and he was executed in November.

Although no new troops arrived from Spain after 1816, the greatest problem that the military faced was financial. As the decade progressed, the task of maintaining military strength presented fiscal challenges that could not be met. The operating costs of army units and pay for soldiers absorbed every available source of revenue. Soldiers whose pay was in arrears robbed civilians and caused local disturbances. Already on the verge of bankruptcy, the army faced disaster in 1820 when the restored Constitution of 1812 allowed municipalities to terminate the hated *contribuciones militares*. In late October 1820, Viceroy Apodaca himself promulgated a royal order stipulating that no army officer could collect taxes in his district. The Constitution provided for recruitment of a national militia to replace the now disbanded royalist army, but most ayuntamientos ignored the law. The royalist military effort collapsed.

Perspectives on the Achievement of Independence

If the immediate achievement of independence entailed a political restructuring that left most existing social and economic inequalities unaltered, the upheaval of the era of struggle had affected a wide spectrum of Mexico's people and regions. Although after independence the political arena encompassed relatively few players and remained vulnerable to the ambitions of strong military leaders *caudillos* who had emerged during the years of conflict, nevertheless the experience of the insurgency and mobilization for political and other objectives left a mark on Mexico's people that could not be expunged. The turmoil of the years culminating in Mexico's independence had touched the lives of nearly everyone in New Spain, cutting across class, race, gender, loyalties, and interests. Women, for example, found new opportunities for engagement in the realm of politics and even in warfare. Women persuaded soldiers to change allegiances, conveyed information and supplies, and organized societies in support of one side or the other. Some women defied husbands or other male relatives to take opposing stands. Doña Leona Vicario, a wealthy orphan in Mexico City, broke with her uncle and guardian, donated much of her fortune to the insurgents, and supplied them with arms and information. Imprisoned in March 1813, she escaped and joined the army of Morelos and married Andrés Quintana Roo, her uncle's former law clerk. She rode with the army and contributed to both military planning and financial administration, giving birth to her first child in a cave.

Mexico emerged into independent nationhood in economic disarray. Damage to haciendas and mines, disruption of trade and production that resulted from warfare, loss of manpower due to military conscription, excessive taxation and forced loans, the death or expulsion of Spaniards, many of whom had played a key role in the maintenance of networks of credit and capital that linked mining to commerce, and wartime mortality, disease, and dislocations of population all brought economic depression or at least stagnation to many parts of the country. In the aftermath of the war travel was difficult and dangerous, and towns and even major cities reflected the impact of years of conflict and neglect. Nor was the political situation any rosier, as regions struggled to assert their autonomy vis-à-vis the center and new political factions formed within the creole group.

Despite the apparently limited achievements of the struggle, the independence era had a considerable impact on Mexican society. The embrace of liberalism, challenged after independence by conservatives and the church, survived as a potent force that eventually culminated in the period of the

Reform and the Constitution of 1857. The mobilization of nonwhite groups for the insurgency and for political purposes also would have significant repercussions throughout the nineteenth century. If the struggle for independence raised social, economic, and regional issues that would not be addressed or resolved with the achievement of political independence, nevertheless the articulation and recognition of these issues would have a powerful impact on shaping the political and social agenda of the new nation well into the twentieth century.

Glossary

alhóndiga   public granary
ayuntamiento constitucional   city or town council elected under the
    Constitution of 1812
Americanos   all those born or living in Mexico
bando   viceregal decree
caudillo   military strongman
contribuciones militares   special taxes to support local militias
Cortes   legislative assembly
gachupín   peninsular-born Spaniard
gavilla   band of thieves, outlaws
jefe político   chief political officer
junta   governing council
tierra caliente   tropical lowlands

Questions for Discussion

1.   How did events in Spain affect the course of the struggle for independence in Mexico?

2.   Why did many upper-class Mexicans support the royalist side and fail to make common cause with working-class insurgents?

3.   How did the revolts led by Hidalgo and Morelos differ from earlier colonial rebellions? What were their objectives?

4.   What position did Morelos assign to Catholicism in the new nation? How did he propose to deal with Spaniards and foreigners?

5.   How did the viceregal government respond to the insurgency and why did it ultimately fail?

6.   What was the compromise that resulted in Mexican independence?

Suggested Reading

Anna, Timothy. "The Independence of Mexico and Central America," in Leslie Bethell, ed., *The Cambridge History of Latin America*, Vol. 3. Cambridge: Cambridge University Press, 1985. Basic overview of the independence period in Mexico by a leading scholar of the period.

Archer, Christon I., ed., *The Wars of Independence in Spanish America*. Part II: "Insurgency and Counterinsurgency in New Spain." Wilmington, Del.: Scholarly Resources., 2000. Includes articles by Peter Guardino and Virginia Guedea, as well as documents related to the viceregal military effort, annotated by Christon Archer.

Benson, Nettie Lee. *Mexico and the Spanish Cortes, 1810–1822: Eight Essays.* Austin: University of Texas Press, 1966. Articles focusing on the participation of Mexicans in the deliberations of the Cortes and the impact of the Cortes on events in Mexico.

Guedea, Virginia. "The Old Colonialism Ends, the New Colonialism Begins," in Michael C. Meyer and William H. Beezley, eds., *The Oxford History of Mexico*. Oxford and New York: Oxford University Press, 2000. Brief overview of events of the independence and immediate postindependence era.

Hamill, Hugh. *The Hidalgo Revolt*. Gainesville: University of Florida Press, 1966. Classic study of Miguel Hidalgo and the revolt.

Rodríguez O., Jaime E., ed. *The Origins of Mexican National Politics, 1808–1847*. Wilmington, Del.: Scholarly Resources, 1997. Articles by Jaime E. Rodríguez O., who also introduces the volume, Christon I. Archer, Virginia Guedea, and Barbara A. Tenenbaum on aspects of the independence struggle and transition to postindependence era.

Taylor, William B. "Banditry and Insurrection: Rural Unrest in Central Jalisco, 1790–1816," in Friedrich Katz, ed., *Riot, Rebellion, and Revolution: Rural Social Conflict in Mexico*. Study of the background to, participants in, and events of the insurrection in Jalisco.

Tutino, John. *From Insurrection to Revolution in Mexico: Social Bases of Agrarian Violence, 1750-1940*. Princeton, N.J.: Princeton University Press, 1986. Relates participation in the insurrection to socioeconomic conditions in the Bajío and central Mexico.

Van Young, Eric. "Islands in the Storm: Quiet Cities and Violent Countrysides in the Mexican Independence Era," *Past and Present* 118 (1988): 130–55. Offers an explanation for the lack of urban revolt or protest during the struggle for independence.

———. *The Other Rebellion: Popular Violence, Ideology, and the Mexican Struggle for Independence*. Stanford: Stanford University Press, 2001. Important study of the participants in the struggle for independence by a major scholar in the field.

Eighteen

Colonial Legacies

In the year 2000, Mexico's population reached approximately one hundred million, a figure that excludes the more than twenty- two million Mexican American/Chicano and Mexican immigrants living in the United States. These huge numbers are the result of the modern expansion of basic medical services. Mexico's population did not reach its prehispanic levels of density until 1940. In contrast with the colonial era, when the vast majority of the population lived in small rural settlements, most Mexicans now live in large cities. The largest numbers of people still live on the central plateau, the region that dominated Mexico politically at the Spanish conquest. The arid north, despite having some substantial cities, particularly along the border with the United States, for the most part remains sparsely populated

Today most Mexicans participate in the labor market as salaried work- ers and pay taxes as citizens of the republic, while in the colonial era the majority of New Spain's population consisted of Indians and castas who paid tribute because of their subordinate racial status. Most Mexicans today speak Spanish as their first language, with indigenous languages surviving mainly in economically marginal parts of the country. Most contemporary Mexicans have attended at least primary and secondary school, institutions funded and run by the government, and have an average life expectancy of more than sixty years. They consider themselves to be citizens of the nation-state of Mexico and vote in elections that have real political meaning. In contrast, in 1800 only a tiny minority of people could read, write, or sign their names, and life expectancy barely reached thirty years. Colonial New Spain's Indians, castas, and Spaniards lacked a collective sense of national identity.

At the end of the colonial era New Spain's territory included the present-day U.S. states of Texas, New Mexico, Nevada, Arizona, and California, as well as parts of Utah, Colorado, and Wyoming. To the south the Captaincy of Guatemala—today the modern Central American countries of El Salvador, Guatemala, Nicaragua, Honduras, and Costa Rica—also formed part of the viceroyalty of New Spain. In 1823 most of that territory separated peacefully from independent Mexico, which reannexed Chiapas in 1824. With the exception of the south the new nation-state of Mexico encompassed the old viceroyalty New Spain.

For Mexico the most traumatic losses of land in the period after inde- pendence resulted from conflicts with the United States, beginning with the independence of Texas, which had been settled by slaveholding Anglos from the United States at the invitation of the Mexican government. The U.S.-Mexican War (1846–8) concluded with the Treaty of Guadalupe Hidalgo, which turned over much of Mexico's north and northwest to the United States. That treaty guaranteed the rights of the Mexican population living in the ceded territories, and the failure of the United States to honor those rights has been a long-standing source of resentment for Mexican-Americans.

The final boundary between the United States and Mexico was set when the bankrupt government of President Antonio López de Santa Anna sold territory bordering the recently lost region of Arizona, an act that helped to precipitate his fall from power in 1854. Since the sale of the Mesilla Valley, known in U.S. history as the Gadsden Purchase, Mexico's northern border with the United States has been fixed at the Río Grande, from the twin border cities of Matamoros-Brownsville to Ciudad Juárez–El Paso, extending westward along an artificially imposed line that reaches the Pacific Ocean, some miles south of San Diego Bay; Tijuana–San Diego is the largest twin city of all. That mid-nineteenth-century transfer of what had been New Spain's northern territories had an enormous impact on the future development of both the United States and Mexico.

The territorial divisions created by the Spanish Crown—kingdoms, captaincies, provinces, high courts, and intendancies—ceased to exist formally after independence, but the eighteenth-century intendancy divisions became the basis for state boundaries when Mexico became a republic in 1823. There no longer is a Nueva Galicia or a Nueva Vizcaya, but many territorial divisions still bear their colonial names, among them the U.S. states of New Mexico (Nuevo México) and California (Alta California). Tlaxcala's services to Hernando Cortés in the conquest earned it an enduring status; it exists today as is a state of the modern federal republic. A map of modern Mexico includes many names and places that would be familiar to a colonial official or traveler. Nearly all its leading cities date to the colonial period, some of them, such as Guadalajara and Puebla de los Angeles, founded in the sixteenth century. Others, including most prominently the national capital, have prehispanic origins. The very name "Mexico" means "place of the Mexica," the Aztecs of Tenochtitlan whom Cortés defeated in 1521. In some cases colonial names have fallen into disuse. The Chinantec village that was known in the colonial period as San Pedro Yolox is again simply Yolox. The struggle for independence did put new names on the map, including states named after heroes Miguel Hidalgo, José Maria Morelos, and Vicente Guerrero.

Mexico City, built on the ruins of Tenochtitlan, embodies the prehispanic and colonial past. Its huge main square, officially called the Plaza of the Constitution but universally known as the Zócalo, is a showpiece for symbols of Mexican power. Surrounding it are the National Palace, the seat of civil government, the cathedral, and the City Hall, housing the municipal government for a city of twenty million. All are colonial buildings that have survived earthquakes that toppled modern skyscrapers.

The Zócalo, with its vast expanse of concrete, is one of the world's great public squares, the site of mass public ceremonies, such as the annual waving of the Mexican flag by the president on the balcony of the National Palace on September 16, the anniversary of Father Hidalgo's Grito de Dolores. Crowds throng the Zócalo during such celebrations, while on normal work days the plaza is host to demonstrators of various kinds and to tourists who witness the daily lowering of the massive Mexican flag by an honor guard at sunset. Indigenous flutists, drummers, and dancers perform modern renditions of Aztec dances.

Just off the Zócalo the Hospital of Jesus, founded by Hernando Cortés, still functions as a medical facility. In the opposite direction, the Monte de Piedad, the national pawnshop founded in the eighteenth century by the Count of Regla to provide cash for Mexico's poor, also still operates. A few blocks from the Zócalo is the Alameda, a park that once witnessed autos de fe but has long served as a popular place to stroll, to see and be seen. In the Plazuela de Santo Domingo the building that once housed the Inquisition retains that institution's coat of arms above the entranceway.

Much of what is beautiful and memorable in the capital originated in colonial times, but there are also spectacular reminders of the prehispanic era, particularly the excavations of the Great Temple of the Aztecs, once buried in the rubble of the postconquest reconstruction. In the late twentieth century, sewer workers found the sculpture of the goddess Coyolxauhqui. This discovery initiated the search for the temple complex. The excavations have yielded enormously important finds, including eight-feet-tall terra

Figure 18-1 **Sor Juana Inés de la Cruz**. Known as the "Tenth Muse," this brilliant seventeenth-century nun wrote poetry and plays in her convent cell. She is Mexico's most famous and honored woman, seen on this high denomination banknote. Courtesy Sarah Cline.

cotta eagle warriors, painted statuary, and sacrificial knives with almost sur-realistic decorations of faces on them. The Great Temple ruins lie immedi-ately adjacent to the Metropolitan Cathedral, something the Spanish conquerors consciously planned, although they hardly anticipated the reap-pearance of the Aztec temple.

The Franciscan church in Tlatelolco (now part of the capital) was one of the first built in Mexico. The surrounding modern complex, known as the Plaza of the Three Cultures, is a colonial site where momentous modern events occurred. The slaughter of hundreds of peaceful demonstrators who protested the Mexican government's vast expenditures on the 1968 Olympics brought this conquest-era locale into national consciousness. Only in the late 1990s did a small plaque appear in the Plaza of the Three Cultures to mark the site.

Mexicans—including (and perhaps especially) those of Mexican her-itage living in the United States—take tremendous and understandable pride in their past, consciously glorifying the prehispanic achievements of indigenous civilizations. In Mexico the government controls the preserva-tion of ancient sites through the National Institute of Anthropology and History (INAH). Interestingly and perhaps tellingly, colonial-era sites and culture are less prominently chronicled and preserved. While the spectacu-lar Museum of Anthropology, with its treasures from the prehispanic past and contemporary ethnographic exhibits, stands in Chapultepec Park in the heart of the capital, the Museum of the Viceroyalty, which houses a huge col-lection of colonial-era art, is located in an ex-Jesuit colegio in Tepozotlan, twenty-five miles from Mexico City.

Mexico's most famous modern art form, muralism, appears promi-nently in some of the oldest and most important colonial buildings, includ-ing the National Palace and the palace of Cortés in Cuernavaca. Murals were used in both prehispanic Mexico and Renaissance Europe. In prehispanic Mexico murals such as the Maya ones at Bonampak depicted scenes of indigenous history. In Renaissance Europe church frescoes presented scenes from the lives of Christ and the saints to illiterate common folk, offering didactic and edifying messages. Colonial-era churches in Mexico were opu-lently decorated with murals, some the work of indigenous artists.

In Mexico murals were revived in the 1920s by brilliant artists of the post-Revolutionary era. Diego Rivera, José Clemente Orozco, and David Alfaro Siquieros decorated many of Mexico's colonial-era public buildings with murals, creating new visual narratives of Mexican history. Mexican muralists present the indigenous past as a lost golden age, portraying the conquest and subjugation of the indigenous population in bloody detail. In the anticlerical postrevolutionary period muralists depicted conquest-era clerics as twisted and grotesque figures.

Mexico became one of the world's first republics, after its brief experi-ment with monarchy in the wake of independence from Spain. According to the Constitution of 1917, the document that provides the framework for the present political system, Mexico is a federation of independent states with powers divided among executive, legislative, and judicial branches.

The notion that the head of state is the protector and patron of the church has disappeared, but that change came about only after a protracted series of civil wars starting in the 1850s with the Liberal Reform and culminating in the Mexican Revolution of 1910–20. Anticlericalism was as rigidly intolerant of religious expression as the colonial-era church was intolerant of any religion but orthodox Catholicism. Presidents of modern Mexico took the lead in the religious struggles, and church-state relations have changed according to the head of state's interest in the religious question. President Avila Camarcho's 1940 declaration, "Soy creyente" (I am a religious believer), effectively put an end to church-state tensions

In the political sphere Mexico's colonial legacy is manifest in the idea that government should benefit those at the top; that public offices are a source of private enrichment for officeholders; and that officials are creatures of the ruling group or party, not civil servants. The centrality of the executive in the structure of the state is another legacy of the colonial era, with presidents of Mexico wielding tremendous power, unchecked by a weak legislative branch, which has no colonial precedents, or the judiciary, which lost its independence in the national period.

Although since independence Mexico's process of choosing leaders has been nominally democratic, effective democracy at the state and national level only took hold in the last ten or fifteen years of the twentieth century. The era of one-party government at the national level came to an end with the election of Vicente Fox from the pro-Catholic opposition National Action Party (PAN) in 2000 in elections generally considered both inside and outside Mexico as free and fair.

Under the Constitution of 1917, the framework of government that was drafted by the winning factions of the Mexican Revolution, the Mexican state claimed powers once exercised by the Spanish Crown. In particular, Article 27 gave the state the power to expropriate land. In the colonial era the Crown protected Indian communities by mandating the creation of the *fundo legal*, a minimum guaranteed expanse of land to support their residents. In the immediate postrevolutionary period Mexican presidents embarked on land reform, expropriating estates and dividing the land into *ejidos* for the use of Indian peasants, conferring protected status on Indian communities.

Article 27 of the 1917 Constitution also empowered the Mexican state to assert sovereignty over its mineral wealth. In the colonial period the Crown retained ownership of mines and leased mining rights to men who paid a percentage of production in taxes while the Crown retained ownership. The idea of national sovereignty over resources embodied in the 1917 Constitution harked back to the colonial era. The intellectual father of Article

27, Andrés Molina Enríquez, studied colonial history and drew directly on the writings of the eighteenth-century Spanish intellectual Jovellanos.

One of the obvious legacies of the colonial era is Roman Catholicism. In Mexico, Catholicism is based on the veneration of the Virgin of Guadalupe and to a lesser extent other devotions, all of which reflect much local input and refashioning that for the most part originated in colonial times, such as the cults of the Santo Niño de Atocha, the Virgin of San Juan de los Lagos, the Christ of Chalma, and San Judas Tadeo. Despite the anti-clerical policies of nineteenth-century liberals and the postrevolutionary regimes of the twentieth century, Mexico remains a stronghold of Catholicism.

Mexican Catholics have broken down the old colonial racial barriers to full (male) participation in the church. Juan Diego, the Indian to whom the Virgin of Guadalupe is reputed to have appeared, was officially canonized in 1992, along with a number of Mexicans martyred during the Cristero Rebellion of the 1920s. The papacy of John Paul II has canonized more saints than any other in history, and Mexico has received its share of recognition. The canonization of Juan Diego, despite considerable doubts expressed even by clerics in Mexico itself about his existence, created a saint who resonates with Mexico's millions and is a source of national pride. The day when a Latin American becomes Pope, a possibility that colonial Mexican intellectuals could only dream of, is no longer so remote. On the basis of sheer numbers Mexico, with its millions of at least nominal Catholics, potentially could produce a successful papal candidate.

Religion in Mexico has evolved considerably since the colonial period, giving rise to what Fray Virgilio Elizondo has called "Mestizo Christianity," a synthesis of European and indigenous practices and beliefs. Catholic Mexicans acknowledge the native sources of many practices, including such colorful celebrations as the Days of the Dead on November 1 (All Saints' Day) and November 2 (All Souls' Day), when families remember their departed loved ones with home altars, special foods, and vigils in the cemeteries where they are buried. The Catholic hierarchy increasingly welcomes Mexican or ethnic manifestations of religious faith, especially in the face of the challenge of Protestant churches that have forged new religious communities that are particularly welcoming to urban migrants in Mexico or Mexican immigrants in the United States.

In the United States, the majority of Catholics soon will be Mexicans, Chicanos, and other Hispanics. Masses conducted in Spanish are no longer unusual, and masses with mariachi music are celebrated in Chicago, El Paso, and Los Angeles as well as in Guadalajara, the birthplace of that music. Mexican venerations are fast becoming part of mainstream Catholicism, with chapels devoted to the Virgin of Guadalupe becoming increasingly standard. The weekly bilingual Sunday mass broadcast from the San Fernando cathedral in San Antonio, Texas is by far the most popular religious ceremony televised in the United States. Mexican and Mexican-American/Chicano communities in the United States have made December 12, the day of Our Lady of Guadalupe, a major celebration on both sides of the Río Grande.

Another colonial legacy is the complex situation of Greater Mexico's north, where the old territory once held by New Spain now is split between Mexico and the United States. Indigenous and Hispanic populations incorporated into the United States suffered from social and legal discrimination and disadvantages that only now are being seriously addressed. The boundary between the United States and Mexico is lengthy and permeable, in some respects artificially dividing a blended cultural region. For both Mexico and the United States, the borderland region is geographically far removed from their national capitals and centers of power. For both nations the region historically was a frontier (*la frontera*) characterized by small, racially mixed, and relatively poor populations, weak control by the central government, and little in the way of wealth or culture from the mainstream perspective. The culture and society of the borderland developed as a result of centuries of contact among diverse peoples, first Spaniards, castas, and Indians in New Spain and then Anglo-Americans (often a more diverse group than the commonly used term "Anglo" implies). Perhaps ironically, today the border region is the fastest growing, economically most dynamic part of both nations, which has political implications at both the national and state levels.

The legacy of the colonial past of Greater Mexico is carried by Mexican migrants to the United States in cultural attitudes and practices, but Spain's colonial legacy also is evident in those parts of the United States once ruled by Spain. Matrimonial law and water law are legacies of the Spanish colonial past in most states of the American southwest. "Community property," the idea that property accumulated during marriage is owned equally by both spouses, is fundamental in Spanish law. When divorce became more common in the United States, the principle of community property in the division of marital assets became more widespread. Water law in the United States differs in the East from the West, with the West following Spanish legal principles guaranteeing access to water to those who do not have direct frontage on streams.

Another obvious legacy of the colonial era in Greater Mexico is the use of the Spanish language. In the U.S.-Mexican borderlands, Spanish has rapidly evolved into a new mainstream language that has spread beyond the traditional boundaries of family, culture, and music. Today in the United States major corporations advertise their products in Spanish and English and have Hispanic divisions dedicated to developing the Spanish-speaking market. Targeted advertising can take some interesting turns. Miller Lite beer, for example, became the official sponsor of the Mexican national soccer (*fútbol*) team, outbidding offers from other U.S. beer companies as well as the major Mexican breweries. In places like San Diego, Los Angeles, and San Antonio, Spanish-language stations compete successfully with the major

Figure 18-2 **Priest blessing a car.** Roman Catholicism remains a potent force among Mexicans. Given high rates of automobile accidents, having one's car blessed also may be a form of insurance.
Photo by Juan Javier Pescador.

networks for prime time ratings. Nearly all substantial U.S. cities have Spanish-language radio stations and newspapers.

In public schools across the United States, Anglo students study Spanish as their second language, far outdistancing French, which has lost its cachet as the international language of the elite. It has been replaced by English, which many upwardly mobile Mexicans now study. Mexican Spanish has many regional variations, with indigenous words making their way into everyday speech, particularly names of foods, plants, and animals and increasingly in the names that parents give their children to reaffirm their real or perceived indigenous heritage.

Other, less positive, legacies of the colonial era include racial and class attitudes that denigrate the living descendants of Mexico's indigenous and racially mixed people. Racial and ethnic perceptions in contemporary Mexico shape and condition the lives of millions of citizens in ways that are reminiscent of the social and ethnic constructs of the colonial world. Millions of Indians in Mexico still suffer from discriminatory practices and are ignored by federal and state governments. The roots of the 1994 Zapatista rebellion in Chiapas, which began as the North American Free Trade Agreement came into force, can be traced to long-standing patterns that stretch far back in time. Mexico's Indians are often seen by urban dwellers as ignorant, rude, lazy, and prone to criminal behavior and assumed to be culturally conservative, even reactionary, religious fanatics who represent an obstacle to Mexico's progress as a modern nation in a global economy.

In the Mexican media, which are heavily influenced by American and European notions of beauty and fashion, stout Indians and dark-skinned Mexicans appear only sporadically. In Mexican sitcoms, Indian women are regularly featured as housemaids for urban middle-class families, a stereotype based on social and economic realities. These Indian domestic workers usually have names intended to be humorous—Petronila, Pancrasia, Domitilia—and the Indian woman's role as the foil to her upscale employers hinges on her ostensible ignorance, lack of manners, or just plain stupidity. Intended to represent backwardness, the Indian housemaid provides a counterpoint to the lifestyle of the family members, who speak, dress, think, and live as modern Mexicans.

Racial hierarchies continue to influence the lives of Mexicans in many ways, and the Spanish heritage is still privileged in professional, artistic, and political circles. College professors, politicians, and artists boast of real or imagined ancestors from Spain. Hispanic elites living in the U.S.-Mexico border region often prefer to identify with a *sui generis* Spanish ancestry rather than embracing their mestizo past. This fantasy heritage, a colonial creation reinforced by the discrimination that Mexicans and Chicanos face in the United States, has given rise to numerous civic, social, and cultural activities in New Mexico, Texas, Arizona, and California in which some Spanish-surnamed families proudly embrace the Spanish conquerors as their direct ancestors.

In the United States, the Spanish past, real or imagined, is commemorated in monuments and streets, and national and state parks bear the names of Spanish conquerors, celebrating the arrival of the first Europeans in the Southwest. Other aspects of popular culture in the United States also reflect Spanish and Mexican influence. Quiz shows, such as the long-running *Jeopardy*, include questions on historical figures such as Hernando de Soto, Vázquez de Coronado, and Cabeza de Vaca.

Among elites in Mexico there is a strong inclination in recent years to privilege Spanish heritage. Whether at academic conferences or social gatherings, people of Spanish ancestry speak affectionately of their origins, and they consider their journeys to Spain and Europe as fundamental stages in their careers and lives. Considered a rite of passage by members of the Mexican upper class, the trip to Spain and Europe mirrors the mentality of the colonial creole, who searched for affirmation and validation in the Iberian peninsula. Elite families still consider Spanish immigrants, now a demographically insignificant group in Mexico, to be ideal marriage choices. In promoting their products many corporations use Spanish culture to symbolize refinement, nobility, honesty, tradition, success, and purity. At the end of the twentieth century the Spanish presence once again became significant in Mexico. As Mexico becomes increasingly integrated into the world economy, Spanish firms have expanded their presence and levels of investment in Mexico. Spanish financial corporations from Cantabria and the Basque country presently own two of the three largest banks in Mexico.

Just as the colonial Mexican upper class created an elaborate terminology for racially mixed people that reflected their own insecurities and desire to distance themselves from the masses, modern Mexican elites show their contempt for those masses through a vocabulary of epithets for those who are darker, rural, and less sophisticated, calling them *nacos* in southern Mexico or *cholos* in the north. The term naco reflects both racial and social prejudice and is all but indistinguishable from the colonial terms *plebe* or *lépero*. In Mexican television sitcoms, the naco usually plays the supporting role of the sidekick, characterized by a blunt sense of humor as well as the inability to see beyond such immediate concerns as food, alcohol, and sex. Among Mexican elites the term naco also refers to the upwardly mobile whose dark skin bars them from further social ascent or people who belong to provincial nonelite families.

Working-class and rural Mexicans do not identify with Spain and Spanish culture, nor do they suffer the insults of Mexican elites without resentment. One achievement of the Mexican Revolution and the Institutional Revolutionary Party that ruled Mexico for seventy years was to bring legitimacy to Mexico's mestizo and indigenous past and empower mestizos in the new political order. Revolutionary ideology glorifying the indigenous heritage still is rooted in the colonial past. In Mexico the conquest of the Aztecs is not generally seen as the triumph of a superior European culture over an inferior indigenous one but rather the crushing of Mexico's own high civilization. To sell out Mexican national interests is to practice *malinchismo*, relegating Malinche (Doña Marina) to the role of traitor. As the five-hundredth anniversary of the conquest of Mexico approaches (2019–21) its commemoration both inside and outside Mexico will reflect a great deal about modern attitudes toward the event.

In Mexico the vestiges of colonial dismissal of Indian culture are manifest in institutions of higher education, where courses in Indian languages are seldom offered, whereas English and French are standard curricular requirements. Mexican intellectuals use European and American theoretical frameworks to undertand the Mexican past and present. The National School of Anthropology has more instructors from Europe and the United States than from Mexican indigenous groups. Indians participate in this school mainly as language instructors, valued for their linguistic skills and cultural insights.

Mexico's desire to preserve the records of its colonial past, however, has seen the creation of the National Archives (AGN) and the National Library (BN) as well as the INAH. These rich collections of records in indigenous languages and Spanish, together with pictorial documents, allow scholars from Mexico and abroad to reconstruct the colonial past in meticulous detail.

Regional differences are still evident in Mexico, products of the natural environment and human adaptations to it over the centuries as well as politics. Regional differences carry social weight, dividing people from the capital from the rest of the country, people from the north from those of the south, and urban residents from campesinos. Each state has a derogatory term for people in bordering states; *Chilangos* (the slang term for people from Mexico City) are despised by everyone else. In Mexico the historic socioeconomic, cultural, and administrative predominance of Mexico City continues to translate into notable economic, educational, and cultural advantages for those who live in the Federal District.

The patterns and direction of economic change and development that characterized New Spain during the colonial period are also still evident. The northward movement that began with the discovery of silver in Zacatecas in 1546, drawing thousands of Indians from their homes in central and western Mexico, has burgeoned in modern times. As the border region develops economically, cities such as Ciudad Juárez and Tijuana continue to grow exponentially, drawing migrants from other parts of Mexico. As the migration of Mexicans to the north accelerates, its logical extension is the movement of Mexicans into areas that once belonged to New Spain and now are part of the United States. Settlements that originated as precarious northern presidios, missions, and towns such as Los Angeles, San Francisco, San Diego, Albuquerque, El Paso, and San Antonio are now vibrant metropolises with significant populations of Mexican origin. Other smaller centers draw tourists and upscale residents in part because of their colonial architecture and beautiful surroundings, such as Taos and Santa Fe in New Mexico and Carmel and Santa Barbara in California.

The modernization of Mexico, based on the displacement of native communities and transformation of Indian peasants into urban laborers, has deep colonial roots. The incorporation of local populations into a global economy, initiated with the Spanish conquest, has dramatically accelerated in modern times; today the Mexican economy is integrated into the capitalist world economy. In the year 2000 the greatest sources of revenue for the Mexican economy were oil and manufacturing exports, remittances sent home by immigrants working in the United States., and tourism. In the 1980s and 1990s, the Institutional Revolutionary Party dismantled mercantilist policies and ones that give special protection to Indians pursuing subsistence agriculture. This initiative culminated in the repeal of Article 27 of the 1917 Constitution and the signing of the North American Free Trade Act with the United States.

Patriarchal and kinship principles inherited from colonial times continue to play a major role in Mexican households. The extended family, together with godparents—compadres and comadres—still constitutes the most important circle for social interaction for Mexicans everywhere. Extended families continue to perform the economic, social, and political roles that developed in colonial times, as seen in both politics and business, which still rely on and reflect kinship and family strategies. The experience of Mexican immigrants in the United States also mirrors the central role of the family as an economic and social unit. Not only do family members follow one another to the United States, immigrants maintain close contact with their relatives in Mexico, sending home money and visiting, and sending or taking their children who may have been born in the United States to visit their Mexican relatives.

Family hierarchies also reflect traditional practices. It is not unusual for the male members of a household to be served their food before the women. The Mexican mother remains the pillar of the household and spiritual center of the family, with the Día de las Madres (May 10) strictly observed by practically all Mexicans. Insults that refer to a person's mother are considered the most offensive of all. Male homosexuality is anathema in Mexico, and the spread of HIV/AIDS has been accelerated by cultural taboos that discourage disclosure of practices that promote its spread among men. A double standard still exists with regard to sexual behavior, tolerating men's extramarital liaisons while condemning women's. Divorce exists in Mexico, but many may be discouraged from pursuing it due to the Catholic Church's stance on lifelong marriage, whatever the circumstances. Sexual violence against women still plagues Mexican society, with wife-beating a common occurrence. In the larger world women are vulnerable without male protectors, and in the absence of an effective social welfare system women often remain in abusive relationships. For some families that have converted to evangelical Protestantism, the strict ban on drinking, gambling, and extramarital liaisons and emphasis on sobriety, thrift, and marital fidelity mean that although patriarchal and traditional gender roles are upheld (men as breadwinners, women as wives and mothers), women's roles are validated. The Catholic Church also has undertaken programs to promote better relations between spouses and their families in the *cursillo* movement.

Despite women's crucial role in the household, they still confront gender inequalities in modern Mexico and have far to go before they achieve equality in the job market. In the political sphere, women only secured the right to vote in Mexico in the 1950s. The reluctance to allow women to vote stemmed in part from patriarchal notions of a woman's proper place and in part from the view of many members of the Institutional Revolutionary Party that women are more religiously inclined than men. Anticlerical politicians worried that enfranchising women would increase the power of the Catholic Church in politics.

Even in more mundane aspects of Mexican life the legacies of the past are notable. There is no better example than that of Mexican cuisine, a hybrid of a myriad of European and indigenous products. There is no traditional Mexican food (be it *tamales, burritos, mole, pozole, enchiladas, menudo,*

Figure 18-3 **House of Tiles, Mexico City**. This colonial-era elite residence continues to be a landmark in the historic city center.
From Nick Caistor, *Mexico City: A Cultural and Literary Companion*. New York: Interlink Books, 2000, p. 202.

barbacoa, or *huachinango al mojo de ajo*) whose origins can be traced solely to one side of the Atlantic. Contemporary Mexican cuisine developed in New Spain as a result of the encounter of Mediterranean and Mesoamerican foodstuffs, spices, and forms of food preparation (usually in the hands of those native women whom elites despise as backward and lazy). Traditional tamales cannot be made without lard, and the paste with which mole is made requires both Old World and indigenous spices for its flavor. In Mexico even the most traditional prehispanic beverages, such as chocolate, are prepared and consumed according to colonial tastes rather than prehispanic ones.

In Mexico City today, Sanborn's restaurant in the highly decorated colonial building known as *Casa de los Azulejos* or House of Tiles suggests some of the cultural contradictions of the country's past and present. The food is a mélange of national cuisines and international dishes, designed to appeal to elite customers. The U.S. firm Walgreen's Drugstores Inc., Sanborn's parent company, bought the building in 1919. Its previous occupant, the high-tone and exclusive Jockey Club, folded during the Mexican Revolution, to be transformed briefly into a "Workers' House" under President Venustiano Carranza.

The House of Tiles has a long history. Originally constructed by Indian laborers in 1596, it was rebuilt early in the eighteenth century as the residence of a wealthy hacendado, the Count of Orizaba. With its blue and white tiles designed in Spain and stone quarried in Mexico, it was as remarkable then as it is now. Mexico's past and present come together in this place as in countless others throughout the country, living legacies of her indigenous and colonial history.

Glossary

Casa de los Azulejos   House of Tiles
ejido   communally owned land
frontera   frontier, border region
fútbol   soccer
lépero   vulgar, lower-class person
malinchismo   betrayal of Mexican interests (from Malinche)
maquiladora   assembly plant
naco   derogatory Mexican term for people of the lower class

Questions for Discussion

1.   To what extent do racial categories still figure in Mexican society?

2.   What are the colonial roots of contemporary Mexican Christianity?

3.   How has the colonial legacy shaped family values and gender differences?

4.   How has modern economic development followed colonial patterns?

5.   In what ways do contemporary Mexican elites resemble their colonial counterparts?

6.   What are the greatest differences between colonial-era and contemporary Mexicans?

Suggested Reading

Brenner, Anita. *The Wind that Swept Mexico: The History of the Mexican Revolution, 1910–1942.* Austin: University of Texas Press, 1973. Includes photos of the Mexican Revolution, including one of Zapatistas at the lunch counter of Sanborn's.

Caistor, Nick. *Mexico City: A Cultural and Literary Companion.* New York: Interlink Books, 2000. Lively account of major landmarks of the capital.

Candell, Jonathan. *La Capital: The Biography of Mexico City.* New York: Random House, 1988. Accessible history of the capital.

Cline, Howard F. *The United States and Mexico.* New York: Athenaeum Press, 1963. Overview of Mexican history with particular attention to U.S.-Mexico relations.

Cypess, Sandra Messinger. *La Malinche in Mexican Literature: From History to Myth.* Austin: University of Texas Press, 1991. Thorough examination of Doña Marina and her place in Mexican culture.

Krauze, Enrique. *Mexico: Biography of Power.* Translated by Hank Heifetz. New York: HarperCollins, 1997. Major work by one of Mexico's premier historians, emphasizing the impact of individual leaders on its modern history.

Nutini, Hugo. *Todos Santos in Rural Tlaxcala: A Syncretic, Expressive, and Symbolic Analysis of the Cult of the Dead.* Princeton, N.J.: Princeton University Press, 1988. Modern anthropological study of the beliefs and observances surrounding this holiday.

Paz, Octavio. *The Labyrinth of Solitude.* New York: Grove Press, 1961. Classic essays on Mexican culture and identity by Mexico's Nobel Prize–winning poet.

Riding, Alan. *Distant Neighbors: A Portrait of Mexicans.* New York: Knopf, 1985. Lengthy examination of Mexican society and politics by an American journalist, emphasizing U.S.-Mexican relations.

Schaefer, Claudia. *Textured Lives: Women, Art and Representation in Modern Mexico*. Tucson: University of Arizona Press, 1992. Examination of well-known women in Mexican culture, including Kahlo, Castellanos, and Poniatowska.

Toor, Frances. *Mexican Folkways*. New York: Crown, 1947. A collection of essays and anecdotes on popular culture in Mexico during the 1930s and 1940s.

Suggested Reading in Spanish

Chapter 1: Mexican Peoples and Cultures

Carrasco, Pedro and Johanna Broda, eds. *Economía política e ideología en el México prehispánico*. Mexico: Editorial Nueva Imagen, 1978. Important anthology of articles on prehispanic central Mexico by major ethnohistorians.

Caso, Alfonso. *Los calendarios prehispánicos*. Mexico: UNAM, Instituto de Investigaciones Históricos, 1967. Classic study by one of Mexico's leading scholars postulating the existence of a single calendrical system in ancient Mexico with regional variations.

Codex Boturini (Tira de Peregrinación). Mexico: Libraría Anticuaria, 1944. Facsimile of the pictorial screenfold showing the migration of the Aztecs to central Mexico.

Historia Tolteca-Chichimeca. Paul Kirchhoff, Lena Odena Güemes, and Luis Reyes García, eds. Mexico: Instituto Nacional de Antropología e Historia, 1976. Facsimile of an important manuscript in Nahuatl with full color pictorials on prehispanic Nahua history.

Huehuetlatolli. Mexico: Comisión Nacional Conmemorativa del V Centenario del Encuentro de Dos Mundos, 1988. Facsimile and translation of a collection of classical Nahuatl texts of speeches parents deliver to children on moral and political matters collected by Franciscan Juan Bautista.

Matrícula de Tributos. Commentary by Frances F. Berdan and Jacqueline de Durand-Forest. Graz: Akademische Druck, 1980. Facsimile of a major Nahua codex dealing with tribute and other economic data.

Chapter 2: Spain in the Era of Expansion

Bennassar, Bartolomé. *La España del siglo de oro*. Trans. by Pablo Bordonava. Barcelona: Editorial Crítica, 1983. Overview of the Golden Age by a leading French historian of early modern Spain.

Ladero Quesada, Miguel Angel. *España en 1492*. Madrid: Editorial Hernando, 1978. Brief examination of aspects of Spanish society, economy, and politics by a leading Spanish historian of the late Middle Ages.

Moya Pons, Frank. *Después de Colón. Trabajo, sociedad y política en la economía del oro*. Madrid: Alianza Editorial, 1986. Study of the first thirty years of Spanish activity in the Caribbean (mainly Hispaniola).

Nebrija, Antonio de. *Vocabulario de Romance en Latín* (1516), Gerald J. MacDonald, ed. Madrid: Castalia, 1973. Edition of the 1492 dictionary, which served as a model for mendicant dictionaries of Mesoamerican languages.

Chapter 3: Conquest and Colonization

Zavala, Silvio. *La encomienda indiana*. Madrid: Centro de Estudios Históricos, 1935. Classic study of the encomienda by a premier Mexican historian.

———. *Tributos y servicios personales de indios para Hernán Cortés y su familia*. Mexico: Archivo General de la Nación, 1984. Extracts from the national archives concerning Cortés's early holdings.

Chapter 4: Narratives of Conquest

Baudot, Georges and Tzvetan Todorov. *Relatos aztecas de la conquista*. Mexico: Grijalbo, Consejo Nacional para la Cultura y las Artes, 1983. Native sources on the conquest in both Nahuatl and Spanish.

Chapter 5: Mexico and the Columbian Exchange

Rojas Rabiela, Teresa. *Las siembras de ayer: La agricultura indígena del siglo XVI*. Mexico: Secretaría de Educación Pública, 1988. In-depth study of sixteenth-century indigenous agricultural techniques.

Von Wobeser, Gisela. *La formación de la hacienda en la época colonial: El uso de la tierra y el agua*. Mexico: Universidad Nacional Autónoma de México, 1983. Study of the development of haciendas and land usage in central Mexico with extensive use of colonial maps.

Chapter 6: Christianity in Colonial Mexico

Cuevas, Mariano, S.J. *Historia de la iglesa en México*. 5 volumes. Mexico: Editorial Porrúa, 1921–8, 1992. Unsurpassed general history of the church in Mexico by a Jesuit historian.

Churruca Peláez, Agustín, S.J. *Primeras fundaciones jesuitas en Nueva España, 1572–1580*. Mexico: Editorial Porrúa, 1980. Useful work by a Jesuit on the Society's earliest years in Mexico.

Códice franciscano: siglo xvi. Mexico: Chávez Hayho, 1941. Compilation of sixteenth-century Franciscan reports on the early spiritual conquest.

Dávila Padilla, Agustín. *Historia de la fundación y discurso de la Provincia de México de la orden de Predicadores*. Mexico: Editorial Academia Literaria, 1955. History of the Dominican Order in the sixteenth century.

Gómez Canedo, Lino. *Evangelización y conquista*. Mexico: Editorial Porrúa, 1988. Analysis of Franciscan evangelization in the New World.

León Alanís, Ricardo. *Los orígenes del clero y la iglesia en Michoacán, 1525–1640*. Universidad de Michoacan de San Nicolás Hidalgo: Instituto de Investigaciones Históricas, 1997. Analysis of the evangelization of several religious orders and of the formation of the diocesan clergy.

Mendieta, Fray Gerónimo de. *Historia eclesiástica indiana*. Mexico: Editorial Porrúa, 1971. Important chronicle by a sixteenth-century Franciscan.

Toribio Medina, José. *Historia del tribunal del Santo Oficio de la Inquisición en México*. Mexico: Editorial Miguel Angel Porrúa and Coordinación de Humanidades UNAM (1908), 1987. Classic history of the institution from its founding to the independence era.

Torquemada, Fray Juan de. *Monarquía indiana*. 3 vols. Mexico: Editorial Porrúa, 1969. Facsimile of the history of the Franciscan evangelization of Mexico.

Torre Villar, Ernesto de la and Ramiro Navarro de Anda, eds. *Testimonios históricos guadalupanos*. Mexico: Fondo de Cultura Económico, 1982. Collection of texts on the Virgin of Guadalupe, with introductory notes.

Vetancurt, Fray Agustín de. *Teatro mexicano: Crónica de la Provincia del Santo Evangelio de México (1698)*. Mexico: Editorial Porrúa, 1971. Facsimile of the chronicle of the seventeenth-century Franciscans.

Uchmany, Eva Alexandra. *La vida entre el judaísmo y el cristianismo en la Nueva España, 1580–1606*. Mexico: Archivo General de la Nación and El Colegio de México, 1992. Careful examination of two Inquisition trials of a crypto-Jewish family and the larger cultural context.

Chapter 7: Mesoamerican Indians under Colonial Rule

Carrasco, Pedro and Jesús Monjarás-Ruiz. *Colección de documentos sobre Coyoacan*. 2 vols. Mexico: Instituto Nacional de Antropología e Historia, 1976, 1978. Early documents in Spanish and Nahuatl with Spanish translations for a major central Mexican Nahua town.

Códice Osuna. Mexico: Edición del Instituto Indigenista Interamericano, 1947. Facsimile edition of a Nahuatl and pictorial complaint to Spanish authorities about Spanish cruelties.

De la Torre Villar, Ernesto. *Las congregaciones de los pueblos de indios*. Mexico: Universidad Nacional Autónoma de México, 1995. Collection of documents dealing with *congregación* for individual communities.

García Martínez, Bernardo. *Los pueblos de la sierra: El poder y el espacio entre los indios del norte de Puebla hasta 1700*. Mexico: El Colegio de México, 1987. Regional study of changes in Nahua towns.

Prem, Hans J. *Matrícula de Huexotzinco*. Graz: Akademische Druck, 1974. Facsimile of the sixteenth-century codex with an introduction by Pedro Carrasco.

Reyes García, Luis, ed. *Documentos sobre tierras y señoríos en Cuauhtinchan*. Mexico: Instituto Nacional de Antropología e Historia, 1978. Compilation of documents in Nahuatl and Spanish.

Chapter 8: Economy and Society in the Middle Period

García-Abasolo, Antonio F. *Martín Enríquez y la reforma de 1568 en Nueva España*. Seville: Diputación Provincial de Sevilla, 1983. An examination of an important reformist viceroy, with chapters on mining, agricultural production, herding, and royal treasury.

Miranda, José. *La función económica del encomendero en los orígenes del régimen colonial (Nueva España, 1525–1531)*. Mexico: Universidad Antónoma Nacional de México, 1965. Important study of early encomiendas in Mexico.

Peña, José F. de la. *Oligarquía y propiedad en Nueva España, 1550–1624*. Mexico: Fondo de Cultura Económico, 1983. Examination of sources of wealth and the economic activities of New Spain's wealthiest citizens.

Ruiz Medrano, Ethelia. *Gobierno y sociedad en Nueva España: Segunda Audiencia y Antonio de Mendoza*. El Colegio de Michoacán, 1991. Detailed examination of the activities of the second audiencia and its relationship with the encomendero and corregidor groups.

Sánchez Rubio, Rocío and Isabel Testón Núñez. *El hilo que une: Las relaciones epistolares en el Viejo y el Nuevo Mundo (siglos XVI–XVIII)*. Mérida: Universidad de Extremadura y Junta de Extremadura, 1999. Letters written to and from men and women in Spain and New Spain.

Viquera, Carmen and José I. Urquiola. *Los obrajes en la Nueva España 1530–1630*. Mexico: Consejo Nacional para la Cultura y las Artes, 1990. Study of the development of early textile workshops in central Mexico.

Zavala, Silvio. *Libros de asientos de la gobernación de la Nueva España*. Mexico: Archivo General de la Nación, 1982. Extracts from the national archives of Mexico concerning agriculture, transportation, mining, and Indian communities during the term of Viceroy Velasco, 1550–2.

Chapter 9: The Northern Frontier

Saravia, Atanasio G. *Apuntes para la historia de la Nueva Vizcaya.* 2 vols. Mexico: Universidad Nacional Autónoma de México, 1978. Monographs on the settlement of Nueva Vizcaya; the city of Durango; northern Indian revolts; and missionaries who died in the north.

Chapter 10: The African Presence in New Spain

Beltrán, Gonzalo Aguirre. *La población negra de México.* Mexico: Fondo de Cultura Económica, 1972 (2nd ed.) Fundamental study of Africans in colonial Mexico that includes consideration of the slave trade, ethnic origins, and Africans' experiences in slavery and freedom.

Montiel, Luz María Martínez, ed. *Presencia africana en México.* Mexico: Consejo Nacional para la Cultura y las Artes, 1994. Articles by various scholars on Africans in Puebla, Michoacan, Guanajuato, Nuevo León, Colima, Campeche, Tabasco, Tamaulipas, and Veracruz.

Chapter 11: Elite and Popular Culture

Argudín, Yolanda. *Historia del teatro en México.* Mexico: Panorama Editorial, 1985. Concise history of theater in Mexico from the prehispanic era to the twentieth century.

Garibay, Angel María. *Historia de la literatura Náhual.* 2 vols. Mexico: Editorial Porrúa, 1953. Examination of Nahual texts of the sixteenth century.

Gómez Canedo, Lino. *La educación de los marginados durante la época colonial.* Mexico: Editorial Porrúa, 1982. Study of schools and colegios for Indians and mestizos in New Spain.

Horacasitas, Fernando. *El teatro nahuatl.* Mexico: Editorial Porrúa, 1974. Major account of Nahuatl theatre in the immediate postconquest period.

Lavrin, Asunción. "La vida feminina como experiencia religiosa: Biografía y hagiografía en Hispanoamérica colonial," *Colonial Latin American Historical Review* 2 (1993): 27–52. Biographies of individual Mexican nuns and a discussion of ideals of holiness in the colonial era.

Muriel, Josefina. *Conventos de monjas en la Nueva España.* Mexico: Editorial Jus, 1995. Important study of nuns and convents, with fascinating illustrations.

Poot-Herrera, Sara, *Sor Juana y su mundo: Una mirada actual.* Mexico: Universidad del Claustro de Sor Juana, 1995. A major anthology of writings on Sor Juana and her cultural milieu.

Sartor, Mario. *Arquitectura y urbanismo en Nueva España, siglo xvi.* Mexico: Grupo Azabache, 1987. Examination of ecclesiastical and civil architecture of the early colonial period.

Tovar de Teresa, Guillermo, *La ciudad de México y la utopia en el siglo XVI.* Mexico: Seguros de México, 1987.

————. *Pintura y escultura en Nueva España (1557–1640).* Mexico: Grupo Azabache, 1992.

Weckman, Luis. *La herencia medieval de México.* Mexico: El Colegio de México, 1983, 1984 (English: *The Medieval Heritage of Mexico,* New York: Fordham University Press, 1992). Wide-ranging examination of the impact of medieval Spanish culture on the development of civil and religious institutions, as well as popular secular and religious practices.

Chapter 12: Rebellion and Crime

Lozano Armendares, Teresa. *La criminalidad en la ciudad de México 1800–21.* Mexico: Universidad Nacional Autónoma de México, 1987. Analysis of criminal records for the late colonial period.

Martin Norman F. *Los vagabundos de la Nueva España, siglo XVI.* Mexico: Jus, 1957. Examination of vagrants in colonial Mexico.

Chapter 13: Race, Class, and Family

Gonzalbo, Pilar, coord. *Familias Novohispanas, siglos XVI al XIX.* Mexico: El Colegio de México, 1991. Studies of marriage, gender, family, and household in colonial and early republican Mexico.

Gonzalbo Aizpuru, Pilar y Cecilia Rabell Romero, coords. *Familia y Vida Privada en la historia de Iberoamerica.* Mexico: El Colegio de México, UNAM, 1996. Studies of family and gender in Latin America.

"La Demografía histórica mexicana," in *Estudios Demográficos y Urbanos* no.19. Mexico: El Colegio de México, 1992.

"La Pintura de Castas," in *Artes de Mexico,* no. 8. Mexico, 1998. Examination of the pinturas de castas by historians and art historians.

Pescador, Juan Javier. *De Bautizados a fieles difuntos: Familia y Mentalidades en una parroquia urbana, Santa Catarina de Mexico, 1568–1821.* Mexico: El Colegio de México, 1992. Sociodemographic study of a central Mexico City parish.

Chapter 14: Economy and Society in the Late Colonial Period

Florescano, Enrique. *Precios del maíz y crisis agrícolas en México (1708–1810).* Mexico: Ediciones Era, 1969. Study of trends of maize prices and their implications in late colonial Mexico City.

Florescano, Enrique and Isabel Gil Sánchez. *Descripciones económicas generales de Nueva España, 1784–1817.* Mexico: Instituto Nacional de Antropología e Historia, 1973. Primary sources for the economic history of Mexico generated during the viceregal term of Revillagigedo.

———. *Descripciones económicas regionales de Nueva España, Provincias del Centro, Sureste y Sur, 1766–1827.* Mexico: Instituto Nacional de Antropología e Historia, 1976. Primary source information on the economy from diverse regions of Mexico during the late colonial period.

Chapter 15: The Bourbon Era

Vázquez, Josefina Zoraida, coord. *Interpretaciones del siglo XVIII mexicano: El impacto de las reformas borbónicas.* Mexico: Nueva Imagen, 1992. Articles by Josefina Zoraida Vázquez, Horst Pietschmann, Brian R. Hamnett, Pedro Pérez Herrero, Carlos Marichal, and David A. Brading.

Chapter 16: The Northern Borderlands

Alessio Robles, Vito. *Coahuila y Texas en la época colonial.* Mexico City: Editorial Cultura, 1938. Important work based on archival sources.

Gomez Canedo, Lino, ed. *Primeras exploraciones y poblamiento de Texas.* Monterrey: ITESM, 1968.

Tamaron y Romeral, Pedro. *Demostración del vastísimo Obispado de la Nueva Vizcaya, 1765: Durango, Sinaloa, Sonora, Arizona, Nuevo Mexico, Chihuahua y porciones de Texas, Coahuila y Zacatecas.* With an introduction, bibliography, and notes by Vito Alessio Robles. Mexico City: Antigua Librería Robredo, de Jose Porrua e hijos, 1937.

Chapter 17: The Struggle for Independence

Alamán, Lucas. *Historia de Méjico desde los primeros movimientos que prepararon su independencia en el año de 1808 hasta la época presente.* Mexico: Imprenta de J. M. Lara, 1850. Major multivolume history written by a leading conservative Mexican historian.

Bustamante, Carlos María de. *Cuadro histórico de la revolución mexicana, comenzada por el ciudadano Miguel Hidalgo y Costilla, cura del pueblo de los Dolores, en el obispado de Michoacán.* Mexico: Imprenta de J. M. Lara, 1843–6. Multivolume history by a major nineteenth-century historian.

Guedea, Virginia. *En busca de un gobierno alterno: Los Guadalupes de Mexico.* Mexico: UNAM, 1992. Study of the clandestine group of supporters of the insurrection in Mexico City.

Chapter 18: Colonial Legacies

Anguiana, Marina, et al. *Las tradiciones del Día de los Muertos en México.* Mexico, 1987. Descriptions of regional celebrations in Mexico.

Poniatowska, Elena. *Las siete cabritas.* Mexico: Biblioteca Era, 2000. Essays by a major Mexican intellectual on important modern women.

Index

Abad y Queipo, Bishop Manuel 345–46
abasto 181,182, 286, 297
Academy of San Carlos 303
Acapulco 65, 155, 175, 177,179,180, 182–83, 358
Acaxee 252
Acoma 323
Act of Consolidation of 1804, 289, 311
adelantado 54
Africans 41, 97, 100, 149, 166, 204–224, 264 (see also slavery)
agriculture 12–13, 21, 40–41, 111, 163, 166–67, 194, 200, 285–89, 331, 334
Aguayo, Marqueses de 197, 211, 286, 329
Aguilar, Fray Francisco O.P. 80
Aguilar, Gerónimo de 56, 58, 79
Alamán, Lucas 355
Albuquerque 323, 325, 372
alcabala 36, 50, 153, 306
alcalde 50, 147, 158
alcalde de crimen 307, 317
alcaldes mayores 312, 317
Alfonso X *"el sabio"* 29, 40
alhóndiga 248, 256, 344, 360
Allende, Ignacio 344, 346, 348
almaceneros 296, 297
Alta California 131, 332–33, 363
altepetl 145, 158
Alva Ixtlilxochitl, Don Fernando de 20, 68, 82–84, 90, 146, 234
Alvarado, Pedro de 54, 58, 59, 63, 67, 69–70, 77, 79–80, 250–251
Americanos 347, 360
Anasazi 14, 16
Anza, Juan Bautista 325, 333, 336
Antequera (see also Oaxaca) 65, 126, 221
Apaches 200, 252, 320, 325, 330, 331, 334–35, 336, 337, 338
Aparicio, Fray Sebastián O.F.M. 135
arancel 312–13, 317
Aragón 34, 35, 36, 38, 41, 46
Arizona 190
Arizpe 306
Army of the Three Guarantees 350
arrieros 155, 179, 182

artisans 68, 151, 172, 175, 180, 210, 222, 236, 295 (see also guilds)
audiencia 35, 49, 50, 69, 70, 162, 191, 195, 293, 309–10, 313, 317, 343
Augustinian Order 37, 124–25
auto de fe 121, 128, 136, 237, 244, 364
aviadores 178, 182, 292
Aztec Empire 7–8, 17, 19–20, 23–24, 61, 63, 64, 145
Aztecs 16, 17, 18–19, 73

Baja California 131, 332–33
Bajío 163, 173, 287, 288, 344, 346, 354, 356
bakeries 175,181, 295
ball game 15
bando 360
barrio 180, 182
Basques 28, 32, 40, 45, 136, 168, 193, 296, 197, 302, 303, 322, 371
beata 130
Black Legend 90
Borda, José de la 291, 292
Bourbon dynasty 300, 302, 312, 341, 342–43
Bourbon policies 284, 294, 290, 297, 334, 354, 356
bozal 206, 208, 222
Britain 293, 296, 297, 302, 313, 341
bullfights 45, 226, 238, 304

caballería 182, 297
cabecera 145, 148, 182
Cabeza de Vaca, Alva Núñez 186–87, 370
cabildo, indigenous 67, 147; Mexican 181
cacao 11, 14, 64, 107, 176, 179, 296, 297
cacicazgo 145, 159
caciques 47, 48, 50, 54, 73, 78, 82, 145, 151, 157, 158, 159, 264, 270
Cádiz 40, 296, 297, 342, 343, 352
cah 145, 159
Calleja, Félix María 346, 351, 357, 358
caja de comunidad 148, 159
Caja Real 338
calidad 197, 261, 279
California 190, 320, 338
calpulli 16, 24
Camino Real 192, 201, 325, 336

Campeche 165, 285, 301
Canary Islands 46, 53, 329
cannibalism 23, 78
capellanía 127, 137, 157
capitán 290, 297
capitulaciones 56
Caribbean 46–50, 53, 54, 63, 97, 100, 180, 204, 206, 207
Carlos of Texcoco, Don 128
Carjaval, Luis 195
castas 265–67, 279
caste paintings 277–78
Castile, 28, 32, 34, 35–36, 41, 168, 182
Castilian language 28, 38, 79
Catholic Monarchs 27, 35–37
Catholicism, Spanish 29
Catorce 291, 292, 293
cattle 40, 105, 110, 165, 167, 168, 207, 322, 329–300, 348
caudillo 359, 360
Cempoala 57
cenote 10, 24
Cervantes de Salazar, Francisco 89, 228
chancellería 35, 50
Charles V 35, 37–38, 41, 62, 69, 79, 236
Chiapas 11, 15, 23, 64, 107, 123, 135, 147, 254, 308, 362
Chicano 91, 362, 367–68, 370
Chichimeca 191–92, 202, 214–15, 249, 250, 251–52, 320, 321, 334
Chihuahua 169, 170, 192, 196, 201, 252, 294, 320, 322, 323, 334
chili peppers 108–09
Chilpancingo Congress 347–48
Chimalpahin 110–11, 129, 230
China Poblana 135
chinampas 20, 24, 153, 157
chocolate (see also cacao) 14, 107–08, 175, 375
Cholula 57, 58
Christianization (see also evangelization, missionization) 80, 82, 84, 194, 198; resistance to 249, 250–52
Church 115–39 (see also cofradias, diocesan clergy, secular clergy, indigenous Catholicism)
church buildings 45, 117, 119, 126, 156, 227, 237, 253, 365
Church finance 45–46, 116, 127, 128, 130, 131–32, 168, 227, 311–12,
Church organization 36, 116–117, 119, 125–28, 136, 148, 227, 312–13
Church racial divisions 122–23, 127, 128, 130, 132, 148, 274–75, 313
Church-state relations 36, 50, 68–69, 115, 116–17, 126, 127, 130, 131–32, 227, 244, 246–47, 312–13, 355–57, 366
Cibola (see Seven Golden Cities)

cimarrón 214–15, 216, 222
Cisneros, Cardinal Francisco Jiménez de 36
cities, Iberian 28, 30, 32, 34, 38–39, 41–42, 44, 296
cities and towns, Mexican Spanish 65–66, 68, 105, 130, 136, 163, 180–82, 191, 193, 196–97, 222, 244, 263, 267, 282, 351
city-states, indigenous 7, 11, 18, 19, 20, 22, 24, 57, 82, 145, 148
Clavigero, Francisco, S.J. 90–91, 129
Coahuila 321, 326–330
cochineal 106, 153, 165, 173, 293, 296
cofradía 45, 50,132, 136, 156, 215, 221–22, 226, 254, 265, 312
colegio 131, 317, 328, 332, 344
Colegio de Santa Cruz Tlatelolco 103, 122–23
Columbian exchange 97–112
Columbus, Christopher 7, 27,28, 46–48
Comanche 200, 320, 325, 335, 337, 338
comercio libre 292, 296, 298, 301, 306 (see also trade)
compadrazgo 158, 176, 372–73
compañía 176, 182, *compañías volantes* 336–37
composición 152, 165, 182
Concho 200
conciliar government 36
confraternity (see cofradia)
congregación 105, 112, 148,159
conquest 53–59, 63–64, 116
conquest narratives 73–92
Conquistadora, La 136, 323 illustration 324
Constitution of 1812, 341, 342, 349, 351, 352, 353, 358–59
Consulado 178, 182, 283, 296, 297, 298, 316, 343
contribuciones militares 358, 360
convents 44, 122, 129–30, 168, 211, 227, 228, 230–31, 232, 269
convivencia 31, 32, 50
conversion, indigenous 83, 84
conversos 31, 45, 50
corn (see maize)
Coronado, Francisco Vázquez de 189–90, 198, 370
corporate organization 43, 244
corregidor 38–39, 50, 67, 264
corregimiento 67, 146, 306
Cortes 36, 50, 342, 350, 351, 353, 360
Cortés, Hernando 21, 49, 54, 55, 56–60, 62–66, 69–70, 73, 74, 75–77, 79–80, 81, 86, 87, 90, 92, 103, 107, 117, 119, 144, 147, 166, 190, 211, 216–18, 236, 363, 364, 365
cotton 16, 283, 285, 294
Council of the Indies 35–36, 69, 124, 356
Council of Trent 45, 85, 128, 135
Coyoacan 60, 62

Coyolxauhqui 364
creoles 261, 308, 309, 343, 349, 350, 352
crime 244–46
criollo 208, 209, 222
Cruz, Sor Juana Inés de la 232–34, 236, 364
Cuauhtemoc 19, 58, 60, 63–64
Cuba 49, 54, 56, 57, 285, 294
Cuernavaca 65, 69, 147, 365
Culhuacan 18, 20, 157
Cuitlahuac 19, 58, 101

dádiva 192, 202, 251
dance 236–237, 275
Days of the Dead 275, 367
deforestation 106
De León, Alonso 327–28
Desagüe 106, 112, 151, 159
Díaz del Castillo, Bernal 3, 54, 58, 73,
    77–79, 91–92
Diego, Juan 133, 134, 367
diezmo 131, 137
diocesan clergy 68, 116, 117, 227 (see also
    secular clergy)
doctrina 119, 137
Dominican Order 32, 37, 68, 80, 117, 119,
    120, 123–25, 332
dowry 44
Durán, Fray Diego O.P. 85–86
Durango 127, 201, 252, 271, 276, 306, 325,
    331, 338

economy, Mexican 64–65, 100–01, 104–105,
    131–32, 150–55, 162–182, 282–297, 325–26
economy, Spanish 30, 39–41, 44,
education 30, 42–43, 77, 121–23, 129, 130,
    225, 227–31, 233, 302, 303, 311, 316–17
ejido 375
El Paso (del Norte) 194, 201, 252, 320, 325,
    326, 338, 363, 367, 372
Enlightenment 301, 302–04, 345, 356
entrada 54, 70
encomendero 47, 50, 64, 67, 68, 119, 123, 125,
    144, 146, 175, 264
encomienda 47, 50, 53, 61, 62–65, 74, 76, 82,
    123, 124, 144, 145, 147, 150, 162–63, 193,
    195
español 277, 279 (see also Spaniard)
estancia 164, 167, 182
evangelista 231, 238
evangelization 68–69, 116–125
epidemics 46, 61, 97–103, 135, 136, 199, 333

Ferdinand I, King of Aragón (see also
    Catholic Monarchs) 27, 38
Ferdinand VII 341, 342, 344, 351, 352,
Feyjóo y Montenegro, Gerónimo 302
fiscal 148, 159
France 41, 300, 326–27, 328, 341

Franciscan Order 37, 115, 117,119–23,
    199–200, 251–52, 323, 325, 326, 327–28,
    329, 332–33, 335, 365
fueros 34, 50, 116, 127, 219, 222, 310, 312,
    314, 315, 316, 317
fundo legal 152, 159, 366

gachupines 248, 256, 279, 341, 350, 356, 360
Gage, Thomas 107–08
gañanes 289
Gante, Fray Pedro de 121, 230
Gálvez, Jose de 305–06, 309, 310
gavilla 348, 360
Gelves, Márques de 246–47
General Indian Court 149–50
genízaros 196–97, 202, 253, 256
Genoese 46, 206
gente decente 245, 256
gente de razón 261, 279
geographical zones 5, 10–11
godparenthood see *compadrazgo*
gold 47, 49, 53, 60, 64, 83, 162, 169
Gómara, Francisco López de 59, 77
"Greater Mexico" 6, 8, 9–11, 53, 73–74,
    368
Grijalva, Juan 55, 58
Guadalajara 65, 153, 162, 169, 221, 228, 229,
    235, 250, 271, 282, 283, 286, 294, 297, 306,
    363, 367
Guanajuato 282, 283, 291, 292, 293, 306, 308,
    310, 313, 344, 345
Guatemala 6, 15, 23, 63, 79, 123, 127, 162,
    173, 175, 176,178, 179, 180, 191, 210, 228,
    297, 306, 331, 362
Guerrero, Vicente 216, 350, 363
guilds (see also *Consulado*) 136, 151, 172,
    178, 211, 263, 291, 295, 316
Guzmán, Nuño de 63, 69, 70, 126, 150, 186,
    187, 249–50

Habsburg dynasty 37–38, 41, 302
hacendado 167–68, 182
haciendas 164, 167–68, 170, 193, 213, 216,
    286–290, 311–12 *de beneficio* 291; *de carbon*
    170, *de minas* 170, 213
Hawkins, John 195
heresy 30, 32
Hernández de Córdoba, Francisco 54–55,
    58
Hidalgo y Costilla, Miguel 216, 297, 308,
    344–47, 348, 353, 354, 355, 356, 357, 363,
    364
Hispanization 84, 144, 148–49, 155, 159,
    166, 196, 206, 267, 273–74, 338
Hispaniola 47, 48, 49, 326
honor 268
Hopi 16, 189, 200, 201, 323, 337
horses 60, 110–11. 112, 171, 192, 250, 334

hospitals 103–04, 125, 221, 234, 364
House of Tiles 374, 375
House of Trade 49
Huatulco 177,180
Huejotzinco 122, 150, 242–43
huerta 40, 50
Huitzilopochtli 18, 21, 59
Humboldt, Baron Alexander von 101, 107, 303
human sacrifice 5, 19, 21–22, 78, 124

idolatry 78, 121, 199–200
illegitimacy 43, 44, 271–272, 276, 279
immigration, Spanish 49–50, 63, 65, 67, 68, 177, 178, 216, 263, 370
Independence struggle 337, 341–361
"Indian" 7, 47, 123, 264, 266, 370 (see also individual groups)
Indians, Mesoamerican 143–161
Indians, Northern 185–203, 320–338
Indian special status 122–23, 143, 149, 201, 230, 243, 264, 269, 277, 315, 316, 372
indigenous Catholicism 80, 148, 156–58, 253–55, 275
indigenous languages 7, 86, 112, 120, 128, 155, 158, 229, 362, 371–72
indigenous towns 67, 143–48, 166, 250, 253–55, 264, 267, 286, 366, 372
indigenous writing 81, 86, 147–148, 152, 155, 231, 234
indigo 106, 173, 285, 297
ingenio 167, 182
inheritance 43–44, 105, 269
Inquisition, Holy Office of 45, 128–29, 204, 213, 221, 231, 232, 244, 247, 351, 353, 364
intendancy system 305, 306–09, 313, 317
Isabel, Queen of Spain 27, 28, 35, 36, 47, 143
Iturbide, Agustín de 348, 350, 354, 357, 358
Iturrigaray, José de 343

Jalapa 297
jefe político 360
Jesuits 45, 87, 90, 103, 116, 128, 129, 131, 148, 196, 198–99, 212–13, 229, 288, 289, 303, 305, 309, 310–11, 317, 330, 332, 325, 344, 365
Jesús, St. Felipe de 135
Jews 27, 29, 31, 37, 121, 128, 244
judaizantes 128–29, 195
junta 317, 342, 343, 360

kachina 200, 202
Kino, Eusebio S.J. 330
kiva 199–200, 202

labor 163, 166–67, 172, 362
labor, African 210–212

labor, Mesoamerican (see also *encomienda, repartimiento*) 17, 150–151, 166, 212. 264
labor, Northern 172, 195–96, 200, 207
labor, women's 154, 284, 294–95
labores 288, 298
labrador 40, 50
Lake Texcoco 9, 18, 20, 153
land holding, Mesoamerican 16–17, 151–53, 284
land holding, Spanish 163–65
ladino 144, 159, 206, 222, 254, 256
Lampart, Don Guillén de 129
Landa, Fray Diego de O.F.M.120, 121
LaSalle, Rene Robert 326–27
Las Casas, Fray Bartolomé de O.P. 77, 80, 90, 124
law, indigenous 20–21
law, Spanish 29, 127, 147, 149–50, 205–06, 242–246, 265, 267 (see also *fueros*)
lépero 375
letrado 36, 50
Liberalism 343, 346, 359–360
limosna 131, 137
limpieza de sangre 37
literacy 42, 86, 122, 147, 230–31, 254
Lizardi, José Joaquín Fernández de 278–79, 352
Los Angeles 333, 368, 372
Louisiana 294, 313, 326, 328
Loyola, St. Ignatius de 45 (see also Jesuits)

macehualtin 16
magic 103, 157
maize 11, 12–13, 64, 106–07, 109, 154, 285, 286, 287, 289, 290
Malinche (see Doña Marina)
malinchismo 371, 375
Manila Galleon trade 65, 179, 181–82, 297
manufacturing 173–75, 293–95
Marina, Doña 56, 58, 78–79, 81, 82, 87, 90, 371
markets, indigenous 3, 14
marriage patterns 269, 272–273
Maya 10, 15, 17, 22–23, 55, 63, 66, 74, 87, 97, 121, 145, 159, 253–255
Mayo 198, 200, 330
mayorazgo 145
mayordomo 166, 182, 226
mayordomía 226, 238
medical treatment (see also hospitals) 103–04
mendicant orders 37, 68–69, 84–86, 116, 136, 235
Mendoza, Viceroy Don Antonio de 69, 122–23, 230, 149, 186, 189, 190, 211, 249–51
mercader 177–78,182
mercantilism 301

merced 74–75, 92
merchants 17, 40, 42, 128, 153, 175, 176–77, 178, 179, 283, 295–97, 322, 325
mercury 169,170, 171, 290–91
Mérida 66, 165, 210, 282, 286
Mesoamerica 6, 10, 24, 73, 74
Mesta real 40, 50
Mexica (see also Aztecs, Nahuas) 18, 73, 74, 85, 196
Mexican Spaniards 308, 309, 312, 349, 351
Mexico City 6, 61, 101, 103, 106, 125, 126, 132, 148, 149, 151, 153, 155, 162, 176, 177, 245–249, 271, 282, 286, 294, 295, 297, 304, 315, 351, 372
mestizo 68, 82, 127, 136, 146, 180, 197, 204, 265–67
Michoacan 11, 63, 64, 73, 74, 84, 88, 89, 124, 125, 136, 149, 169, 208, 210, 221, 250, 306, 310, 313, 344
migration 148–49, 196–97
military (see also *presidios*) 19,-20, 21–22, 23, 219–220, 264, 310, 313–16, 320–22, 335, 338, 346, 349, 350, 354, 357–59
military orders 34, 47
mining 47, 106, 153, 162, 168–172,181, 191–93, 282–83, 284, 290–93, 297, 325, 331,349, 366
missions 111, 131, 196, 198–201, 252–53, 327–28, 330, 332–33, 337, 372
Mixtecs 7, 16, 123, 145, 147, 149, 355
Mixtón War 63, 249–251
Monclova 195, 330, 334, 338
Moctezuma 18, 55, 56, 57, 58, 59, 60, 61, 78, 87, 88, 101, 104
Molina, Fray Alonso de O.F.M. 120
Monte Alban 14
Monte de Piedad 227, 238
Montejo, Francisco 63
Montesinos, Fray Antonio de O.P. 48, 124
Montúfar, Fray Alonso de O.P. 125, 132, 220
Moors 29, 50
Morelos, José María 216, 346–49, 353, 354, 355, 358, 359, 363
Morelos region 144, 210, 212, 285
moreno 208, 222
Moriscos 41, 50, 265
Motolinia, Fray Toribio de Benavente O.F.M.120
Moya y Contreras, Pedro 126, 235
Mozarabs 31
mules 111, 171 (see also *arrieros*)
mulatos 208, 222, 265–267
Muñoz Camargo, Diego 68, 81–82, 86, 121, 146, 174
music 156, 225, 232, 235–36, 237

Nahuas (see also Aztecs, Mexica) 23, 24, 63, 65, 68, 73, 74, 108, 122, 145, 149

Nahuatl 7, 8, 18, 24, 56, 79, 84, 86, 87, 92, 108, 111–12, 117, 122, 124, 134, 148, 152, 155, 229
Napoleonic invasion 341–43
Naváez, Pánfilo 58, 99, 186
Navaho 325, 336
Nebrija, Antonio de 28
New Christians 31, 50
New Laws of 1542, 124
New Mexico 11, 15, 16, 136, 186, 190, 193–194, 196, 199–201, 321, 323–26, 363
New Spain 6, 24, 76
New World 6
Nezahualcoyotl 19
Nezahualpilli 19, 20
Niza, Fray Marcos de O.F.M. 186, 188–89, 190
nobles, Spanish 34, 35, 36, 42, 277, 291, 297
nobles, indigenous 16–17, 20–21, 84, 88, 122, 130,144–45, 146, 151, 158, 165, 263, 267, 274 (see also *caciques, principales*)
Noche Triste 58, 99
novohispano 262 (see also creole)
Ñudzahui 7, 16
Nueva Galicia 63, 162, 186, 189, 191, 193, 210, 215, 250, 363
Nueva Vizcaya 193, 195, 196, 323–26, 327, 330, 363
Nuevo León 194–95, 286, 329
Nuevo Santander 326–330

Oaxaca 7, 11, 16, 23, 64, 69, 123, 144, 149, 153, 169, 210, 286–87, 294, 306, 355
obrajes 173–75, 182, 207, 211, 245, 293
obrajero 174,182
obras pías 227, 238
oficial 222
oidor 317
Olid, Cristóbal de 63, 64
Olmec 9, 10, 13, 14, 15, 16, 17, 21
Oñate, Cristóbal 193
Oñate, Don Juan de 194–95
Ordenanza del Patronazgo 1574, 130
Orizaba 294
Opata 198, 334
Otomí 191, 196, 287
Ovando, Fray Nicolás 47–48

Palafox y Mendoza, Bishop Don Juan 131, 229, 236, 237
palenque 215, 222
panadería 175, 182
Papago 330
pardo 219–220
Parral 169, 193, 194, 197, 252, 323, 325
partido 292, 293, 298
patio process 170
Patronato real 36, 50, 116

patriarchy 268, 276, 372
Pax Hispanica 242, 249
peninsular [Spaniard] 262, 309, 312, 341, 343, 349 (see also *gachupines*)
peones 290, 298
pepena 178, 182
Pericues 337
Peru 49, 63, 67, 128,177, 179, 180, 301
Philippine Islands 38, 135, 166, 175, 176, 177, 179, 180
pigs 40, 98, 105, 288
Pima 198, 320, 330, 331
Plan of Iguala 348, 350, 353, 357
plebe 277, 280, 371
poblador 92
pochteca 17, 24
Popé 252, 253
Portolá, Gaspar de 332
Portugal 34, 35, 41, 128, 204, 206, 342
population size 11, 22, 43, 100, 102, 104–05, 143, 157, 209–210, 282, 333, 362
posada 237, 238
prehispanic era 6, 24
presidios 153, 321–22, 325, 326, 330, 332, 333, 334, 336, 337, 338
primacias 131, 137
primordial titles 87, 152
principales 146, 159, 243 (see also nobles, indigenous)
printing 235, 263
prostitution 246
Protestants 128
Protomedicato 104
Provincias Internas 306, 336
Puebla de los Angeles 65, 80, 125, 135, 163, 168, 173, 174, 209, 212, 219, 227, 235, 271, 276, 282, 286, 293, 306, 313, 315, 316, 363
pueblo 42, 50
Pueblo 16, 189, 190, 194, 199–200, 325, 334
Pueblo Revolt 198, 200, 201, 251, 252–253, 320, 323–324
pulque 110, 165, 226, 245, 284, 288, 289
punishment 17, 108–09, 127, 173, 200, 205, 213, 215–16, 244, 245, 348, 356
Purepecha 7, 19, 22, 24, 73, 74, 88, 89, 125, 186

Querétaro 180, 192, 210, 282, 290, 293, 294, 344, 354
quetzal 11
Quetzalcoatl 21
Quintana Roo, Andrés 359
quinto 54
Quiroga, Vasco de 103, 125
Quivira 190

race 261–267, 268, 370, 371
race mixture 67, 149, 196–97, 208, 220
rancho 164,182, 193, 288

ranchería 185, 200, 202
ranchero 298
reales de minas 169, 182, 191–92, 197, 292, 330 (see also mining)
Real del Monte 292
real hacienda 317
rebellions (see revolts)
recogimiento 271, 280, 304
Reconquest 27, 31, 33, 50, 53
reducción 148, 200, 202 (see also *congregación*)
regidor 39, 50, 147, 159
Regla, Count of 227, 228, 292, 293, 364
regular clergy 115, 116, 117, 137, 356 (see also mendicant orders)
religion, indigenous 20, 21–22, 87, 116, 198, 199–200
religious culture 225–228
repartimiento 47, 150, 166, 172, 215; *de mercancías* 153, 159, 308
república de españoles 261
república de indios 143, 159, 261, 264
requerimiento 92
residencia 317
revolts 87, 198, 215–16, 249–256, 320, 330–31, 332, 337, 344 (see also riots)
Reyes Católicos 27
rice 285–86
riots, Mexico City 227,246–49
Royal Council 35
Royal Road (see *Camino Real*)
Ruíz de Alarcón, Hernando 157

Sahagún, Fray Bernardino de O.F.M. 84–86, 99, 103, 120, 122
saints 135, 136, 156, 274
Saltillo 193, 196, 330
San Antonio 328, 329, 338, 367, 368, 372
San Buenaventura 333
San Carlos Boromeo 333
San Diego 190, 320, 332, 333, 363, 368, 372
San Francisco 333, 372
San Gabriel 333
San Juan Capistrano 333
San Luis Obispo 333
San Luis Potosí 290, 306, 310
Santa Anna, Antonio López de 350, 363
Santa Bárbara 333
Santa Clara 333
Santa Fe, 194, 196–97, 201, 320, 323, 325, 334, 372
Santiago de Compostela 32
Santiago 32, 33, 110–11, 156; military order of 34, 277
Santo Domingo 49, 56
secular clergy (see also diocesan clergy, priests) 68, 69, 116, 123, 125–128, 246, 353, 355–357

secularization of missions 130–31
Seri 198, 331, 337
Serra, Fray Junípero O.F.M. 332
Seven Golden Cities 186–189
Seville 40, 41, 42, 49, 162, 178, 193
sex 127, 128, 271–72
sheep 39–40, 105, 110, 166, 168, 207, 282, 293
Siete partidas 29, 205
Sigüenza y Góngora, Don Carlos 232, 233–34
silk 30, 65, 165–66
silver 65, 162, 170, 194, 325, 331 (see also mining)
slavery, African 41, 49, 81, 100, 130, 167, 172, 174, 196 , 207
slavery, Indian 3, 5, 17, 47, 143, 169, 194, 207, 251, 252, 334
smallpox 60, 98, 99, 101
society, Spanish 41–45
Sonora 330–332
sorteo 315, 317
Spain, history 27–52
Spaniards (see also creole, Mexican Spaniard, *novohispano*, peninsular) 262–63
"spiritual conquest" 61, 115–125, 131, 136
St. James (see Santiago)
State 69–70, 116–17
subdelegado 308–09, 312, 317
sujeto 145, 159
sugar 49, 65, 109, 167, 204, 206, 207, 208, 211–12, 285, 296
Supremo Congreso Nacional Americano (see Chilpancingo Congress)
syphilis 102–03, 112

Taino 47, 48
Tampico 195
Tapia, Andrés 81
Tapia, Cristóbal 77
Tarascans (see also Purepechas) 192, 196, 287
Tarahumara 193, 198, 200, 320
Taxco 169, 170, 355
Tejas 329–30, 338 (see also Texas)
temastianes 201, 202
Tenochtitlan 4, 7, 8, 18, 19, 20, 21, 22, 24, 56, 58, 59, 60, 61, 66 (map), 73, 74, 75, 84, 86
Teotihuacan 14, 15
Tepehuan 193, 198, 200, 252, 320
Texas 321, 326–29
Texcoco 7, 8, 18, 19, 20, 61, 68, 74, 82–83, 109, 128, 174, 176–77
textiles (see also cotton, *obrajes*, wool) 282–83, 293–94
Tezozomoc, Don Hernando de Alvarado 87

theater 120, 225, 234–35, 303–04
tianguis 111, 112, 226, 238
Tiburón Island 331
tierras baldías 50
títulos 152, 159 (see also primordial titles)
Tlacopan 7, 18, 60
Tlaloc 21
tlameme 14, 24, 111, 179
Tlatelolco 78, 85, 87, 92, 122, 148, 365 (see also *Colegio de Santa Cruz*)
Tlaxcala 19, 22, 57–58, 60, 61, 65–66, 68,73, 74, 76, 82, 85, 86, 121, 122, 148, 181, 191, 193, 196, 363
tobacco 109, 284, 294–95, 310
tocinería 295, 298
Toltec 14, 16, 18, 21
Toluca 286, 288
tomato 108, 112
Tonantzin 132
Totonac 57, 58
trade, indigenous 3, 13–14, 15 111, 155
trade, Spanish 49, 162, 173, 176–80, 295–97 (see also *comercio libre*,merchants)
transportation 179–180
trapiche 294, 298
traza 181, 182
tribute 13–14, 16, 19, 22, 104
Triple Alliance 7, 17, 18, 19, 22, 53, 55
tumulto 246–49, 256
Tzeltal Maya revolt 253–55

University of Guadalajara 229, 303
University of Mexico 104, 216, 225, 228–29, 232
Urdinola, Francisco de 193, 286, 329
Utes 200, 325, 336

Valencia, Fray Martín de O.F.M. 119
Valenciana mine 291, 293
Valeriano, Antonio de 122
Vargas, Diego de 323
vaqueros 218, 222
vecino 34, 50, 163, 182, 263
Velázquez, Diego de 55–57, 59, 63, 64, 75–76
Venegas, Francisco Javier 344, 351, 352
Veracruz 57, 65, 75, 119, 155, 177, 178, 180, 181, 209, 220, 221, 282, 296, 297, 304, 306, 313, 315, 316
Vetancurt, Fray Agustín de O.F.M. 234
Vicario, Doña Leona 359
viceroy 36, 69, 126, 195, 221, 225, 246–47, 248, 304, 306, 309, 333, 343, 344, 346 349, 350, 351, 352, 358
Vidosola, José Antonio 336
Virgin of Guadalupe 132–135, 226, 234, 253, 275, 344, 347, 348, 355, 367, 368
virgins 135–36, 254–55, 323, 367

visita 119, 137, 317
Vizcaíno, Sebastian 332

warfare, indigenous 21, 22–24, 185–86
wheat 109, 286
wills and testaments 105, 156–57, 158
wine 109–10
women 130, 269–70, 271, 302, 303,, 359 304,
    350, 373
women, African 212, 215
women, lower class 270–71
women, indigenous 12, 13, 14, 16, 17, 67,
    68, 85, 90, 100, 105, 121, 127, 130, 151,
    152, 154, 174, 256, 270, 303, 370, 375
women, Spanish 39, 40, 44, 49, 67, 68, 74,
    175, 302
wool 39–40 (see also *obrajes*, sheep, textiles)

Xixime 252

Xochimilco 20, 86, 153
xochiyaotl 21–22

Yanga 215
Yaqui 198, 200, 330, 331, 337
Yermo, Gabriel de 343–44, 350
Yucatan 10, 11, 64, 66, 79, 84, 120–21, 127,
    135, 147, 165, 210, 285, 301, 306
Yuma 198, 330, 333, 336, 337

Zacatecas 169, 170, 171, 177, 178, 191, 192,
    194, 201, 276, 283, 286, 292, 293, 323
zócalo 363–64
Zapotec 123, 147, 148
Zorita, Alonso de 147
Zumárraga, Bishop Don Juan de 68, 125,
    126, 134, 186, 188, 230
Zuni 188, 189, 198, 199, 200, 323